Public Interest Design Education Guidebook

Public Interest Design Education Guidebook: Curricula, Strategies, and SEED Academic Case Studies presents the pedagogical framework and collective curriculum necessary to teach public interest designers. The second book in Routledge's Public Interest Design Guidebook series, the editors and contributors feature a range of learning competencies supported by distinct teaching strategies where educational and community-originated goals unite. Written in a guidebook format that includes projects from across design disciplines, this book describes the learning deemed most critical to pursuing an inclusive, informed design practice that meets the diverse needs of both students and community partners.

Featured chapter themes include Fundamental Skills, Intercultural Competencies, Engaging the Field Experience, Inclusive Iteration, and Evaluating Student Learning. The book consists of practice-based and applied learning constructs that bridge community-based research with engaged learning and design practice. SEED (Social Economic Environmental Design) academic case studies introduce teaching strategies that reinforce project-specific learning objectives where solving social, economic, and environmental issues unites the efforts of communities, student designers, and educators. This comprehensive publication also contains indices devoted to learning objectives cross-referenced from within the book as well as considerations for educational program development in public interest design.

Whether you are a student of design, an educator, or a designer, the breadth of projects and teaching strategies provided here will empower you to excel in your pursuit of public interest design.

Lisa M. Abendroth is a professor in the Communication Design program at Metropolitan State University of Denver in Colorado, USA. She is a SEED Network founding member and a recipient of the SEED Award for Leadership in Public Interest Design. Her work focuses on the social, economic, and environmental impacts of design created within the contexts of underserved people, places, and problems. Abendroth is a coeditor of the *Public Interest Design Practice Guidebook: SEED Methodology, Case Studies, and Critical Issues* (2016).

Bryan Bell founded Design Corps in 1991 with the mission to provide the benefits of design for the 98 percent without architects. Bell has published three books on public interest design. His work has been supported by the American Institute of Architects Latrobe Prize and through a Harvard Loeb Fellowship. His designs have been exhibited at the Venice Biennale and the Cooper Hewitt, Smithsonian Design Museum. Bell holds degrees from Princeton University, USA, and Yale University, USA. He teaches at North Carolina State University, USA.

Public Interest Design Education Guidebook

Curricula, Strategies, and SEED Academic Case Studies

Edited by Lisa M. Abendroth and Bryan Bell

Routledge
Taylor & Francis Group
NEW YORK AND LONDON

First published 2019
by Routledge
711 Third Avenue, New York, NY 10017

and by Routledge
2 Park Square, Milton Park, Abingdon, Oxon, OX14 4RN

Routledge is an imprint of the Taylor & Francis Group, an informa business

© 2019 Taylor & Francis

The right of Lisa M. Abendroth and Bryan Bell to be identified as the authors of the editorial material, and of the authors for their individual chapters, has been asserted in accordance with sections 77 and 78 of the Copyright, Designs and Patents Act 1988.

All rights reserved. No part of this book may be reprinted or reproduced or utilised in any form or by any electronic, mechanical, or other means, now known or hereafter invented, including photocopying and recording, or in any information storage or retrieval system, without permission in writing from the publishers.

Trademark notice: Product or corporate names may be trademarks or registered trademarks, and are used only for identification and explanation without intent to infringe.

Library of Congress Cataloging-in-Publication Data
A catalog record for this title has been requested

ISBN: 978-1-138-64663-6 (hbk)
ISBN: 978-1-138-64665-0 (pbk)
ISBN: 978-1-315-62745-8 (ebk)

Typeset in Univers LT Std
by Apex CoVantage, LLC

Contents

Acknowledgments — ix

Foreword: Can Public Interest Design Be Taught? *Rahul Mehrotra* — xi

Introduction: Public Interest Design Pedagogy, *Lisa M. Abendroth and Bryan Bell* — 1

Part 1, Public Interest Design Curricula — 7
1. Whole-Systems Public Interest Design Education: Department of Landscape Architecture, University of Washington, *Jeffrey Hou, Benjamin R. Spencer, and Daniel Winterbottom* — 8
2. Educating the Next Generation of Social Innovators: Designmatters at ArtCenter, *Mariana Amatullo, Dan Gottlieb, Penny Herscovitch, and Susannah Ramshaw* — 22
3. Changing Practice, Practicing Change: The Graduate Certificate in Public Interest Design at Portland State University, *R. Todd Ferry and Sergio Palleroni* — 34
4. A Comprehensive Public Interest Design Curriculum: College of Design, North Carolina State University, *Bryan Bell, Robin Abrams, and Gene Bressler* — 46
5. Connecting Classrooms and Publics: The University of California, Davis, Center for Design in the Public Interest, *Susan Verba, Sarah Perrault, and Tracy Manuel* — 59

6. Design (Education) to Create Meaningful Change: The Design for Social Impact Master's Program at the University of the Arts, *Anthony Guido with Jeremy Beaudry, Jamer Hunt, Sharon Lefevre, Michael McAllister, and Jonas Milder* ... 70
7. Collaborating for Change in New Orleans: Small Center for Collaborative Design, *Maggie Hansen and Emilie Taylor Welty* ... 82
8. From the Ground Up: Envisioning an MFA in Public Interest Design at Metropolitan State University of Denver, *Lisa M. Abendroth, Kelly Monico, and Peter Miles Bergman* ... 93

Part 2, Educating the Public Interest Designer ... 105
Fundamental Skills
9. Fundamental Skills: Developing Social Literacy Through Practice-Based Learning, *Lee Davis and Mike Weikert* ... 107
10. The Edge Effect: PROJECT RE_, *John Folan* ... 111
11. Preparing to Design With: IMPACT Orientation, *Megan Clark and Shalini Agrawal* ... 117
12. Democratic Civic Engagement: The USAER XXXIV Training Center for Special Education, *Pedro Pacheco* ... 122

Intercultural Competencies
13. Intercultural Competencies: Teaching the Intangible, *Ursula Hartig and Nina Pawlicki* ... 131
14. Creating Design Leaders: The African Design Centre, *Christian Benimana* ... 135
15. Teaching *Intra*personal Development, Improving Interpersonal and Intercultural Skill Sets: The Transforming Mindsets Studio, *Lisa Grocott and Kate McEntee* ... 141
16. Addressing Air Pollution Impacts on Senior Citizens in Beijing, China: The International Urbanization Seminar, *Deland Chan* ... 147

Engaging the Field Experience
17. Engaging the Field Experience: Integrated, Interdisciplinary, On-Site, Enduring, *Benjamin R. Spencer* ... 155
18. iZindaba Zokudla (Conversations About Food): Innovation in the Soweto Food System, *Angus Donald Campbell and Naudé Malan* ... 158
19. Building Partnerships and Awareness: Healing an Urban Stream, *Brian Gaudio* ... 165
20. Advancing Resiliency: The Huxtable Fellowship in Civic Engagement and Service Learning, *Benjamin Peterson* ... 171

Inclusive Iteration
21. Inclusive Iteration: Participation as Method in Design Theory and Practice, *Eduardo Staszowski* ... 179

22.	"Making" Change *Together*: Rust to Green's Placemaking Praxis, *Paula Horrigan*	182
23.	Building User Capacity Through Iterative Processes: Ten Friends Diner, *Edward M. Orlowski and Julia Jovanovic*	189
24.	Examining Collaborative Efforts to Visualize Community Transformation: Alexandra Youth Precinct Project, *Chris Harnish*	195

Evaluating Student Learning

25.	Evaluating Student Learning: Engaging Experience to Create Agents of Change, *Nadia M. Anderson*	202
26.	Assessing Experiential Learning in Design Education: The Practice Department at the Boston Architectural College, *Bethany Lundell Garver*	206
27.	Merging Research, Scholarship, and Community Engagement: Roche Health Center, *Michael Zaretsky*	214
28.	Reflecting Through Razor Wire: The Environmental Justice in Prisons Project, *Julie Stevens*	220

Part 3, SEED Academic Case Studies — **227**

29.	The SEED Process for Academia, *Lisa M. Abendroth and Bryan Bell*	228
30.	SEED Academic Case Studies, *Lisa M. Abendroth and Bryan Bell*	231
	A. Design in Partnership With the Lama Foundation	232
	B. Pleasant Street Pedestrian Project	237
	C. A Social Approach to Design	243
	D. Cooperative Education at the Detroit Collaborative Design Center	248
	E. Com(m)a	254
	F. The Farm Rover	261
	G. On Site: Public Art and Design	266
	H. South of California Avenue	273
	I. With Sacramento	279
31.	Afterword: A Public Interest Design Educational Platform, *Thomas Fisher*	285

Part 4, Appendix — **291**

Glossary	292
Biographies	302
Reading List	315
Appendix A: Learning Objective Index	318
Appendix B: Program Considerations Index	328
Image Credits	333
Index	340

Acknowledgments

There are many individuals who have been vital to this publication. First, we wish to acknowledge the contribution of our authors, their students, and community partners. Without their sustained efforts in the realm of community-based pedagogies this publication would not have been possible. They are the inspiration that has driven this publication from the very start.

Our deep appreciation goes to our peer-review team[1] who extended their generosity of time and spirit in their assessment of projects for publication. Also, the five invited authors/teams in Part 2 have imparted a unifying vision to this part of the book. We are thankful for their contribution: Mike Weikert and Lee Davis, Nina Pawlicki and Ursula Hartig, Eduardo Staszowski, Benjamin R. Spencer, and Nadia M. Anderson.

The SEED Network founders, partners, members, and collaborators have our heartfelt thanks for evolving the vital exchange of knowledge we have today.

We wish to recognize Shannon Turlington for her prudent recommendations during the editing process. And we thank Eric Field for the technical creation and smooth operations of the SEED Evaluator.

Routledge has provided us with this opportunity for which we are grateful; thank you to our editorial team for ongoing publication development advice.

Thank you to our respective educational institutions, Metropolitan State University of Denver and North Carolina State University, which have supported our work in important and diverse ways.

Bryan would like to thank, for their valuable long-term support, the Board of Directors of Design Corps[2] and the Edward W. Rose III Family Fund of the Dallas Foundation.

Our families have our unending gratitude. We thank you for your patience, love, and support. Lisa imparts her appreciation to her husband, Eric, and her parents, Peter and Nancy, for their enduring encouragement. Bryan would like to especially thank his wife, Victoria; his parents, Rubie and Bryan; and his children, Sky and Cole.

Lastly, we are thankful for the inspiration provided by our students who drive the requirement for enhanced understanding and application of public interest design pedagogies today and into the future.

Recognizing this work as the deep collaboration that these acknowledgments represent, and seeing this collective work as part of a broader discourse on the interconnected relationship between practice and pedagogy, we envision a future where public interest design practitioners are more and more supported through thoughtfully constructed and engaged learning pedagogies.

Notes

1. Nadia M. Anderson, Greta Buehrle, Shannon Criss, Lee Davis, Ursula Hartig, Nina Pawlicki, Michael Rios, Jota Samper, Benjamin R. Spencer, Eduardo Staszowski, and Mike Weikert.
2. Beth Chute, Emily Axtman, Andrew Sturm, Aaron Bowman, Evan Harrel, Elisa Iturbe, Drew Kepley, Jeremy Knoll, Melissa Tello, Melissa Threatt, and James Wheeler.

Foreword
Can Public Interest Design Be Taught?
Rahul Mehrotra

Today, the physical structures of human settlements around the globe are evolving—becoming more malleable, more fluid, and more open to change than the technologies and social institutions that generate them. Urban environments face ever-increasing flows of human movement, more frequent natural disasters, and iterative economic crises that modify the global investment of capital and affect the physical form of cities and their extended hinterlands. Furthermore, a general sense of inequity is emerging as one of the largest challenges for imagining the built environment. At a time in which change and the unexpected are the new normal, approaches to design—whether of the built environment or as a broader intervention in people's lives—need to be more flexible. In this context, attributes like reversibility and openness are critical elements for articulating a more sustainable form of our habitats. How can we imagine transitions in this unpredictable, emerging landscape of demographic and economic shifts? How do practitioners concerned with the built environment partner with people to make these transitions happen? How does design become more vested in the public's interest for the present as well as the future?

Starting in the 1960s, many alternative practices of engaging with the built environment emerged globally as a counterpoint to the perceived eraser of tradition, as well as nonparticipatory models that the "modern" project perpetuated. These alternative models first manifested themselves in the form of the architect as craftsperson—working directly with the builders and often with the community, essentially eliminating drawings as a medium to communicate design intentions. In other words, drawings and documents as the only means of instruction in the building process were deemed inadequate. Vigorous use of local materials and vernacular construction techniques characterized the buildings that these practitioners created. The method of direct communication created a truly participatory process, with the bulk of the decisions left to the artisans and builders to make.

The early treatise by Christopher Alexander and others in the seminal book *A Pattern Language: Towns, Building, Construction* (New York: OUP USA, 1977) and, later, the more systemic approach in *Supports: An Alternative to Mass Housing* by John N. Habraken and Jonathan Teicher (Gateshead, UK: Urban International Press, 1999) are two examples of the theorization of this model. The representative work of Laurie Baker in Kerala, India, and Rural Studio in the United States grew out of this genre of practice. In this approach, flexibility in design intentions and open-endedness, where the construction process determines the final product, facilitate the easy incorporation of symbols, icons, and—most importantly—local building practices as a way to link architecture to the larger social and cultural traditions and economy of the region. In these practices was inherent the seed of public interest design as we have come to see it today.

The idea of placing the public interest at the center of design engagement was reenergized with new vigor in the 1990s, with the onslaught of globalization and the marginalization and displacement that ensued. This model of practice now encompasses architect activists and practitioners who have consciously chosen to be more reflective, to consider the consequences of their actions and ways they can effectively counter the global flows that marginalize both traditions and people. These practitioners enter into a potentially more fulfilling relationship with the site, its history, the community of users whose needs they address, and the members of the workforce who are their collaborators. Mainstream practitioners view this model of practice with great suspicion—perhaps as it challenges the more orthodox patterns of professional practice? These experiments are, in fact, carried on at the margins of conventional practice. By choosing to operate at the boundaries of the dominant structure of capital, these alternative practitioners, who work explicitly in the public's interest, have made overt their moral choices in the face of globalization.

This model of practice is innovative in the matter of patronage; projects are sometimes supported by the state or the corporate sector in a compassionate mood (trusts, foundations, and so on), but more usually by nongovernmental organizations, charities, and similar patrons. In the same spirit, practitioners reject certain sources of patronage, such as developers and real estate speculators, and treat with suspicion technologies of mass production, such as reinforced cement concrete, steel, and an obsessive use of glass. In this way, the model demonstrates new directions and interpretations of sustainable design in the global context.

Exploration of alternative technologies and building methods is a recurring theme in this model. All decisions are based on community participation, resuscitating architecture from formal production processes by focusing on the lived experiences of users. This form of practice also acts as an important counterpoint to the protocol-driven corporate pattern of architecture and planning. The practice emphasizes an intimacy of scale, a direct involvement with building, and an activist preoccupation with political and civic issues that impinge on architecture. Practitioners make an argument for architectural diversity and acknowledge the differences that are critical to the evolution of relevant architecture. Moreover, recognition of human creativity acquires special meaning in the age of atomizing privatism. This access to a wider base of skills and concerns is especially important in the face of globalization, which has reduced the character of the built form to a thin veneer of glamour. Most critically, practitioners have the public's interest in the outcomes of any design intervention at the center of their agenda; the goal is to have the public participate and, more importantly, benefit.

While public interest design often operates at a limited scale, this model of practice is firmly embedded in the socioeconomic milieu of the region. The model facilitates the engagement of social networks in the process of building and is characterized by cost-effective solutions—often derived from the conversion of social assets into financial ones in the way labor is engaged or material procured. Not overwhelmed by issues of architectural and aesthetic concerns, these buildings are often conceived with a looseness that allows for flexibility in terms of materials and the building process. Although this mode of practice has seen popular support among institutions, nongovernmental organizations, and intellectuals and has produced a significant amount of building, it often lacks cohesion in physical articulation and is sometimes reduced to caricatures of regional icons and images. While public interest design seemingly extends traditions and attempts to express an economy of means, its literal visual translation often subverts rather than extends vernacular traditions and can lack the aesthetic robustness that makes the vernacular idiom timeless.

Ironically, this position of privileging the visual should not be seen as contrary but rather as being a simultaneously valid aspiration. However, pedagogy seems to address one over the other. Thus, what does this recognition of alternative practices of design in the public interest mean for pedagogy? While there are currently more questions than answers, some of these questions open up a conversation for the future. How does education address this issue—does it accept and work with reinforcing this pluralism or try to recast the profession in a singular model? Can education simultaneously embrace these counterpoints to create schizophrenic architects, or is conformity a better alternative?

The real question in this discussion of orienting pedagogy for the public interest designer is whether reconciling these varied aspirations is possible at all. Practices that focus on public interest questions often evolve. Conventional practitioners stumble on these issues out of circumstance or while pursuing their own passions and commitments. Alternative practitioners interested in public interest design typically come from the institutions or practices that serve as incubators to nurture these alternative approaches and are often in circumstances where peer learning and support result in new directions. So can public interest design practice be taught?

Public Interest Design Education Guidebook: Curricula, Strategies, and SEED Academic Case Studies, edited by Lisa M. Abendroth and Bryan Bell, fills a crucial gap in grappling with this critical question. The two themes dominating the book are interdisciplinary public interest design education and the Social Economic Environmental Design (SEED) process, which suggest new ways that the authentic learning from projects around the globe can inform pedagogy and vice versa. While the projects presented in the book are diverse, tackling specific challenges of participating partners and communities, the persistent thread is education: the education of student designers, the frameworks of public interest design pedagogy, and the communities affected by this work. All are crucial ingredients in the formation of the alternative practitioner for whom the public interest is at the heart of the practice.

The challenge of reorienting pedagogy to educate those students who might become alternative practitioners is the primary theme of the book. All of the contributors—educators, students, and project partners—share this mission. In addition to posing questions about the issues that need to be addressed in achieving this pedagogical mission, the book's admirable ambition is articulating the SEED process, which asks, "What is the specific vision of success?" and "How is that vision to be measured?" The authors propose that *learning objectives* function as the much-needed lens through which to analyze student-centered *learning outcomes* to provide a universal reference within the language of pedagogy. The term for measurement in this context is *assessment*. These commonly accepted academic terms link design education to critical questions that the book seeks to answer in public interest design pedagogy and within the broader process of SEED.

This critical feedback loop and the structure in a pedagogical framework that the authors have established make this book an important resource for educating the public interest designer more globally. The book facilitates a network of practices by constructing a structure that allows and actually encourages all sorts of feedback loops, which support thinking and practice around public interest design. Addressing an academic audience of educators, students, scholars, and administrators, the *Public Interest Design Education Guidebook* explores how public interest design practice demands specialized instruction that embraces many core values. These values range from a deep investment in working locally through participatory practices with diverse and underrepresented stakeholders to the pursuit of an issue-based approach to problem solving that promotes longevity and sustainability.

The book also covers implementation of evaluation that is embedded in community-centered design work from a project's start—that is, how to build community partnerships, how to assess student learning in conjunction with project development, how to incorporate service-learning and internships, and more. The book creates a tool kit for the practitioner and educator, as well as for the patron, to understand their own relationships. Its most powerful suggestion is that there is a blurring between the practice of advocacy in the interest of the public and the tools of advocacy. Today, these two things have to be intrinsically linked and coevolved by the advocate and the community.

Any shift in values and modes of practice that we bring to the profession has to be founded on a solid base of education—on values that inform how we practice. Society invests in our training as architects with the express intention that we help imagine spatial possibilities in which human beings can lead better lives. In fact, public service and interest are intrinsically central to our purpose as design practitioners. Perhaps our training has to reclaim this mission once again to retrieve it from an amnesia that has engulfed us in the final decades of the twentieth century. The *Public Interest Design Education Guidebook* is a guide to nurturing this sensibility in a generation of designers to come.

Introduction
Public Interest Design Pedagogy

Lisa M. Abendroth and Bryan Bell

The goal of this publication is to advance the rigors of a comprehensive public interest design education and collective curriculum. The editors, along with a team of project peer-reviewers, have undertaken the vital task of identifying the best methods and pedagogical techniques embedded within public interest design education today. Subsequently these documented learning competencies together with teaching strategies help shape a vital landscape where academic and community-based goals unite. The inherent challenge was to ensure the information presented here is communicated in the clearest terms and in a manner that promotes relational understanding across audiences. The editors and contributors strive in earnest to move the profession forward by presenting a dialectic of pedagogies, a detailed account of the educational processes, systems, and interactions that empower engaged learning within communities and with community stakeholders. While a mutuality of efforts has galvanized public interest design as a viable profession, it is the attentive pedagogy of educators that will sustain it, offering new standards and practices that define this ever-evolving field.[1]

In this publication, the term *public interest design*[2] functions as a unifier of diverse approaches and descriptions of inclusive community-based practices from across the fields of design.[3] In recent years and the more distant past there has been steady momentum shaping a context for what public interest design might mean to the education and the practice of a designer. In his foreword to *Expanding Architecture: Design as Activism* (Bell and Wakeford 2008) Thomas Fisher (2008) ponders how education might respond to the necessary evolution of architectural practice in new and differing contexts (10). Donald Schön (1985) has also examined the evolution of architectural design education in the wake of "community architecture." He points to the question of whether a "traditional architectural education" best serves students stepping into previously undefined roles (Schön 1985, 3–4). Originally published in 1971, in *Design for the Real World: Human Ecology and Social Change*, Victor Papanek (1985) radically asserts, "The main trouble with design schools seems to be that they teach too much design and not enough about the ecological, social, economic, and political environment in which design takes place" (291).

The call to action has been palpable for quite some time. Today, the evidence of many individual and unified efforts to build transferrable knowledge of this field through pedagogy *and* practice is apparent.[4] Yet, while there are a number of qualified public interest design educators, each offers a unique range of knowledge and experience. This variety has been productive in building pedagogical discourse but has yet to yield the fully developed, transparent, and interconnected cross-disciplinary scale needed within academia. The adverse result is that very often neither administrators, educators, nor students know what a *complete* education in public interest design includes.[5]

The demand for design professionals capable of guiding this practice is growing. Students, educators, and administrators must be prepared to tackle the challenges and benefits of a pedagogy of engagement. An opportunity is presented in the creation of new theoretical frameworks that imagine future iterations for applied learning. A new era of education demands continued and dedicated research that maps, for example, educational approaches to the convergence of metacognitive and technical skill development. While educators are thoughtfully developing engaged teaching and research activities, much work remains. There is a need to understand the impact of these activities, both project results and student learning outcomes, on students themselves, the community partners, and institutions. The relatively recent evolution of diverse degrees, programs, and formats of study in this field fuel the necessity for this conversation.

The evidence of public interest design pedagogies are presented here in three primary sections of this publication. This structure was created to provide a baseline for examination of curricular perspectives, thematically driven project-based work along with case studies that demonstrate the rigor and evolving standard of pedagogy embedded within public interest design education.

Part 1: *Public Interest Design Curricula* presents eight chapters from faculty in distinct educational settings—public and private, research-based and teaching-based, undergraduate and graduate levels—from across design disciplines and throughout the United States. The authors reflect on the comprehensive nature of their integrated course work by presenting pedagogical goals and learning outcomes. These create a bridge between Part 1 chapters, demonstrating core curricular and learning takeaways helpful in comparing programs and approaches. Featured projects offer evidence that links educational frameworks with community-based efforts. Project goals, learning objectives, project outputs, and documentation of student learning through assessment of project results are discussed. Together these authors reveal an important transformation shaping schools that moves beyond typical design studio scenarios to deeply contextualized problem solving working mutually *with* communities (NERCHE 2016)[6] toward collectively identified goals and often in embedded situations.

Part 2: *Educating the Public Interest Designer* presents twenty chapters expressed through five themes that underscore the timely relevance of engaged pedagogy. Each thematic section begins with an introduction from an invited author who orients the theme within the landscape of public interest design pedagogy and connects the individual efforts of contributors in that section to a broader discourse. Fifteen double-blind, peer-reviewed chapters identified through an international call for projects constitutes the volume of this section. These chapters articulate a range of critical community-based methods and teaching strategies through applied project-based and practice-based learning that will help design educators envision new possibilities in their own pedagogies.

Chapter themes in Part 2 include the following topics:[7]

- As noted by authors Lee Davis and Mike Weikert in their introduction to the theme *Fundamental Skills*, two interwoven yet fundamental concepts emerge: "(1) elevating social literacy to expand students' capacity for understanding the complex, systemic nature of social problems and change; and (2) employing immersive, collaborative, and participatory practice-based learning experiences to expose students to real-world problems" (see pages 107–110). Thematic topics further address ethics, leadership, immersion, social responsibility, mutuality, building trust, and practicing empathy.
- Ursula Hartig and Nina Pawlicki share perspective on the theme *Intercultural Competencies* stating, "a profound understanding of the specific local context and a deep investment in the place are required" (see pages 131–134) for intercultural understanding to emerge. Projects in this section demonstrate the importance of metacognitive skill development along with the imperative for translating social and cultural meaning and for considering cultural immersion through the interpretation of political, economic, environmental, and social frameworks.
- In *Engaging the Field Experience* Benjamin R. Spencer introduces readers to the Scholarships of Application and Engagement (SAE) as "a platform for educators to take public interest design out of the classroom and into the field" (see pages 155–157). Design research in local, national, or international contexts requires a clear understanding of culturally appropriate engagement. Featured authors in this section delve into the processes and contexts that have shaped project outputs through community collaborations.
- Eduardo Staszowski positions *Inclusive Iteration* as "an experimental, iterative process, where project phases and activities often repeat or overlap, allowing for the disparate needs, motivations, and ideas that exist among the different participants to proliferate and align" (see pages 179–181). Thematic projects reveal ways of generating and gathering effective feedback, which can inform an iterative and participatory design development strategy that promotes access and inclusion.

- The theme of *Evaluating Student Learning* is introduced by Nadia M. Anderson who poses the question, "Do students see themselves, as a result of the course, as dialogical people participating in mutual exchange with others, or do they see themselves as individuals separate from others?" (see pages 202–205). Authors in this section reflect on the relational quality of student–university–community partnerships in engaged programs where the role of evaluation is vital to understanding learning outcomes and project results as well as long-term and short-term impacts within applied learning contexts.

Part 3: *SEED Academic Case Studies* demonstrates nine educational projects that highlight project-specific learning objectives paired with a selection of teaching strategies that elucidate the skills required within a resulting public interest design practice. Projects developed into case studies were selected by the editors from within the previously discussed peer-reviewed call for projects. The faculty representing selected case study projects also submitted their work to the SEED Network using the SEED Evaluator to further their case study development. The resulting cases offer important evidence of the variables found within community-based applied learning that address social, economic, and environmental issues; the community-based challenge; pedagogical goals; and project results and learning outcomes. These uniquely divergent perspectives, unified by a consistent SEED case study format useful for comparison/contrast analysis, make tangible the sometimes-intangible aspects of public interest design pedagogy. To further the accessibility of this content, learning objectives in Part 3 and from throughout the book have been collated in Appendix A (Part 4, pages 318–327) and offer a comprehensive set of learning goals as a useful reference.

In the foreword to Paulo Freire's *Pedagogy of the Oppressed* (2013), Richard Shaull offers perspective on the tacit relationship between education, transformation, oppression, and justice. He reminds us, "There is no such thing as a neutral educational process" (34). This prompt signals the implicit responsibility of educators who, in the context of this publication, seek to empower students and communities through the mutuality of thoughtfully derived public interest, community-centered work. Shaull goes on to translate the important message of Freire's work where education "becomes the 'practice of freedom,' the means by which men and women deal critically and creatively with reality and discover how to participate in the transformation of their world" (34). A proposal for a comprehensive, collective curriculum of public interest design endangers itself in its codification and instead must acknowledge the requirement for intentional, meaningful engagement in the social contexts that define communities and *their* needs. The emphasis on pedagogy itself as a transformative experience liberated beyond that of a singular set of strategies (Macedo 2013, 24–25) is necessary. The editors of this volume are hopeful that the projects, ideas, and approaches presented here together embody a philosophy of education that transcends a reliance on the technological qualities of design education today. Through a rigorous immersive pedagogy and ethical professional practice, public interest designers can be poised to decisively address the systemic needs of today's global society.

Notes

1. The editors are indebted to the fine work of the many scholars and affiliated organizations who have pioneered progress on the aligned topics of community engagement, democratic engagement, civic learning, and engaged learning. Please see the Reading List in the *Part 4: Appendix* (pages 315–317) for recommended reading.

2. In the *Public Interest Design Practice Guidebook* (Abendroth and Bell 2016), public interest design is defined as "[a] design practice composed of three tenets—democratic decision making through meaningful community engagement, an issue-based approach, and the requirement for design evaluation" (308).

3. See *Wisdom from the Field: Public Interest Architecture in Practice* (Feldman et al., 2011) for a description of public interest design in "Appendix 5: Survey Instrument" (112, para 2). See also "Appendix 8: Survey Findings Report" for an expanded definition of public interest design adapted from *Building Community: A New Future for Architecture Education and Practice: A Special Report* (Boyer and Mitgang 1996, 9) which emphasizes "putting creative abilities to use to improve quality of life in communities" (129, para 2). These publications have been pivotal in shaping the discourse around public interest design education today.

4. See the panel discussion summary from the Structures for Inclusion 2016 conference session, "Public Interest Design Education Open Forum" moderated by Lisa M. Abendroth and hosted at North Carolina State University College of Design on March 19, 2016. https://designcorps.org/sfi16-panel-4/.

5. The editors acknowledge the inherent significance and challenges in conducting work with communities as part of the higher education experience. This publication's editors have made a priority of celebrating the desirable attributes of this pedagogy, many of which follow here. First, the requirement for mutuality of benefits between community partners and participating institutions should serve as a baseline for coproduced projects developed through the lens of "community engagement" (NERCHE 2016). Further, an emphasis on the integrated nature of "democratic purposes and processes" can demonstrate an alignment with publically meaningful and purpose-driven "democratic engagement" that strives to "alleviat[e] public problems through democratic means" (Saltmarsh, Hartley, and Clayton 2009, 6). Fostering long-term relationships that are built upon trust through collective skill- and knowledge-sharing can promote and strengthen community-identified goals. Honing skills in culturally appropriate communication (both visual and verbal) and design facilitation that respects people and place should benefit both students and community partners alike. Last, the power of exercising humility and building empathy cannot be over stated as necessary twenty-first-century design skills.

6   See the Carnegie Foundation's definition and stated purpose of community engagement: http://nerche.org/index.php?option=com_content&view=article&id=341&Itemid=92#CEdef.

7   Some of the themes included in this publication were inspired during an invited luncheon of over fifteen participants hosted by Design Corps and conducted during the Structures for Inclusion 2015 conference in Detroit on April 12. The meeting provided a forum to explore topics of significance to educators pursuing and/or practicing public interest design and helped establish a space for critical inquiry of these in this publication.

References

Abendroth, Lisa M., and Bryan Bell, eds. 2016. "Glossary." In *Public Interest Design Practice Guidebook: SEED Methodology, Case Studies, and Critical Issues*, 306–9. New York: Routledge.

Boyer, Earnest, and Lee Mitgang. 1996. *Building Community: A New Future for Architecture Education and Practice: A Special Report*. Princeton, NJ: Carnegie Foundation for the Advancement of Teaching.

Feldman, Roberta, Sergio Palleroni, David Perkes, and Bryan Bell. 2011. *Wisdom from the Field: Public Interest Architecture in Practice*. FAIA Latrobe Prize Research Report. Washington, DC: College of Fellows of the American Institute of Architects. Accessed August 23, 2014. https://issuu.com/designcorps/docs/latrobe_prize_research_-_public_int

Fisher, Thomas. 2008. "Foreword: Public-Interest Architecture: A Needed and Inevitable Change." In *Expanding Architecture: Design as Activism*, edited by Bryan Bell and Katie Wakeford, 8–13. New York: Metropolis Books.

Macedo, Donaldo. 2013. "Introduction." In *Pedagogy of the Oppressed*, by Paulo Freire, 11–27. New York: Bloomsbury Academic.

New England Resource Center for Higher Education (NERCHE). 2016. "Carnegie Community Engagement Classification." Accessed October 12, 2016. http://nerche.org/index.php?option=com_content&view=article&id=341&Itemid=92#CEdef.

Papanek, Victor. 1985. *Design for the Real World: Human Ecology and Social Change*. Chicago: Academy Chicago Publishers.

Saltmarsh, John, Matthew Hartley, and Patti Clayton. 2009. *Democratic Engagement White Paper*. New England Resource Center for Higher Education. Accessed February 10, 2017. http://repository.upenn.edu/gse_pubs/274.

Schön, Donald A. 1985. *The Design Studio: An Exploration of Its Traditions and Potentials*. London: RIBA Publications for RIBA Building Industry Trust.

Shaull, Richard. 2013. "Foreword." In *Pedagogy of the Oppressed*, by Paulo Freire, 29–34. New York: Bloomsbury Academic.

Part 1
Public Interest Design Curricula

1
Whole-Systems Public Interest Design Education
Department of Landscape Architecture, University of Washington

Jeffrey Hou, Benjamin R. Spencer, and Daniel Winterbottom

Program Philosophy

Public interest design has a long tradition at the University of Washington (UW). Dating back to the 1960s and 1970s, when faculty and students led efforts to preserve Seattle's beloved landmarks and develop new public parks, this focus remains strong through ongoing initiatives in service-learning, community engagement, and design activism. Rather than confining the study of public interest design to a single course or a small set of courses, as is typical of most design programs, the UW Department of Landscape Architecture has fully integrated public interest design into the curricula of its two professional degree programs: Bachelor of Landscape Architecture (BLA) and Master of Landscape Architecture (MLA). Our focus not only motivates our pursuit of projects in underserved communities but also influences the way we approach issues of urban green infrastructure, physical and psychological health, ecological planning and design, and social justice.

Public interest design is embodied in our programs at multiple levels. Our strategic plan recognizes five focal areas of exploration: design as activism, design for ecological infrastructure, design for ecological learning and literacy, design for human and environmental health, and design for social and environmental justice. These strategic focuses guide the directions of our curricular development, resource investment, student and faculty recruitment, and community outreach. Most, if not all, of our advanced design studios involve working with community groups, civic organizations, and public agencies on projects ranging from eco-district planning to design of community gardens. These courses are taught not by just one or two individual faculty members but rather by the entire departmental faculty.

Despite a wide variation in interests and specializations, all of the faculty consider public engagement to be a critical component of our scholarship, teaching, and practice. We believe that involving diverse stakeholders in deliberations and actions is critical to the social and environmental resilience of our cities and communities and critical to empathetic design. Our focus on design activism in turn attracts students who share such passion and conviction. Over the years, we have developed long-term collaborative relationships with community groups, civic organizations, and public agencies through service-learning projects. These projects provide the experimental ground for public interest design education.

Program Curriculum Overview

Like most professional design programs, both the BLA and MLA programs at UW are organized around a sequence of design studios. The first-year curriculum in both programs consists of a series of foundational design studios focusing on basic concepts and skills with regard to social, ecological, and spatial forms and processes. In the second-year sequence, public interest and community engagement are integrated into studio projects.

Undergraduates in LARC 402 and LARC 403, the Neighborhood Design and Cultural Landscape studios, work with community "clients," or partners, focusing on actual sites and projects in the community. Recent projects include design for neighborhood greenways and visions for a historic Japanese American garden now open to the public. Community partners range from American Indian tribes to immigrant communities in the Pacific Northwest. As the culmination of the BLA program, Daniel Winterbottom directs LARC 474/475, our Design/Build Capstone Studio. Each year, students under Winterbottom's supervision work with an underserved community to design and implement a project in collaboration with community partners.

At the graduate level, students in LARC 501, the Ecological Urbanism Studio, work on urban-scale projects in Seattle, focusing on public-space design in partnership with civic organizations and city agencies; students in LARC 502, the Design Activism Studio, typically work with informal urban communities in Peru; and students in LARC 503, the Urban Agriculture Studio, explore urban food issues and design of community gardens in partnership with local communities. Specific studios can be linked to a long-term initiative, such as the Informal Urban Communities Initiative (IUCI), a multiyear effort focusing on empowering the community of Lomas de Zapallal in Lima, Peru. Similarly, a series of advanced studios has contributed to an ongoing community-driven design process in Seattle's Chinatown-International

Whole-Systems Public Interest Design Education

District since 2002 (Hou 2011, 2014), leveraging over $2 million in funding and resulting in renovated neighborhood parks and streetscapes.

Aside from these regular courses, students have access to study-abroad programs with a focus on public interest design and community engagement. Recent opportunities have included a series of design/build courses in Latin America (Mexico and Guatemala), Eastern Europe (Bosnia and Herzegovina and Croatia), and Asia (China). In Guatemala and Eastern Europe, students worked with communities traumatized by war, poverty, and mental illness. IUCI has also recently expanded its footprint beyond Peru to Cambodia through a study-abroad studio. These courses experiment with integrating service-learning and public interest design education with study-abroad experiences.

Seminars and lectures are also important parts of our whole-systems approach to public interest design education. These courses include LARC 561, Human Experience of Place; LARC 570, Theory and Scholarship; and LARC 571, Advanced Research Methods, which incorporates methods of community engagement.

Design/Build Capstone Studio

The UW Design/Build Capstone Studio was founded in 1994 to strengthen our curriculum and fulfill a university goal of public service. The design/build methodology brings BLA and MLA students the experience of discovering the evocative connection between design, making, and material expression. Without the experience of building, students cannot apply knowledge from construction lecture classes. Teaching models that integrate design and the art of building allow different ways of thinking to enlighten one another, promoting responsive and expressive design. Over the years, the studio has increasingly worked with underserved communities, applying therapeutic and social-justice design principles. We advance the idea that landscape architecture is a unique vehicle for social and ecological activism and hope that our students will carry that idea on into their professional careers.

In *The Eyes of the Skin*, Juhani Pallasmaa (2012, 25) describes the banality of vision that threatens the significance of designed environments:

> Current industrial mass production of visual imagery tends to alienate vision from emotional involvement and identification, and to turn imagery into a mesmerizing flow without focus or participation. The cancerous spread of superficial architectural imagery today, devoid of tectonic logic and sense of materiality and empathy, is clearly part of this process.

Pallasmaa defines (landscape) architecture as "the art of reconciliation between ourselves and the world, and this meditation takes place through the senses" (77).

Noted sociologist Richard Sennett (2008, 160) discusses learning challenges, curiosity, and the role of fear:

Diminishing the fear of making mistakes is all important in our art. In performance, the confidence to recover from error is not a personality trait, it is a learned skill. Technique develops, then, by a dialectic between the correct way to do something and the willingness to experiment through error.

The two sides cannot be separated. If the young musician is simply given the correct way, he or she will suffer from a false sense of security. If the budding musician luxuriates in curiosity, simply going with the flow of the transitional object, she or he will never improve.

The design/build capstone studio aligns with Sennett's goals: students understand the art of building through an exploration of materials and form while also responding to community needs.

Design/Build Studio Pedagogical Goals

The goals of the design/build capstone studio are expansive and vary depending on each project and the needs of the particular community being served (Winterbottom 2002). A specific educational goal is developing a deeper understanding of, and competence in, making and craft. Students explore the multisensory properties of materials to engage users fully and to create appropriate, meaningful places. Communication skills are honed as we work in a participatory design process. We incorporate recycled materials and green building techniques with a view toward sustainable design. Nearly all project clients come from traumatized or marginalized communities, providing a unique opportunity for students to explore issues of social justice and activism (Winterbottom 2014). Through dialogue, students discover normative values and assumptions that contribute to some members' continued disadvantage. In response to trauma, illness, and personal or societal disruptions, we create effective therapeutic environments that reduce stress and improve well-being through the interplay of nature, form, and materials (Winterbottom 2011).

Over the years, a study-abroad version of the design/build studio, open to both undergraduate and graduate students, has been developed. In projects abroad, we embed ourselves in the community: homestays in Guatemala, rooms in a Croatian mental hospital, or dormitories inside a Chinese sculpture park (Wagenfeld and Winterbottom 2015). In our Seattle-based projects, we are on-site twenty hours per week, building community relationships that grow deeper as time goes on. This familiarity transforms community building into a social, physical, and spiritual art. Through storytelling, spontaneous conversations, and collaborative building, we see cultural, personal, and professional exchange flourish.

Design/Build Studio Outcomes

Students who immerse in this intensive iterative experience understand that design, as William Carpenter (1997, 55) notes, is a "circular, reflective process, from idea, to building and back to idea, linking the thinking about and the act of place making." Our design process is collaborative yet competitive at the outset. While elements from all team proposals are included in the final design, one or two designs serve as its foundation. Moving into construction, the process becomes intensely collaborative and interdependent. Students must adjust the individual drive that may have guided them through design. They take on multiple shifting roles, as in a professional environment that calls for flexibility and adaptability. When working in the context of another culture, students test their comfort zones and experience personal and intellectual growth. They acquire an expanded global perspective of their roles as change makers and as socially aware citizens. According to student feedback, individual outcomes include growth in leadership ability, self-confidence, and empathy. Students attain a more comprehensive understanding of the political, humanitarian, and practical implications of design, which they hope to bring to their professional work.

The crafting of the studio is a continuing process, and each project offers new insights for improvement and change. According to their feedback, students highly value the nonstructured interactions with the community and volunteers, especially in international projects where cross-cultural enlightenment is of particular interest. Asking students to voice and articulate their ideas, missions, and goals increases their retention in ways that lecturing cannot achieve. Many students enter the design/build program wanting clear, predictable directions. They leave with the crucial realizations that "real life" is innately and wonderfully unpredictable and that flexibility and adaptability are essential for success. Their self-confidence and empowerment increase as a result.

Design/Build Capstone Studio Sample Project: Puget Sound Veterans Administration Healing Garden

The recently completed Healing Garden at the Puget Sound Veterans Administration offers a verdant place for escape, contemplation, and respite, a calming oasis from the stress and anxiety common among veterans and exacerbated by the institutional hospital setting. In an extensive participatory process, students worked with staff, patients, and administrators to understand their needs and desires. Students engaged in focus group discussions, visual preference exercises, and brainstorming sessions as they studied the site (see Figure 1.1). They then analyzed the feedback to inform their designs. Six schematic design proposals were created and presented to the community. Two were merged and elements borrowed from the others to compose the final design.

The Sky Room features a view of the sky framed by the buildings and offers a sense of escape and expansiveness in the courtyard garden. The seating arrangement fosters social interaction and is used for group therapy sessions. The Earth Room, at the other end of the L-shaped site, is contained on three sides by the building and prompts an inward focus. It is private and used for meditation and modest physical therapy. A fountain sits between the two "rooms," linking earth to sky with running water. Native materials infuse a sense of place and region, in accordance with the veterans' wishes. Images of mountains are cut into privacy screens, and native plants ensure a lush, verdant natural environment where users can escape the monotony and harshness of medical wards and hallways (see Figure 1.2).

1.1
Engaging the patients and staff in a photo-preference exercise to better understand their preferences. University of Washington Design/Build Program, Puget Sound Veterans Administration Healing Garden, Seattle, Washington, 2016.

1.2
Students with little construction experience take on the fabrication, refining their skills over the project and creating community amenities in the process. University of Washington Design/Build Program, Puget Sound Veterans Administration Healing Garden, Seattle, Washington, 2016.

Whole-Systems Public Interest Design Education

Students with little construction experience fabricated all elements, including bent and welded steel and wood (see Figure 1.3). Community members donated services, such as irrigation and lighting, and worked with the students to complete the installations. Student leaders, responsible for material ordering, budgets, and scheduling, managed the construction teams.

The stories exchanged between students and patients were an unplanned benefit of fieldwork. Most students knew little about the military or the postconflict effects on veterans. This experience dismantled the walls of ignorance, and students gained a deeper understanding of the innate physical and mental challenges of life after war. They saw how gardens can help people cope, endure, and thrive.

1.3
Mother and child using the Healing Garden prior to a medical appointment. University of Washington Design/Build Program, Puget Sound Veterans Administration Healing Garden, Seattle, Washington, 2016.

Informal Urban Communities Initiative

IUCI confronts the challenges of urban slum development through community-driven participatory design intervention. Founded in 2010 by faculty, students, and professionals from UW and Architects Without Borders–Seattle (AWB–Seattle), the initiative integrates public interest design practice, engaged scholarship, and design education.

IUCI's approach is based on an understanding of the enormous hardships that slum residents face, a belief in the strength and vitality of their communities, and a dedication to grounded action. It acknowledges and builds on existing incremental processes of slum development and attempts to empower community members to improve human well-being in their own neighborhoods through an emergent-convergent design process (Spencer and Bolton 2016). Students, faculty, and professionals work with community members to design and implement small-scale *emergent* interventions in community infrastructure that are relatively easy to build with local resources and have the potential for replication. They also help community members articulate their long-term development goals. Over time, emergent interventions accumulate and *converge*—both with one another and with the community's evolving long-term goals. The perspectives of community members and the IUCI team also converge as they build trust and mutual understanding through repeated collaboration.

Two primary activities contribute to this approach: UW campus-based design activism studios and on-site projects. During design activism studios, graduate students design small-scale, distributed infrastructure prototypes and formulate conceptual designs at the scale of the site that respond to community-expressed priorities. The students articulate how their small-scale prototypes might accrue over time and contribute to longer-term neighborhood development. During on-site projects, graduate and undergraduate students from multiple disciplines work with community members to design and implement built interventions and to monitor and evaluate their impacts. These on-site projects draw loosely upon the conceptual ideas developed during studios and ground them in real-world circumstances.

IUCI Pedagogical Goals

Both the design activism studios and the on-site projects emphasize learning objectives that foster students' emergent-convergent design skills and provide a foundation for the future pursuit of public interest design:

- **Informal urban development**: Having had little exposure to the challenges of slum development worldwide, students are introduced to the processes of urbanization, the development of urban slums, and the profound hardships that slum dwellers face through a combination of theoretical exploration and firsthand engagement.

- **Multiscalar thinking**: Slum development can be both massive in scope and driven by individuals and communities working to improve their lives through a bottom-up process. With this in mind, IUCI courses challenge students to design at multiple scales concurrently. Students posit design ideas at the scale of the household and the neighborhood with the potential for replication in other slum communities.
- **Interdisciplinary collaboration**: The challenges facing slum communities are complex and multifaceted. They require integrated, multisectoral solutions that draw on expertise ranging from engineering to environmental sciences to public health. Interdisciplinary collaboration during studios and on-site projects introduces students to diverse perspectives through which they interpret design challenges.
- **Participatory design**: Design that responds to local priorities, draws on local knowledge and skills, and asks community members to invest their own resources strengthens project outcomes and helps ensure long-term project sustainability. Students learn how to conduct participatory exercises, such as community mapping, priorities assessment, and participatory drawing and modeling, and how to facilitate community-driven implementation.
- **Design communication**: Students develop their skills in digital representation, hand rendering, and diagramming, as well as both digital and physical modeling, as a means of sharing their conceptual design ideas during participatory workshops. In preparation for project construction, students produce design manuals illustrating construction tools, materials, and processes of assembly. Iterative prototypes, full-scale mock-ups on-site, and ongoing design modification throughout the construction process help students and community members further articulate and refine their design ideas.
- **Hands-on implementation**: Project implementation requires firsthand knowledge of material assemblies and construction techniques. In studios, students strengthen their construction skills through the iterative fabrication of distributed infrastructure prototypes. On-site, they learn about local construction techniques from faculty members, professionals, and local craftspeople.
- **Personal resilience**: Community-driven, participatory design processes in urban slums seldom unfold according to plan. Unforeseen intracommunity conflicts, scheduling difficulties, and technical challenges can derail projects at any time. Students learn the value of patience, flexibility, persistence, and adaptability.
- **Long-term relationships**: Working with communities whose collaborative relationship with the IUCI spans many years, students learn about the trajectory of project evolution and participate in the monitoring and evaluation of previous projects. Through long-term relationships with partner communities, students and faculty build trust with community members and gain a deeper understanding of community dynamics.
- **Design matters**: Design is a synthetic approach to problem solving that integrates social, environmental, technical, and aesthetic considerations. It is

both a process and a product that builds social capital and instills dignity and a sense of pride. Students learn that design matters—especially in communities where resources are limited.

IUCI Outcomes

Students involved in IUCI projects in Lomas de Zapallal have contributed to the design and implementation of a park; a stairway and terraced garden; a classroom at Pitágoras School; as well as forty-seven household gardens, fog-collection pilot projects, and a large-scale fog-collection system in the Eliseo Collazos (EC) neighborhood (Spencer, Bolton, and Alarcon 2014; Feld, Spencer, and Bolton 2016). The design and implementation of a fog-irrigated park in EC is currently under way (see the Fog Water Farms sample project).

IUCI has begun to branch out from Lomas de Zapallal-based projects. In the floating community of Claverito in Iquitos, Peru, IUCI students are designing and implementing garden technologies and researching their impacts on human and environmental health.[1] In the Pongro Senchey neighborhood of Phnom Penh, Cambodia, students recently completed a six-hundred-meter road and community gathering space.[2] Participatory impact assessment, focus group interviews, on-site observation, and quantitative surveys indicate that IUCI projects are benefiting community members. After repeated engagement, the IUCI team has become increasingly adept at project implementation. At the same time, we continue to learn from our experiences.

Student evaluations of IUCI service-learning projects have been highly favorable, and many students count their participation in the IUCI courses as one of the most transformative experiences of their design education. They gain an appreciation for the complexities of cross-cultural, collaborative design and their potential as agents of change. Some students elect to participate in multiple on-site projects during their time at UW.

Although we have yet to conduct a comprehensive survey of alumni, anecdotal evidence suggests that the program has had a lasting impact on student activities following graduation. Some former students have contributed to IUCI as professional volunteers for AWB–Seattle. Others have served as professional volunteers on IUCI projects or have undertaken related public interest design efforts. For example, one former IUCI student became the president of Engineers Without Borders–USA's West Coast region. IUCI's Peruvian cofounder and on-site coordinator and another IUCI graduate are leading the IUCI projects in Iquitos mentioned previously.

IUCI projects are published on a regular basis and have received awards from the American Society of Landscape Architects, the Environmental Design Research Association, the Social Economic Environmental Design Network, and the Council of Educators in Landscape Architecture. By continuing to engage students, faculty, and professionals; assess project impacts; and disseminate project outcomes, IUCI hopes to make a small contribution toward improving the conditions of informal urban communities and promoting the practice of public interest design.

IUCI Sample Project: Fog Water Farms[3]

Fog Water Farms (FWF) responds to a lack of public green space in Lima's informal urban communities and the threat of increasing water insecurity due to climate change and the disappearance of Andean glaciers. Leveraging the presence of fog in Lima for seven months each year and the initiative of community members, the project serves as an example of community-scaled, point-of-use water infrastructure. FWF represents the convergence of two of IUCI's previous projects: SQWater, a fog-collection pilot project that assessed the feasibility of fog collection as an alternative water resource and developed new materials with the potential to increase fog-collection yields; and Gardens Green Space and Health, a project involving the design and construction of twenty-nine household gardens and the measurement of their impacts on social capital, health, and well-being.

In June 2015, students, faculty, and professional volunteers initiated the first phase of the project. They facilitated a series of participatory workshops (see Figure 1.4) and helped community members design four large fog collectors, expand the twenty-nine household gardens previously constructed, and construct an additional eighteen household gardens and a small community garden. Operational by the latter part of the 2015 fog season in Lima, the fog collectors captured fog water as a source of irrigation for the gardens (see Figure 1.5).

The second phase of the project is currently under way and draws upon lessons learned during Phase I. Fewer UW students are directly engaged in Phase II. However, several AWB–Seattle professionals who were involved in IUCI as students have taken on leadership roles and are building on their previous experiences. During Phase II, the IUCI team is working with community members to improve and expand the Phase I fog-collection system and to design and implement a community park that includes fog-water storage, terraced gardens, a sports court, and areas for gathering and play (see Figure 1.6).

1.4
Participatory fog-collector modeling workshop at Eliseo Collazos Community Center. University of Washington IUCI Team, IUCI Fog Water Farms, Lima, Peru, 2016.

1.5
Fog collectors on the hillside overlooking Eliseo Collazos. University of Washington IUCI Team, IUCI Fog Water Farms, Lima, Peru, 2016.

1.6
Fog-water-irrigated community park in Eliseo Collazos. University of Washington IUCI Team, IUCI Fog Water Farms, Lima, Peru, 2016.

Whole-Systems Public Interest Design Education

Notes

1. Funding for the IUCI project in Iquitos is provided by the Centro de Investigaciones Tecnologicas, Biomedicas y Medioambientales, the Landscape Architecture Foundation Olmsted Scholars Program, the University of Washington Center for One Health Research, the National Institutes of Health Fogarty Global Health Fellowship Program, the UW Department of Global Health Thomas Francis Jr. and Go Health Fellowships, and University of Washington Global Innovation Funds.
2. Funding for the IUCI project in Phnom Penh, Cambodia, was provided by University of Washington Global Innovation Funds.
3. Funding for the Fog Water Farms project in Lima, Peru, is provided by the Robert Rauschenberg Foundation.

References

Carpenter, William J. 1997. *Learning by Building, Design, and Construction in Architectural Education*. New York: Van Nostrand Reinhold.

Feld, Shara, Benjamin R. Spencer, and Susan Bolton. 2016. "Improved Fog Collection Using Turf Reinforcement Mats." *Journal of Sustainable Water in the Built Environment* 2 (3): 1–8. doi:10.1061/JSWBAY.0000811.

Hou, Jeffrey. 2011. "Differences Matter: Learning to Design in Partnership with Others." In *Service-Learning in Design and Planning: Educating at the Boundaries*, edited by Tom Angotti, Cheryl Doble, and Paula Horrigan, 55–69. Berkeley, CA: New Village Press.

Hou, Jeffrey. 2014. "Life Before/During/Between/After Service-Learning Studios." In *Community Matters: Service-Learning and Engaged Design and Planning*, edited by Mallika Bose, Paula Horrigan, Cheryl Doble, and Sigmund C. Shipp. London: Earthscan.

Pallasmaa, Juhani. 2012. *The Eyes of the Skin: Architecture and the Senses*. West Sussex, UK: John Wiley and Sons, Ltd.

Sennett, Richard. 2008. *The Craftsman*. New Haven, CT: Yale University Press.

Spencer, Ben, and Susan Bolton. 2016. "Emergent Convergent: Technology and the Informal Urban Communities Initiative." In *Innovations in Landscape Architecture*, edited by Jonathon R. Anderson and Daniel H. Ortega, 205–22. London: Routledge.

Spencer, Ben, Susan Bolton, and Jorge Alarcon. 2014. "The Informal Urban Communities Initiative: Community-Driven Design in the Slums of Lima, Peru." *International Journal of Service Learning in Engineering*, 9 (1): 92–107.

Wagenfeld, A., and Daniel Winterbottom. 2015. *Therapeutic Gardens: Design for Healing Spaces*. Portland, OR: Timber Press.

Winterbottom, Daniel. 2002. "Building as Learning." *Landscape Journal*, 21 (1): 201–13.

Winterbottom, Daniel. 2011. "Effecting Change Through Humanitarian Design." In *Service-Learning in Design and Planning: Educating at the Boundaries*, edited by Tom Angotti, Cheryl Doble, and Paula Horrigan, 189–204. Berkeley, CA: New Village Press.

Winterbottom, Daniel. 2014. "Developing a Safe, Nurturing, and Therapeutic Environment for Families of the Garbage Pickers in Guatemala and for Disabled Children in Bosnia and Herzegovina." In *Greening in the Red Zone: Disaster, Resilience and Community Greening*, edited by Keith G. Tidball and Marianne E. Krasny, 410–37. New York: Springer.

2
Educating the Next Generation of Social Innovators
Designmatters at ArtCenter

Mariana Amatullo, Dan Gottlieb,
Penny Herscovitch, and
Susannah Ramshaw

Department Philosophy

Through research, advocacy, and action, Designmatters engages, empowers, and leads an ongoing exploration of art and design as a positive force in society.

Implicit in the mission statement of the Designmatters department at ArtCenter College of Design is the mandate to bring real-world and real-time issues into the curriculum of the college as the source of experiential learning about the role of the arts and design disciplines in catalyzing social-innovation outcomes, which we define as new products, processes, environments, and systems that satisfy unmet needs and enhance society's capacity to act (Mulgan et al. 2007). As an educational department at ArtCenter, Designmatters is integrated into an institution that has had more than eighty-five years of lasting impact in educating artists and designers using a conservatory approach, supplemented by intercultural and interdisciplinary dialogue with leading practitioners. The college's emphasis on project-based learning, rigor, and preparation under the guidance of an expert professional faculty is found in all of the department's educational offerings. Throughout its sixteen-year history, the department's philosophical orientation has remained consistent: to foster an open, forward-thinking, entrepreneurial culture of socially responsible design through a range of learning activities, both curricular and cocurricular.

Designmatters has grown significantly in scope since its inception as a college-wide program in 2001.[1] The growth pertains to the infrastructure and reach of the Designmatters curriculum, as well as to the measurable outcomes that Designmatters has garnered through projects and special initiatives with partner organizations. In 2009, Designmatters transitioned from a college-wide program of curated courses, special projects, and publications to a full-scale, non-degree-granting educational department.[2] Today Designmatters champions the mission and principles of public interest design at the college.[3] The department acts as a horizontal curricular hub at ArtCenter, fostering collaboration across all design disciplines taught at the college and partnering with many public and private organizations that take an innovative approach to addressing pressing societal challenges for public benefit.[4]

Four thematic pillars—sustainable development, public policy, global health, and social entrepreneurship—are brought together under the Designmatters curriculum, allowing students to apply their skill sets and creativity to engage in societal issues that often require an interdisciplinary, human-centered approach to innovation. The department's educational offerings range from individual elective courses open to students seeking an experience in design for social innovation as part of their education at ArtCenter to a structured course of study for undergraduates pursuing a public interest design specialization through the Designmatters minor.[5] Cocurricular workshops with thought leaders in social innovation design, internships in the social and public sectors, and the Designmatters Fellowship program expose students to promising career pathways in the field.[6] The department also collaborates with ArtCenter's Media Design Practices (MDP) in a graduate track known as MDP: Field, which partners with the UNICEF Innovation division to inform the field-experience and design-research opportunities offered to students within this Master of Fine Arts curriculum.

Department Curriculum Overview

The Designmatters pedagogy has two objectives: (1) to provide students with an enriching set of learning outcomes by working collaboratively at varying levels of complexity and community in public interest design and (2) to support partners with design knowledge and capacity in the critical phases of implementing projects conceived through the department.

To achieve these goals, the department is organized as a hybrid educational and administrative structure with three roles:

1. an educational magnet that provides content-based challenges and opportunities for transdisciplinary research in design for social innovation
2. an incubator that supplies students with the know-how and resources needed to implement their ideas or launch their own social enterprises
3. a center for collaboration with innovative organizations and networks that are committed to public interest design

Educating the Next Generation of Social Innovators

A key pillar of the department's pedagogical model is co-creation and collaboration through participatory research methods. Design briefs are structured within a collaborative framework that includes field research and multiple touch points for feedback from external stakeholders and potential beneficiaries of the interventions. This process exposes students to perspectives and expertise from multiple disciplines. The model emphasizes unique participatory research methodologies that build empathy with the end users; the objective is to address users' needs in a holistic way that engages the participants in cooperatively informing the creative problem-solving process as much as possible.

Another important hallmark of Designmatters studios is a transdisciplinary, team-based approach to collaboration. Students from across design disciplines form teams to solve real-world challenges in a "reflection-in-action" (Schön 1983) mode of inquiry. This approach enables students to experiment and to incorporate experience-based insights, judgment, and intuition. Students bring their individual life experiences, diverse cultural upbringings, and varied strengths in design skill sets from their core academic design disciplines. The collaborative process facilitates dialogue, feedback, critical thinking, delegation, leadership, and, ultimately, teamwork. This process also promotes the flexibility, adaptive learning, and confidence building necessary for working with the interdependent, complex challenges of the social-design briefs that students encounter in Designmatters studios.

Finally, Designmatters studios integrate the broad-based learning opportunities of ArtCenter's liberal arts curriculum (overseen by the Department of Humanities and Sciences), allowing students to connect their questions and concerns with a sense of ethical and civic responsibility and a critical understanding of the social issues that they are tackling. Domain experts from various fields of the social and hard sciences are invited as guest faculty or in advisory capacities to inform students' research into their design briefs, preparing students to make relevant connections and to apply this knowledge to their ideation process.

Example Initiative: Safe Agua Course Series

The Safe Agua initiative from the Designmatters portfolio exemplifies how the three pedagogical pillars manifest in practice. Safe Agua is an ongoing transdisciplinary series of design-research and social-innovation courses hosted in the Environmental Design department, in which students develop products and services to meet the challenges of access to safe water for populations of urban slum dwellers in Latin America. The initiative was developed in partnership with TECHO, a prominent Latin American nongovernmental organization (NGO) that serves slum communities, and SociaLab, a consultancy and incubator for social-innovation start-ups spun off TECHO's Innovation Center. Safe Agua has also relied on participation of community members in each of the urban field-research settings where three subsequent phases of the initiative have taken place: Santiago, Chile (2009); Lima, Peru (2011–2012); and Bogotá, Colombia

(2013–2014). Each iteration of the Safe Agua courses was designed by building on the insights of previous studios; all three iterations have fostered effective models for design-centric social enterprises, services, products, and built-environment solutions that have reached various levels of pilot testing with the communities engaged in the research (Amatullo and Herscovitch 2012; Amatullo, Becerra, and Montgomery 2011).[7]

In addition to design, Safe Agua integrates social-entrepreneurship instruction in part through a partnership with the Marshall School of Business Brittingham Social Enterprise Lab at the University of Southern California (USC). The director of the program and graduate students collaborate with lead Environmental Design faculty on key modules and various stages of project incubation that emphasize business skills and entrepreneurship methods within the social mission of the initiative. The partnership with USC Marshall has allowed students to not only develop innovative products and systems but also map strategies and begin to understand the complex commercial ecosystem involved in bringing their ideas to fruition.

Safe Agua Course Series Learning Objectives

The Safe Agua course framework guides students through a sixteen-week research and design process to create outcomes with the potential to take on an entrepreneurial life, working toward the aspiration of real-world impact beyond the class. As a result of the Safe Agua course series, students will be able to:

- use field research to develop a sense of empathy and to give further insight to the problem by understanding core values, aspirations, physical environments, and so on
- engage community members, stakeholders, and audiences in the co-creation and prototyping phases of the design process
- develop sustainable, scalable solutions with a potential for real-world outcomes
- develop radically affordable products and services for Base of Pyramid (BoP) families who are living on under two dollars per day[8]
- develop a sustainable business plan, including sourcing, pricing, and marketing
- research and identify potential partners and manufacturers to bring the products to market

Safe Agua Course Series Pedagogical Goals

The Safe Agua course series follows an iterative, human-centered design process, educating students in the sequence of social-design methodologies outlined in Figure 2.1. At the same time, the course provides an opportunity for students to use their creative passion and original thinking to address entrenched social problems. The course ultimately seeks to empower students to apply this thinking process to future design challenges.

2.1
Timeline, activities, and milestones for the Safe Agua course series.

Weeks	Phase	Key Activities	Goals and Outputs
1–2	Field research	Uncover needs, constraints, and aspirations through immersive field research with families and community partners. Guide students through participatory, qualitative, and quantitative research methodologies using method cards. Conduct community-action exercises.	Establish empathy and deep connections with local families. Identify important, relevant problems to address that apply both locally and globally. Seek powerful, yet realizable, design opportunities.
2–3	Research analysis and problem definition	Organize and analyze research collected. Define problems where design can make an impact. Communicate and analyze the problem visually using storyboarding and problem mapping.	Identify the most salient problems and begin to address those challenges in collaboration with community leaders and partner organizations.
4–5	Creation of opportunity areas	Cross the problem with values and resources, consumption patterns, and aspirations. Ask questions like "How might we...?" and "What if...?" Apply filters and criteria: potential to make a significant impact on lives; alignment with families' top priorities and students' passions; and potential to scale up.	Define opportunity areas: spaces to begin to generate a range of solutions. Prioritize opportunity areas to create social impact and align with students' passions.
6–9	Design ideation and iteration	Brainstorm, mind map, sketch, do "thinking through making" exercise, and create iterative prototypes.	Generate design concepts within opportunity area. Develop, test, and refine initial design solutions.
6–9	Business model development	Engage in social entrepreneurship lectures, exercises, and critiques.	Consider the value chain and articulate preliminary business models.
9–10	Midterm review and refinement	Present design proposal options, as well as the key elements of the process.	Receive feedback from guest critics with diverse perspectives in how to develop designs.
11–12	Field-testing and prototype iteration	Field-test working prototypes of products, services, systems, and business models with community and partners. Make specific refinements to designs (or pivot) based on field-testing response.	Elicit community feedback, essential to incubating and iterating designs to create the most value for users.
12–16	Final design execution	Fabricate final models, renderings in context, drawings, and presentations.	Create a functioning prototype of the product, system, or service.
12–16	Business model revision	Conduct a strategy-mapping workshop. Draft and revise business model canvas, value proposition, and value chain.	Develop proposal for business and implementation strategy.
16	Final presentation	Create a professional presentation to share with an audience of educators, partner organizations, and professionals.	Identify potential for future project refinement, piloting, development, and implementation through discussion and feedback.

Evolution of Programming: Development Seminar

Unlike in many traditional design studios where students' final presentations conclude the class, in Safe Agua the "final" is truly a departure point. To nurture projects with strong potential, Designmatters has created the Development Seminar, an elective extension of the core Safe Agua course into the following term. The Development Seminar emerged to meet the projects' needs, based on the learning that students and their projects thrive with structured support after the end of the studio. A platform for development, this seminar shepherds highly motivated student teams as they set goals and strategies for advancing their projects to the next level. During the seminar, teams identify new advisers and team members, apply for grants and awards, plan and conduct a further round of pilot testing and design iteration, and pitch to potential strategic partners.

While the Development Seminar has established a track record of yielding grants, international accolades, and publicity, a key challenge that remains is how to propel projects to reach "escape velocity" so that they can survive beyond graduation, when real-world financial and career pressures emerge. Although faculty mentorship continues informally beyond the Development Seminar, Designmatters faculty have identified the need to develop a stronger institutional infrastructure for supporting team members after graduation and are currently exploring how best to foster career pathways in social entrepreneurship within the context of a small private design college.

2.1
Community members from Cerro Verde engaged in the research-methodology process to identify key challenges and opportunities. Safe Agua Peru, Cerro Verde, Peru, and Pasadena, California, 2011.

Educating the Next Generation of Social Innovators

> **Sample Project: GiraDora, Safe Agua Peru**
>
> In fall of 2011, Designmatters hosted the transdisciplinary studio Safe Agua Peru, building on the investigations and experiences of the award-winning Safe Agua Chile initiative in 2009. Designmatters once again partnered with the Latin American NGO TECHO and its Innovation Center to co-create innovative design solutions to overcoming water poverty; the partners worked with families living in Cerro Verde, a thirty-thousand-person slum perched on the hillsides surrounding Lima, Peru.
>
> Safe Agua Peru followed an iterative, human-centered design process, educating students in a sequence of social-design methodologies. Each key activity of the sixteen-week studio correlated with measurable goals and learning outcomes for the students.
>
> Beginning with two weeks of immersive field research, students established deep connections with approximately twenty families in Cerro Verde, enabling the students to seek powerful design opportunities with end users (see Figure 2.1). By defining the problem where designs could make an impact, students identified the most salient issues and began addressing these challenges collectively with community leaders and the partner organization. Creating opportunity areas allowed students to ask questions like "How might we...?" and "What if...?" to better understand the families' priorities and the students' personal passions. Design ideation and iteration created brainstorming and mind-mapping sessions where multidisciplinary teams developed and refined the initial design solutions. Designmatters invited guest lecturers to the studio to discuss business-model development, including exercises and critiques, for the students' budding social enterprises. Following the midterm review, students moved to field-testing and iterating prototypes to elicit feedback from the community, essential to creating the most value for the consumer. Students then executed their final designs by producing functioning prototypes and revised their business models to solidify a value proposition and create an implementation strategy. Finally, students presented their fully developed projects to an audience of educators, partners, and professionals, who helped identify future project refinement, development, and implementation.
>
> GiraDora, a project implemented by Safe Agua Peru, is a combined clothing washer and spin dryer that saves water, does not require electricity, reduces the time to wash a load of laundry, and improves the experience of washing clothes for families living without access to running water (see Figure 2.2). Conceived by a team of product- and environmental-design students, GiraDora's development exemplifies the driving principles of co-creation and social enterprise. GiraDora was one of three prototypes sent to Cerro Verde leading up to the studio, providing the students returning to the community a valuable opportunity to test the viability of the product and to uncover insights with the BoP consumer. During field-testing, community members identified an innovative solution that converted the working prototype, a single-function wringer, into a dual-function washer and wringer (see Figure 2.3).
>
> Since the culmination of the course, the GiraDora team has founded Blue Barrel Concepts, LLC, a social enterprise under which GiraDora is the core product. GiraDora has gone on to win design awards and seed grants, as well as to garner global interest from private-sector companies and social-impact investors. The product currently has a contract with a prominent Latin American manufacturer of domestic goods for pilot testing in the Mexican market.

Course Outcomes and Challenges

The Safe Agua initiative presents powerful empirical evidence of the opportunities and challenges that are inherent to integrating social entrepreneurship into public interest design curricula. The sample project, GiraDora, exemplifies the challenges of trying

2.2
GiraDora is a human-powered clothing washer and dryer designed with slum-dwelling residents during the 2011 Safe Agua Peru course. Alex Cabunoc, product design, and Ji A. You, environmental design, Safe Agua Peru, Cerro Verde, Peru, and Pasadena, California, 2011.

to meet societal needs while nurturing students through a pedagogical framework to develop successful social ventures. For example, realizing a social venture requires sustained time and commitment, well beyond the core course and Development Seminar. For faculty, the challenge lies in guiding students to balance an emerging

Educating the Next Generation of Social Innovators

2.3
A student observes early user testing with a GiraDora prototype. Alex Cabunoc, product design, and Ji A. You, environmental design, Safe Agua Peru, Cerro Verde, Peru, and Pasadena, California, 2011.

social venture with their academic course load and nurturing that venture so it can thrive after students graduate and transition into their design careers.

One key lesson learned is how to balance the design curriculum with the fluid nature of collaboration, the needs of multiple stakeholders, and real-world constraints. This challenge can become a teaching opportunity. The pedagogical emphasis has to take into consideration multiple design-client relationships at once. These relationships are often complex in public sector design; for students, the interdependent dimension of collaboration can become an opportunity to learn how to reframe their missions and projects depending on the audience—for example, in presenting to community members, a nonprofit partner, a potential grant funder, or a business partner.

From the perspective of the project management and design faculty team, how do we inspire design students to embrace social-impact design and social-entrepreneurship models as exciting and viable career pathways? How do we overcome the challenges of following a syllabus with traditional expectations within the limited timeframes of the academic setting and reconcile design-instruction goals with field research in a foreign country and highly disadvantaged socioeconomic context? This is a balancing act for the faculty. It requires adhering to the learning outcomes stipulated in a course's syllabus while simultaneously preparing students to acquire the skill set and confidence to build their own social enterprises as a continuum to their educational experiences.

The following are some further reflections on how to address these challenges:

- Challenge students to accept that they will have to work in circumstances where everything is a moving target and the unexpected will occur; ingenuity and adeptness at taking advantage of the resources at hand are key ingredients of success.
- Resist the urge to predetermine the design brief and its deliverables in too narrow a fashion. Do not bring in preconceived notions or assumptions about

course outcomes, but rather anticipate and be as rigorous as possible in "front-loading" the process (for example, line up partners who can support the challenging step of taking the product to market, such as business faculty and other local experts, in advance).

- Secure and nurture trust with organizational partners in the project to ensure access to the community in a way that will allow the design team to form sustainable ties with the project participants.
- Develop ongoing strategies and channels for communication with users to maximize co-creation throughout every step of the process.
- Rely on—or, if necessary, build—an institutional infrastructure that can maximize a continuum of learning and adequately incubate projects. Ensure that students receive faculty mentorship and access to diverse expertise that can prepare students to create the value network they will need to take their social enterprise forward into the marketplace.
- Remember that while partners are essential to social-innovation projects that aspire to go beyond the studio and have a long-term impact on society, adding more stakeholders to the process also adds more complexity that will need to be confronted and managed.

These strategies and lessons learned have helped Designmatters programs like Safe Agua begin to overcome the limitations encountered in traditional design-education models and supporting infrastructure.

The Safe Agua course series is an exemplar of the Designmatters Department's commitment to experiential design education and public-sector design. Safe Agua, rich in design-entrepreneurship outcomes, illustrates some of the key opportunities and recurrent challenges that still remain for educators and students who engage in projects of such complexity. Our experience suggests that what "success" looks like by the end of the course is as much about the tangible designs that might be ideated for products and services as it is about accepting a new threshold of flexibility and ingenuity in what often feels like uncharted terrain.

Notes

1 Designmatters was launched at ArtCenter in 2001, during the presidency of Richard Koshalek, as part of an overall institutional commitment to bring a renewed infusion of innovation and global engagement into the organizational culture and curricula. It was one of several programs of the college's former International Initiatives Department, led by Erica Clark, cofounder of Designmatters with Mariana Amatullo and a former senior vice president at ArtCenter. The program was modeled after a select number of social-design initiatives in European institutions, including a program led by Liz Davis at ENSCI–Les Ateliers, Paris. The Designmatters task force was in place during the program's first two years

and was responsible for developing the organizational principles of the program and ensuring its integration within the fabric of the institution. Critical to the work of Amatullo and Clark in the initial years was building the necessary institutional capacity and effective processes to coordinate the external partnerships that would inform the program's scope of activities.

2. The "projects" and "library" sections of the Designmatters website (www.designmattersatartcenter.org/) provide a robust archive of case studies and publications in the portfolio of the department.

3. While the term *public interest design* is not used in the articulation of the social-innovation mission of the department, Designmatters is closely aligned with the foundational belief of the movement: "Every person should be able to live in a socially, economically, and environmentally healthy community" (Abendroth and Bell 2016).

4. Commitment to partnerships as a source of experiential learning has been a cornerstone of the Designmatters vision since its founding. Structured collaborations with local, national, and international organizations that bring an influx of public interest design issues to bear are key to the pedagogical model of Designmatters. One of the most notable alliances, established by Designmatters in the early years of the program, is with the United Nations and a number of its agencies and funds. Through Designmatters, in 2003 ArtCenter became the first design institution in the United States to be granted nongovernmental organization status with the UN Department of Public Information; other formal alliances followed. For further reference about Designmatters' partnership strategy, see Amatullo and Breitenberg, "Designmatters at ArtCenter College of Design," 2006.

5. The elective courses are referred to as *transdisciplinary (TDS) courses*; they typically cross several disciplines to create a holistic approach to problem solving, with outcomes of the course generally aimed at implementation. TDS courses are team taught by faculty from different fields and vary every academic term. To graduate with the Designmatters minor in social innovation, ArtCenter students are required to complete two or more TDS courses. For further reference on the portfolio of these courses, see the "projects" section of the Designmatters website (www.designmattersatartcenter.org/proj/).

6. The Designmatters Fellowship is an honors internship initiative that places an average of six to eight of the most talented ArtCenter students in international development organizations, government agencies, research and development divisions of industry, and social enterprises on an annual basis. For further reference and documentation about the Designmatters Fellowship Program, see www.designmattersatartcenter.org/fellowship-program/.

7. For detailed outcomes of each Safe Agua course, see the Designmatters website project section (www.designmattersatartcenter.org/proj/); the Safe Agua Chile and the Safe Agua Colombia courses were each documented in print publications available for download from the site. The Safe Agua Peru

course was the subject of a documentary, *Hands in the Mist,* directed by Erik Anderson and available at https://vimeo.com/designmatters/.
8 Espoused by the influential US business-school academics Prahalad and Hart (2002), the Base of Pyramid theory suggests that new business opportunities lie in designing and distributing goods and services for poor communities.

References

Abendroth, Lisa M., and Bryan Bell, eds. 2016. *Public Interest Design Practice Guidebook: SEED Methodology, Case Studies, and Critical Issues.* New York: Routledge.

Amatullo, Mariana, Liliana Becerra, and Steven Montgomery. 2011. "Designmatters Case Studies: Design Education Methodologies as a Tool for Social Innovation." VentureWell Open Conference, Washington, DC, March 24–26. www.designmattersatArtCenter.org/wp-content/uploads/Design-Education-Methodologies-as-a-Tool-for-Social-Innovation.pdf.

Amatullo, Mariana, and Mark Breitenberg. 2006. "Designmatters at ArtCenter College of Design: Design Advocacy and Global Engagement." Cumulus Working Papers, Nantes, France, July 16.

Amatullo, Mariana, and Penny Herscovitch. 2012. "Perspectives About Design Education for Social Innovation: The Safe Agua Case Study." Cumulus Working Papers, Santiago, Chile, November 25. www.designmattersatArtCenter.org/wp-content/uploads/Projecting-Design-paper-publication_Safe-Agua-case-study.pdf.

Mulgan, Geoff, Simon Tucker, Rushanara Ali, and Ben Sanders. 2007. *Social Innovation: What It Is, Why It Matters, and How It Can Be Accelerated.* Oxford, UK: Skoll Centre for Social Entrepreneurship. http://youngfoundation.org/wp-content/uploads/2012/10/Social-Innovation-what-it-is-why-it-matters-how-it-can-be-accelerated-March-2007.pdf.

Prahalad, C. K., and Stuart L. Hart. 2002. "The Fortune at the Bottom of the Pyramid." *Strategy + Business* 26 (First Quarter). www.strategy-business.com/article/11518?gko=9a4ba.

Schön, Donald A. 1983. *The Reflective Practitioner: How Professionals Think in Action.* New York: Basic Books.

3
Changing Practice, Practicing Change
The Graduate Certificate in Public Interest Design at Portland State University

R. Todd Ferry and Sergio Palleroni

Program Philosophy

The Center for Public Interest Design (CPID) is a research, education, and community design center whose mission is to investigate, promote, and engage in inclusive design practices that address the growing needs of underserved communities worldwide through sustainable methods. Based in the School of Architecture (SOA) at Portland State University (PSU) in Oregon, CPID activates the university's motto, "Let knowledge serve the city," by fostering opportunities for transdisciplinary collaboration among faculty, students, professionals, and community partners. CPID's goal is to advance positive social change through the power of design. The creation of a Graduate Certificate in Public Interest Design supports this effort and is at the heart of CPID's work.

The certificate program and the work of CPID seek to advance the potential for design to improve the lives of all people—not just the few that can afford it—as demonstrated perhaps most notably by the design/build programs growing out of the social movements of the 1960s and 1970s. CPID's founding director, Sergio Palleroni, was an early leader in this movement, and nearly three decades ago, he cofounded the Building Sustainable Communities Initiative (BaSiC), an international academic program focused on offering design and building services to communities. This service-learning program was both a response to the needs of vulnerable communities around the globe and a desire to expand the capacity of architects to address social and environmental issues. Through the immersive experience of

BaSiC, students living in the communities that they served began to appreciate that the building itself was only a small part of what would be produced through their collaboration with the community. The other outcomes, such as building the capacity of communities to undertake similar projects for themselves, were what Palleroni termed the "unseen 90 percent." BaSiC focused on teaching students this crucial understanding along with the skills to create *with* the community. This lesson was carried forward as a fundamental principle of CPID's work and pedagogy.

Design/build remains a cornerstone of many of CPID's fieldwork initiatives and is often incorporated into the center's planning, engagement, and design work to demonstrate immediate action while working with community partners toward larger efforts. We believe that public interest design cannot be taught without embedding students into a project's context and giving them the means to observe and participate in the processes that make a community and frame a project. CPID also aims to expand the role of designers to make significant impact through a range of approaches, which can take the form of design services, planning processes, community engagement, research, or, frequently, a combination of all of these.

One of CPID's most distinguishing features is the range of projects it undertakes, from initiatives to address homelessness, gentrification, and environmental sustainability in Portland and the Northwest region to international design/build projects in Haiti, Argentina, and India. The diversity of projects at CPID underscores the range of research by CPID Faculty Fellows and professional collaborators.[1] This diversity also supports a key aspect of the center's mission to research the entire field of public interest design and to offer students opportunities for research, design, and fieldwork in a variety of areas that align with their professional goals, recognizing that there is not one path toward public interest design practice.

We are creating an environment that promotes critical discourse by combining course work with practice. CPID facilitates this discourse by acting as a hub for students, faculty, community members, and design professionals to discuss the vast array of issues surrounding public interest design practice. While we were very intentional about the framework and choices of transdisciplinary course offerings when developing our certificate program, our goal is not to offer a certificate that merely provides answers and verifies completed credit hours at our institution. We strive to foster leaders who enter into meaningful practice anchored by thoughtful questioning continuously informed by lessons learned in the field.

Program Curriculum Overview

The Graduate Certificate in Public Interest Design was created as a means to prepare future leaders in architecture, urban planning, community development, and other fields to aid currently underserved populations through transdisciplinary design approaches. With no precedent for an academic certificate of this nature, the curriculum was informed by an in-depth study of the field, as well as of successful certificate programs in departments with similar missions at PSU and other universities. The certificate is offered to both current graduate students and professionals with a previous degree. The program consists of a minimum of eighteen credit hours of course options from several disciplines, with a focus on the *triple bottom line* of sustainability: social, environmental, and economic; these course offerings range from Social Entrepreneurship (PA 541) to Environmental Sustainability (ESM 588) to Concepts of Citizen Participation (USP 550). The course work is anchored by an Introduction to Public Interest Design seminar (Arch 433/533) and culminates with students embedded in fieldwork or a practicum on a real-world project at CPID.

Graduate Certificate in Public Interest Design (Minimum Eighteen Credit Hours Total)

Course Work (Minimum Fourteen Credit Hours)

Required course for all certificate participants:

Contemporary Issues Seminar: Public Interest Design in Practice (Arch 533), Four Credits

Social (One of the Following Courses)
- Design Thesis (Arch 585) with public interest design focus, architecture students only, six credits
- Design Thinking for Social Innovation (MGMT 521), online, four credits
- Creating Collaborative Communities (PA 543), three credits
- Concepts of Citizen Participation (USP 550), four credits
- Urban Poverty in Critical Perspective (USP 552), three credits

Environmental (One of the Following Courses)
- Building Science Research Topics (Arch 563), four credits
- Environmental Sustainability (ESM 588), four credits
- Urban Ecology (ESM 528), four credits
- Sustainable Cities (Geog 532), four credits
- Sustainable Development Practices (USP 588), three credits

Economic (One of the Following Courses)
- Topics in Professional Practice (Arch 543) with public interest design focus, four credits
- Grant Writing for Nonprofit Organizations (PA 525), three credits
- Social Entrepreneurship (PA 541), three credits
- Money Matters for Social Innovation (MGMT 522), online, four credits
- Political Economy of Nonprofit Organizations (USP 580), three credits
- Green Economics and Sustainable Development (USP 590), three credits

Fieldwork (Arch 541), Minimum Four Credit Hours

Introduction to Public Interest Design Seminar

The Introduction to Public Interest Design seminar kicks off the certificate course sequence and provides an overview of guiding principles, issues, and best practices of public interest design work. The seminar's framework and learning objectives mirror that of the larger certificate.

As a result of this course, students are able to:

- analyze foundational definitions, history, and present trends in the field of public interest design
- develop engagement strategies in underserved communities to identify issues, map assets, and work toward a collective solution
- demonstrate knowledge of funding models for public interest design projects
- interpret the fundamentals of sustainability
- demonstrate real-world experience on a public interest design project
- compare metrics for creating and evaluating the efficacy of a public interest design project

The course's primary components are weekly discussions and debates, case studies in public interest design, and hands-on experience in an ongoing public interest design project at CPID. The seminar meets twice weekly during the quarter, for about two hours each class. Each week explores a different theme within public interest design (such as the potential role of design in disaster relief and resiliency, project funding, or community partnerships), sparked by a particular discussion question or provocation led by different students and, often, a guest practitioner. The students leading the discussion research supporting materials and case studies for both sides of these provocations and moderate a class debate that is often extremely lively. The following are a few examples of these prompts:

- Should public interest designers respond only to challenges and opportunities brought forth by a community, or should they use their backgrounds to identify challenges and opportunities in a community and propose a project?
- What are the considerations for whether public interest designers should or should not work outside of their communities, cities, cultures, or languages? Should public interest designers only work within their immediate contexts?
- Should the person or organization first inviting a designer into a community decide what constitutes the community, or is it the role of the designer to help determine who should be included in the community?

The point of these prompts is not to arrive collectively at a conclusive answer but to bring up the complexities within public interest design work and to help students develop their own identities as designers and practitioners, informed by guiding principles, readings, case studies, and hands-on experience in the ongoing projects that the seminar offers.

Students in the seminar research case studies representing best practices, chosen from the complete list of Social Economic Environmental Design (SEED) Network award winners.[2] In groups of two or three, the students analyze their chosen projects and study the practitioners and context of the work; prepare presentations on the projects to deliver to the other students; and evaluate the social, economic, and environmental strategies represented. Students also reflect on the work by creating analytical diagrams of each project and noting important takeaways that can apply to the projects that they undertake in the seminar.

Students then break up into groups that will each contribute to an active CPID project in a different stage of development. These projects provide an entry point to fieldwork where the seminar students can interpret theory and put lessons learned into action. While they vary in type and stage of process, the projects collectively offer an opportunity for students to gain a comprehensive understanding of different approaches to public interest design through comparing their own experiences to those of their peers working on other initiatives. In 2016, student groups designed a bus stop that could double as a community center in support of California's carbon-credit initiative to serve underserved neighborhoods in Sacramento, researched material reuse as a strategy for addressing Portland's housing crisis, and advanced an ongoing campaign to prevent the displacement of African Americans from Portland's quickly gentrifying city center by creating an engagement tool for community partners. At the end of the quarter, each group submits an extensive report detailing previous work on the project, the seminar group's contribution, and thorough suggestions for next steps. Crucially, this reporting also offers an opportunity for reflection and evaluation of the project. The seminar informs the elective courses that students take toward their certificates as they consider their developing interests and desired skills.

Electives

Students must complete three elective courses for the certificate, one each from the social, economic, and environmental categories. Because there are many different pathways and focus areas of work under the umbrella of public interest design, a range of elective options across disciplines is offered to ensure that the certificate is flexible in both content and scheduling. This flexibility acknowledges that each individual may have a different area of interest or hope to attain a different skill set and so accommodates for distinct focus areas. The five or six course options in each category come from such fields as urban planning and design, public administration, engineering, business, and architecture.

Two online options are also available, including a course on Design Thinking for Social Innovation (MGMT 521) that CPID faculty codeveloped and teach with faculty from the Business School. We often hear from people around the world interested in the certificate who express their frustration that the program is not fully offered online. While we are strong advocates of expanding education in public interest design to more people, we do not presently feel that we could properly support the exchanges, discourse, and fieldwork at the heart of the program through an online experience.[3]

Fieldwork

The fieldwork component (Arch 541) of the certificate is much like a thesis, asking students to take a leadership role on a project and reflect on it. Ideally taken at the end of the certificate sequence, the fieldwork can vary from an effort researched and developed over a year to a short but intensive period of engagement, design, and possibly construction. In each case, the fieldwork concludes with a portfolio documenting the student's certificate course work and outside projects that informed the work and methodology. Importantly, this documentation also provides an opportunity for students to evaluate the project, reflect on takeaways, and make recommendations to others who will work on similar projects.

While most students choose to fulfill the fieldwork requirement with CPID, they can complete this work elsewhere through an approved alternative. For example, we placed a student, Nada Maani, in the office of Estudio Teddy Cruz to accomplish her fieldwork by contributing to his Cross-Border Initiative and our ongoing collaboration with him. This was an appropriate match because Maani's thesis explored the space of women and children in Jordan's Zaatari refugee camp, another strong border condition. This type of exchange benefits the student, the host organization, and CPID, as research and collaboration with leading public interest design practitioners allows us to learn from best practices and apply them to our teaching and community work.

Program Pedagogical Goals

The Graduate Certificate in Public Interest Design cannot be properly understood as simply a series of required courses conducted in isolation; rather, it is a crucial part of the forum promoted as the core of the CPID experience, in which discussion, debate, and exploration of issues around public interest design are encouraged. Supplemental programs, such as talks with key practitioners and thinkers, a CPID Student Fellows program, and ongoing collaborative events and projects designed to invigorate thinking and practice for certificate students, make CPID a vibrant place to work, visit, and study (see Figure 3.1).

CPID Talks represent a primary opportunity for students to expand their exposure to emerging ideas and enterprises in the field. Continuing a tradition since its founding, CPID hosted sixteen talks during the 2015–2016 academic year. Speakers, representing a range of disciplines, included nationally recognized public interest design leaders, anthropologists, engineers, activists, and local thought leaders. These talks, which are open to the public, have greatly informed the discourse on issues related to public interest design at CPID. The talks are often scheduled by topic to inform active projects or to anticipate forums or charettes that the center is undertaking, and they are widely attended.

The CPID Student Fellows program is a key initiative that provides additional opportunities to certificate students for deeper engagement and leadership. An

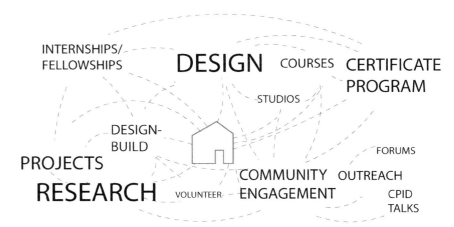

3.1
In search of a comprehensive approach to teaching public interest design and serving communities. CPID Diagram, 2015.

obvious challenge with having students work in a community is that the relationships and trust built during the project can be disrupted by the academic calendar if not carefully planned for in advance. The CPID Student Fellows program addresses this issue while giving outstanding certificate students the opportunity to gain valuable experience outside the classroom through participation in a public interest design project for a minimum of one year. Students accepted into this competitive program are each given a leadership role on an active CPID project under the guidance of one of its Faculty Fellows or professional collaborators, which limits the available spots to the number of visiting scholars, Faculty Fellows, and current collaborators. Projects that student fellows have worked on include the design of a sustainable community center in Inner Mongolia, a pop-up porch to serve as a venue for African American artistic and cultural programming in Portland, and a healthy, affordable modular classroom.

The certificate program aims to prepare students from a variety of disciplines to tackle pressing social, economic, and environmental issues. It also endeavors to make them leaders, teachers, and practitioners who share their knowledge and experience in public interest design with others. CPID is structured in such a way as to provide students earning the certificate with leadership experience through fieldwork, supplemental programming, and project-based employment opportunities at CPID and PSU's School of Architecture.

Program Outcomes

Response to the Graduate Certificate in Public Interest Design has been overwhelmingly positive, and it consistently ranks as one of the top reasons students identify for choosing to pursue a Master of Architecture degree at PSU. By operating as a professional community design center and working closely with students on ongoing projects, we continually reevaluate the skills and experience needed to support students' ability to practice public interest design successfully, a process that has led to several significant improvements in the program's first three years. That said, the program has not been without its challenges.

Other universities considering a similar certificate program might learn from our framework of transdisciplinary course options and supplemental programming to enrich educational opportunities. However, it is worth noting that including courses offered by departments outside the SOA severely limits our control of course offerings by term or year, and the financial benefits of increased student enrollment in these courses remain within the department offering the course. The supplemental activities give life and camaraderie to the certificate program, but they require a significant amount of work, which needs to be considered. As student interest in the certificate continues to rise, identifying meaningful fieldwork opportunities can be a significant hurdle.

Finally, students considering pursuing the certificate want to know what kinds of jobs it will directly result in when they graduate, a question with no easy answer. We provide students with the best preparation and work experience we can, but the field of public interest design is broad and evolving, and our degree program is still new. In lieu of a definitive answer, we offer the following profiles from our first cohort of graduates. These profiles provide snapshots of the students' backgrounds, paths to complete the certificate, and subsequent employment.

Karina Adams, Graduate Certificate in Public Interest Design, Fall 2015

Seminar Project
Gateway Park Community Engagement Project

Fieldwork
Adams took her efforts in the seminar class further with the design and erection of a temporary pavilion to host community engagement with neighborhood residents to anticipate and inform the design of a new park in an underserved area of Portland.

Other Notable Work
Adams fulfilled one of her courses through a project with visiting professors Belinda Tato and Jose Luis Vallejo of the Madrid-based design firm Ecosistema Urbano. Adams's chosen project centered on addressing the large number of bird deaths that occur because of building design. She has continued to contribute to bird-friendly design efforts with the Audubon Society of Portland and the Portland Bureau of Planning and Sustainability, and she has assisted with language adopted by the Portland City Council in its Green Building Policy, which now includes bird-safe building design practices.

Current Work
Adams currently has her own design practice, Karina Adams Design, and continues her advocacy work with the Audubon Society of Portland. She has continued her relationships

with Horatio Law, the resident artist on the Gateway Park Community Engagement Project, and with Therese Graf, a CPID intern who also worked on the project, by working together on a community engagement project in Seattle's South Park community. Like her peers Julia Mollner and Nada Maani, graduates of the first class of the certificate program, Adams is now an adjunct studio instructor in the SOA at PSU.

Reid Weber, Graduate Certificate in Public Interest Design, Fall 2015

Seminar Project
Northern Cheyenne Resilience Project

Fieldwork
Weber was a leader in rebuilding efforts on the Northern Cheyenne Indian Reservation in 2014 following devastating wildfires. He has returned many times to contribute to ongoing community engagement and resiliency efforts on the reservation.

Other Notable Work
Weber was a 2014–2015 CPID Student Fellow. In this role, he participated in a design/build project in Haiti and worked on the design of a sustainable community center for an elderly population in rural Inner Mongolia. Weber recently traveled to the project site in Inner Mongolia to oversee the start of the building construction. As a preliminary winner of the PSU Cleantech Challenge in 2013, Weber worked with a team of his peers and CPID Faculty Fellow Margarette Leite to develop waxed cardboard insulation as an alternative building product, with the goal of diverting a material unable to be recycled from the landfill.

Current Work
Weber works at SERA Architects, Inc., as a project assistant in the hospitality studio. He is currently leading a team at SERA on a CPID-led effort to work with local firms

3.2
CPID design/build project on the Northern Cheyenne Indian Reservation. CPID with American Indian Housing Initiative, Spang Family Barn, Ashland, Montana, 2016.

Sample Project: American Indian Resilience Project

In 2014, CPID undertook a new chapter of work with long-time partners in southeastern Montana on the Northern Cheyenne and Crow Indian Reservations. We were asked to create a resilience plan when devastating wildfires in 2012 revealed that no working emergency plan was in place. We were hearing from the Northern Cheyenne Tribe that they wanted to ensure that they were prepared for the next disaster, rather than simply rebuild. Over three summers (and multiple trips in between), CPID worked toward understanding the social and political issues that contribute to the preparedness and resiliency of the tribe in the event of another disaster, while providing immediate assistance through the design and reconstruction of affected buildings. The center has also been active on the Crow Indian Reservation, working with the Center Pole Foundation, a nonprofit focused on youth development and environmental and cultural sustainability, to construct an earth lodge for tribal ceremonies.

These actions build on the relationships formed over two decades by CPID Director Sergio Palleroni, collaborating with Professor David Riley from Penn State University. Their work in straw-bale construction through the American Indian Housing Initiative, focusing on developing local capacity in sustainable building, is evident in multiple structures on the Northern Cheyenne Indian Reservation, Crow Indian Reservation, and other American Indian locations in the region. The first straw-bale home they constructed in 1999 was for Center Pole Foundation founder Peggy Wellknown Buffalo.[4] While the goal initially was to collaborate on assisting friends in need, the capability of design to continue to play a role in improving lives in the area became apparent, and the experience for students was truly life changing. Students were immersed in a culturally rich experience that exposed them to a range of important public interest design issues, including community engagement, social equity, disaster relief, resilience planning, and sustainable design. The work that CPID students contributed to in these communities represented a true exchange where all parties benefited and were stronger for the relationship.

Projects included a barn for a family affected by the wildfires and whose livelihood depended on their horses (see Figure 3.2), a temporary pavilion at the annual powwow to facilitate community input and discussion on resilience (see Figure 3.3), and an earth lodge classroom based on historic tribal structures (see Figure 3.4). Students participated in these efforts in a variety of ways. A group in the Introduction to Public Interest Design Seminar reviewed the resilience plans and research, spoke with partners on the reservation, and designed the concept of a temporary pavilion for community engagement at the powwow. Students in a summer service-learning course traveled each summer to advance design/build efforts, which have also informed the tribal conversation on promoting sustainability and resilience. Three students have taken leadership roles in planning and executing the summer initiative to complete their fieldwork toward the Graduate Certificate in Public Interest Design. These certificate students reflected on and evaluated the work through a project portfolio, while making recommendations for future work. The CPID Student Fellows have contributed to the work and conducted illuminating follow-up interviews as part of a trip in the fall that served as an orientation into the fellows program, emphasizing the importance of meeting with partners to evaluate a project collectively.

Like many of the initiatives at CPID, this project is a transformative experience for students who are able to participate through multiple entry points, depending on their interests and skill levels. The project has benefited from long-standing partnerships and a framework that allows the work to be addressed from multiple angles. For students in the Graduate Certificate in Public Interest Design, the project represents just one option for course work, fieldwork, and leadership at CPID, emphasizing community engagement, environmental sustainability, and social and economic resilience.

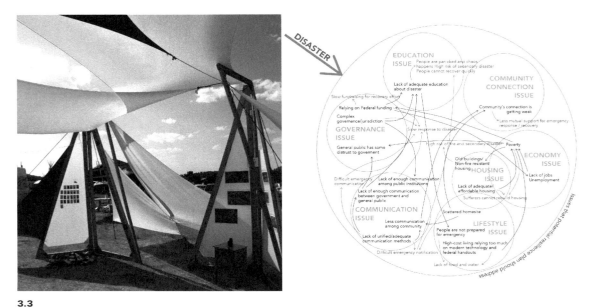

3.3
Understanding resiliency on the Northern Cheyenne Indian Reservation. CPID, American Indian Resilience Project, Lame Deer, Montana, 2015.

3.4
CPID design and construction of the earth lodge at the Center Pole Foundation, Crow Indian Reservation. CPID, Center Pole Earth Lodge, Gerryowen, Montana, 2016.

on the design and construction of microhousing prototypes to house homeless Portlanders. He also volunteers with Portland Forward, a group that promotes civic engagement for the next generation by building connections with civic leaders.

Notes

1. Faculty and professionals are invited to work with CPID through fellowships where they mentor students, contribute to CPID programming, and collaborate on work. Founding Faculty Fellows include Travis Bell, R. Todd Ferry, Margarette Leite, Sergio Palleroni, and B. D. Wortham-Galvin.
2. These awards presented by Design Corps and the SEED Network represent best practices in sustainability and impact and make an ideal case-study source for students new to public interest design.
3. Currently, CPID accepts no more than ten students in the program per year, resulting in no more than twenty active certificate students at a time.
4. This project and others completed through the American Indian Housing Initiative are documented in *Studio at Large: Architecture in Service of Global Communities*, Sergio Palleroni and Christian Eichbaum Merkelbach (University of Washington Press, 2004).

4
A Comprehensive Public Interest Design Curriculum
College of Design, North Carolina State University

Bryan Bell, Robin Abrams, and Gene Bressler

Program Philosophy

The built and natural environments, the spaces in which we live and work, the products we consume, and the messages we receive have a powerful impact on how we function in society. Good design requires attention and sensitivity to social, economic, political, cultural, and behavioral issues. Public interest design links design education and professional practice with the knowledge and skills to address global issues. The curriculum in public interest design at the College of Design at North Carolina State University (NC State Design) takes a multidisciplinary approach that emphasizes the triple bottom line of sustainable design, which encompasses environmental, economic, and social challenges. At the same time, it exposes students to the role of good governance, which must be in place for sustainability to reach reality. Related courses seek to broaden access to the benefits of design to all of the general public. By connecting the design process to global issues, public interest design communicates the value of design to a broader audience and provides designers with a larger platform to affirm the value of all the design disciplines.

Under the leadership of Dean Mark Hoversten, one new addition to NC State Design's mission to improve society through design, teaching, and research is the Public Interest Design Certificate. This new program allows NC State Design to build on past leadership in public service and to strengthen the institution's role as a global leader in this realm. The curricular content, which is research and design based in both the classroom and the field, educates students and professionals in how to use design to address the critical challenges that communities face in the world. This program provides an opportunity to align the teaching, research, and outreach of the College of Design and to further the college's strategic plan.

4.1
The strength of public interest design at NC State University extends back into the mid-1960s, and the College of Design has a recognized history of using design to address the social, economic, and environmental challenges of communities. Henry Sanoff, a pioneer of participatory community design, began teaching at NC State College of Design in 1966. Current faculty who are furthering this field include Robin Abrams, Tania Allen, Tom Barrie, Bryan Bell, Kofi Boone, Gene Bressler, Andrew Fox, David Hill, Sharon Joines, Robin Moore, Celen Pasalar, Sarah Queen, and Art Rice.

As a graduate-level program, the Public Interest Design Certificate provides much-needed education in this rapidly emerging field. The field of public interest design has grown out of the design disciplines over the past ten years. Similar to public health, public interest design has a broad scope that goes beyond traditional roles of practice to consider the whole of society. Like public interest law, public interest design seeks to provide services to the general public, not just to the individuals who can pay a fee for such services.

> Design for social impact has been gaining momentum for some time. Most of the early luminaries are still active. ... At the same time, the next generation of designers focused on social impact are now establishing themselves, and as they do we are witnessing a shift. In part, this is characterized by an evolution in identity. 'Public Interest Design' has emerged as a label that effectively organizes the collective efforts of those working in the social impact sector.
> (Dewane 2015)

> Public interest design is transforming architectural practices. This transformation can be seen as a wide-spread response to the concern that the conventional model of practice responds solely to the paying client, thus limiting the profession's capacity to address the problems of our time.
> (Feldman et al. 2011)

> As landscape architects we vow to create places that serve the higher purpose of social and ecological justice for all peoples and all species. We vow to create places that nourish our deepest needs for communion with the natural world and with one another. We vow to serve the health and well-being of all communities. ... To fulfill these promises, we will work to strengthen and diversify our global capacity as a profession. We will work to cultivate a bold culture of inclusive leadership, advocacy and activism in our ranks.
> (LAF 2016)

4.2
The Triangle Greenway was the original vision of NC State Design landscape architecture student, Bill Flournoy, Jr. His graduate project, "The Benefits, Potential, and Methodology for Establishing the Capital City Greenway," is a model of professional practice in public interest design. The Greenway now has over one hundred miles of trails, four thousand acres, and more than 750,000 users per year. Raleigh, North Carolina. Photo: Courtesy of North Carolina Museum of Art. Sculpture: *Gyre* by Thomas Sayre.

Addressing a New Educational Need

Both the millennial generation and current architecture and landscape architecture practitioners want to know how to use their design education and professional skills to serve the public. The motivation to "improve quality of life in communities" has been documented as the second primary reason that people enter the profession of architecture (Boyer and Mitgang 1996, 9).

In 1996, Ernest L. Boyer and Lee D. Mitgang surveyed architecture students on their primary reasons for entering the architecture profession. Forty-four percent of respondents ranked "putting creative abilities to practical use" as their most important reason for entering the profession; 22 percent stated that "improving quality of life in communities" was their top motivation (Boyer and Mitgang 1996, 9). Combining these two reasons gives a useful working definition of public interest design: "the desire to improve quality of life in communities" by "putting creative abilities to practical use."

Two more recent surveys, one of American Institute of Architects (AIA) members and another of a sample of students at the Harvard Graduate School of Design (GSD), document the current strong interest for a public-based practice. Figure 4.3 presents the results of a 2011 survey of graduate students in all design degree programs at GSD, conducted through the GSD Student Services with Bryan Bell as principal investigator.

The survey of students at GSD also found confirmation of a desire among students for education and training, specifically for a Public Interest Design Certificate program (see Figures 4.4 and 4.5).

Research among current architecture professionals confirmed a similarly strong interest in public interest design. A 2011 survey of a representative national sample of AIA members assessed interests of current design professionals to pursue further education in the field with the following results (Feldman et al. 2011):

4.3
Rankings of most important reasons for entering the architecture profession by Harvard GSD students.

Reason for entering the architecture profession	Percentage of students who ranked:		
	As first reason	As second reason	As third reason
Putting creative abilities to practical use	63%	17%	20%
Improving quality of life in communities	26%	46%	28%

4.4
Survey results showing interest in public interest design education among Harvard GSD students.

Question asked	Percentage of students who answered:	
	Very likely	Somewhat likely
If a certificate in public interest design were available to you now in addition to your current degree program, how likely—if at all—do you think you would be to pursue this?	13%	42%
If training in public interest design were available to you now, how likely—if at all—would you be to pursue it?	26%	52%

4.5
Methods that Harvard GSD students indicated they would choose to gain additional expertise and training in public interest design.

Method option	Percentage of students who indicated interest
Classes at my school	73%
An independent service program like a summer design/build studio	68%
Independent training sessions organized by and located at a university	24%
Online webinars	7%

- Fifty-four percent of survey respondents identified the lack of "necessary identified expertise and training" as an obstacle to successful practice of public interest design.
- Seventy-two percent identified the lack of on-the-job training in public interest design as an obstacle.
- Seven specific learning objectives were identified as needed for a successful practice in public interest design.
- Twenty percent of survey respondents knew architects who had left the field because of dissatisfaction with how it served local communities.

A Comprehensive Public Interest Design Curriculum

This survey clearly identified the need for training in public interest design. The results provided evidence that the lack of training was a major obstacle in succeeding in a career in public interest design and that failing to accomplish this goal had resulted in a clear and tangible loss for the profession in terms of trained and licensed practitioners. These data also suggested a demand for certificate programs among both professionals and students.

Currently, only one other certificate program in public interest design is offered nationally at an accredited design school. With this certificate, NC State Design has further built on its historic legacy and the strength of many expert faculty by offering a specific program of study in a highly sought field.

Program Curriculum Overview

Courses for the Public Interest Design Certificate at NC State Design are drawn from the four academic departments in the College of Design: Architecture; Landscape Architecture; Art + Design; Industrial and Graphic Design.

In the School of Architecture (SOA) and the Department of Landscape Architecture (LAR), students and faculty are developing the knowledge and skills to address complex contemporary issues: "stewardship of scarce resources, promotion of livability in cities, mitigation of poverty through provision of humane housing, research and development of ecologically responsive building materials and integrated building systems, and understanding history as a means of creating a better future" (NC Design 2016). These two programs have rich legacies and reputations built on preparing graduates for the rigors of professional practice, leadership, community engagement, and research.

Faculty in the SOA are pursuing cutting-edge research in the areas of energy and technology in architecture, city design, and architecture in the public interest, which includes initiatives focused on affordable housing, sustainable communities, and home-environments design. Similarly, faculty in the LAR are leaders in areas such as the interdependence of human health and well-being, the ecological health of the land, and understanding the consequences of human actions on the land. These varied perspectives create a healthy ecosystem of collaboration and expertise applicable to a number of complex social, economic, and environmental design problems.

In addition to the diversity of design disciplines ideal for pursuing multifaceted problems, public interest design practices rely on diverse stakeholders to achieve positive impact. Rather than the professional-client transactional relationship of traditional design practice, public interest design takes a shared-expertise approach, where the assets of multiple stakeholders are recognized, respected, and applied to the design solution—including stakeholders such as governmental entities, funders, community members, and others ranging well beyond the design disciplines.

> Most practitioners found they needed to expand their conventional professional roles and services to include planning, research, advocacy strategies, and others to meet the public needs of a project. This required cultivating new skills and strategies and building relationships with experts in other fields, representatives of various non-profits, and/or government officials to facilitate projects. Working in collaborative teams not only improves projects, it allows practitioners to engage in larger scale work. Collaborations with governmental entities are often necessary and productive to address ongoing community needs and disaster relief. In the U.S., federal and local governments' financial investment in social issues has been a boon for public interest practices, providing an important source of commissions.
>
> (Feldman et al. 2011)

To accommodate the diversity of practices, students pursuing a Public Interest Design Certificate at NC State Design may take up to twelve credits from other university programs that offer graduate-level course work related to public interest design.

Program Pedagogical Goals and Outcomes

In NC State Design's Public Interest Design Certificate program, students learn concepts of effective practice and leadership in using design to address the critical challenges that communities face globally. The program develops the student designer's perception, knowledge, skills, and problem-solving abilities in preparation for a career in public interest design. As a result of this program, students will be able to:

- analyze precedents of how public interest design can be a meaningful part of professional practice
- describe one model of professional practice in public interest design
- identify public need for design that can address community challenges
- identify a design project's social, economic, and environmental impact on a community
- identify stakeholders and assets that can address project challenges
- test a step-by-step method of working with a community as a design partner
- apply a collaborative process with multiple stakeholders

To demonstrate that these learning objectives have been accomplished, students are required to provide evidence of successful completion of each outcome. Documentation—such as the featured sample projects—must be provided that addresses critical criteria for each outcome.

Flexible Course Work

To receive a Public Interest Design Certificate, a student must complete fifteen hours of course work. Each student must provide evidence that learning objectives are met (see Figure 4.6 and the following for examples). Course work can be completed within the existing curricula of the Master of Architecture and the Master of Landscape Architecture programs. Additionally, it is possible to earn this certificate as a postbaccalaureate, non-degree-seeking student.

Three options allow a mix of seminars and design studios to meet the credit hours required. Students can take up to three studios or four seminars for credit from the following options:

1. one required public interest design seminar (three credits) and two approved studios (twelve credits)
2. one required public interest design seminar (three credits), one approved studio (six credits), and two approved seminars (six credits)
3. one required public interest design seminar (three credits) and four approved seminars (twelve credits)

Public Interest Design Seminar: Case Studies and Current Issues is a required seminar, but the other twelve credit hours of courses are electives. Students may select these electives from several preapproved courses or propose for approval an individual course of study from the many course options available across NC State University, allowing students to customize their own curricula (see Figure 4.7). This scope of possibilities acknowledges that public interest design is a wide and growing space, with many of the most innovative successes coming from hybrid knowledge in two or more fields. The following departments offer relevant courses: Sociology and Anthropology; Public Administration; Management, Innovation, and Entrepreneurship; Social Work; Educational Leadership, Policy, and Human Development; Business Management; Forestry and Environmental Resources; Economics; and, Parks, Recreation, and Tourism Management.

4.6
The Public Interest Design Incubator Studio taught by Bryan Bell generated this example of evidence of meeting the learning outcome "test a step-by-step method of working with a community as a design partner." Lotte Van Miegroet, North Carolina State University, Raleigh, North Carolina, 2016.

4.7
The Public Interest Architecture seminar developed by Georgia Bizios, Bryan Bell, Katie Wakeford and Jamey Glueck provided this SEED case study as an example of meeting the learning outcome "analyze precedents of how public interest design can be a meaningful part of professional practice." Sarah Lower, North Carolina State University, Raleigh, North Carolina, 2017.

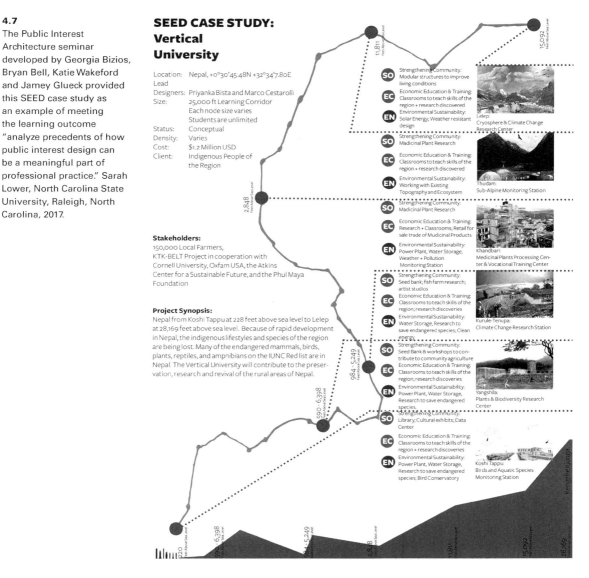

SEED CASE STUDY: Vertical University

Location: Nepal, +0°30'45.48N +32°34'7.80E
Lead Designers: Priyanka Bista and Marco Cestarolli
Size: 25,000 ft Learning Corridor
   Each node size varies
   Students are unlimited
Status: Conceptual
Density: Varies
Cost: $1.2 Million USD
Client: Indigenous People of the Region

Stakeholders:
150,000 Local Farmers, KTK-BELT Project in cooperation with Cornell University, Oxfam USA, the Atkins Center for a Sustainable Future, and the Phul Maya Foundation

Project Synopsis:
Nepal from Koshi Tappu at 228 feet above sea level to Lelep at 28,169 feet above sea level. Because of rapid development in Nepal, the indigenous lifestyles and species of the region are being lost. Many of the endangered mammals, birds, plants, reptiles, and amphibians on the IUNC Red list are in Nepal. The Vertical University will contribute to the preservation, research and revival of the rural areas of Nepal.

One preapproved course within the Public Interest Design Certificate is the NC State University Coastal Dynamics Design Lab Studio taught by David Hill and Andrew Fox, in which students produce graduate-level work that designs resiliency and hazard mitigation into coastal communities and develops productive relationships among institutional, governmental, and professional practice communities (see Figure 4.8). To achieve these goals, the studio organizes students into a laboratory for confronting coastal issues in a comprehensive way. Participating students work in conjunction with numerous colleges and universities, institutions, and agencies, including planners, marine and earth scientists, nonprofit organizations, and engineers. The studio employs a collaborative process with multiple community stakeholders.

A Comprehensive Public Interest Design Curriculum

4.8
The Coastal Dynamics Design Lab Studio taught by David Hill and Andrew Fox provided this example of evidence of meeting the learning outcome "identify a public need for design that can address community challenges." Students documented conversations with community residents and stakeholders on video to understand people and place. Mahta Nazari Khoorasgani, Fishing Harbor Park, Beaufort, North Carolina, 2016.

The studio educates students and stakeholders through direct exposure to state-of-the-art environmental design techniques, enhances statewide understanding of coastal adaptation strategies, and creates outcomes that benefit both university students and coastal communities. The studio generates understanding in academic and community-centered endeavors by integrating research, teaching, and public engagement activities into a synthetic process that enables stakeholders to identify and assess individual and group needs through scenario testing, dialogue, and consensus building.

In a recent project with the town of Beaufort, North Carolina, the studio developed a series of Proactive Recovery Community Structures: resilient landscapes, architecture, and site plans that address this coastal town's urban-design issues, challenges from climate change, and the effects of acute Atlantic storms. Students produced analysis videos—including stakeholder interviews—as tools for understanding people and place, ultimately resulting in more responsible and responsive design solutions. Frequent meetings with town leaders provided a forum for exchanging ideas. Together, stakeholders and students identified and programmed twelve projects that students developed further through iterative design processes.

Another graduate-level seminar within the certificate program, DIY Cartography taught by Tania Allen and Sara Queen, explored mapping—analyzing and making meaning of raw data—as a comparative analytic tool to uncover hidden meanings between data and reality (see Figure 4.9). Students in this course analyzed, synthesized, and visualized the history of Raleigh, North Carolina; they engaged in field research as comparative analysis and investigated and reflected on the effect of the mapping process

4.9
DIY Cartography taught by Tania Allen and Sara Queen provided this example of evidence of meeting the learning outcome "identify stakeholders and assets that can address project challenges." Researching the history of educational access in Raleigh, Master of Architecture student Rebecca Ryan created a series of maps that visualized how location, income, and race influence access to education for students in Raleigh. Rebecca Ryan, North Carolina State University, Raleigh, North Carolina, 2016.

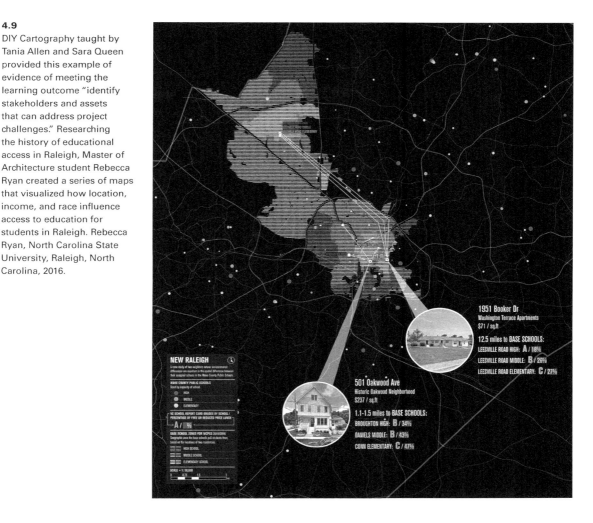

on how data are understood. Through intense observation and interaction with census data, the physical environment, and the official and unofficial archival history of Raleigh, students engaged in a rich, triangulated approach to historical and social research.

Within the course, students examined current urban research methods through precedent projects and employed a variety of mapping tools to conduct urban and community-based research themselves. By looking specifically at the history of Raleigh, not just as a physical environment but also as a socially dynamic one, students were encouraged to make tangible connections between the ways that design contributes to, and is affected by, social interactions and tensions.

Course and Program Assessment

Ongoing evaluations through an annual feedback loop are built in for both individual classes and the program overall. For the required seminar, an anonymous student self-assessment is used to track changes in perceived knowledge. The example, from the spring 2014 Public Interest Design Seminar taught by Bryan Bell, shows the percentage change in self-perceived knowledge level over time, as assessed at the beginning of the class and again at the end of the class (see Figure 4.10).

This survey facilitates students' self-assessment of what they have learned and shows what the course provides that is not available from other sources. For example, students had an average before-course score of 4.8 for "moving beyond LEED to measure the social, economic, and environmental impact on communities," while they gave an average 6.3 before-course score for "maximizing a design project's positive impact on a community." Further research could assess whether they felt they had gained this level of knowledge through other courses and how the overall curriculum could work more efficiently as a whole.

Another assessment method is to collect evidence that a specific learning objective has been met. For example, the following letter demonstrates how one student, Jason Patterson, met the goal of "leveraging partners and assets to address project challenges." This letter was written after the design phase of the project by a key stakeholder, Dr. Elisabeth Potts Dellon, of the pediatric palliative care team at the North Carolina Children's Hospital:

> Pediatric palliative care is medical care focused on quality of life for children with serious medical conditions and their families. Our team endeavors to support children and families as they face difficult decisions, intense stress related to serious illness, and end of life. One of our biggest challenges has been improving the experience of death in the hospital. We unfortunately don't have

4.10
Student self-assessment responses from the Public Interest Design Seminar.

Please assess and rate your current level of knowledge in each of these learning objectives from 1 to 10, with 10 being the highest level of understanding.

Objective	Before	After	Percentage change
Understanding public interest design and how is it reshaping the design professions	5.1	8.9	+75%
Moving beyond LEED to measure the social, economic, and environmental impact on communities	4.8	8.9	+85%
Maximizing a design project's positive impact on a community	6.3	9.3	+48%
Using a step-by-step process of working with a community as a design partner	4.9	9.4	+92%
Finding public interest design projects	5.4	7.7	+43%
Leveraging partners and assets to address project challenges	4.5	8.1	+80%
Understanding how public interest design can be a meaningful part of professional practice	5.6	9.3	+66%

the resources or space to design less sterile, more home-like hospital rooms for end of life care, so we decided to try temporarily transforming hospital rooms to more comfortable spaces for dying children and their families.

Jason volunteered to take on the challenging task of designing a complex, mobile piece of furniture that simultaneously stores comfort items for families, functions as a gathering spot for meals and for siblings to play and do artwork, and fits in seamlessly within the existing design of hospital rooms with varying dimensions and layouts. He met with multiple stakeholders, including bereaved parents, health care providers, and hospital design and engineering staff, and created some truly unbelievable pieces for us. We cannot wait for these to be built and put into use. His thoughtful, incredibly skilled work will be much appreciated by countless families and health care providers. We are extremely grateful for the tremendous time and effort Jason has donated to the children and families we serve.

(Elisabeth Potts Dellon, pers. comm.)

In addition to assessments of individual courses and learning objectives (see Figure 4.11), the Public Interest Design Certificate program measures the success of providing an educational experience that satisfies the expectations of its graduates. These outcomes are documented through an exit survey administered annually by a third party, the NC State University Graduate School. The survey assesses whether students completing the program are satisfied with the following aspects of the certificate program:

4.11
The Design/Build Lab taught by Randall S. Lanou and Ellen C. Cassilly provided this evidence of meeting the learning outcome "apply a collaborative process with multiple stakeholders." North Carolina State University, Benevolence Farm Barn, Alamance County, North Carolina, 2014.

A Comprehensive Public Interest Design Curriculum

- usefulness in enabling students to achieve their professional goals
- appropriateness of the courses in providing the knowledge or training needed for their professional goals
- frequency and timeliness of courses offered for the certificate
- quality of teaching
- overall educational experience

These assessment tools give feedback on how well the program provides necessary tools and meets the goals of each student. Iterative feedback is a best practice in public interest design and can provide continual incremental improvement in the development of educational models as well.

Developing a comprehensive curriculum in public interest design is a key next step in the growth of the field. While the recent period of individual projects and people have developed new examples and models of best practices, the need is for *systemic* inclusion of public interest design in society for it to reach its full potential to serve the public. Providing a comprehensive curriculum and thorough education in this emerging field is one of the most effective means for this systemic change to be realized.

References

Boyer, Ernest L., and Lee D. Mitgang. 1996. *Building Community: A New Future for Architecture Education and Practice*. Stanford, CA: Carnegie Foundation for the Advancement of Teaching.

Dewane, David. 2015. "Navigating the Frontiers of Public Interest Design." *Design Intelligence*, December 23. www.di.net/articles/navigating-the-frontiers-of-public-interest-design/.

Feldman, Roberta, Sergio Palleroni, David Perkes, and Bryan Bell. 2011. *Wisdom from the Field: Public Interest Architecture in Practice*. FAIA Latrobe Prize Research Report, Washington, DC: College of Fellows of the American Institute of Architects.

LAF (Landscape Architecture Foundation). 2016. "The New Landscape Declaration." https://lafoundation.org/news-events/2016-summit/new-landscape-declaration/.

NC State Design. 2016. "Architecture." NC State University College of Design. Accessed December 21, 2016. https://design.ncsu.edu/academics/architecture/.

5

Connecting Classrooms and Publics

The University of California, Davis, Center for Design in the Public Interest

Susan Verba, Sarah Perrault, and Tracy Manuel

Program Philosophy

Founded in 2014 with a seed grant from the University of California, Davis Grand Challenges initiative, the Center for Design in the Public Interest (DiPi) brings together teams of creative people from different fields to solve community problems through research-based design and to study how interdisciplinary groups work, investigating the question: What does democratic design look like?

DiPi focuses on projects related to civic engagement, community health, public safety, energy, and sustainability. This work is highly interdisciplinary. Susan Verba, the center's director, is a professor in the Department of Design at the University of California, Davis (UC Davis), and Sarah Perrault, the codirector, is a professor of writing and rhetoric in the University Writing Program. Affiliated faculty come from the communication; computer science; anthropology; and gender, sexuality, and women's studies departments. The center also employs undergraduates, graduate students, and recent graduates as designers, researchers, and staff. Student assistants and researchers have diverse backgrounds, including in design, art history, art studio, cinema and digital media, computer science, community development (human ecology), technical communication, English, and managerial economics. This rich collaboration creates exceptional opportunities to explore new tools and methods, including innovative ways of approaching design education.

DiPi has connections with a number of courses in the Department of Design at UC Davis. These courses were developed with a public interest design focus at a university that "is committed to the land-grant tradition on which it was founded, which holds that the broad purpose of a university is service to people and society" (Regents of the University of California 2016). The Department of Design has been linked with this land-grant mission from its start in 1966 in the College of Agriculture and Environmental Sciences. Design became part of an interdisciplinary department in 1980 and later moved to the College of Letters and Science, becoming a standalone department in the Division of Humanities, Arts, and Cultural Studies. In 2009 the Master of Fine Arts (MFA) was established, graduating its first students in 2011. Today the Department of Design draws on the strengths of a multidisciplinary research environment; individual faculty contribute research and teach in areas as diverse as information design and wearable technologies, connecting with disciplines ranging from the humanities to engineering.

Program Curriculum Overview

Over five hundred undergraduate majors in the Design Bachelor of Arts program benefit from a liberal arts education emphasizing critical thinking, visual literacy, and foundational skills in various design areas. Emphasis on public interest design begins in Introduction to Design (DES 001), which addresses the role of the "designer and products in contemporary culture including social responsibility and sustainability" (Office of the University Registrar 2016, 235) and continues throughout the curriculum. MFA students encounter a blend of design theory and creative practice that prepares them for leadership jobs in academia, in the design industry, or for entrepreneurial opportunities. At both undergraduate and graduate levels, courses stress a multidisciplinary research environment in which students engage in cross disciplinary and collaborative work; many courses also integrate aspects of public interest design.[1] Overall, the department aims to be nationally and internationally recognized as a leader in socially progressive, sustainable design research and development. This desire to contribute to the public good is reflected in the two courses described in this chapter.

Design for Understanding

Students in Design for Understanding (DES 159), an elective senior capstone, use the tools of creativity and analysis to collectively redesign everyday artifacts and experiences, making them easier to understand and navigate. Drawing on texts such as Tufte's *Envisioning Information* (2008) and Visocky O'Grady's *The Information Design Handbook* (2008), the course combines lectures and discussions that build students' understanding with workshops that provide opportunities for experimentation, observation, and practice, focusing on unmet social design needs. Students learn to improve the "clarity, density, and dimensionality of information," practice "user-centered methods of investigation," and "design strategies ... to improve clarity and meaning in communication" in ways that "open up new possibilities for using design to solve everyday problems" they care about (Verba 2016).

The course outcomes state that students will be able to:

- develop an understanding of public interest design with a user-centered focus
- investigate and put into practice strategies for noticing what is not working and for improving daily lives through better design
- explore typography as a tool for enhancing clarity and legibility in complex communications
- hone collaborative making and thinking skills
- see beauty in surprising places

As befits a senior capstone class, these outcomes correspond to all levels in Bloom's taxonomy of educational objectives.[2] Students write about what they know, defining and labeling concepts (level one); explain, summarize, and paraphrase information from primary and secondary research (level two); apply their knowledge to constructing outcomes (level three); analyze options, comparing and contrasting different approaches to solving problems through design (level four); hypothesize about what might work and then create, design, invent, and develop prototypes (level five); and judge and critique designs for themselves and one another, justifying these critiques as well as their own design decisions (level six). Students meet the objectives through a series of exercises and a final project.

For the first five weeks, students analyze real-world design artifacts, identify problems, and propose improvements to "explore user-centered design strategies for the visual/experiential presentation of information" (Verba 2016). Students sometimes work individually and sometimes collaboratively, and each exercise includes critique sessions.

In Exercise 1, "Get Out Safe," students work on a fire safety instruction sheet. The sheet, from the pocket of a hotel room-service folder,[3] has several problems:

1. Instructions are given as a numbered list of fourteen steps, even though they are not intended to be a step-by-step procedure.
2. There is no visual hierarchy; other than the heading "Fire Safety" at the top of the page, the document uses the same type size throughout.
3. The decision point—whether to leave the room based on if the door is warm or not—is not clear.

Students create three new versions of the sheet, altering the layout and text and then adding images or icons.

Exercise 2, "Are You Driving Drunk?" tasks students with improving a Department of Motor Vehicles (DMV) mailer, the "Alcohol Impairment Chart" (California Department of Motor Vehicles 2016, 81). To come up with a better design for this confusing graphic depicting blood alcohol levels, students are asked to focus on two objectives: improve the user experience by making the graphic educational and easy to understand; and use familiar language, clear information hierarchy, and other design devices to make it evident when it is safe to drive and when it is not. Although they are permitted to rewrite the headline and copy, students cannot leave out any important information. Students work together to research relevant information and to analyze the graphic for what is and is not working. They create an inventory of the different kinds of information included and the ways that hierarchy is (or is not) created and present their findings in class. Next, as homework, each student explores and tests a variety of concepts and formats, resulting in a proposal for a graphic that is clear and easy to understand. Students then present the proposed graphics, along with sketches, research methods, and user methodology, for in-class critique.

In Exercise 3, "Radiation in Everyday Life," students analyze the effectiveness of a Japanese information display (Japan National Tourism Organization 2016) meant to communicate radiation risk and exposure to the public. Students choose and research a specific area of radiation education, specify an audience and a point of view, and identify a hypothetical agency that might sponsor such a project. In a brief written proposal outlining their choices, students answer questions about their concepts: Why does this information matter? Who is the audience? What is the authorial position? The goal is to create an educational piece that provides a context for the information and engages and communicates with the identified audience. To ensure that this exercise moves students toward greater independence in conceiving and developing solutions, the outcome is not predetermined, and the exercise has resulted in a variety of proposals, including a radiation board game, a music video to engage high school students, and a child-friendly interactive video display.

For their final projects, students identify a public health, education, or safety need that they care about and might begin to address through a five-week research-based design intervention. Students think deeply and widely about this real-world problem, ask provocative and insightful questions, and seek answers to those questions in multiple ways: conducting secondary source research; engaging in primary research with stakeholders and participants via interviews, surveys, and other user-centered research activities (guided by IDEO's Method Cards);[4] learning from classmates via discussion, feedback, and reviews; and making experimental prototypes and capturing responses to those prototypes. Students present their explorations and findings—including next steps for moving the project toward implementation—in a process workbook and in-class presentations.

While specific problems vary, projects fall into a range of categories: redesigning documents, such as jury summonses, DMV forms, or hospital emergency room discharge forms, for greater understanding; improving experiences, such as through better wayfinding or wearable technologies; and educating people to promote behavior change, as when groups create games or apps to alleviate the stigma around mental health needs. All are problems that design can address in ways that will better many people's lives, and all require students to connect with stakeholders through user-centered research. Thus, while stakeholders and outcomes vary, the public interest aim of the class remains constant.

Since DiPi launched in April 2014, eighteen students in Design for Understanding have completed projects related to DiPi's work. Verba and Perrault (2015, 2016) describe some projects related to DiPi's Communicating Pain Project: a flipbook-style pain-tracking log, type studies of pain words for possible use in a pain scale, and a prototype tablet app for self-assessment of pain. Another student's project, a combination of community radio and participatory design, is featured in the sample project (see the sidebar). Most recently, a student chose to work on developing a pain self-management tool. Like the exercises, these final projects challenge students to develop and refine their abilities at all levels of Bloom's taxonomy. In addition, creating the process workbook gives students a chance to reflect on their decisions and their own learning processes.

Professional Practice and Ethics

At the graduate level, Professional Practice and Ethics (DES 223) investigates issues of professional design practice, including agency, ethics, and social responsibility. Each year the course has a specific theme. In Winter 2016, the class focused on public interest design, with the *Public Interest Design Practice Guidebook: SEED Methodology, Case Studies, and Critical Issues* (Abendroth and Bell 2016; henceforth *PIDPG*) providing a conceptual framework for students to make sense of their professional experiences to date and to explore the kinds of work they would most like to do when they enter or reenter the design world. Even for students who will not focus on public interest design, the text offered a means to probe ideas about meaningful work, to consider ethical issues in user-centered research, to discuss how to define and evaluate success, and to examine other questions that are relevant to critical design practice.

The learning objectives for the class state that students will be able to:

- explore notions of design agency as a way to gain insight into the role of the designer, present and future
- probe ideas of meaningful work and the value of making "with" rather than "for"
- connect theory and practice
- consider ethical issues in planning and carrying out user-centered research and activities that engage the public in the design process
- discuss different ways to define and evaluate success in a project and explain how they are appropriate for different situations

During the first half of the course, students explored questions about public interest design: what it is and how it might relate to their own intended design careers. To this end, students completed a series of short reading responses on the class blog, in which they answered specific questions based on their readings from *PIDPG*. For example, students read Fisher (2016, 36) on "Professional Responsibility and Ethics," which describes how the "foundational ideas" of moral foundations theory (MFT)[5] "guide people's judgments about right and wrong across many different cultures." Students were asked to choose one MFT idea and explain on the blog how it played a role in a design situation they have been in, answering questions about the decisions and tensions that were involved and how the specific MFT idea might have helped them negotiate the situation. Students wrote about the MFT ideas of care/harm in relation to waste of resources, loyalty/betrayal in learning to recognize when design differences are actually rooted in cultural differences, and fairness/justice in framing a process of developing shared rules for resource use. The group also cooperatively developed a collective list of readings and resources to aid their thinking about agency, ethics, and critical practice. Individually, each student delved into a selected case study from *PIDPG*, researched one public interest design case study of their choice not included in the book, and presented these case studies to the class for discussion.

In the second half of the course, each student developed a final project that connected both inward- and outward-facing representations of who they were as designers. The final project included developing professional presentation materials (such as a résumé, business card, cover letter, LinkedIn profile, and visual framework for a portfolio) and writing a statement of personal design philosophy.

Course Pedagogical Goals

Projects for the course Design for Understanding met the pedagogical goals by addressing the five public interest design principles (Bell 2016, 14):

1. **Advocate with those who have a limited voice in public life.** Because the course emphasizes identifying and designing for unmet needs, every project followed this principle, but some projects especially focused on underserved or socially excluded groups. For example, one project sought to improve bus-riding experiences for people with invisible mobility impairments, while another worked to address the unmet sex education needs of LGBTQIA individuals.
2. **Build structures for inclusion that engage stakeholders and allow communities to make decisions.** All projects included structures for inclusion in the research phase, and some students also designed artifacts that reify community involvement on an ongoing basis. One student created a multilingual booklet and poster to help connect Asians and Pacific Islanders with a community counseling center that serves the local Asian-Pacific community. Another student designed a gardening kit and journal that can lower barriers for parents and small children who are starting to grow their own food.

3. **Promote social equality through discourse that reflects a range of values and social identities.** One project used 'zines to foster accessible conversations about sex, noting that changing the discourses can change how people view sex. Another project, a coloring and self-care book, included quotes from activist women of color and visually represented different ethnicities and body types.
4. **Generate ideas that grow from place and build local capacity.** The coloring and self-care book for student leaders of color was meant to support and sustain community members who, research showed, were prone to subordinating their own needs to the needs of their communities. Other examples of projects that grew from place included a plan for universal design-based signage and wayfinding on the UC Davis campus, a map of gender-neutral restrooms on campus, and a UC Davis bicycle safety instructor's guide.
5. **Design to help conserve resources and minimize waste.** Students took this principle into account when deciding on the medium for their designed artifacts, such as carefully considering whether a specific design intervention needed to be produced in paper or digital form and taking into account aspects of reuse like sharing and repurposing printed materials.

Connection to the public interest design principles was diffused throughout the Professional Practice and Ethics course. Being informed about the ethics of user-centered research, one of the main themes of the seminar, is very important in public interest design. *PIDPG* exposed students to public interest design ideas and helped them think about the kinds of jobs or roles they wanted to play as designers. The course also expanded students' ideas about what public interest design is; for example, a student in fashion design initially thought she was not interested in public interest design but eventually decided that her thesis project would include a focus on conserving resources and minimizing waste. Overall, students found public interest design concepts useful for articulating the nexus of skills, desires, and curiosities that drive many designers; the readings and the exercises based on the book helped students connect their values and beliefs to their career goals. Even for those students who want to become commercial designers, that grounding will help.

Challenges and Successes

Establishing DiPi came with challenges that any center is likely to face—getting funding and finding a space, for example—and connecting DiPi's work to design classes also came with unique challenges. Connecting curricula to ongoing design projects takes more time to provide the extra scaffolding needed when students work on wicked design problems.[6] Since projects can vary widely between groups and years, much of this scaffolding has to be developed as projects unfold and cannot be done during breaks or preparation time. Ensuring productive student critiques

> **Sample Project: Outpatient Radio**
>
> In 2015, Tracy Manuel was a senior design major in Design for Understanding and an intern working on DiPi's Communicating Pain Project. Outpatient Radio (see Figure 5.1), a community radio program that aired on KKRN 88.5, began as her class project, and materials created for class were key in helping secure the approval of KKRN's board of directors.
>
> Community radio has a scrappy activist history of striving to counter top-down corporate broadcasting, and many community radio stations have developed to spread social change in ways that have everything to do with "voice." In Shasta County, California, a region where people with chronic pain have limited access to health education and resources, Outpatient Radio broadcasts will empower patients, community members, and health-care providers to share stories and knowledge in ways that exemplify public interest design. Featuring interviews with chronic pain patients, Outpatient Radio will "advocate with those who have a limited voice in public life" (Principle 1) by amplifying an often-unheard community: chronic pain patients in a remote rural area.
>
> Interviews will also be integral to "structures for inclusion" (Principle 2). In design, interviews usually happen as part of problem mapping or user-centered feedback; in radio, they are not a means but an end, constituting the stories and information that are distributed. Another structure for inclusion will be live listening events, where Manuel and the DiPi team will air the show and record feedback to incorporate into the broadcast. Thus, listeners will hear how the show is put together, how it changes, and how it focuses and refocuses; some will even hear themselves speak.
>
> The show will promote social equity through discourse "that reflects a range of values and social identities" (Principle 3). Whereas official experts usually dominate medical discussions, Outpatient Radio will redraw the boundaries of expertise to include individuals whose personal experience and regional knowledge are often overlooked. Similarly, Outpatient Radio will "grow from place and build local capacity" (Principle 4) since all stakeholders—patients, care providers, and community members—will have a voice in the broadcast, with each person presented and honored as an individual. The show's iterative nature will ensure that it is built around the community's responses to itself as ideas and themes develop organically over time.
>
> Finally, Outpatient Radio will "help conserve resources and minimize waste" (Principle 5) by using existing equipment, not adding infrastructure, and not requiring participants to buy anything. Radio is simpler technology than many contemporary design solutions like mobile apps; radio is also more accessible and reliable than Internet in vast areas of California.
>
> Overall, Outpatient Radio will facilitate discussions about chronic pain, treatment options, and obstacles and pathways to healing. Chronic pain can be isolating, stigmatized, and misunderstood; Outpatient Radio will use dialogue and narrative to increase community understanding and engagement, eroding patients' isolation and offering them greater understanding of chronic pain (including treatment options, history, common pitfalls, and everyday solutions), as well as a modality for reflecting on and sharing their progress to help others.

also takes more time and attention when there are dozens of different projects since students are not always engaged with and informed about one another's projects.

For undergraduates, another challenge is lack of time and connections since students have only five weeks to interact with stakeholders. This shortage of time and connections, combined with lack of experience with user testing, means that

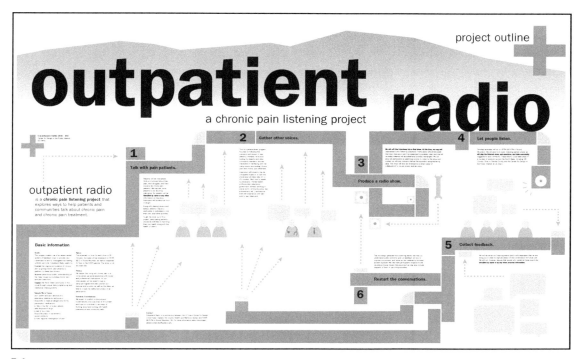

5.1
A poster that folds into a booklet provides a visual roadmap to engage stakeholders and participants in the project. Tracy Manuel, Outpatient Radio, UC Davis Center for Design in the Public Interest, Davis, California, 2016.

students tend to engage friends and family or conduct online surveys (via Facebook, for example). Students require instruction and guidance on how to develop effective surveys and how to interview users for their research. Because students are not accustomed to open-ended, poorly defined problems, the larger challenge is to help students realize that design includes not just producing final outcomes but also making tools to help engage others in the process, to imagine possible futures together with stakeholders, participants, and one another.

The hard work pays off as students learn to create as well as use tools, to work across disciplinary boundaries, and to explain their design decisions to nondesigners. While a five-week project allows little time for implementation, students can opt to have their work feed into the larger ongoing process at DiPi. We see such implementation as one of the greatest benefits of linking design curriculum to DiPi.

At the graduate level, students sometimes struggle to see how public interest design principles are relevant even in client-driven work; they ask how to incorporate public interest design into professional practice when they have to take care of client needs and wonder if they could do so only via pro bono work on the side. Through the readings and ongoing discussions, students eventually began to see how some of the public interest design principles can apply to and help guide any project, even those driven by clients' needs. The public interest design focus also helps greatly with another challenge: MFA students come from a wide range of backgrounds and have different goals. The shared readings and exercises focused on public interest design concepts help forge a common vocabulary and provoke meaningful discussion about how these principles resonate with each student's past experiences and future goals.

Extending learning beyond the classroom is the ultimate goal of education, whether undergraduate or graduate, in design or in any other field. Integrating public interest design into the undergraduate and graduate curriculum has been richly fulfilling. As Bell (2016, 13) says, "Without a mission, design can be seen merely as an advanced technical skill," and these courses build on the breadth of UC Davis's design curriculum by connecting design activities to larger social goals. The approaches used in these courses offer some ways to make such connections and to extend public interest design pedagogy by connecting classes with larger public interest endeavors.

Notes

1. For example, Professor Mark Kessler works with interior-architecture students to design and implement a nonprofit, pay-as-you-wish café for a local church, and Professor Helen Koo taught a course in fashion design and wearable technology that included projects to assist those with disabilities. Professor Emily Pilloton teaches courses in sustainable design and three-dimensional design incorporating aspects of public interest design (e.g., a project pairing design students with a fifth-grade class in Davis to design and build cardboard chairs that encourage creativity and engagement).
2. Benjamin Bloom's taxonomy of educational objectives lists educational goals as a pyramid. The base is Remember, because in order to perform other functions, students must be able to "recall facts and basic concepts." The levels, starting from this base, are Understand, Apply, Analyze, Evaluate, and Create. Each objective has associated key words; for example, the key words for Create include *design*, *assemble*, *construct*, and so on. For more about the taxonomy, see Patricia Armstrong's description at https://cft.vanderbilt.edu/guides-sub-pages/blooms-taxonomy/ and also Lorin W. Anderson and David R. Krathwohl, *A Taxonomy for Learning, Teaching, and Assessing: A Revision of Bloom's Taxonomy of Educational Objectives* (New York: Longman, 2001).
3. Many thanks to Professor Rebekka Andersen for providing material for this exercise.
4. For more information about IDEO Method Cards, see www.ideo.com/post/method-cards.
5. For more on the development of moral foundations theory, see, for example, Haidt and Joseph (2007) and Graham et al. (2013).
6. For more on this, see Verba and Perrault (2015, 2016).

References

Abendroth, Lisa M., and Bryan Bell, eds. 2016. *Public Interest Design Practice Guidebook: SEED Methodology, Case Studies, and Critical Issues*. New York: Routledge.

Bell, Bryan. 2016. "The State of Public Interest Design." In Abendroth and Bell, *PIDPG*, 11–18.

California Department of Motor Vehicles. 2016. "Get a DUI—Lose Your License!" *California Driver Handbook*. Accessed January 7, 2017. www.dmv.ca.gov/web/eng_pdf/dl600.pdf.

Fisher, Thomas. 2016. "Professional Responsibility and Ethics." In Abendroth and Bell, *PIDPG*, 35–44.

Graham, Jesse, Jonathan Haidt, Sena Koleva, Matt Motyl, Ravi Iyer, Sean P. Wojcik, and Peter H. Ditto. 2013. "Moral Foundations Theory: The Pragmatic Validity of Moral Pluralism." *Advances in Experimental Social Psychology* 47: 55–130, January 1.

Haidt, Jonathan, and Craig Joseph. 2007. "The Moral Mind: How Five Sets of Innate Intuitions Guide the Development of Many Culture-Specific Virtues, and Perhaps Even Modules." In *The Innate Mind*, edited by Peter Carruthers, Stephen Laurence, and Stephen Stich, vol. 3, 367–91. New York: Oxford.

Japan National Tourism Organization. 2016. "Radiation in Daily-Life." *Japan Travel Updates After the 3.11 Earthquake*. Accessed July 7, 2016. www.jnto.go.jp/eq/eng/04_recovery.htm.

Office of the University Registrar. 2016. *UC Davis General Catalog: 2016–2017, 2017–2018*, vol. 48.

Regents of the University of California. 2016. "Mission Statement: Philosophy of Purpose." Accessed October 21, 2016. http://catalog.ucdavis.edu/mission.html.

Tufte, Edward R. 2008. *Envisioning Information*. Reprint. Cheshire, CT: Graphics Press.

Verba, Susan. 2016. "Design 159 Syllabus."

Verba, Susan, and Sarah Perrault. 2015. "Design for Understanding: Creating Open-World and Open-Ended Design Experiences for Undergraduates." *IIID Vision Plus 2015 Symposium Papers, Abstracts, and Speaker Biographies*, 83–89. Birmingham, UK, September 3–4. www.iiid.net/downloads/IIID-VisionPlus-2015-Proceedings.pdf.

Verba, Susan, and Sarah Tinker Perrault. 2016. "Unbounded: Integrating Real-World Problems into an Undergraduate Information Design Course." *Information Design Journal* 22 (3): 266–80.

Visocky O'Grady, Jennifer, and Kenneth Visocky O'Grady. 2008. *The Information Design Handbook*. Cincinnati, OH: How Books.

6

Design (Education) to Create Meaningful Change
The Design for Social Impact Master's Program at the University of the Arts

Anthony Guido with Jeremy Beaudry, Jamer Hunt, Sharon Lefevre, Michael McAllister, and Jonas Milder

Program Philosophy

We believe in the power of design to create meaningful change in the world.

Dedicated to educating students in the arts and design, the University of the Arts (UArts) encourages students to collaborate across disciplines. This commitment to cross disciplinary, collaborative approaches to creative work also informs the two-year, sixty-credit Master of Design (MDes) program in Design for Social Impact (DSI). The MDes DSI program prepares students to become leading agents of social change, instrumental in fostering strategic creativity, organizational learning, and community engagement. The program promotes a social-design process that produces actionable models to create sustainable change. This hands-on process is action oriented and highly visual. It puts the needs of people and organizations at the center of the work and balances ecological, social, and economic values in the development of innovative solutions.

The values and mission of UArts as a whole informs and supports the graduate design program. UArts articulates its core values as commitment to "integrity and to respect for diversity, experience, ideas, and self-expression." The university further aims to "inspire, challenge, and support the unconventional thinkers, dreamers, and doers who are passionate about using their creative works to make an impact on society." It promotes community outreach, dedicating itself to connecting "the performing, visual, and communication arts in both the classroom and the community, expanding artistic possibilities, outcomes, and lives through creative collaboration" (UArts 2016).

What creates meaningful change in a community? How can public interest designers more fully engage the ideas, social capital, and co-creative design opportunities for change by working more fully *with* communities? And how might this change connect better to design (and design education) currently and in the future? The faculty, students, and community partners of the UArts DSI program actively engage in these questions, with their related challenges and opportunities, through applied academic research, participatory design projects, and collaborative realizations in the local context. The collective program ethos can be summarized as "Real people. Real places. Real projects."

The DSI curriculum balances classroom learning and real-world application through partnerships with local, national, and international organizations in sectors such as health care, social services, technology, and education. The program's pedagogy puts learning into practice by focusing on project-based community collaborations that can produce meaningful change. The program strategically meshes a multicultural group of students with experienced faculty from diverse design, social science, and business disciplines. Students and faculty are united in attempting to understand the needs of people, communities, and organizations so that a truly human-centered design process can make a constructive difference in how people live, play, and work.

Alumni are hired into leading companies and design firms, such as IBM Design, SAP SE, Electronic Ink, Comcast Interactive Media, and the University of Pennsylvania Health System's Center for Health Care Innovation. Many graduates start their own design consultancies and initiatives. A funded one-year postgraduate fellowship offers the opportunity to implement and measure the impact of thesis work within the Philadelphia community, as well.

Program Background and Strategic Evolution

To understand the DSI program's current participatory community design pedagogy and relationship to public interest design, a brief review of the evolution of the graduate design program at UArts is important. The program is the collective result of the applied social-design research of four previous graduate program directors: Charles Burnette, PhD; Jamer Hunt, PhD; Jonas Milder; and Jeremy Beaudry. The program's current director, Anthony Guido, continues this applied-research trajectory by expanding definitions, methods, research, and practices via community-engaged design projects.

An Interdisciplinary Graduate Program for Design Education and Research

Charles Burnette launched the original Master of Industrial Design (MID) graduate program in 1993 with a Federal Highway Administration–funded research project into the future of "advanced driver interface design and assessment" (Burnette 2015, 1). After years of work as a design educator, design thinking tools researcher, and author, Burnette astutely sensed fundamental shifts in design, expanding beyond the physical design of objects and evolving toward smarter interfaces via human-experience-informed design. New approaches in design thinking and education were his ultimate goals: "We were not interested in or capable of designing highways, but were very interested in designing safer controls for cars and better ways to assess human factors, usability, and safety on the highway" (Burnette 2015, 1).

Although this innovative, pragmatic, and successful interdisciplinary project ended in 2000, it created opportunities for venturing into the emerging human-centered design research arena. This timely shift coincided with other UArts "sustainability-oriented" design education approaches and new career-path options (Elkington 1990).

Rebooting a Graduate Industrial Design Program

In 2001, the newly appointed graduate director, Jamer Hunt, who originally trained as a cultural anthropologist, sensed an opportunity to redress the self-evident irony of design education in a postindustrial city like Philadelphia in the twenty-first century. He, together with the other industrial design faculty members, immediately engaged in a radical rethinking of what it meant to teach design skills at a time when thoughtful design practitioners addressed issues like the environmental impact of rampant consumerism and globalism's effect on managing humane work conditions.

Hunt created the tagline, "UArts MID: A graduate laboratory in postindustrial design." Borrowing the term *postindustrial* from Daniel Bell's *The Coming of Post-Industrial Society* (1976), which by that point was already twenty-five years old, Hunt hoped to create a graduate research program in design that did not teach incoming students what design was, but rather explored what postindustrial design could be. The faculty strongly emphasized critical thinking tied to design; in particular, every student took an introductory industrial design seminar, Concepts and Contexts, as an orientation to the shifting social, technological, and ecological context and theories of design practice. The aim was to demonstrate that design as a process and practice was both historically determined and contingent, which meant that it was also open to evolving. The faculty emphasized that designers should understand the political and environmental stakes of industrial design and better align practice to politics.

The studio courses also attempted to rethink the context of industrial design practice and explore the limits and possibilities of new forms of design. The projects themselves triangulated between conceptual and critical approaches to design (influenced by the work of Anthony Dunne and Fiona Raby at the Royal College of Art in London),[1] applied community-based projects, and explorations into new social technologies. Collaborations began with active community groups in Philadelphia trying to rebuild the physical and social infrastructure, whether or not the engagement was framed as design. While it was necessary to rely on a form of the design process to do this (explore, ideate, envision, propose, materialize, and assess), students and faculty more often searched for more effective ways to use design to redress industrial devastation and reimagine future possibilities.

Toward Strategic Design and Community Engagement

In 2007, Jonas Milder became the director of the MID program. The new enrollment plan made several major changes. The program became postdisciplinary, accepting students with design and nondesign degrees. Focus shifted from the design and making of objects to the third and fourth orders of design practice (Golsby-Smith 1996): a human-centered design approach that explored human experience in communities and design of organizations, systems, and environments (Buchanan 1992). The front end of the design process focused not just on problem solving but on problem definition.

The new curriculum emphasized small-group dynamics and facilitation of co-creative processes. Working with a psychologist as well as a leadership coach and using the observation-based Tavistock model of learning about group relations, students were able to build emotional intelligence as part of their skill sets (Goleman 2005). Building on work by Elizabeth Sanders, among others, the program began to develop design tools and practices that could be transferred across different projects and collaborations. Sharing design tools and thinking in a co-creative setting, rather than working *for* a particular client or partner (see sample project sidebar), allowed the program to seed design culture in communities that were not previously exposed to design practice.

Projects allowed students to learn in the world, facing and responding to real-world challenges. Informed by the global scale, studio projects were framed in a local context. The program partnered with a range of for-profit and nonprofit organizations to engage sustainable, multiyear change through design. Some of the partnerships actually proved to be transformational, as organizations adopted design as a new practice.

Design for Social Impact

In 2013, Jeremy Beaudry led the transition to the current DSI program with the next iteration of the graduate industrial design program (which included important pedagogical threads drawn from the undergraduate industrial design program). With its emphasis on preparing students to use design as an instrument of positive social change, the program responded to contemporary trends in social design, innovation, and entrepreneurship, all framed within the methodology of human-centered design and design thinking. This was a step further toward the expansion of the boundaries of industrial design (and of design, broadly understood).

The change of the program name to Design for Social Impact and the degree offered changed to Master of Design, as well as the revised curriculum, were all intended to establish the field of social design as a distinct educational and career pathway. Given the rise of other graduate programs, centers, and institutes focused on social innovation, the DSI program followed a logical progression begun several years earlier at UArts and unequivocally shed the mantle of industrial design. As a practice-based design studio program, the major studio and thesis projects were organized as partnerships with businesses, government agencies, nonprofit organizations, and community groups. The multifaceted nature of these collaborations and design explorations ventured into the ambiguous territory of complex systems, organizational cultures, and business strategies. The curriculum evolved to equip students to take on this complexity by supplementing more traditional design content with course work in design research, organizational psychology, emotional intelligence and facilitation, and business fundamentals (Goleman 2005).

Partnership projects gravitated toward health care, social services, technology, and education, with project outcomes such as new service models; design for user experience; strategies and tools for community engagement; and the development of social entities, organizations, new businesses, and initiatives. The program found its most willing and accessible partners in the public and nonprofit sectors, which was as much a matter of convenience as it was program philosophy. Public and nonprofit organizations are often resource challenged with limited capacity. The offer of highly skilled, energetic graduate students to help these organizations work through complex and often ambiguously defined problems is greatly valued. At the same time, these partnerships align perfectly with the DSI program's mission to demonstrate the efficacy and power of design to work in the interest of the public good.

Program Curriculum Overview

Today the DSI curriculum, consisting of sixty credits, is structured around a careful balance of classroom learning, reflection, and real-world application of design practice. The curriculum is project based: each semester's course content is integrated with studio-based projects. Seminars, lectures, workshops, and critiques from faculty and leading outside professionals create a dynamic studio environment. Academically, students have great freedom to engage in self-directed, independent projects, including a final thesis project that reflects the student's personal design interests.

Because design is a collaborative profession, most studio projects are team based. During the first and third semesters of study, first-year students work with second-year students and an industry partner in a shared studio. The second and fourth semesters are focused on more independent student-driven projects. The final semester of the two-year program is devoted to a master's thesis, in which social-design students work independently with faculty and outside professionals to develop a thesis project that advances their chosen fields of study.

Curriculum Exemplar: The DSI Design Methods Sequence

Of particular importance to the program is the synergetic blend between the studio, methods, and seminar course work. Figure 6.1 presents the evolutionary, highly connected path of learning human-centered design methods (IDEO 2011) and participatory, collaborative, generative design processes (Sanders and Stappers 2013). Informed by team-based collaboration experiences, these methods play a significant role in working successfully in the community client-based studios and on thesis projects (see Figure 6.2).

6.1
Years one and two of the DSI program sequence.

Year 1, Fall **Design Methods I (IDES 604)**	Year 1, Spring **Design Methods II (IDES 606)**
Emphasis: design fundamentals	Emphasis: design tools in practice
Methods and tools exercises: • digital design tools • visual communication design concepts • complex systems mapping and data sets • storytelling and presentation • prototyping skills	Methods and tools exercises: • boundary objects • cultural probes • ethnography • generative tools and facilitation • stakeholder mapping • backcasting and affinity diagramming • concept evaluation • tool construction • video narratives • narrative structures
Year 1–2, Summer **Optional Methods Workshop**	Year 2, Fall **Advanced Design Methods (IDES 704)**
Extracurricular, nonrequired weekend workshops	Emphasis: service and experience design; information design (advanced)
Methods and tools exercises: • visual communication design • three-dimensional prototyping • storytelling and presentation	Service and experience design methods: • service models • service blueprints • service maps • user scenarios • wireframes • storyboarding • four-dimensional design methods (motion graphics, audio, and video)

6.2
Graduate design methods class reviewing book spreads of project documentation. Studio NEXT, Philadelphia, Pennsylvania, 2009.

Additional Cross-Linked DSI Course Examples

The graduate seminar and workshop Collaboration and Co-design (DESN 630) examines the theoretical underpinnings of effective collaboration and co-design within the contexts of organizations and communities relevant to designers working in several fields. Emphasizing the creation of successful consultant relationships between designers and their clients, the course explores such topics as systems thinking, facilitation and leadership, emotional intelligence (Goleman 2005), consulting dynamics, co-design, and participatory design frameworks. Through theoretical study combined with practical applications and tactics, students understand how to better craft and maintain collaborative relationships in the context of their design practice.

The Design I and II studios (IDES 603 and 703) are structured around collaboration with businesses, for-profit and nonprofit organizations, and community groups. Projects focus on organizational development, service design, and design for user experience. Studio teams combine first- and second-year MDes students. As first-year students are introduced to the human-centered design process and methodology, second-year students take on leadership roles as team managers and facilitators. Design research, synthesis, and visual communication are emphasized. The prototyping and practice are additionally supported through Design Methods I and II (IDES 604 and 704).

Program Pedagogical Goals

As a result of the DSI MDes curriculum, graduate students will be able to:

- practice DSI through real-world design projects in partnership with businesses, government agencies, nonprofit organizations, and community groups

- examine the contextual, theoretical, and historical evolution of DSI practices and techniques and relate these to current philosophies and best practices in the field
- foster a collaborative, participatory co-design process that places people at the center of the design process
- use design tools for community engagement, conversation, and collective learning to facilitate a participatory co-design process
- develop emotional intelligence, facilitation, and leadership skills that support the design student's ability to maneuver effectively in complex organizational and social situations
- relate expertise in the use of a range of design methods and tools drawn from a variety of design disciplines
- use design-research methodologies to understand the specific stakeholders, context, and issues of a given design opportunity
- apply inductive reasoning through quantitative and qualitative research data to identify patterns, insights, and design opportunities
- construct iteratively developed design prototypes in a range of fidelities and formats that can be tested with stakeholders
- develop clear metrics and assessment criteria to evaluate the impact of design interventions and prototypes
- analyze fundamental business and entrepreneurial practices as they apply to the field of design
- create visually compelling, narratively rich documentation and presentations that effectively communicate the design process and project outcomes

Program Outcomes

The UArts DSI program is the culmination of several years of master's level design inquiry, design curriculum evolution phases, continued academic experiments in participatory co-design with a diverse set of community partners, and the diligent work of many graduate students and faculty. There have certainly been many challenges and successes along the way for co-learning. In support of the university mission and specifically the DSI program ethos, faculty, students, and partners believe in the power of design to create meaningful change in the world through the following observable and measurable outcomes:

- expertise in applying human-centered design processes, methods, and tools—research, synthesis, ideation, prototyping, and user testing—to the development, production, and iteration of innovative design interventions in a range of situations and formats
- practical experience in the use of design tools for community engagement, conversation, and collective learning to facilitate a participatory co-design process

- understanding of fundamental business and entrepreneurial perspectives, terminology, and practices as they apply to the opportunity for design and designers to have measurable impact in these domains
- successful completion of an independently directed design thesis project that demonstrates expertise in the use of methods and tools for DSI as applied in real-world contexts
- ability to embark on numerous professional pathways that require expertise in design process and thinking, design research, strategic planning and organizational change, community engagement, and collaboration and that are supported by visual thinking, visual communication, and strategic thinking

---

Sample Project: The Remás Project: Building Trust Through Community Design Partnerships

The bi-level course combined project studios: Community Design Partnerships (IDES 603 and 703) mixes first-year graduate students in their first design studio and second-year students also working on the project who mentor the first-year students. This project-based design studio introduces the concepts of building connections, team diversity, collaborative outreach, and sharing the human-centered design process as a foundation to working in an actual community on real issues.

    This 2010 course was taught by Professors Michael McAllister and Jonas Milder and included students Georgia Guthrie, Alaina Penda, Donovan Preddy, and Dominic Prestifilippo on the graduate design research team. In a project called Remás: Rethinking How Mexican Immigrants Send Remittances, the research team worked with Brendan McBride, a community partner who has dedicated much of his career to studying and building housing for people with low incomes. McBride's work raised his awareness of the significant role played by remittances, earnings sent home by immigrants abroad. Many families rely on these remittances to improve their living conditions. However, the money transfers often require high fees, and many workers are significantly hindered by not having bank accounts. Furthermore, McBride saw an inherent flaw in a system that transfers earnings to individuals with no benefit to the recipients' communities.

    McBride asked the team to help him try to transform the money-transfer industry. His goal was to make it easier and cheaper for the workers to send remittances, and he wanted fees in excess of costs to go to development in the recipients' communities.

    In this multifaceted project, students researched how migrant farmworkers send money home and explored how to expand and transform this process. Philadelphia and southern New Jersey were the loci for research. The stakeholders were migrant farmworkers, the Remás nonprofit organization, and local bodega owners (see Figure 6.3). The goal was to address financial issues and related needs that would benefit immigrants and their communities.

As a result of this project, students were able to:

- develop confidence in applying the design process to problems and contexts in the public realm
- demonstrate research skills using both primary and secondary methods
- formulate methods of observation, such as storytelling, interviewing, and surveys
- synthesize complex research and the often-conflicting needs of multiple stakeholders into a clear direction

- experience direct engagement with clients and stakeholders
- learn how to interact professionally in environments outside the context typical for traditional designers
- develop cultural sensitivity
- use iterative prototyping to gain feedback from users and stakeholders for continual improvement

Although McBride, the primary stakeholder, held preconceived notions that a kiosk supporting online remittances was the answer, the team ultimately chose a different direction. McBride's preconceived solution afforded students a classic client–consultant challenge: How do you encourage the removal of presuppositions? Research took students into the migrant-farming community, where they had to build trust in order to discuss as sensitive a topic as money. Facing cultural, language, literacy, and legal barriers, students built trust by attending Catholic Mass on Sundays in the community and ultimately by developing a relationship with the parish priest. It took time and perseverance just to be able to interview and survey migrant farmers. Surveys had to be carefully crafted and translated into Spanish, and they had to provide anonymity for workers who might be in the country illegally. Ultimately, students developed low-tech, easily comprehensible materials to extend knowledge and understanding of banking and extra-banking choices, while building trust and brand familiarity. Once migrant workers understood the alternative means for remitting, then high-tech methods could also be offered online.

The following were the design-process outcomes (see Figure 6.4) of this project:[2]

- a culturally sensitive, graphic-heavy pamphlet explaining banking, fees, requirements for opening a bank account, and benefits of a bank account
- a certification system for institutions interested in becoming immigrant friendly
- a cell phone financial information service
- a website for financial information, price comparisons, and a rating system
- a kiosk in local bodegas or transportation hubs for those who did not have computer access

6.3
Remás project design research and remittance location site documentation. Dominic Prestifilippo, Remás: Rethinking How Mexican Immigrants Send Remittances, Philadelphia, Pennsylvania, 2010.

Design (Education) to Create Meaningful Change

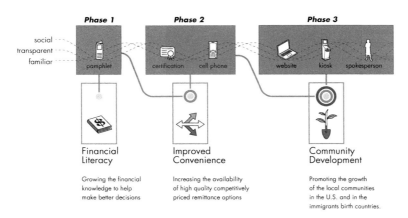

6.4
Illustrated design research mapping phased sequences of multitiered solutions. Georgia Guthrie, Alaina Pineda, Donovan Preddy, and Dominic Prestifilippo, Remás: Rethinking How Mexican Immigrants Send Remittances, Philadelphia, Pennsylvania, 2010.

Notes

1   For more information on their work, see Dunne and Raby's 2013 publication *Speculative Everything: Design, Fiction and Social Dreaming* (Cambridge, MA: MIT Press).
2   For more information, see the final student publication documenting this project at https://issuu.com/mid_uarts/docs/remas/.

References

Bell, Daniel. 1976. *The Coming of Post-Industrial Society: A Venture in Social Forecasting*. New York: Basic Books.

Buchanan, Richard. 1992. "Wicked Problems in Design Thinking." *Design Issues* 8 (2): 5–21.

Burnette, Charles. 2015. *An Interdisciplinary Graduate Program for Design Education and Research*. Philadelphia, PA. Accessed February 10, 2017. www.academia.edu/20045170/An_Interdisciplinary_Graduate_Program_for_Design_Education_and_Research.

Elkington, John. 1990. *Cannibals with Forks: The Triple Bottom Line of 21st Century Business*. Oxford, UK: Capstone Publishing.

Goleman, Daniel. 2005. *Emotional Intelligence: Why It Can Matter More Than IQ*. New York: Bantam Dell Publishing Group.

Golsby-Smith, Tony. 1996. "Fourth Order Design: A Practical Perspective." *Design Issues*, 12 (1): 5–25.

IDEO. 2011. *Human-Centered Design Toolkit: An Open-Source Toolkit to Inspire New Solutions in the Developing World*. Bloomington, IN: AuthorHouse.

Sanders, Elizabeth B.-N., and Pieter Jan Stappers. 2013. *Convivial Toolbox: Generative Research for the Front End of Design*. Amsterdam: BIS Publishers.

UArts (The University of the Arts). 2016. "Core Values and Mission." Accessed December 20, 2016. www.uarts.edu/about/core-values-mission.

7
Collaborating for Change in New Orleans
Small Center for Collaborative Design

Maggie Hansen and Emilie Taylor Welty

Program Philosophy

The Albert and Tina Small Center for Collaborative Design (formerly Tulane City Center) is the community design center of the Tulane School of Architecture (SOA) in New Orleans, Louisiana. Since its founding in 2005, the Small Center has addressed a gap in the design field by providing technical services for traditionally underserved organizations and groups. At the Small Center, we are working to expand the role of designers and the impact of good design in our home, New Orleans, by creating space for more voices in the design process.

At Small Center we act on the belief that our built environment affects all citizens and that everyone should be empowered to participate in the decisions that shape their environment. As a result, deep engagement and collaboration are critical components of our work. We use the design process as a powerful coalition-building tool, and our role in many projects extends beyond architecture to diplomacy, education, and facilitation.

Our design process is structured to ensure that stakeholders have a voice—that they are viewed as the experts on their communities and on the issues that their organizations seek to address (Till 2005). Stakeholders work alongside technical consultants as expert advisers. We host design conversations around specific questions and invite the organization's stakeholders and leadership, constituents, academic researchers, policymakers, and technical consultants, each with a unique and valuable perspective for the discussion's theme (Till 2005). We present our design work and facilitate a conversation not only to receive input on the design, but also to talk through the larger issues of the project and begin to build a coalition with expertise from lived experience and representatives in a position to make change. Throughout the design process, this coalition grows, helping to envision the project and building capacity toward expanded multimodal effects long after our design work is complete (Pitera 2014). The design process offers a framework and an impetus for these conversations to develop deeper questions and to define and create shared goals of broader change within a coalition. Our role as designers is to create space for these conversations, listen, develop the spatial implications, and make connections to develop the nonspatial goals. We are also able to prove the value of design excellence in our city and shift conventions (both in perception and reality) around whom architects serve, what they work on, and how we approach designing for a more equitable city.[1]

In 2005 our city was devastated by floodwaters caused by Hurricane Katrina and the federal levee failures that followed. These events and the subsequent rebuilding efforts influenced the center's focus, as well as the ethos of Tulane University and our partner organizations. Small Center has emphasized equitable rebuilding, meaningful outcomes, and inclusion as part of the design process. Our architectural efforts benefit from parallels in other departments. Tulane University mandated service-learning activities as a core requirement for graduating students following Hurricane Katrina. This university-wide focus on students' being productive members of a rebuilding community reinforced efforts already under way within the SOA to take the curriculum outside the classroom.

In our first ten years, Small Center has completed more than eighty-five projects, involving over five hundred students, thirty-five faculty, and seventy-four partner organizations. The students who participate primarily attend the Tulane SOA and include graduate and undergraduate students. The SOA has several affiliated degree programs, including a Master of Preservation Studies and a Master of Sustainable Real Estate Development, whose students also participate when needed. Student involvement in Small Center projects is elective, and we benefit from the enthusiasm of students who opt in.

Program Curriculum Overview

All projects originate as proposals from community-based organizations through our annual request for proposals. New Orleans–based nonprofits are invited to submit a simple proposal for technical assistance. A jury, consisting of representatives from past project partners, faculty and professional architects, and peer institution leaders, reviews the proposals and ranks the applications based on impact, feasibility, creative potential, and learning opportunities. We facilitate a discussion with the jury and provide a scorecard to make certain that equal consideration is given to all proposals. The transparency and structure of this process ensure from the beginning that the work is grounded in an actual need from our community and help to build trust at the outset of every project.

Selected projects begin with a scoping exercise, in which our team meets with the organization's leadership to define the goals of the project and to discuss parameters. The exercise is a facilitated discussion based on a template of simple questions intended to spark conversation in the group, set a tone of trust, and identify points of confusion, misinformation, and potential problems:

- What is the primary goal we are trying to achieve together?
- How will we measure this project's success?
- Who are the stakeholders (constituents and naysayers) in this project?
- What are the most effective methods of engaging the stakeholders?
- How can we build capacity within our community?
- What are the student learning objectives?
- What readings does the partner organization recommend to frame the design investigation?
- How are we educating the public about broader issues for New Orleans citizens?
- How do we mark the project's conclusion (a crawfish boil, a press release, a day of action, etc.)?

Framing these questions for ourselves, with our partner organization and often with our students, allows us to arrive at a set of common achievable goals for the project, set clear expectations, and quickly build trust within our team. Using the responses, we strive to create and define goals within three categories: an appropriate design product (object, space, and tool), a stronger coalition for advocacy (organizational capacity), and education of young designers (a public interest design experience for students).

This scoping conversation forms the basis of a simple agreement document that informs the creation of the design team and the timeline of the project and that frames the team's work together. Some projects are structured as course work where students earn credits; others are paid design internships focused on a particular project. Determining whether to use a course-based or internship structure depends on the project's size, funding source, and schedule, which often does not correspond to the constraints of the academic semester schedule. We offer two studio design/build courses and a seminar on design in the public interest as options within the curriculum each year. Outside the curriculum, we also offer project-based internships and a summer fellowship as paid opportunities.

We believe it is important for students to experience a full phase of a project, so we structure all student opportunities to result in a meaningful deliverable for the partner organization. For design/build studios, this creates a constraint on the scale of our work, as the project must be designed and constructed in the fourteen weeks of the semester. For all projects, we create a publication describing the project that the partner organization can use for fund-raising and marketing. As designers, we think through intentional making, and the graphic and physical products of our investigations are benefits of working with us.

All projects are developed in a collaborative process that engages the organization's constituents and stakeholders to better shape the final product and to strengthen the organization's network at a moment of change. Each team is composed of SOA faculty and students, with support and guidance from our staff. Project goals may identify needs that fall outside of our architectural expertise, requiring external consultants and university partners who can address them. Collaborators frequently include structural engineers, landscape architects, real estate development students, planners, public health students, and former project partners.

Students participate in predesign research through teach-ins with the partner organization, assigned readings, and independent research. This team-oriented approach offers students an opportunity to hone their technical expertise while managing the complex dynamics of schedules, budgets, and teammates—experience that typically doesn't occur until professional practice. The resulting project must meet the stated aims of the partner organization and a social need in the city; however, the standards of innovation, design excellence, and artful representation still apply.

Often with projects involving participatory practices, there is a misperception that architecture is a passive vehicle for community desires or that collaboration results in mediocrity. Our students experience the participatory process as an exchange of expertise, in which the power of design excellence and innovation builds on the insight gained through robust engagement. These participatory processes are tools used to produce outcomes that are useful, beautiful, empowering, and greater than the sum of their parts.

Building Capacity and Community

Our engagement process is tailored to each project's needs, yet it always includes these key steps:

- understanding what our partner organization wants to achieve
- determining the most productive way we can insert ourselves into the process
- opening the conversation to a vast network of collaborators and consultants
- executing the project as a team
- celebrating as a team, as the beginning of the organization's next steps

The organizations we work with often have pressing needs that cannot be addressed through architecture alone. We see the design process as an opportunity to strengthen the relationships within the organization's network, to make new strategic links, and to identify other goals for the organization's future (Johnson 2011). We also recognize that participation and inclusion do not equal power, and we work to co-create meaningful momentum to bolster larger social movements. Our responsibility as designers is to advance solutions that enhance the organization's ability to do its work, which means we need to design a building that it can realistically afford to build and maintain but often also requires facilitating tough conversations about whether the organization's aspirations for its future are realistic. These conversations are not strictly architectural but often have great impact on our design proposals.

During each project's engagement process, we are working to build the capacity of our partner organizations while educating students and stakeholders alike. The design process presents an opportunity for the organization to strengthen its own network around a shared set of goals, and we encourage our partners to use our collaboration as an excuse to invite in strategic allies. This capacity-building work demands that we flex our nondesign skills as communicators, empathetic and curious people, and true collaborators, as we seek outside experts to lead much of this work alongside our design work.

Being part of that community for an extended period of time is important (Perkes 2009). This is not an adventure-based design project where we swoop in, design, and leave. This is our home, and we participate as members of the community through the application of our talents and training, as well as through our commitment to our fellow community members. These are lasting relationships, and we recognize that continued partnership is critical to chipping away at the larger systemic issues that we are all grappling with. Our partnership continues after construction concludes: we are here to take the calls when there is a problem with the building, or a client wants us in city hall to help plead a case, or there is a wedding, a birth, or a crawfish boil. Our students experience that one small change in the city's fabric can catalyze change of larger systems, and they see that good designers are also good citizens.

Student Skill Development and Learning Objectives

All of our courses and internships emphasize skills and experience in collaborative design that will apply to future work as professional designers. Students learn the following:

- development, testing, and representation of design ideas individually and as a part of a team
- presentation of design ideas to reviewers from outside the architecture discipline at multiple stages of the design process
- methods of asking questions and soliciting useful feedback
- basic engagement and research methodologies, including simple observation, interview techniques, and design critique, as tools for understanding human context in relation to the built environment
- introduction to professional design ethics and a designer's responsibility to clients
- introduction to issues of equity and social justice through the lens of the built environment

As a result of our design/build courses, students are able to:

- plan a project from an initial client–partner interview through design to completion of construction
- develop basic construction skills (including welding, woodworking, details, and joinery), with emphasis on understanding the logic of material assembly and design details
- manage a limited materials budget and construction timeline
- delegate responsibilities across a team

Our students learn that seeing a project through from idea to completion is a long, difficult, and joyful struggle that takes a team to accomplish, and to gain the trust of that team, students must take the time to be a part of it. Impact is also related to the level of trust established in a community.

Program Pedagogical Goals

In working on our projects, students are asked, often for the first time, to consider engagement and to create a process for conducting design research and feedback—a process that sets them up to be more thoughtful and proficient design professionals. The most important lessons of the studio occur when initial assumptions are challenged in doing the actual project work. Students often identify critical turning points in the semester as the moments that challenged their preconceptions: of a community's expertise, of the real barriers to accessing resources, or of the simplicity of a construction detail. It can be difficult to fit all the student objectives of engagement, construction proficiency, and collaborative design into a single semester while also ensuring that the partner organization gets a functional, beautiful, and useful outcome to its design question, but we work to structure each student opportunity to begin and end a project phase, to allow these opportunities for reality checks along the way.

The projects are often the first opportunities students have to navigate a real client relationship and to present their work to nondesigners. We challenge students to manage the schedule, budget, delegation, and presentation of the work. The process frequently reveals the importance of developing modes of representation that are quickly accessible to a variety of people—teammates, clients, and future employers—and of shifting presentation language based on audience. As a recent example, a review of a design for a bookstore interior included architecture professors and bookstore staff. After several minutes of jargon-heavy feedback from the designers, one of the bookstore clerks interrupted to ask that the designers use words everyone could understand. In the postreview discussion, students were struck by how hard it was for their professors to shift their language for a new audience and how important vocabulary is to its specific context.

Sample Project: Sankofa Mobile Market

In the fall of 2015, our design/build studio partnered with Sankofa Community Development Corporation, a nonprofit based in the Ninth Ward of New Orleans, to design and build a more efficient and eye-catching mobile produce stand. Sankofa's organizational mission is to support the creation of a local environment that promotes positive health outcomes and long-term community well-being. The resulting Sankofa Mobile Market increased the organization's capacity to serve senior centers and health clinics around the city.

The "site" of the design/build project was the bed of Sankofa's Toyota Tundra pickup truck, which presented unique challenges that the students addressed with skill, thoughtfulness, and creativity through a rigorous engagement and collaborative development process (see Figure 7.1). In the process, they experimented with materials and with their capacities, learned new skills (such as welding steel and aluminum), experienced the value and process of collaboration and communication (with our community partner, end users, material suppliers, and one another), and explored larger issues of food access and local power dynamics in finding productive ways to create positive change.

The students in the Small Center design/build studio (DSGN 4200/6200) took on the design challenge: how to design a mobile produce stand that draws in customers and provides functional, durable food display and sun protection while physically representing Sankofa's brand. The Small Center design/build studio included undergraduate and graduate architecture students who had completed three years of design studio courses, but most had no experience with tools, detailing, or client interaction. The design team included Sankofa's leadership, with stakeholder groups composed of Sankofa Fresh Stop and Mobile Market workers, leaders of other local food-justice organizations, and the customers (primarily seniors) who relied on the Mobile Market at five different locations across the city.

The result of the fourteen-week studio is an insert for storing produce in the bed of the truck, with a mechanized market stand above. When parked, the market expands in a single motion, allowing setup by one person, to reveal an angled frame for supporting baskets of produce and a shade cloth to protect people and vegetables from the sun (see Figure 7.2). The new Mobile Market has been on the road since February 2016. Before our collaboration, the market required thirty minutes or more to set up baskets of produce on a table for an hour of sales at each location. The new, more efficient market setup now takes a few minutes and increases the time devoted to sales on each site. The standardization of display-crate sizes and the sequencing of the selection-to-purchase process create a streamlined customer experience with a consistent look and feel. The previous market could display between six and nine items and required on-site staging, while the new design allows an average of twelve and a maximum of twenty display items, so more variety is visible.

In a more qualitative way, both staff and customers appreciate the shade since it allows some relief from the relentless summer heat. Seniors engaged in the design process feel a personal affinity to the design and pride in seeing their market appear each week (see Figure 7.3).

A challenging moment comes in every project when students confront the limits of design as a tool to address the myriad needs of our partner organizations. We see more and more students interested in design for the opportunity to contribute to positive social change, and we work to engage these interests directly while grounding the work in true constraints and challenges. Much of our early work is in framing the architectural intervention and its role, while identifying resources

7.1
Mobile Market design feedback at Mercy Endeavors Senior Center. Small Center studio team, design lead Doug Harmon, Sankofa Mobile Market, New Orleans, Louisiana, 2016.

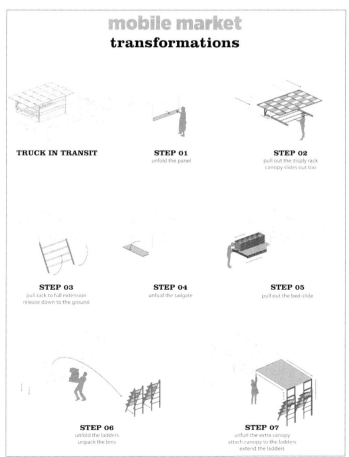

7.2
Diagram of the Mobile Market transformation. Small Center Design/Build Studio, Sankofa Mobile Market, New Orleans, Louisiana, 2016.

Collaborating for Change in New Orleans

7.3
Mobile Market as built and in use at a senior center. Small Center studio team, design lead Doug Harmon, Sankofa Mobile Market, New Orleans, Louisiana, 2016.

to address other needs. It is important for students to experience that true change results from the work of many hands and strategic timing. Design is a road into these broader conversations but cannot be a solution in isolation.[2]

True collaborative work requires a lot of time and energy—effort that is often invisible and underestimated by those outside the project. Yet the results of an inclusive project that engages stakeholders in meaningful ways create buy-in for the projects and produce a set of advocates, motivated coalitions, and maintenance partners that are invested in the life of the project. By experiencing the fulfillment of developing a project alongside its users, as well as the frustrations that come with real-world work, students are better equipped to navigate their own professional contributions to the field and to leverage their design voices to create spaces for more voices in the process.

Program Outcomes

Small Center projects range in scale, scope, timeline, deliverables, and capacity of our partnering organizations. For example, while we were developing the Sankofa Mobile Market (see sidebar), we were also working with Women With a Vision, Inc., a group dedicated to improving the health and wellness of marginalized women. The project was to create a schematic design booklet as a tool for raising funds for a new office after the group's office was intentionally burned down. In addition to these examples and other site-specific projects, we often use our graphic and spatial analysis skills to develop advocacy and education campaigns, such as our collaboration with the Greater New Orleans Fair Housing Action Center on a project aimed at improving the rights of renters in New Orleans.

We are careful to match the needs of our partner organizations with our own capacity and our students' skills, and a lot of our work is in communicating with partner organizations before, during, and after design about expectations and shared goals. The metrics for our students' success are consistent from project to project (teamwork, true participation, true collaboration, innovation, and attention to details), but the metrics for the success of each project are tailored to the needs of the partner organization.

Measurement of success ranges from evaluating the dry numbers to understanding the harder-to-quantify impact on education and quality of life. The coalitions built around projects like Circle Food Store, Grow Dat Youth Farm, Jane Place, and Parisite DIY Skatepark[3] have together raised over $10 million; they have brought food, affordable housing, and recreation to thousands across the city and founded new projects with the momentum built from the initial design collaborations. Harder to quantify are the influences on community members, students' educations, and perceptions of the design profession and the effect design can have on people's lives.

As a small but meaningful example of the power of this inclusive design process, several of our former project collaborators have enrolled in degree programs in design schools. Two collaborators from Parisite DIY Skatepark are now studying landscape architecture, and a collaborator on numerous projects in the Lower Ninth Ward just completed a degree in sustainable real estate development. Additionally, our public interest design work in the community and our work across traditional academic silos have drawn both graduate and undergraduate students. We have seen an increase in the number of young designers who are interested in issues of equity and impact and who want to learn how they can work within design disciplines to be in service of larger societal justice. This work, particularly in an educational setting, moves the profession toward a more equitable version of itself and of the built environment.

Notes

1   We are indebted to and inspired by the work of our colleagues at the Design for Equity Initiative (www.designforequity.org) in outlining the importance and complexity of design work toward equitable outcomes.

2   "Critical thought requires looking beyond architecture towards an enhanced understanding of the whole to which it belongs ... in relation to other issues of education, healthcare, transportation, recreation, law enforcement, employment, the environment, the collective community that impacts on the lives of both the rich and the poor," writes Sam Mockbee in an essay from *Architectural Design: The Everyday and Architecture,* eds. Sarah Wigglesworth and Jeremy Till (London: Academy Editions, 1998).

3   Many exceptional community-based organizations are working to improve the quality of life of New Orleans citizens, and we are lucky to have had the

opportunity to work alongside them. Visit small.tulane.edu for more information on our projects. The following organizations were mentioned in this chapter:

- Circle Food Store (http://circlefoodsnola.com/about_us/)
- Greater New Orleans Fair Housing Action Center (www.gnofairhousing.org/)
- Grow Dat Youth Farm (http://growdatyouthfarm.org/)
- Jane Place Neighborhood Sustainability Initiative (http://jpnsi.org/)
- Parisite DIY Skatepark (Transitional Spaces; www.parisitediy.org/)
- Sankofa Community Development Corporation (www.sankofanola.org/)
- Women With a Vision, Inc. (http://wwav-no.org/)

References

Johnson, Cedric G. 2011. "The Urban Precariat, Neoliberalization, and the Soft Power of Humanitarian Design." *Journal of Developing Societies* 27 (3–4): 462.

Perkes, David. 2009. "A Useful Practice." *Journal of Architectural Education*. 62 (4): 64–71.

Pitera, Dan. 2014. "Leading from the Side: Leadership, Civic Engagement and the Built Environment." In *Syncopating the Urban Landscape; More People, More Programs More Geographies*. Detroit Collaborative Design Center, 187–92.

Till, Jeremy. 2005. "The Negotiation of Hope." In *Architecture and Participation*, edited by Peter Blundell-Jones, Doina Petrescu, and Jeremy Till, 25–44. London: Routledge.

8

From the Ground Up
Envisioning an MFA in Public Interest Design at Metropolitan State University of Denver

Lisa M. Abendroth, Kelly Monico, and Peter Miles Bergman

Founded in 1965, Metropolitan State University of Denver (MSU Denver) is uniquely positioned to provide a comprehensive education to a diverse student population. MSU Denver is among the nation's most affordable public universities (MSU Denver 2017a); it operates within a context of "diversity, access, entrepreneurship, respect, and community" (MSU Denver 2017b). These values holistically define the university and the student population while supporting a vision for teaching, research, and practice that connects purpose with people and place. The university's 2020 strategic plan furthers this motivation through such relevant themes as "community engagement and regional stewardship" (MSU Denver 2015), which inspire and guide programmatic development.

Between 2009 and 2010 the Colorado Commission on Higher Education approved MSU Denver's first master's degree programs (MSU Denver 2010, 17). This long-anticipated outcome was the impetus to shape a distinct path of innovation for the field of design: a vision for a proposed Master of Fine Arts (MFA) in Public Interest Design.[1] Building on undergraduate course work catering to a program legacy of community-based and design research practices, the Communication Design faculty began crafting a regionally unique, nationally competitive, and first of its kind MFA that differentiated itself based on its breadth of interdisciplinary interest and need.

Laying the Groundwork: Communication Design Undergraduate Program

The Communication Design program, housed within the National Association of Schools of Art and Design (NASAD)–accredited Department of Art, offers the Bachelor of Fine Arts (BFA) in Communication Design degree. This program delivers a robust set of skills across three primary pillars: design fundamentals (storytelling, branding, systems, history, and theory), emergent practices (public interest design, human-centered design and strategy, and design research), and emergent media (data, ambient, spatial, responsive, and user experience). These skills combined with a focus on design pragmatics, semantics, and syntactics have enabled the program to connect with distinctly community-centered problems. Studio courses, such as Community-Based Design I (running regularly in various course iterations since 2004) and II (CDES 4100 and 4101; service-learning-designated courses), Studio M (CDES 4650; a service-learning-designated course) Design Research Methods (CDES 3222), and the lower-division theory seminar Design Inquiry (CDES 2226), have established essential undergraduate course content and anchored program orientation toward engagement with problems located outside and well beyond campus.

The evolution of study abroad offerings have further supported undergraduate level course work. The course Community-Based Design in the Dominican Republic (CDES 390A) for example ran for three weeks with thirteen interdisciplinary art and design undergraduate students who collaborated on-site with the Dominican-Haitian community of La Piedra and the partnering organization Centro Cultural Guanin. The locational immersive design process applied in this course demonstrates how design can function as a tool for outreach and address a community's needs as defined by its members. Students develop leadership skills by collaborating with partner organizations and community leaders to create long-term, sustainable change. Working in the field, side by side with community members, teaches students to be citizen designers and expands their cultural perspective.

This backdrop of undergraduate program development contextualizes the intent of the proposed master's degree as part of a comprehensive pedagogy. The lessons the faculty has learned along the way can be of value to other educators seeking to craft similar programs.

Visioning the Future: Program Philosophy[2]

The MFA philosophy is anchored in several well-tested engagement foundations, including the Social Economic Environmental Design (SEED) Network, Campus Compact, and the Carnegie Community Engagement Classification (CCEC). Each of these frameworks advances concepts of democracy, engaged citizenship, and responsibility as core tenets of life and learning fundamental to a new program of study.

The emphasis on public-serving projects reinforces the mission and principles of the SEED Network. The SEED Network prompts a process for pursuing public interest design, also vital in constructing structures for engaged learning (especially through the SEED principles). The mission of "advanc[ing] the right of every person to live in a socially, economically, and environmentally healthy community" (SEED 2017a; Bell 2016, 13) triangulates the primary issues of contemporary life and practice. The balance between these needs creates space for identifying issues that span public- and private-sector work. The SEED Network principles also promote *activism*, *inclusion*, *equity*, *capacity building*, and *conservation*.[3] When taken individually or leveraged as a group, these principles present a powerful case for activated learning with community partners. Finally, the importance of design evaluation cannot be overstated. There is a need for design practitioners who can deliver on analysis that substantiates and translates lessons learned while leveraging transferrable knowledge, accomplishments, and unresolved challenges.[4]

A member of Campus Compact of the Mountain West (CCMW), MSU Denver received the 2014 CCMW Engaged Campus award, which acknowledges the enduring inclusion of a range of engagement benchmarks across the campus community. These benchmarks include purpose-driven curriculum and pedagogy developments, research advances, and mutually beneficial campus-community partnerships, to name a few (CCMW 2014). Campus Compact's Indicators of an Engaged Campus (Campus Compact 2016b) offer twelve qualities[5] that help define a civically vital campus culture and thus inform programmatic vision and philosophies, such as those embedded in the public interest design degree.

The CCEC provides a critical framework for understanding the expectations of a public interest design master's program. CCEC defines community engagement as an integrated relationship between universities, their programs, and the surrounding communities, operating on a range of scales and proximities that are responsive to shared outcomes (NERCHE 2016). CCEC describes the purpose of such engagement: "to enrich scholarship, research, and creative activity; enhance curriculum, teaching, and learning; prepare educated, engaged citizens; strengthen democratic values and civic responsibility; address critical societal issues; and contribute to the public good" (NERCHE 2016). Introduced in 2005 (Campus Compact 2016a) and based on voluntary participation, the First-Time Classification framework supports public-good activities that emphasize working *with* community partners. The shared quality of those relationships is essential in that both partners gain from the benefits of education, asset development, and competency building while contributing to commonly held "issues of public concern" (Carnegie Foundation 2015, 2).

The proposed MFA program is dedicated to expanding the viability and visibility of design in the public interest. Graduate students, working collaboratively and beyond the confines of the campus studio, will be provided the space to cultivate a design practice based on human values. The program pedagogy supplies the necessary tools for student engagement with on-the-ground, community-driven problems investigated through the lenses of communication, theory, research, and practice. This pedagogy supports collaboration with traditionally under-resourced people, environments, and issues. The degree prioritizes three conditions of public interest design practice: (1) community engagement that is integral to the design process, (2) problem solving through an issue-based lens, and (3) prioritization of design-evaluation criteria and assessment-tool development (Abendroth and Bell 2016, 308).[6][7]

Program Pedagogical Goals

The MFA program's mission is to provide a critical graduate design education focused on the emerging field of public interest design inclusive of an issue-based approach, an engagement praxis, and a methodology for the analysis of outputs and outcomes. Students from a broad spectrum of design experience will embrace social, economic, and environmental equity issues while working locally with disinvested communities directly affected by need.

Twelve pedagogical goals define the program and reinforce course-specific learning objectives:[8]

1. identify and engage in design problem solving for people and groups traditionally not served by design
2. use human-centered design methodologies to generate understanding
3. triangulate social, economic, and environmental justice issues
4. cultivate field scholarship through codevelopment of community-driven projects
5. develop and implement a research plan that addresses community-prioritized goals
6. create frameworks for documenting and evaluating the short-term and long-term impacts of design solutions in community contexts
7. analyze and interpret outcomes
8. foster individual leadership skills
9. promote interdisciplinary practices across fields of design
10. champion inclusivity
11. empower civic discourse through design decision making
12. evaluate design outputs in the public sector

The following measurable student learning outcomes are indicators of what students should be able to do (skills) and what they should understand (knowledge) upon completion of this degree:[9]

1. demonstrate advanced applied proficiencies in human-centered design research methodology (research planning, data collection via participatory practices, empathy building, iteration, and adjustment)

2. initiate, analyze and problem solve, execute, and assess a community-driven public-sector design project through planning and facilitation
3. display proficiencies in culturally appropriate communication (verbal, written, and visual), effective collaboration, and leadership

Structure of the Public Interest Design MFA

This traditionally structured, two-year, sixty-credit MFA degree is meant to anchor community-based design practice within an institution committed to service-learning opportunities and collective community building. The curriculum is designed around NASAD accrediting guidelines. According to a NASAD and American Institute of Graphic Arts (AIGA) accreditation white paper on research practice orientations at the graduate level,

> students enter these programs to develop design research skills and to speculate on emerging issues and areas of practice. They are less concerned about (re)entering the field as it is currently practiced and more interested in developing the body of knowledge about design and the emerging research culture.

The guidelines further emphasize possible course work options:

> Course work may include: (1) study of research in non-design disciplines that hold significance to the understanding of design (example: perspectives from anthropology, cognitive science, linguistics, cultural theory, computer science, etc.), and (2) studios that address issues beyond those of the typical design office.
> (AIGA and NASAD n.d., 4–5)

Within the structured course of study, students are empowered to research problems that either support their individual unique capabilities or locate their research within contexts of distinct need. Navigating the space between personal affiliation and externalized "call to action" is part of the fundamental study embedded in the program. Research focuses on the role of assessment and the evaluation of design systems, services, and processes relative to outputs and outcomes. Students will not only conduct assessments but also critique and create evaluation tools applicable to their own research.

Interdisciplinarity of the Public Interest Design MFA

The program provides a point of entry for students from various design backgrounds motivated by a desire to delve into unfamiliar problem-solving spaces. These contexts require students to be open to exploring diverse relationships with one another and with their evolving communities of practice beyond traditional disciplinary silos. Students will work broadly across the fields of design, responding to the range of problem solving required of citizen designers today while leveraging their existing technical design expertise. This vision allows the students to move beyond limitations of anticipated outcomes based on consequences and instead focus on the inherent nature of the problem as defined by the community or audience and on desired outputs, such as activities, products, participation, or engagement.

An alternative to the two-year program is offered as a three-year option: applicants who do not have a previous baccalaureate degree in a related design discipline must complete a supplemental year (between twenty-four and thirty credits) of design-supportive course work in Communication Design at the undergraduate level. With the student's incoming disciplinary background as a grounding element, the MFA provides expertise beyond the technical skills of a single design discipline and instead caters to the methodology of a publicly engaged practice.

Program Curriculum Overview

The proposed MFA in Public Interest Design program has been designed to meet the needs of full-time students. Students will complete five consecutive semesters (including the summer session between years). The program plan (see Figure 8.1) includes a typical complement of required courses and electives and a suggested sequence. Specific course content has been constructed to support ongoing thesis-project development beyond semester-driven limitations. A series of studio-seminar pairings support reciprocal community–student relationships and projects. Studio courses are six–credit hour experiences, whereas seminars are offered at three credit hours each.[10]

8.1
The proposed two-year MFA program of study.

Year One	
Semester One	*Semester Two*
Public Interest Design Studio I: Problem Seeking (6 credits)	Public Interest Design Studio II: Strategic Partnerships (6 credits)
Public Interest Design Seminar I: Theoretical Perspectives (3 credits)	Public Interest Design Seminar II: Methods, Tools, and Tactics (3 credits)
Designated university elective (3 credits)	Public Interest Design Practicum: Designing Research (3 credits)
Summer	
Public Interest Design Field Research (6 to 12 credits)	

Year Two	
Semester One	*Semester Two*
Public Interest Design Studio III: Implementation and Analysis (6 credits)	Public Interest Design Studio IV: Exhibition (6 credits)
Public Interest Design Seminar III: Realization and Evaluation (3 credits)	Public Interest Design Seminar IV: Publication and Thesis (6 credits)
Designated university elective (3 credits)	

Core Courses: Year One[11]

The Theoretical Perspectives seminar is designed to reinforce themes in the companion studio course, Problem Seeking; both are taken during the first semester. The seminar introduces the frameworks required to interpret, understand, and practice public interest design in a manner that respects people and facilitates relationships. The course praxis prioritizes theories of inclusion and exclusion and examines these from across design disciplines thus informing the interdisciplinarity of the field. Topics include agency, empowerment, oppression, otherness, altruism, and ethics. Critical frameworks, such as actor-network theory, semiotic theory, evidence-based design, and postcolonial theory, are used in case-study analysis to activate connections between theoretical underpinnings and the complex realities of practice in the public realm.
   Select learning objectives for this course include the following:

- defend premises and principles evinced in ethical public interest design practices
- evaluate agency and empowerment through the framework of actor-network theory
- appraise the functions of altruism and humanitarianism as related to professional practice and fee-for-service frameworks

The studio course, Problem Seeking, introduces the field of public interest design, serving as a primer for connecting students to contexts where design solutions are community driven. Students explore topics and premises for responding to community- and audience-specific design prompts in what will become a multiyear project commitment. Students investigate the convergence of sites, communities, and needs generated by a combination of localized community-based research and critical inquiry. An introduction to issue-based practice (understanding problem scaffolding integrated through social, economic, and environmental lenses) supported by community partnerships is a core aspect of the course; this framing can motivate the early students to identify the early parameters of their work and how they wish to engage publicly. The course praxis prioritizes issue identification.
   Select learning objectives for this course include the following:

- formulate projects based on critical inquiry and personal perspective within public interest design
- analyze how place, community, and culture fuse in the creation of social, economic, and environmental design issues
- define the theoretical realm that informs the development of the design problem as well as shapes the context in which designers work

In the second semester, the seminar Methods, Tools, and Tactics supports approaches for engaging in generative research with the people, problems, and places affected in the evolving thesis project. Students experiment with best-practice community-participation models and strategies as defined by project research requirements. Students analyze, deconstruct, and reinvent community-engagement tool kits to inform ways of working with diverse and distinct audiences. Adapting or creating new models from existing literature reviews promotes design thinking about community-centered problem-solving methods. The course praxis prioritizes engagement tool kit creation and analysis.
   Select learning objectives for this course include the following:

- construct a methodological framework for conducting research that builds on literature review and analysis
- analyze outcomes and adjust methodologies for different audiences and social, political, economic, and environmental concerns
- synthesize discoveries into a program protocol

Taken during the same semester, the Strategic Partnerships studio emphasizes a course praxis of design facilitation and serves as a primer for cultivating community relationships. Working from a position of collaboration, outreach, and trust building, students establish specific research-problem parameters, verify community partnerships, and respond to their evolving roles as design facilitators and embedded community members. Studio goals emphasize communication with diverse stakeholders, identification of key partners and associates, and demonstration of leadership capacity. At the conclusion of the semester, students submit a thesis-project proposal for approval.

Select learning objectives for this course include the following:

- assess processes that promote outreach and invite inclusion from community participants
- develop leadership skills that support the designer's ability to succeed in facilitation
- explain and defend the thesis-project proposal

Designing Research is a hybrid seminar and online course taken in conjunction with second-semester field-research activities. Students are guided through a process for designing their research plans using evidence-based design methodology. As part of the formulation, students are introduced to the university policy for working with human subjects, which serves as the course praxis. Students complete training modules online and, as determined by the nature of the research, submit to the Institutional Review Board (IRB). This three-credit course is intended to bring added clarity to the purpose of the research and those whom it affects.

Select learning objectives for this course include the following:

- plan and establish a protocol for field-research activities
- assess the role of and impact on human subjects relative to evolving research
- defend and modify relevant IRB materials pertinent to anticipated thesis research

The summer session is an important time to conduct longer-term on-site work. Public Interest Design Field Research varies in credit hours (six to twelve credits) to accommodate the needs of students conducting international travel or back-to-back semesters of study; it provides the opportunity for students to conduct original research while embedded within a specific locale. The experience validates the thesis research questions and identified practical or theoretical frameworks through input collection and data analysis. Based on the approved thesis-research proposal, students perform their research plans in domestic or international contexts. Students implement qualitative and quantitative research strategies developed in previous course work. Field-research outcomes emphasize enhanced understanding of the problem context and stakeholder needs, and assess limitations for realization.

Select learning objectives for this course include the following:

- articulate on-site research goals and outcomes
- assess cultural requirements inclusive of social, economic, and environmental conditions
- analyze case studies to support thesis research, test hypotheses, and expand critical awareness of issues embedded within design problems

Core Courses: Year Two

In the second year, the Realization and Evaluation seminar analyzes the in-progress development and benchmarking of the thesis work. A growing discourse in design evaluation supports the role of assessment across design fields and specifically within public interest design. Students investigate evaluation criteria, standards, and practices where design evaluation is the identified course praxis. Evaluation case studies link scenarios from the field with individual or team-based student research. Students create rubrics for measuring project goals, results, and impacts based on community-generated inputs. Reflection on adjustments to design processes based on anticipated results is integrated into the course experience.

Select learning objectives for this course include the following:

- evaluate bias within assessment scenarios and determine ways to represent inclusivity of participant voices in outcomes
- create and test schemes for analysis of project impacts
- analyze case-study data and relate to research

Implementation and Analysis, a counterpart studio to the seminar, is a systems course that advances thesis work generated in the summer Field Research course. Students codify and interpret their research by identifying trends and analyzing strategies for innovation while exploring actionable opportunities revealed in collected field-research data. The course praxis embraces data-analysis translation and visualization: students incorporate relevant technologies and techniques, including interaction design and data visualization, to demonstrate project evidence. Students activate previously identified methodologies in collaboration with their community partners or audience members to move toward a series of recommendations that embody the thesis.

Select learning objectives for this course include the following:

- design artifacts and visual responses to the thesis problem that empower communities and build collective knowledge
- synthesize and apply knowledge gained of assessment systems to the thesis project whereby results and reflection are articulated and quantified with research data
- compose critical analyses of structures and systems based on design evaluation

In the final semester, two six-credit courses conclude the MFA sequence: Publication and Thesis and Exhibition. While directed as individual courses, together they manifest complementary results. Students are responsible for a comprehensive written assessment (the thesis publication) of their community-driven research processes, results, implementation, and impacts. This written document is also presented through a public exhibition that delivers conclusions. As evidence of their original research, students submit the written thesis encompassing methods, foundational theories, and impacts while emphasizing transferrable knowledge. Demonstration of public, community, and professional leadership is required, as is the ability to align community-identified issues with results.

Select combined learning objectives for these two courses include the following:

- relate contexts for project evaluation and analysis whereby historical, critical, and theoretical implications are evident
- defend expertise using public interest design methodologies (issue-based approaches and inclusive engagement processes) as applied to the thesis project and assessed in the written and visual documentation
- articulate theoretical and applied perspectives that evolve the discourse of public interest design

Program Opportunities and Next Steps

MSU Denver is a relatively young institution with an equally emergent proposed degree. We have been fortunate to learn from other programs of study that encompass the fields of design in cultivating this MFA. In the end, however, this program is distinct to the mission and vision of MSU Denver and seeks to be responsive to the needs of the community where our campus is embedded.

Our ability to provide a broad-based degree that acknowledges the distinct technical skills of our graduate cohort while honing "nontechnical" skill development in the context of design is rare. It is not every day that a faculty team is afforded the privilege of crafting a new graduate degree program from scratch. With this in mind, our proposal is motivated by the requisite for informed, connected, and aware design professionals who are committed to communities and *their* values. The challenges of engaged learning *and* working are vast. Public interest designers in pedagogy and practice have the unique opportunity to reflect on the ethical underpinnings of the field and the constantly changing nature of the communities we partner with in order to evolve the discourse. The process of envisioning, developing, and proposing this degree has allowed us to build on our strengths while attending to the educational needs of our students today and into the future.

Notes

1. The Phase One MFA in Public Interest Design graduate program proposal (consisting of academic and business plans) was submitted for review in September 2016. While both department and college levels recommended the proposal, it was not recommended by MSU Denver's Graduate Council. At the time of writing, a revised submission is underway that addresses strategies for university return on investment and an increased inclusivity across departments and/or colleges.
2. Some language in this chapter is derived in whole or in part from the *MSU Denver Phase One Review Process for New Degree Programs* document (titled "MFA in Public Interest Design Spring 2016 Submission"), written by the coauthors of this chapter. Whenever possible, notes have been included to acknowledge this.
3. The SEED Network principles include the following: "advocate with those who have a limited voice in public life; build structures for inclusion that engage stakeholders and allow communities to make decisions; promote social equality through discourse that reflects a range of values and social identities; generate ideas that grow from place and build local capacity; design to help conserve resources and minimize waste" (SEED 2017a; Bell 2016, 14).
4. See the SEED Evaluator 4.0, an online tool provided by the SEED Network to "guide, document, evaluate, and communicate the social, economic, and environmental outcomes of design projects" (SEED 2017b).
5. See http://compact.org/initiatives/advanced-service-learning-toolkit-for-academic-leaders/indicators-of-an-engaged-campus/.
6. This paragraph presents language from "Program Description" in the *MSU Denver Phase One Review Process for New Degree Programs* document.

7   The definition of *public interest design* is used here to help frame the desired outputs and outcomes of students pursuing this degree.
8   Learning objectives reproduced from page 18 of the *MSU Denver Phase One Review Process for New Degree Programs* document.
9   Learning outcomes reproduced from page 20 of the *MSU Denver Phase One Review Process for New Degree Programs* document.
10 The few exceptions to this rule include Public Interest Design Seminar IV: Publication and Thesis (six credits), Public Interest Design Seminar Practicum: Designing Research (three credits), and Public Interest Design Seminar Field Research (repeatable up to twelve credits).
11 The description of courses provided in this chapter are derived in whole or in part from MSU Denver Regular Course Syllabi, written by the coauthors of this chapter. Syllabi are not required to be submitted in Phase One Review and thus have remained with the authors. Learning objectives were written for inclusion in official course syllabi and may have been refined or rewritten between 2014 and 2016 in order to hone language through goals and learning outcomes. Should the program be approved with resubmission, further refinements to program documentation, including course descriptions and learning objectives, are expected. Course numbers have not yet been assigned as the course syllabi have not been submitted or approved for implementation.

References

Abendroth, Lisa M., and Bryan Bell, eds. 2016. "Glossary." In *Public Interest Design Practice Guidebook: SEED Methodology, Case Studies, and Critical Issues*, 308. New York: Routledge.

AIGA and NASAD (American Institute of Graphic Arts and National Association of Schools of Art and Design). n.d. *Degree Programs and Graphic Design: Purposes, Structures, and Results*. Briefing paper, AIGA/NASAD. Accessed November 29, 2016. https://nasad.arts-accredit.org/wp-content/uploads/sites/3/2016/03/AIGA_NASAD_GD_degree_programs.pdf.

Bell, Bryan. 2016. "The State of Public Interest Design." In *Public Interest Design Practice Guidebook: SEED Methodology, Case Studies, and Critical Issues*, edited by Lisa M. Abendroth and Bryan Bell, 11–18. New York: Routledge.

Campus Compact. 2016a. "Carnegie Community Engagement Classification." Accessed January 3, 2017. http://compact.org/initiatives/carnegie-community-engagement-classification/.

Campus Compact. 2016b. "Indicators of an Engaged Campus." Accessed November 29, 2016. http://compact.org/initiatives/advanced-service-learning-toolkit-for-academic-leaders/indicators-of-an-engaged-campus/.

Carnegie Foundation (for the Advancement of Teaching). 2015. "2015 Carnegie Elective Community Engagement Classification: First-Time Classification

Documentation Framework." Accessed October 12, 2016. http://nerche.org/images/stories/projects/Carnegie/2015/2015_first-time_framework.pdf.

CCMW (Campus Compact of the Mountain West). 2014. "Engaged Campus Award." Accessed January 3, 2017. www.ccmountainwest.org/awards/engaged-campus-award.

MSU Denver. 2010. "Metro State Academic and Student Affairs Subcommittee Meeting Agenda-Revised." May 12. Accessed March 20, 2017. https://msudenver.edu/admissions/apply/adultstudents/.

MSU Denver (Metropolitan State University of Denver). 2015. *2015–2020 Strategic Plan Refresh June, 2015*. Accessed January 3, 2017. www.msudenver.edu/media/content/aboutmsudenver/documents/Strategic_Plan_Summary_Sheet.pdf.

MSU Denver. 2017a. "Admissions: Adult Students." Accessed January 3. https://msudenver.edu/admissions/apply/adultstudents/.

MSU Denver. 2017b. "Metropolitan State University of Denver Strategic Plan 2020." Accessed January 3. www.msudenver.edu/about/strategicplan2020/.

New England Resource Center for Higher Education (NERCHE). 2016. "Carnegie Community Engagement Classification." Accessed October 12. http://nerche.org/index.php?option=com_content&view=article&id=341&Itemid=92#CEdef).

SEED (Social Economic Environmental Design Network). 2017a. "Mission." Accessed February 21, 2017. https://seednetwork.org/about/mission/.

SEED (Social Economic Environmental Design Network). 2017b. "SEED Evaluator 4.0." Accessed February 21, 2017. https://seednetwork.org/seed-evaluator-4-0/.

Part 2
Educating the Public Interest Designer

Fundamental Skills

9
Fundamental Skills
Developing Social Literacy Through Practice-Based Learning

Lee Davis and Mike Weikert

The pedagogy of public interest design is, and *should* be, as varied as the complex social problems it is intended to address. Programs offered by educational institutions to prepare public interest designers—including the three featured in this section at California College of the Arts, Carnegie Mellon University, and Tecnológico de Monterrey—differ based on the people leading them, the contexts in which they operate, the expertise represented in their faculty, the demographics and interests of their student body, and the nature of the problems they choose to address.[1]

Given that it is transdisciplinary in nature, public interest design curriculum is also varied, incorporating aspects of many other disciplines. However, as the cases in this section illustrate, two unconditional guiding principles are fundamental: (1) elevating **social literacy** to expand students' capacity for understanding the complex, systemic nature of social problems and change; and (2) employing immersive, collaborative, and participatory **practice-based learning** experiences to expose students to real-world problems.

Public interest design education develops the social literacy of students by focusing on "real challenges for real people."[2] Students must develop a holistic perspective of complex problems, analyze issues at multiple levels, and examine the interconnected causes of social problems. Students should develop skills in framing problems and learn that the design process is intended to better understand social systems, not necessarily to solve problems.

Public interest design pedagogy should emphasize that practice is contextual and differs based on the goals, scale, and level of intervention. This is illustrated in the Social Design Pathways (see Figure 9.1),[3] a tool developed collectively by nearly

Social Design Pathways

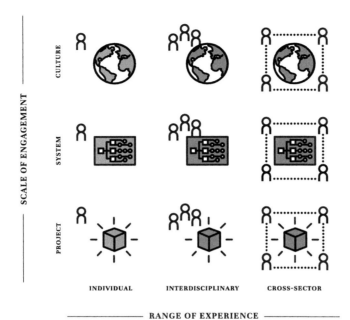

9.1
Social Design Pathways.
Winterhouse Institute,
Hamden, Connecticut, 2013.

twenty leading educators at the Winterhouse Symposium on Design Education for Social Impact. In the matrix, the range of expertise axis refers to the collections of expertise brought to bear on a problem: an individual designer, an interdisciplinary team, or a cross-sectoral collective. The scale of engagement axis describes the level and scale at which the design intervention aims to make change happen: at a project, system, or cultural level.

The Social Design Pathways is a useful tool for students to map social problems to understand how to address them at multiple levels, to frame them from diverse perspectives, and to design interventions to achieve various levels of change. Each quadrant requires different skills for designers to engage effectively. Projects often extend across multiple quadrants, necessitating a mix of experience, expertise, and skills.

Heightening the social literacy of public interest design students also requires building their critical sensibilities and their capacity to navigate complex social contexts. Students should understand the ethics of community engagement practice, the role and social responsibility of the designer, and the public purpose of the discipline, and they should learn to "address challenges with honesty and sensitivity."[4] Students should cultivate a self-reflective practice through active listening, empathy, and humility. They should learn to value diverse people, perspectives, and forms of knowledge beyond the academic, including community and life experience. Students must develop an understanding of the interconnectedness of people, their livelihoods, and their physical environments.

Fundamental to practice-based learning is improving students' skills in facilitating a socially inclusive co-design process *with*, rather than *for*, various stakeholders. This process should build students' leadership capacity as well as enable the capacity of community stakeholders to grow. Students should practice methods to articulate a common vision, values, goals, roles, and responsibilities with stakeholders.

Practice-based learning allows educators to expose students to the complex but critical process of building authentic, trusted relationships based on mutuality—the principle of shared objectives, benefits, and learning. Partnerships should allow for the "sustained daily full-time contact"[5] necessary to overcome the arbitrariness of academic calendars and their misalignment with longer-term goals, community commitments, and expectations.

Students must balance—respectfully and transparently—the educational goals of their work with the goals of other stakeholders and the wider social-impact goals of an initiative. Assessing impact can be especially challenging when balancing educational learning outcomes (the impact on students), design outcomes (the specific impact of an intervention), and social outcomes (the impact on the community, stakeholders, and society). Students need exposure to methods for assessing the results of their work, but they must also recognize that design impact is but one element of a much broader collective effort with stakeholders and partners to articulate social impact.

Public interest design educators should also challenge students with questions about the sustainability of practice at multiple levels:

- **Student sustainability**: As student ownership of practice increases, how might educators prepare students to sustain their work beyond the classroom?
- **Community sustainability**: How might students enable stakeholder capacity to sustain collective work and livelihoods?
- **Financial sustainability**: How might educators help students to develop skills in various business models, fund development, and entrepreneurship to sustain project interventions financially?
- **Artifact sustainability:** How might educators prepare students to anticipate and plan for maintenance, repairs, and/or removal of project artifacts over time?

Whatever the term used—hands-on education, service-learning, learning by doing—students gain confidence and skills in place-specific, real-world settings. Each case highlighted in this section represents a unique pedagogical approach, context, and process, but all share a commitment to raising students' social literacy through authentic practice-based learning.

- The USAER XXXIV Training Center for Special Education (pages 122–129) explores the emergent pedagogical methodology of democratic civic engagement, wherein students create knowledge through an awakening, transformative experience in collaboration with others.

Fundamental Skills

- The Urban Design Build Studio at Carnegie Mellon University with its PROJECT RE_ program (pages 111–116) celebrates a context-specific approach that emphasizes transactional mutuality and multiyear cross-community partnerships, allowing for the sustained contact necessary for students to develop empathy, understanding, and trusted relationships.
- The Center for Art + Public Life's IMPACT Orientation (pages 117–121) calls for a more deep and responsive community-engagement pedagogy, whereby students gain confidence in real-world settings and are challenged to question and disrupt their assumptions about identity, power, privilege, and positionality.

Practice-based and place-based learning as a pedagogical paradigm is not new. As public interest design education continues to evolve and a new generation of designers and educators emerges, fundamental skills may also shift. However, the need for heightened social literacy and deep, practical immersive learning will always be a pedagogical priority.

Notes

1. See, for example, the varied list of more than twenty-five educational programs among the Founders Circle of the Winterhouse Institute, a network of leading design educators dedicated to articulating the value of education in social impact. www.winterhouseinstitute.org
2. See "Democratic Civic Engagement: The USAER XXXIV Training Center for Special Education," page 124.
3. For more information and case studies of the Winterhouse Institute's Social Design Pathways tool, visit www.winterhouseinstitute.org. Figure 9.1 is used with permission from the Winterhouse Institute, © 2018 Winterhouse Institute, licensed under a Creative Commons Attribution 3.0 Unported License.
4. See "Preparing to Design With: IMPACT Orientation," page 118.
5. See "The Edge Effect: PROJECT RE_," page 112.

10
The Edge Effect
*PROJECT RE_*

John Folan

In ecology, the **edge effect** refers to changes in population or community structures occurring at the boundary of two habitats (Levin 2009, 780). Where ecosystems overlap, the influence of bordering communities on one another creates a greater diversity of life. Although the form of transformation varies based on specific places and conditions, the concept of the edge effect is universally transferable (see Figure 10.1). This sensibility informs the work of the Carnegie Mellon University (CMU) Urban Design Build Studio (UDBS) and the formation of PROJECT RE_. Consistent with many university-affiliated design/build entities, the work of UDBS is firmly tied to its context: the social and economic conditions of Pittsburgh, Pennsylvania. While place specific, UDBS public interest design work is process and strategy based so that the relevance of learning remains universal.

UDBS projects are predicated on addressing the needs of marginalized communities. Although situations vary based on neighborhood or region, the baseline characteristics of these communities reflect the impact of catastrophic population loss and the urban decline cycle. These baseline characteristics include a history of low or poorly targeted investments from the public and private sectors, poor connectivity with institutions, segregation from economic vitality, high crime rates, and racial or class segregation that often severely limits opportunity. In Pittsburgh and the surrounding region of western Pennsylvania, the natural topographic condition creates a physical environment that has exacerbated these challenges.

As these issues are interrelated, they must be addressed holistically. The objective in UDBS public interest work is to empower neighborhood residents through the development of knowledge, skills, relationships, interactions, and organizational structures that enable positive, future-oriented outcomes. Borrowing

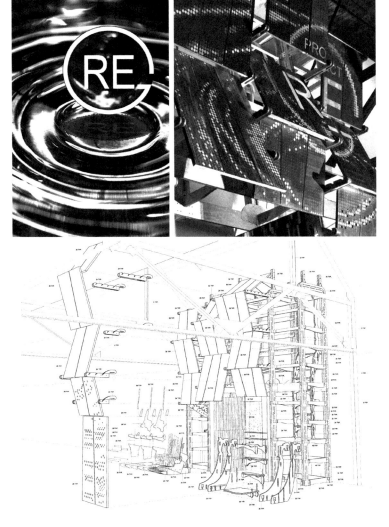

10.1
PROJECT RE_ entry marquee illustrating the inclusion of edge effect and ripple graphic content, translation of that content through digital fabrication techniques developed in collaboration between UDBS and TIP on harvested door panels, and technical drawing illustrating the integration of building prototypes developed for the entry. Urban Design Build Studio, PROJECT RE_, Pittsburgh, Pennsylvania, 2015.

from the sensibilities engendered in the concept of the edge effect, UDBS specifically collaborates with residents to create cross sector, cross community partnerships that provide potential for the implementation of meaningful projects and the development of self-sustained, internal capacity. PROJECT RE_ developed out of a desire to increase the efficacy of UDBS work in these two areas.

Partnering to Achieve Impact at Scale

PROJECT RE_ is the product of a partnership between three nonprofit organizations: UDBS; Construction Junction (CJ), the region's leading material-repurposing center;

and Trade Institute of Pittsburgh (TIP), an apprentice-training program for populations reentering society. Leveraging the assets of each partner, PROJECT RE_ has the following mission:

1. rebuild communities by strengthening the capacity of local residents
2. facilitate landfill diversion through the reuse of materials
3. restore lives by teaching people trade skills necessary to secure a living wage

PROJECT RE_ exists physically and organizationally. As an organization, it functions as a transactional entity fostering collaboration between the partnering organizations and an extended network of community stakeholders. Physically, the facility serves as a community education center, job-training facility, workshop, and prefabrication center for value-added products ranging from furniture to buildings. Educational programming and building-product prototypes developed at PROJECT RE_ are used to sustain the operation of the center, to fund subsequent community-outreach projects, and to create community-based entrepreneurship opportunities for residents.

The physical facility is the result of a three-year design and construction process that involved interdisciplinary collaboration between undergraduate architecture and engineering students, architecture engineering and construction management (AECM) graduate students, residents, stakeholders, and consultants. UDBS students participated in the project through a series of advanced studio options (eighteen credit units per semester) offered in the fourth and fifth years of the professional-phase undergraduate curriculum. A series of corequisite electives (nine credit units per semester) focusing on the development of relevant public interest and technical skill competencies complemented the studio courses.

The CMU School of Architecture curriculum is organized as a three-plus-two program that addresses National Architectural Accrediting Board competencies in the first three years of undergraduate education, enabling UDBS studios and elective courses to be offered sequentially and providing students the opportunity to remain engaged on the project for as long as two years. Graduate students in the AECM program were involved with the project as a rotating cohort each semester over the three years through an eighteen-credit unit UDBS Masters Synthesis course (ARC48_719). Interdisciplinary work was managed through independent studies and course work offered by allied faculty. All participants were given the opportunity to work on the project during the summer months through a grant-supported internship. Twenty-five undergraduate architecture students, sixteen AECM graduate students, and two allied faculty were involved in the development and construction of the project.

Executed in collaboration with **apprentices in training** representing populations reentering society after sustained incarceration, PROJECT RE_ is firmly grounded in the physical limits of what can be made through hands-on training and emerging knowledge bases. The resulting buildings and spaces developed in collaboration with this cohort of UDBS students represent significant interrelated learning strategies and objectives.

These objectives include the following:

- develop understanding of complex socioeconomic community contexts
- demonstrate leadership through technical and hands-on skills
- create capacity through design-intent documentation and prototyping skills.

Embedded Understanding

Understanding of place and community is best achieved through sustained daily full-time contact. Similarly, collaboration with resident populations on the same timetable fosters greater empathy for people in different situations. The location of PROJECT RE_ and the partnerships established were selectively explored for five years preceding the project's development. Located in the Homewood South neighborhood three miles northeast of the CMU campus, PROJECT RE_ resides geographically at the edge: a four-block-wide swath of territory between the Homewood North and Point Breeze neighborhoods. One neighborhood is characterized by catastrophic disinvestment and the other by affluence. Course work takes place in the neighborhood and in warehouse space made available by CJ.

The partnership with TIP provides an opportunity for UDBS students and TIP apprentices in training to work shoulder to shoulder on a daily basis (see Figure 10.2). This contact has numerous educational benefits. TIP apprentices in training represent communities in Pittsburgh where UDBS works and reflect the demographic profile of Homewood: predominantly African American and having lower income per capita, lower median household income, and higher unemployment averages than city and state averages (Pittsburgh Dept. of City Planning 2012). TIP apprentices in training seek to gain

10.2
John Folan, director of UDBS and executive director of PROJECT RE_, working with UDBS students and TIP apprentices during construction of the community room. Urban Design Build Studio, PROJECT RE_, Pittsburgh, Pennsylvania, 2015.

job skills that will enable them to earn a living wage. A majority are reentering society after incarceration. Statistically, they represent 97 percent of all former incarcerates who return to the communities where they were raised upon release (Guerino, Harrison, and Sabol 2011), those characterized by the socioeconomic challenges previously identified.

By working with TIP apprentices on a daily basis for extended periods of time, UDBS students are able to develop relationships with the apprentices and to have conversations with them that would not happen in traditional participatory design contexts. The benefits to both groups are significant. For TIP apprentices, access to college students from around the world, both graduate and undergraduate, via one-on-one contact builds self-esteem and confidence, elevates hope for future opportunity, and diminishes the perceived correlation between circumstance, intellect, and personal potential critical to empowerment. For UDBS students, the experience fosters empathy, enhances understanding of socioeconomic conditions for people of different situations, and engenders humility, critical sensibilities for educating public interest designers.

Leadership by Example

The buildings and spaces that comprise PROJECT RE_ were designed and built by members of the three partnering organizations. All work is predicated on the demonstration of **Design for Deconstruction (DFD)** principles (Morgan and Stevenson 2005). During the conceptual development of the project, UDBS students and TIP apprentices gained knowledge and experience in the implementation of harvested materials yielded from deconstruction projects. As work advanced, that knowledge was used to develop replicable building strategies employing low- to no-value resources identified by CJ. UDBS students were challenged to develop value-added products and building systems featuring construction materials that would normally go to a landfill. Mass-production strategies were tested through job-training programs administered by TIP.

Through this process, UDBS students learned to rely on standard trade-construction methods in achieving economically efficient, replicable design strategies. Collaboratively advanced in ten-week cycles to align with the TIP apprentice program, the realization of PROJECT RE_ was predicated on identifying appropriate construction methods that could simultaneously support development of skills and opportunity for entrepreneurship. The project included twenty-one viable building-product prototypes, employed 68 percent reconstituted building material harvested from local deconstruction projects, and served as a vehicle for the professional training of 126 TIP apprentices (see Figure 10.3).

Capacity, Entrepreneurship, and Ripple Effect

The realization of the physical facility and formation of a transactional entity created capacity for sustained community benefit, established the legitimacy of the

10.3
Exterior view of the community room, studio, and entrance hall of PROJECT RE_ taken from the industrial woodshop and prefabrication area, illustrating the integration of the reconstituted and harvested building material systems employed. Urban Design Build Studio, PROJECT RE_, Pittsburgh, Pennsylvania, 2015.

partnership in achieving goals, and fostered the trust of the community members who were involved. Construction by UDBS students and TIP apprentices increased technical the capacity of individuals from both groups and allowed for meaningful social interaction between people who may not otherwise have met. More importantly, it established a place for future generations to create and interact.

Community-based entrepreneurship programs developed around prototypes created at PROJECT RE_ have provided students with valuable experience in producing the documents necessary to communicate design intent and decision making. Residents, entrepreneurial mentors, and newly certified apprentices have collaborated to advance the prototypes toward scale production, and the physical and transactional framework is in place for the next set of challenges—at the edge.

References

Guerino, Paul, Paige M. Harrison, and William J. Sabol. 2011. "Prisoners in 2010." *NCJ 236096*, December. Accessed March 19, 2013. www.bjs.gov/content/pub/pdf/p10.pdf.

Levin, Simon A. 2009. *The Princeton Guide to Ecology*. Princeton, NJ: Princeton University Press.

Morgan, Chris, and Fionn Stevenson. 2005. *Design for Deconstruction: SEDA Design Guidelines for Scotland: No. 1*. Glasgow: Scottish Ecological Design Association. www.seda.uk.net/assets/files/guides/dfd.pdf.

Pittsburgh Department of City Planning. 2012. "PGHSNAP Raw Census Data by Neighborhood." Accessed June 3, 2015. www.pittsburghpa.gov/dcp/snap/raw_data.

11
Preparing to Design With
IMPACT Orientation

Megan Clark and Shalini Agrawal

When articulating the ethos of public interest design, practitioners frequently use the phrase "design with, not design for," underscoring the value of designers being invited into partnership by communities. How do design educators support their students in translating this phrase into embodied action?

Educators share technical skills, often discrete activities designed to break down interpersonal barriers, and they build consensus and initiate collaboration among project participants. Educators facilitate project-based learning: mutually beneficial partnerships with community groups through which students develop research and technical skills, reflect on public interest design practice in real time, and gain confidence in real-world settings. And educators provide framing for how students might approach their work, invoking the behavior we expect of guests—respect for, and deference to, our hosts—to upend the power dynamic of practitioner-client relationships epitomized in *Dick & Rick: A Visual Primer for Social Impact Design* (Gaspar et al. 2015), where Dick privileges his design knowledge over the lived knowledge of a community.

Upending these dynamics and professional narratives is crucial to disrupting assumptions and to breaking down our internal barriers to collaborative practice. In addition to these inherently valuable teaching methods, the Center for Art + Public Life at California College of the Arts (CCA) advocates for opportunities to learn more about ourselves and about what we bring to working partnerships.

At the Center, we help our students to explore by asking:

- How might who we are influence our ability to partner and work within a community?

- How might we engage with, and learn about, all of the identities we hold?
- How might our identities intersect with those of our partners and with the unique historical, social, and political realities of a project?

And of ourselves, as educators, we have sought to explore the following:

- How might we develop programming that meets our students where they are?
- How might our educational approach avoid assumptions about students' identities and experiences?
- How might we prevent a similarly static or unidimensional perception of our communities and community partners?

Our Context

The Center for Art + Public Life is an independently run department of CCA in the San Francisco Bay area. Since its founding in 1998, the Center has worked with over two thousand alumni and has evolved from an external hub for community-based practitioners to an internal and external hub that partners CCA students of art, design, and writing with community organizations dedicated to social good. With this shift, we have expanded the educational experiences offered to our students as well as the creative resources offered to our community partners, and we have recognized the associated need for deep, responsive community-engagement pedagogy.

The Center's IMPACT Awards require that interdisciplinary teams of CCA students develop grant proposals in direct response to a social need identified by a community local to the project. As a program focused on student-led projects, IMPACT presents an ideal space to pilot in-depth introspective programming. Teams apply their critical and creative problem-solving skills and outline actionable next steps with communities in the San Francisco Bay area, elsewhere in the United States, and internationally. Once awarded IMPACT funding, teams prepare to collaborate with community experts and local groups.

IMPACT Orientation

To facilitate students' preparation, we developed the IMPACT Orientation, focusing on **identity literacy**, **active listening**, and navigation of power dynamics. At the stage when the orientation is offered, teams have begun building a relationship with their community partners but have not yet begun design or implementation. We aim to ground the students in their own identities and to empower them to address challenges with honesty and sensitivity, while building trust and open communication with one another and with their community partners.

IMPACT Orientation begins with the establishment of community agreements that set the tone for a safer growth environment. We then move into an exploration of self using the Spectrum of Spectrums, a tool developed by Shreya Shah of Saltwater Training, which we will focus on for the purposes of this chapter. The Spectrum was first introduced to CCA as part of school-wide conversations organized by a coalition of staff, faculty, and students, including Center staff. The discussion focuses on the diagram (see Figure 11.1). Components of personal identity are set side by side, each with a vertical spectrum of relative power and oppression. The empty bubbles at the right acknowledge the inherent privilege in who defines the list of identity components, which keeps the list interactive and open for discussion. Once we have discussed and edited the Spectrum, students engage in multiple rounds of pair sharing and group debriefs around their individual experiences with both power and oppression.

In a setting that—while not neutral—has yet to be complicated by project deadlines and the natural tensions of local context, the Spectrum dialogues offer students a framework for recognizing power dynamics and provide the language for discussing them. The conversations, and the Spectrum itself, thereby open the door for students to collaborate as empathetic, multifaceted humans rather than as unidimensional designers. It is the setting of a new and different expectation, one of **radical empathy**, as emphasized by Sue Mobley and Stephen Goldsmith's (2016) Design Futures session, "Centering the Human in Human-Centered Design."

The IMPACT Orientation builds upon this self-exploration by examining power dynamics through a student–community case study, defining and exploring the

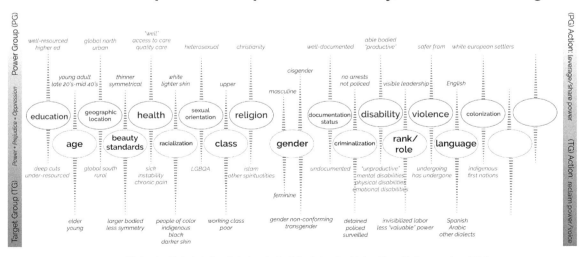

11.1
Spectrum of Spectrums tool, adapted from Saltwater Training's tools. Shreya D. Shah, Saltwater Training (www.saltwatertraining.org 2016).

practice of **allyship**, identifying implicit and explicit communication, practicing active listening, and, finally, developing a framework for setting and evaluating project goals. Together, these exercises and discussions provide a response to our initial question, "How might we develop programming that meets our students where they are?" At the conclusion of orientation, students draft team charters, in which they set forth the project description, mission, vision, goals, responsibilities, timeline, communication plan, and team values.

Learning Objectives and Outcomes

To determine whether the Center has met its learning outcomes for IMPACT orientation, we refer back to the team charters. We compare the teams' initial intentions and mindsets as articulated in their charters with their written reflections during and after fieldwork. These comparisons consistently reflect achievement in the following learning objectives:

- apply inclusive language and regular reflection on power dynamics and privilege
- employ active listening rather than a team's fixed vision to evolve relationships and projects
- practice new communication tools among teammates and with community partners
- experiment with responsiveness and flexibility

The mission of Team Visible Youth, a group of undergraduate design students, proved a particularly powerful compass. Over several months, the team established a mutually exciting partnership with Larkin Street Youth Services, a nonprofit serving homeless and at-risk youth in San Francisco. In spite of good rapport and communication, the roadblocks they hit throughout the summer led all to agree to postpone a built solution. At the final IMPACT presentation, the team was asked, "Why didn't you just build something without Larkin Street?" They responded without hesitation that doing so would have violated their commitment—captured in their mission statement—to develop a project collaboratively with Larkin Street's staff and extended community. That they came to this decision of their own accord underscores deeply held personal convictions about public interest design practice.

Further Examples From Academic Peers

The Center acknowledges that the core practices—identity literacy, contextual grounding, and active listening—have been, and continue to be, tried by professional and academic leaders across the United States. We offer the following highlights from a few of our academic peers and encourage readers to follow up for more information:

- **Albert and Tina Small Center for Collaborative Design, Tulane University**: Sue Mobley, the inaugural community engagement manager at the Small Center, partners with faculty leads and program managers to apply interdisciplinary research skills in teaching design project context and cultural competency; she recently partnered with antiracism facilitators from Tulane's Center for Public Service to pilot peer-led workshops focused on the roles, responsibilities, and identity literacy of students engaged in projects.
- **Department of City and Metropolitan Planning, University of Utah**: In recentering the university's urban ecology program, Professor Stephen Goldsmith grounded the curriculum in relationships between people and place, exemplified by his "Listening to. . . " courses; he collaborates deeply with each of his students to support individual explorations of self and privilege relative to projects and brings in peers from the University of Utah's Office for Equity and Diversity and College of Social and Behavioral Science to engage in broader discussions of race, gender, and power dynamics.
- **Sam Fox School of Design and Visual Arts, Washington University**: Liz Kramer, Sam Fox's assistant director of community-based design and sustainability, has partnered with staff from Washington University's Gephardt Institute for Civic and Community Engagement to adapt their Entering and Exiting Community Workshop for faculty and students interested in community-based practice, focusing on identity literacy and university–community power dynamics.

When designers partner within communities, we step into a living context, one defined not only by the historical dynamic of residents, land, and policies, but also by an entirely new dynamic created by the virtue of our presence. In delving into our own identities, we build a framework for evaluating our inevitable missteps and cultivate sensibilities that help us avoid further errors. Finally, we set the stage for an ongoing self-reflective practice, with results and outcomes responsive to the infinitely broad range of community–designer partnerships.

References

Gaspar, Christine, Theresa Hwang, Liz Ogbu, and Matthew Ledwidge. Ping Zhou, Illustrator. 2015. *Dick & Rick: A Visual Primer for Social Impact Design*. New York: The Center for Urban Pedagogy and Equity Collective. http://welcometocup.org/file_columns/0000/0789/dick_rick.pdf.

Mobley, Sue, and Stephen Goldsmith. 2016. "Centering the Human in Human-Centered Design." Session at Design Futures: Public Interest Design Student Leadership Forum, University of Virginia, Charlottesville, VA, May 25.

12
Democratic Civic Engagement
The USAER XXXIV Training Center for Special Education

Pedro Pacheco

Today more than ever civic engagement finds the appropriate conditions to move society in the direction that protects the common good and in ways that are respectful of human rights. Universities across the globe are slowly but consistently identifying ways to prepare students to create knowledge and find sustainable solutions to the challenges posed by diverse societal groups through collaborative partnerships (Kecskes, Joyalle, Elliot, and Sherman 2017). In this sense, **democratic civic engagement** becomes a transformative and intense process as college students participate passionately in the co-creation of knowledge for the purpose of changing society (Saltmarsh, Hartley, and Clayton 2009; Boyte and Fretz 2010). As a consequence of the democratic civic movement, **experiential learning** strategies such as design/build are becoming more widespread within design schools, not only to educate design professionals but also to promote an integrated approach to education that is place-based, problem-oriented, and transdisciplinary (Kolb 1984; Sanoff 2011; Allen 2012; Raisbeck, Mitcheltree, and Pacheco 2013).

Design/build was employed in the USAER XXXIV[1] Training Center for Special Education (UTC) project as the service-learning instrument in a senior architectural design studio at the Tecnológico de Monterrey (Monterrey Tec)[2] to understand and apply principles of community design, including participatory decision making and community building. Service-learning was also used to illustrate to first-year architecture students the public nature of design and the social responsibility of architects. The UTC facility, located within the Belisario Dominguez Primary School, was designed and built by college students and volunteers for special education training. At seventy-two square meters, it includes an office, a kitchenette, a restroom, and a flexible space used as a meeting room and as a classroom. Teachers are trained at the UTC to work with 284 children with mental or physical disabilities within the Escobedo school district using the inclusive model employed in the regular school system.

UTC demonstrates the collaborative effort of college students and community members to learn by building. As a result of this project, students were able to achieve the following learning objectives:

- build trusting relationships with diverse stakeholder groups by engaging in formal and informal encounters for learning with UTC users; to do so, students collaborated with potential users in defining and evaluating post-occupancy activities
- facilitate communication and design outcomes through participatory strategies, in which users were viewed as experts
- generate understanding in academic and community-centered endeavors that helps identify meaningful opportunities for action
- interpret the public purpose and realize the impact design can have on underserved groups

Building Relationships of Trust

The UTC project was planned, designed, and built from July 2012 to December 2014 on its host site at the Belisario Dominguez Primary School. From the first day, as the UTC's director explained the facility's needs and expectations to the Monterrey Tec students, it was clear that the project could count on the enthusiastic collaboration of the UTC members, who wanted a dignified place to work but did not have the economic resources to accomplish their goal. In the process of building a trusting partnership, the students and UTC members developed a strong sense of ownership and responsibility that sustained the project over time and led to other projects at the primary school, including a shaded outdoor space, a dining area, and a kitchen. As of July 2016, parents from the school were preparing to build the shaded space.

Donaldson and Kozoll (1999) suggest that in the initial stages of collaborative efforts, stakeholders develop social and psychological contracts to guide their work but that formal agreements consolidate these relationships. Collaboration for UTC began as a personal relationship between its director and the design studio professor and was eventually formalized by an institutional agreement. What began as a perceived need developed into the built project that satisfied the space requirements of UTC, fulfilled Monterrey Tec's mission of preparing students to become citizens committed to the sustainable development of their communities and allowed the students to comply with mandatory community work adopted by Tecnológico de Monterrey (Benavides-Ornelas, Pacheco, and Hernandez 2017). The collaboration succeeded in no small part as a result of this informal-formal process that permitted the stakeholders to develop both a shared vision and clear roles and responsibilities (see Figure 12.1).

12.1
Model of interagency collaboration (Pacheco 2003).

Facilitating Design and Communication

Designing for underserved groups is a challenge in a context where resources are scarce and the need for appropriate and dignified spaces is great. Fortunately, for UTC and for many similar projects around the globe, design schools are increasingly adopting experiential learning as an important pedagogical paradigm (Allen 2012). Although hands-on education is not new, it is becoming an alternative for practice among students and young architects seeking meaningful learning experiences.

A key component of the UTC case was the mandatory community work, used from diagnosis to construction. Like other schools within the Monterrey Tec system, the School of Architecture, Art and Design (EAAD) integrates the citizenship component across its curriculum to supervise the 480 hours of community work that students are required to complete as a prerequisite for graduation. Traditionally, the EAAD has integrated the community work requirement into the design studio, thus creating a service-learning strategy to help community groups find solutions to spatial and architectural problems, while at the same time allowing architecture students, along with students from other disciplines, to develop the corresponding disciplinary competencies. In this sense, the work done in the design studio is meaningful for both the students and the beneficiaries because it uses the students' capacities and the community work mandate as resources for addressing real challenges for real people.

In the case of UTC, an advanced design studio was used from 2012 to 2014 to explore the potential of connecting the curriculum requirements and community work with the needs and expectations expressed by the community. In the first phase, during the summer of 2012, students from the University of Melbourne, Australia, and from Monterrey Tec explored ideas for a master plan that eventually guided the UTC project and other projects at the Belisario Dominguez Primary School in collaboration with parents and teachers.

During the second phase, which lasted one year, students developed the architectural design of the building and tested construction techniques using nonconventional materials such as wood pallets, recycled polyurethane, refrigerator doors, and reused glass and doors from the Monterrey Tec campus (see Figure 12.2). In this phase, prototyping was crucial to develop students' sensibility for materials and for the interior atmosphere of the building. In the third phase, during the summer and fall of 2014, the new UTC building was erected according to the technical plans developed by students. In both the second and third phases, students from the architecture school and other disciplines collaborated with parents and teachers from USAER in the exploration of materials, training, and eventual construction of the UTC. Prior to construction, every participant was trained in the use of tools and manipulation of materials.

Collaboration was the keystone of the UTC experience, from diagnosis of the situation through design, construction, and celebration. UTC students, their parents, and their teachers were involved at every step of the process, from problem definition through construction. Most students participated for only one academic period (four months). Those willing to continue did so on a voluntary basis for up to three semesters in a row through the Impulso Urbano program;[3] many did because they had developed a sense of ownership on the project, as expressed by one student: "[We] wanted to see the construction of an idea."

Interaction among stakeholders was accomplished in different scenarios to enable all participants to understand one another's work environments and to

12.2
Students experimenting with materials in the laboratory. Impulso Urbano program, Testing Prototype, Monterrey, Nuevo León, Mexico, 2012.

Democratic Civic Engagement

allow the Monterrey Tec students to absorb the knowledge and experience of the stakeholders, both teachers and students. The Monterrey Tec students, for example, expanded their site investigation to include neighborhood streets and households of elementary school children. Conversely, UTC teachers and students visited Monterrey Tec to understand how architecture students work and to be trained in construction methods. Other opportunities for interaction included searching for construction materials in the city and eating and working together on-site. In all instances, Monterrey Tec students were encouraged to reflect with different stakeholders about the lessons learned and the challenges faced by the group. The result of reflecting in action was always useful in finding better solutions to problems identified at the construction site or to visualized potential additions to the project.

Generating Understanding in Academic and Community-Centered Endeavors

Because of the involvement of indirect users, such as other students in the school district, their teachers, and community volunteers, the UTC experience went beyond its original goal of providing a sufficient, dignified space for training special education teachers. Once the UTC was inaugurated, its director and other stakeholders saw the opportunity to formulate a program for strengthening relationships between students with disabilities and their parents through informal citizenship and human rights courses, a workshop to fabricate a bench and a small wooden easel that was later used for a painting class, and other programs.

Teachers from nearby schools have used the UTC facility for ceremonies and other after-hours social activities. In addition, Monterrey Tec's EAAD is slowly becoming an Engaged Department (Kesckes et al. 2017) by supporting faculty involved in community projects. Since 2015 the Department of Architecture uses the training center as a case study to raise awareness among first-year students about the public purpose of the discipline and the role that collaboration plays in addressing social problems in general. Raising awareness is the first of a four-phase model that Monterrey Tec is implementing to make the mandatory community work an awakening and transformative experience. The other three phases include comprehension, action, and transformation and are embedded within the curricula through the five-year program of all majors.

Perhaps the greatest lesson for all participants, including design students, is learning that our world has become so complex that solving problems now requires the knowledge and capacities of many people, including different disciplines and other stakeholders, working toward the common good.

UTC has become an important reference for all participants, but mainly for Monterrey Tec students, who learned basic principles of democratic civic engagement by designing and building a public facility for special education students and their teachers, one of many underserved groups in society (see Figure 12.3). In the process, the community has been empowered with training in methods that allow them to take greater control of their urban and domestic environments. Connecting people, place, and its problems has provided the ingredients for nonconventional educational methods that allow all participants to become aware of the realities in our society, while gaining the disciplinary capacities and methodologies to address the wicked problems that need attention (see Figure 12.4).

Finally, the USAER XXXIV Training Center has become a success story in part due to the commitment of all stakeholders involved, but mainly due to the assumed responsibilities of beneficiaries and the support from an engaging Department of Architecture that recognize the pedagogical strategy used in the project. At the same time, the UTC represents a challenge for both the academic community and the institution as they explore ways of consolidating the pedagogical strategy.

12.3
Children with special needs performing a play in collaboration with students from the school district. Impulso Urbano program, USAER XXXIV Training Center for Special Education, Escobedo, Nuevo León, Mexico, 2014.

12.4
The UTC building. USAER XXXIV Training Center for Special Education, Escobedo, Nuevo León, Mexico, 2014.

Democratic Civic Engagement

Notes

1. Unidad de Servicio de Apoyo a la Educación Regular (USAER) is a government agency that coordinates and trains special education teachers to help children with special needs (disabled and high performing children) within the traditional classrooms. There are 237 USAER units in the state of Nuevo León to support 39,000 students with special needs (physical, developmental, behavioral/emotional and sensory impaired).
2. Monterrey Tec is a private university with twenty-six campuses in different states of Mexico. The university has a population of 89,641 students of which 26,114 are high school students, 55,565 are bachelor level, and 7,962 are graduate students.
3. Impulso Urbano is a nonprofit organization that partners with families and communities to improve their housing and community conditions through self-help practices and voluntary work. The program is coordinated thought the Department of Architecture within the School of Architecture, Art and Design at Monterrey Tec and works collaboratively with family and community members, social service students, and faculty to design/build housing and community projects. Impulso Urbano is a platform to explore alternative ways to use and reuse resources in the search for a better-built environment in which trash becomes treasure for most projects.

References

Allen, Stan. 2012. "The Future That Is Now: Architecture Education in North America Over Two Decades of Rapid Social and Technological Change." *Places Journal*, March. Accessed July 21, 2016. https://placesjournal.org/article/the-future-that-is-now/.

Benavides-Ornelas, Ernesto, M. F. Pacheco, and Brianda Hernandez Cavalcanti. 2017. "Brigadas Comunitarias in Queretaro Mexico." ed: Hoyt, Lorlene. In *Regional Perspectives on Learning by Doing: Stories from Engaged Universities around the World*, Project MUSE. East Lansing: Michigan State University Press, 2017: 21–36.

Boyte, Harry C., and Erick Fretz. 2010. "Civic Professionalism." *Journal of Higher Education Outreach and Engagement*, 14 (2): 67–90.

Donaldson, Joe F., and Charles E. Kozoll. 1999. *Collaborative Program Planning: Principles, Practices, and Strategies*. Malabar, FL: Krieger Publishing Company.

Kecskes, Kevin, Jennifer Joyalle, Erin Elliot, and Jacob D.B. Sherman. 2017. "Sustainability of Our Planet and All Species as the Organizing Principle for SLCE." *Michigan Journal of Community Service Learning*, Spring 2017: 159–164.

Kolb, David. 1984. *Experiential Learning: Experience as the Source of Learning and Development*. Englewood Cliffs, NJ: Prentice-Hall.

Pacheco, Pedro. 2003. "Partnering Globally: Connecting People, Places, and Ideas for Sustainable Development." Seventh International Conference on Technology, Policy, and Innovation, Monterrey, Mexico, June 10–13.

Raisbeck, Peter, Heather Mitcheltree, and Pedro Pacheco. 2013. "(RE) Thinking Architectural Design Pedagogy." Paper presented at the Reclaim + Remake Symposium, Washington, DC, April 11–13.

Saltmarsh, John, Matthew Hartley, and Patti Clayton. 2009. *Democratic Engagement White Paper*. Boston, MA: New England Resource Center for Higher Education.

Sanoff, Henry. 2011. "Multiple Views of Participatory Design." *Focus* 8 (1): Article 7.

Intercultural Competencies

13
Intercultural Competencies
Teaching the Intangible

Ursula Hartig and Nina Pawlicki

Today's global challenges are greatly transforming society's expectations of architects and designers, and their roles are changing rapidly. Adapting academic curricula by emerging specific competencies is necessary to tackle these challenges, but that can be a slow, bureaucratic process.

Public interest design and design/build projects question the current conventional academic practice. Strongly embedded in "real life," these projects bridge the gap to the nonacademic world by identifying actual needs and stimulating discussion. "Learning by doing could foster our professional debate on 'vocational action competence'" (Birgit Klauck, Dean of Architectural Studies at the Institute of Architecture, Technische Universität Berlin).[1] Although the projects are mostly small in scale, there is a belief in creating something significant, a small change for the betterment of others and a major change in the attitude of the participants.[2]

Academic hands-on projects present a challenge to students, teachers, and facilitators: users and clients may have different backgrounds or belong to marginalized communities, which often cannot afford design and building services. There is an evident need to develop strategies for intercultural communication and participatory approaches, following the paradigm that design processes and outcomes should be relevant, appropriate, and sustainable.

A profound understanding of the specific local context and a deep investment in the place are required to meet these requisites. These requirements apply equally to design/build projects that Western universities implement in countries of the Global South with the support of local communities[3] and to projects in neighborhoods close to the universities where they are designed and developed (see Figure 13.1).[4]

13.1
Map presenting projects, actors, and organizations posted on the dbXchange.eu web platform. It shows the location of the design/build studios (black dots/white numbers) and the projects (white dots/black numbers). Apparently, North American Universities tend to project locations in the neighborhood, whereas European projects are often located in countries of the Global South. Exhibition: *Hands On: Enhancing Architectural Education*, Technische Universität Wien, Austria, 2016. Photo: Carsten Krohn.

Some studios with an international focus cooperate academically with universities in partner countries.[5] Such balanced collaborations are difficult to establish due to significant differences in curricula, funding, and faculty structures. Multiple benefits for the projects and actors may be achieved, however, if students and teachers from local universities hold key positions: they not only secure a well-grounded investigation of the local context, but also create change as future decision makers, developing and sustaining the knowledge that the projects generate.

A challenge results from the insight that the divide between collaborating students of different nationalities (who share similar social backgrounds, academic levels, and cultural affections) is much less than the social and cultural divide between academics and local communities from the same nation (which have considerably different economic and educational structures and are usually strongly embedded in traditional cultures).

To open oneself to an unknown cultural context poses a big hurdle for students, and is as well challenging to the local community partner as a counterpart. The intense engagement in a design/build project—living in a community for several weeks or collaborating with community stakeholders for an entire year—makes a strong impact on both students and hosts. Such engagements often lead to mutual learning, greater respect, and better understanding of cultural differences, beyond professional training.

Critical reflection on the relationship between the international academic and local partners is necessary. Speakers at conferences and lectures about international design/build projects frequently point out that these projects tend to manifest neocolonialist tendencies.[6] For example, Alejandro Vidal, a graduate at the Universidad Nacional Autónoma de México (UNAM), raised the question, "Why always expect someone else to come to Mexico and show us how things should be done?" at a symposium in Berlin in 2012. The speakers blame a paternalistic attitude toward the development of culture and economy but equally toward the migration of architectural typologies and techniques. In one of these discussions,[7] representatives of a Mexican women's cooperative, which had initiated and collaborated on an award-winning design/build project, expressed their wishes for cultural and economic development and their esteem for this kind of appropriate architecture. These different viewpoints show that knowledge and respect of the cultural and social context of all involved stakeholders (academic and nonacademic) are as indispensable as a constant evaluation of attitudes toward knowledge and culture transfer.

The chapters in this section demonstrate ways to teach the intangible **intercultural competencies** while structuring knowledge transfer in sensitive and well-embedded formats:

- Lisa Grocott and Kate McEntee provide insight into their teaching approach at the Transforming Mindsets Studio (pages 141–146), which conveys soft skills to design students to help them navigate unfamiliar cultural contexts, tackle sensitive social issues, and collaborate effectively with multidisciplinary groups. As an integrated format, this approach could complement and help to revise the set of soft skills that are being generated through user-oriented design projects in education.
- The challenge embedded in the international Clean Air Campaign, a project of the International Urbanization Seminar at Stanford University (pages 147–153), is a problem of air pollution and its impact on senior citizens in Beijing. In this chapter Deland Chan explains how experiential learning, empathetic co-design, and ethical research support cross-cultural and interdisciplinary approaches to working with local communities. The project process demonstrates how human-centered design outcomes can be verified and adapted to reveal an approachable and effective product.
- Design/build projects directed by organizations in countries of the Global South are still scarce but offer great opportunities for balanced knowledge exchange.[8] Christian Benimana describes the development of the African Design Centre's (pages 135–140) curricular structure, which emphasizes project-based education to strengthen understanding of context, critical thinking, and leadership skills. Located in Kigali, Rwanda, the African Design Centre has the potential to become a landmark for inclusive, appropriate public interest design education and is a promising partner for intercultural academic projects.

Notes

1 Stated at the Symposium DesignBuild Studio, New Ways in Architectural Education, at Technische Universität Berlin, Germany, in 2012 (see https://issuu.com/cocoon-studio/docs/cocoon_new_ways_in_arch_education_s as well).

2   For more information, see: *Small Scale Big Change: New Architectures of Social Engagement*, exhibition at the Museum of Modern Art, New York, 2010, www.moma.org/interactives/exhibitions/2010/smallscalebigchange/; and Bryan Bell, *Good Deeds, Good Design*: *Community Service Through Architecture* (New York: Princeton Architectural Press, 2004), http://www.papress.com/html/product.details.dna?isbn=9781568983912

3   See, for example:
- BASEhabitat, Kunst Universität Linz (University of Art and Design Linz), Austria, www.dbxchange.eu/node/960
- design.build studio, Technische Universität Wien, Austria, www.dbxchange.eu/node/387
- TUM Design/Build. Technische Universität München, Germany, www.dbxchange.eu/node/986

4   See, for example:
- Parsons The Design Workshop, The New School, United States, www.dbxchange.eu/node/1132
- Rural Studio, Auburn University, United States, http://www.dbxchange.eu/user/3332
- Center for Public Interest Design, Portland State University, United States, www.pdx.edu/public-interest-design/

5   See, for example:
- CoCoon—contextual construction, Technische Universität Berlin, Germany, http://cocoon-studio.de/
- Archintorno, Italy, www.archintorno.org/

6   A critical review of the exhibition *Afritecture* at the Architekturmuseum of the Technische Universität Munich, Germany, by Dankwart Guratzsch addresses this issue: "Die neuen Kolonialisten kommen nach Afrika," *Die Welt* (2013), accessed December 9, 2016, www.welt.de/kultur/kunst-und-architektur/article122849541/Die-neuen-Kolonialisten-kommen-nach-Afrika.html.

7   Public Interest Design Mexico conference and Social Economic Environmental Design (SEED) Network award ceremony at UNAM, September 2014.

8   See, for example:
- Design Build and Design Construction Projects for Community, INDA, Chulalongkorn University, Thailand, http://cuinda.com/work/
- Impulso Urbano, Tecnologico de Monterrey, Mexico, www.facebook.com/diezxdiez/?fref=ts and www.dbxchange.eu/node/1053

14
Creating Design Leaders
The African Design Centre
Christian Benimana

In September 2016, the African Design Centre (ADC) welcomed its inaugural class of eleven fellows in Kigali, Rwanda, with a mission to guide African growth by educating future leaders in **impact-driven design**. Established by the international nonprofit architecture firm MASS Design Group, ADC builds on the success of the firm's design methodology. ADC seeks to make high-impact design more broadly accessible across Africa, complementing existing programs with a curricular strategy that emphasizes project-based education (see Figure 14.1).

Christian Benimana, director of the program, introduced ADC at the first United Nations Solutions Summit in 2015. ADC builds on Benimana's vision: to prepare designers to respond to the critical need for high-quality infrastructure that Africa will face as it experiences rapid population growth and urbanization in the coming decades.

The ADC fellows, recent graduates in design disciplines, have diverse backgrounds and come from across the continent and abroad. With a twenty-month curriculum built around understanding context, ADC will create a community of high-impact designers who can tackle the anticipated challenges that come with the huge infrastructure demands of Africa's growing population.

Program Curriculum

Impact-driven design addresses the ability to use architecture and design as a lever to improve communities. In impact-driven design, each project establishes a core mission: a simple, legible, transmissible idea that speaks to a greater societal goal.

14.1
ADC fellows gain hands-on experience through a design/build project. MASS Design Group, Butaro, Rwanda, 2012.

Through each phase of a project, designers consider how this mission is being achieved, giving special consideration to the direct, indirect, and systemic outcomes of the project.

The core component of ADC's curriculum is the design/build project. Under the guidance of project managers, fellows lead projects through four stages of impact-driven design: immersion, design, construction, and evaluation. In ADC's first years, this design/build component will revolve around constructing primary schools in Rwanda's Musanze District, building on a design framework for child-friendly schools developed by MASS that improves on existing Ministry of Education standards. Fellows will experience firsthand the benefits of the impact-driven design methodology and gain experience in all aspects of the design and building process:

1. During the *predesign immersion phase*, fellows work with teachers, parents, and students to identify constraints and local opportunities that will inform the school's design and construction (see Figure 14.2).
2. The *design phase* builds on the opportunities previously identified, moving from visioning to developing construction documents and ensuring that all decisions align with stakeholders' needs and priorities.
3. The *construction process* is an often-underleveraged opportunity to foster social engagement, training, and equitable hiring. By working with local materials, laborers, and artisans in innovative ways, the fellows foster on-site exchange of ideas and techniques while generating community investment in the building, ensuring its continued success and maintenance. This local fabrication, or Lo-Fab, approach is at the heart of the ADC methodology.
4. In a *post-occupancy evaluation phase*, design fellows evaluate the quantitative and qualitative effects of the design and construction process, recalibrating as

14.2
Women creating mats from local reeds for roof insulation. MASS Design Group, Mubuga Primary School, Musanze, Rwanda, 2015.

needed to maximize sustained impact. Fellows also identify successes and failures to inform the improvement of the built environment.

In addition to the design/build program, fellows follow seminars on topics emphasizing the interdisciplinary nature of design. Fellows also use tools to develop prototypes and conduct research to uncover innovative, context-responsive solutions that counteract reliance on imported and nonrenewable building technologies.

Learning Objectives

Beginning with an intensive foundation course in the first year, the ADC curriculum is designed to help fellows build critical skills that will prepare them to address the challenges facing the African continent. The curriculum addresses several learning objectives in the areas of understanding context, critical thinking, and developing leadership.

Understanding Context

Impact-driven design must be rooted in a detailed understanding of the needs and priorities of a community. The ADC curriculum teaches the soft skills—interpersonal communications, cultural empathy, and creative entrepreneurialism—required to listen to needs and identify opportunities. The curriculum also gives fellows a framework to assess the context and site. This framework represents the immersion phase of the design process, which fellows learn in practice as they conduct research at the start of the project and revisit as they evaluate the project's success.

Fellows develop personal relationships within the community where they are working that will last the duration of the project: with stakeholders who serve as advisers at every stage of design and construction, as well as with local laborers and artisans who contribute to the building.

At the end of the program, fellows will have the ability to gain a complete understanding of any project context. Students will be able to:

- apply observation and information-collection skills to determine, list, and prioritize the real issues faced by the community
- scrutinize which of these issues can be addressed through design
- illustrate the limitations and the internal and external factors that may affect the success of the project
- identify contextual opportunities for impact-driven design solutions
- develop tools to use for including the community in the design process

Critical Thinking

By emphasizing problem solving and innovation, ADC aims to complement design education in the region, which is sometimes restricted to rote memorization and technical skills. As a direct goal of the foundation courses, this focus permeates fellows' expectations at every stage of the design/build process, as well as in seminars and personal research. Graduates will be able to apply an iterative process to solving systemic problems throughout their careers, whether they are addressing infrastructural, management, or policy challenges.

ADC aspires to become a hub of collaborative research by hosting visiting faculty and researchers. It will work closely with other design institutions across East Africa, which together can drive a collective shift in how design is taught throughout the region.

Through the program, fellows will learn critical-thinking skills and gain an understanding of the human-centered design process. Students will be able to:

- define the parameters of the design solution intervention
- apply an iterative, human-centered design process to solve systemic problems
- translate the process and ideas into practical design solutions
- formulate strategies for scaling the impact of the conceived design solutions

Leadership

All ADC fellows are tasked with leading aspects of construction administration on the project; they learn to direct a team on-site, respond to professional and intrapersonal challenges among team members, and handle challenges that arise unexpectedly. Fellows work with artisans with varied skill sets and learn to incorporate these skills into projects in ways that are mutually valorizing (see Figure 14.3).

14.3
Construction using the MASS Lo-Fab building process. MASS Design Group, Mubuga Primary School, Musanze, Rwanda, 2015.

The program curriculum emphasizes communication skills throughout; effective writing and public speaking enable graduates to connect with stakeholders and advocate for the role of design in facilitating systemic development.

As a result of the program, fellows will be empowered to be thought leaders in developing design solutions to global problems. Students will be able to:

- participate in forums in which discussions on solutions to the world's problems take place
- defend the ability of impact-driven design methodology to solve societal problems
- demonstrate leadership through team-building activities to resolve challenges
- demonstrate the ability to understand problems, seek advice, and make design decisions that maximize their positive impact
- develop effective ways to advocate for appropriate impact-driven design solutions to global issues

Mubuga Primary School Project

MASS piloted the pedagogy of ADC's design/build program in overhauling the Mubuga Primary School in Musanze District. MASS upgraded the school, which had suffered from infrastructural failures, in partnership with the M^2 Foundation between 2013 and 2015. In the process, MASS created a framework for the design and construction of better learning and teaching environments, now used in ADC's design/build program, and trained two of the firm's designers on-site.

Under the supervision of a project manager, MASS fellows Annie Peyton and Theophile Uwayezu worked together to schedule project construction, procure materials, oversee the employment of new construction techniques, and troubleshoot on-site challenges. The two developed invaluable knowledge of impact-driven design, leadership skills, and construction administration. They learned to manage a team and project schedule and to oversee project quality, while also navigating the challenges inherent to bringing innovative designs and building techniques to a specific site and community.

Uwayezu describes his experience on-site:

Having the managerial role in construction was key, and I've learned a lot about how to get things done. How to control quality, cost, and timing of the project—to make sure those three go together ... When you see a detail you made is not working on site, it puts the pressure on to come up with a solution, to use every resource that you have. It prepares you to be more proactive in everything.

Peyton describes her experience on-site:

I had never spent time on a construction site before, so the many components that come with that were by far the best learning. For example, learning how concrete is made—I had read about it before, but I had never seen it mixed in front of me and poured into formwork and made into a building.

By 2050, Africa's population will have doubled to 2.5 billion people, and over half of these people will live in urban areas (UN DESA 2015, 1). Recent epidemics, environmental crises, and inadequate living conditions in many informal neighborhoods demonstrate that quality primary infrastructure is critical to supporting dense human settlement. By teaching core skills to practice impact-driven, contextual design, ADC trains the designers who will build that infrastructure in an equitable and sustainable manner, becoming the pillar of Africa's future.

Reference

UN DESA (United Nations, Department of Economic and Social Affairs, Population Division). 2015. *World Populations Prospects: The 2015 Revision, Key Findings and Advance Tables*. Working Paper No. ESA/P/WP.241, United Nations, New York.

15
Teaching *Intra*personal Development, Improving Interpersonal and Intercultural Skill Sets
The Transforming Mindsets Studio

Lisa Grocott and Kate McEntee

Humans are at the heart of the participatory practice of public interest design. Whether designers are creating interfaces, systems, or services, the emergent tools of this relational practice are less about technology and more about connection and understanding. Consider maps that annotate a user's needs in an empathy interview or diagrams that trace the human values being exchanged between services and experiences. The practice of public interest design calls for a generation of designers able to more deeply understand the human experience. It asks designers to use this understanding to navigate unfamiliar cultural contexts, tackle sensitive social issues, and collaborate effectively with multidisciplinary groups.

As we look outward at the interpersonal skills needed to work with collaborative, cross disciplinary teams and the intercultural skills necessary to engage the public, it is as important to look inward at the individual doing the designing. How might teaching students how to interrogate their own habits and **mindsets** influence their capacity to thrive in community-based work? This question was the motivation behind a four-year experiment that introduced pedagogical practices focusing on **intrapersonal skills** in design education. The latest iteration of this experiment was taught in the Transforming Mindsets studio (PGTD 5100) of the Master of Fine Arts in Transdisciplinary Design program at Parsons School of Design.

As a result of this course, students will be able to achieve the following learning objectives:

- recognize the influential role mindsets play in the context of learning
- facilitate **case clinics** to underscore how learning how to learn is key to thriving personally and professionally
- use **serious play** to enhance social and emotional co-creation skills

A research study investigated the effectiveness of this experimental curriculum using real-time self-reporting tools, one-to-one interviews, and a six-month follow-up with students after the completion of the studio. The study disclosed that the focus on inward skills had a deeply transformative effect on students—changing their relationship with learning and their approach to design—while simultaneously leading to studio project outcomes that exceeded previous work. Yet post-studio interviews revealed the challenge of integrating intrapersonal skills and practices into future contexts.

Inside the Activities

The Transforming Mindsets studio was framed as an exploration of the role of design in behavior change. The studio partnered with Riverdale, a K–12 school in the Bronx, to pilot interventions designed to shift learning mindsets. Designs for public interest often lead to proposals that require an individual to shift behaviors, mindsets, or belief systems, such as a public health campaign or a community-composting initiative. The parallel process of having students work toward personal behavior changes or mindset shifts while designing projects to shift others' mindsets proved to be a powerful empathy exercise.

Building on research from social psychology, organizational leadership, and learning sciences, the studio adapted tactical approaches to teach growth mindsets (Dweck 2006), experiential case clinics (Scharmer 2009), and play workshops (Brown 2009). We used a past–present–future concept to frame the intrapersonal work students took on in the studio. Reflective exercises highlighted how a person's *past* influences current practice. Exercises in being *present* tuned mindfulness toward how students approach new contexts and collaborations. Working with how mental models shape *future* behavior and mindsets honed the ability to manifest desired outcomes. Multiple exercises addressed these concepts in the studio, but students reported that three exercises had the greatest impact: Prospective Writing, Learning Mindset Case Clinic, and Performance Gym (see Figure 15.1).

Proposing Preferred Futures

The semester began with a Prospective Writing exercise that students reported had a profound effect on their learning experiences, more so than the reflective writing at the conclusion of the studio. The "Give Yourself an A" exercise asked students to write an argument for how they would earn an A for the studio

15.1
The Performance Gym.
Lisa Grocott, Transforming Mindsets studio, New York, New York, 2015.

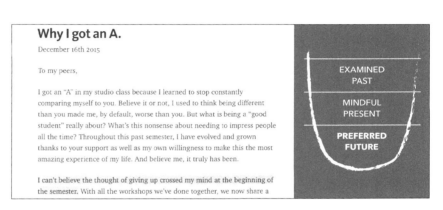

15.2
Student Sophie Riendeau's blog written after the first week of class and postdated for the end of the semester. Sophie Riendeau, Transforming Mindsets studio, New York, New York, 2015.

(Zander 2006). Students postdated the letter for the end of the semester and were encouraged to think about how they might enact a different preferred mindset in advance of the course work (see Figure 15.2). In foreshadowing what success looked like for each individual, the exercise deployed students' intrinsic motivations to succeed and brought attention to students' ability to shape their educational experiences.

Surfacing Limiting Beliefs

The Learning Mindset Case Clinic worked with the premise that one must let go of old ways of thinking to allow new ways of being (Scharmer 2009). The sixty-minute session began with students in small groups presenting the mindsets they most believed were holding back their learning. The case giver traced the current belief back to past experiences, and in return, three or four peers reflected back a visual, felt, and performative account of what they heard. This non-analytical, judgment-free mirror opened up new ways of "seeing" the situation, and led to students generating tactics to overcome limiting patterns of behavior (Presencing Institute 2016).

The Transforming Mindsets Studio

15.3
The Theory U framework, represented in diagram, informed the Case Clinic and Performance Gym. Lisa Grocott, Transforming Mindsets studio, New York, New York, 2015.

Students presented cases that ranged from the inability to manage their workloads to feelings of imposter syndrome. Yet the stories themselves were of less significance than the vulnerability experienced when students communally interrogated their own fixed mindsets (Dweck 2006).

Tuning Behavior Patterns

Dedicating the first ninety minutes of the weekly six-hour studio to serious play was a significant structural change. This Performance Gym was infused into the course with the premise that the way one does anything, is the way one does everything (Brown 2009). The embodied activities demonstrated how students instinctively react in new and collaborative situations, revealing responses that limit the ability to be present and unveiling behavior patterns that usually go unnoticed but still have significant impact on actions (see Figure 15.3).

The exercises surfaced students' comfort levels around risk taking, not-knowing, and uncertainty. Debriefs after each activity encouraged reflection on actions like jumping in to "save" someone else or acting too soon or too late. Real-time feedback allowed students to see how they try to control a situation or abdicate responsibility, embrace risk or shy away from taking the lead.

Student Response

Explicitly dedicating studio project time to working on these noncognitive competencies greatly enhanced students' ability to empathize with the public, collaborate with peers, and design never-before-seen solutions, according to students' reports. Given the studio time dedicated to affective learning outcomes, partner projects were not compromised, and students reported that the projects were some of their best work.

Students described how transformative the deep sense of self-awareness and social belonging was that came from playing together each week in the gym and seeing themselves in one another's stories through the case clinic. The clinic's structure for active listening and empathy left an indelible mark on the collaborative culture of the studio, with one student saying the environment "was like magic, amazing, transformative." Another student described the play as liberating: "We are not so self-conscious of everything we do. That makes us be more open and spontaneous."

The Prospective Writing exercise rejected the notion that student achievement should be measured only by design critiques and project outcomes. One student described how this framing led her to ask, "What does success look like for me, and not simply what do I need to do to please my professor?" Together the exercises shaped a class focused on enhancing collaborations, collective growth, and lifelong learning. Students cited the impact that the learning environment had on building self-confidence, relieving stress, and improving communication skills and group dynamics, directly leading to enhanced community partnerships and more mature project outcomes.

Transferring these skills into future academic and professional projects had mixed results, however. Students reported struggling with translating the empathy, reflection, and collaboration skills into the conventional project-driven environments of the design studio. Some students lamented their inability to advance a collective-growth mindset or to be as secure and open when peers had not had a shared experience.

Several students said the Transforming Mindsets studio stood out as a significantly transformative and unique learning experience. We hope further iterations will disclose how to improve the transferability of the learning outcomes. A change that could make the most significant difference would be to require students to teach their peers how to pursue a more self-aware design practice. Students reported that the studio lacked the opportunity to lead play exercises, develop an embodied curriculum, or design a case clinic of their own. Similar to content-based lessons that students lead, a space for students to facilitate sessions would help make concrete what they have learned tacitly and show the community the transformative impact that such an approach can have on learning over a lifetime. It is possible to imagine how a space dedicated to developing self-awareness and social belonging within an academic or professional cohort could be the cornerstone of a program, leading to enhanced collaboration and project outcomes across courses.

Infusing *intra*personal development into the curriculum hones the communication, understanding, and collaboration skills necessary for successful public interest design. Through a focus on intrapersonal development, designers greatly improve their interpersonal and intercultural capacities. Teaching students to examine past experiences and belief systems, to become more aware of behavior and biases in the present, and to frame desired futures unlocks great potentials for themselves and for the communities for which they are designing.

References

Brown, Stuart. 2009. *Play: How It Shapes the Brain, Opens the Imagination, and Invigorates the Soul*. London: Penguin Group.

Dweck, Carol. 2006. *Mindset: The New Psychology of Success*. New York: Ballantine Books.

Presencing Institute. 2016. "Case Clinic." Accessed August 14, 2016. https://uschool.presencing.com/tool/case-clinic.

Scharmer, Otto. 2009. *Theory U: Learning from the Future as It Emerges*. Oakland, CA: Berrett-Koehler.

Zander, Benjamin. 2006. "Gurus with Benjamin Zander." *Teachers TV* video, 14:01, recorded July 10. Accessed August 14, 2016. http://archive.teachfind.com/ttv/www.teachers.tv/videos/benjamin-zander.html.

16
Addressing Air Pollution Impacts on Senior Citizens in Beijing, China
The International Urbanization Seminar

Deland Chan

China has experienced rapid urbanization and economic growth since 1978, resulting in reduced air quality and growing concerns about air pollution. In Beijing, fine particulate matter concentrations at times exceed World Health Organization safety guidelines (He et al. 2001). Students in the International Urbanization Seminar (IUS)[1] at Stanford University examined air pollution and its impacts on senior citizens in Beijing as a critical question of urban sustainability. Working in a multinational, interdisciplinary team, American and Chinese students collaborated with Clean Air Asia, an international nongovernmental organization (NGO) that promotes better air quality in cities across Asia through technical assistance, to develop public campaign materials targeting Beijing's older adult populations. Over four months, the team researched scientific literature on air pollution impacts, identified barriers and opportunities, translated technical knowledge into public campaign materials, and tested these materials with senior citizens. Through this course, students learned to work across cultures and disciplines to apply **human-centered design** and advance sustainability approaches rooted in cultural humility and respectful collaboration with local communities.

Toward an Inclusive Urban Future

Two-thirds of humanity will be living in cities by 2050, elevating the need for a sustainable and equitable urban future for all (United Nations 2014). Recognizing that cities are complex and extend beyond the ability of a single discipline to tackle their challenges, the author co-founded the Stanford Human Cities Initiative (HCI) to nurture a pipeline of leaders who understand cities to be responsive to diverse human communities.[2] Through education and research, the HCI uses **design thinking** to envision an inclusive human-centered urban future.

Several courses are offered under the HCI that are open to undergraduate and graduate students from across disciplines at Stanford. Courses such as the IUS are offered for academic credit and count toward degree requirements. The author developed and teaches the course along with a trans-Pacific faculty team from the Program on Urban Studies at Stanford University and the Department of Construction Management and Information Art and Design at Tsinghua University in Beijing, China.[3]

Initiated in 2014, the IUS focuses on design thinking and fieldwork strategies for students from *all* disciplines to apply creative problem-solving approaches to urban sustainability. It is structured around three urban labs that guide students through human-centered design, empathy interviews, user observation, and prototype testing. This chapter refers to the Clean Air Campaign undertaken by IUS students as one of three projects in fall 2015.

Seminar Structure

The IUS consists of three phases: a two-week fieldwork studio in Beijing, a ten-week course involving remote collaboration, and a capstone experience at the Human Cities Expo held at Stanford University at the conclusion of the course.

The course sequence begins with Stanford students traveling to Beijing for a two-week studio. They participate in daily seminars with Tsinghua University students, visit local NGOs and sustainability organizations, and engage in immersive activities that allow them to understand the scale and history of Beijing (see Figure 16.1). The studio emphasizes fieldwork where students are divided into multinational, interdisciplinary teams to meet with community partners and engage in site visits.

After the studio, Stanford students return to the United States and continue with a ten-week course during the fall quarter. Students meet twice a week in class to discuss comparative United States–China sustainability issues and participate in a weekly joint teleconference session with their Tsinghua counterparts. During these sessions, students engage with faculty and invited guest experts from both sides of the Pacific and break out into small group discussions. Students are required to work outside the class on project development, guided by assignments focused on urban observation and prototyping in the city.

The course culminates with Tsinghua faculty and students traveling to Stanford to participate in the annual Human Cities Expo (see Figure 16.2). The expo serves as a daylong celebration of interdisciplinary perspectives and strategies for advancing human-centered cities. The expo features interactive exhibits, class presentations, and keynote talks from sustainability scholars and practitioners.

16.1
China Director of Clean Air Asia presents the organization's work and meets the students in the International Urbanization Seminar in Beijing, China, 2015. Photo: Deland Chan.

16.2
Students in the International Urbanization Seminar create interactive exhibits and engage with audience members at the Human Cities Expo as a capstone experience. International Urbanization Seminar, Stanford, California, 2015. Photo: Adriana Baird.

Learning Objectives and Outcomes: Clean Air Campaign

The Clean Air Campaign team consisted of six Tsinghua students and five Stanford students from the fields of environmental systems engineering, construction management, and service design. They partnered with Clean Air Asia to develop a scientifically based educational campaign to reach senior citizens, who are

Addressing Air Pollution Impacts

disproportionately affected by air pollution impacts in Beijing. By engaging in this work, students achieved the following learning objectives:

- comprehend scientific knowledge
- analyze a real-life problem
- synthesize field research into effective ways of addressing air pollution impacts on seniors

Students began the project by researching the health impacts of air pollution on senior populations and effective methods of protection that an individual could take, such as purchasing indoor air purifiers, wearing a respirator mask, or reducing exposure. Students reviewed existing scientific research, interviewed subject experts, and summarized current practices in a technical report.

After the initial literature review, students embarked on exploratory fieldwork to understand the motivations of the senior population. This led to unexpected findings; for example, students discovered that seniors did not initially express concern for their own health but were very concerned about the health of their grandchildren. In turn, the team realized that they could attract the attention of senior citizens by targeting educational materials that describe health impacts on their grandchildren and suggest protections that would benefit the entire family.

Following this discovery, the team analyzed and distilled this knowledge into prototypes of public campaign materials to educate senior citizens about the hazards of air pollution and available methods of self-protective measures. Tsinghua students then tested these flyers at a Beijing senior center (see Figure 16.3) to see if the message targeting the senior citizens' of responsibility as caretakers of their grandchildren resonated and whether they would adapt protection methods as role

16.3
Students in the Clean Air Campaign engage in outreach at a senior community center with their prototypes in Beijing, China. International Urbanization Seminar, Beijing, China, 2015. Photo: Leqi Sun.

models for the next generation. Stanford students contributed to these efforts by testing the collateral with senior citizens of Asian descent in the San Francisco Bay area.[4] This resulted in a deeper understanding of communication preferences and effective messaging from two sites across the Pacific and helped to inform the work of the Beijing-based team members.

The project concluded with students synthesizing user feedback to design collateral such as a video and a print booklet detailing the causes of air pollution, the air quality index, and techniques for individuals to protect themselves from air pollution. Together, the team generated a playbook of techniques that Clean Air Asia could implement in future public education campaigns.[5]

Teaching Strategies: The Three Es

The IUS focuses on three teaching strategies identified by the author as the three Es of the HCI classes: experiential learning, empathic design, and ethical research. Together, these methods create transformative educational impacts and sustained project benefits long after the course ends.

- Experiential learning involves learning about communities through direct interaction. By traveling to Beijing and making intentional choices such as biking and walking rather than traveling in air-conditioned tourist buses, students were encouraged to learn about Beijing by experiencing conditions firsthand. Unlike in other types of architecture or planning studios where learning takes place through desktop research at a distance or limited direct interaction, in the IUS students are themselves users of the site and engage daily with local stakeholders on the ground with the collaboration of their Chinese counterparts at Tsinghua.
- Empathic design encourages students to put themselves in the shoes of someone other than themselves to understand the diverse experiences of urban dwellers. Through guided exercises, students were instructed to navigate Beijing beyond their normalized ways and engage local community members to understand their daily lived experiences. For example, two students rented a wheelchair and traveled throughout the city from the perspective of someone with limited physical ability. This exercise aimed to encourage empathy for people with different experiences and generate insights for working with local populations.
- Ethical research focuses on the use of rigorous and scientific methods to gather truthful information. Fieldwork was done in conjunction with Beijing-based students and in collaboration with Clean Air Asia as the NGO that shaped and defined the research question. Students were trained in methods of **cultural probes** and reflection strategies to understand the significance and impact of their work on real communities and their roles as students entering a community to amplify existing efforts.

Lessons Learned

The next generation of global leaders must collaborate across cultures and disciplines to address complex urbanization challenges (Steiner and Posch 2006). The Stanford HCI nurtures this pipeline by offering project-based courses such as the IUS and opportunities to partner with stakeholders on real-world problems.

The Clean Air Campaign supports the educational benefits of students applying human-centered design to analyze the needs of local stakeholders and devise culturally sensitive approaches. While students sought to work with humility and respect local expertise, the course also emphasized project deliverables that targeted individual actions, rather than broader advocacy for the public or private sectors to regulate air pollution. Future iterations of the course would need to address the delicate balance of working in a foreign country in regard to politically sensitive topics and maintaining collaborative relationships, while ultimately ensuring that the project is sustainable and impactful.

Notes

1. The International Urbanization Seminar is an interdisciplinary course offered at Stanford University through the Program on Urban Studies as Urban Studies 145 and cross-listed in other departments as Civil and Environmental Engineering 126, Earth Systems 138, and International Policy Studies 274.
2. Based in the Program on Urban Studies at Stanford University, the Human Cities Initiative takes a whole-systems approach to the research and practice of sustainable cities. The initiative identifies urbanization challenges at different stages of development and supports human-centered technological, policy, and design strategies that address those challenges. It develops and practices ethical approaches, using frameworks that are inclusive (for many) and participatory (by many) and striving to benefit diverse human communities. For more information, see www.humancities.org.
3. The trans-Pacific faculty team included Kevin Hsu (Program on Urban Studies, Stanford University), Nan Li (Construction Management, Tsinghua University), and Zhiyong Fu (Information Art and Design, Tsinghua University).
4. Stanford students did not return to Beijing to conduct additional fieldwork. However, they engaged San Francisco Bay area senior citizens of Chinese descent in prototype testing. While they could not assume that these populations had the same lived experiences as those in Beijing, there were many commonalities. For example, many had experienced air pollution in other cities in China. Many were also familiar with those issues through the media or anecdotes from family and colleagues. More importantly, these interviews provided insights into effective communication and public campaign materials for the Chinese-speaking diaspora.

5   Project materials can be found at the International Urbanization website at www.internationalurbanization.org.

References

He, Kebin, Fumo Yang, Yongliang Ma, Qiang Zhang, Xiaohong Yao, Chak K. Chan, Steven Cadle, Tai Chan, and Patricia Mulawa. 2001. "The Characteristics of PM 2.5 in Beijing, China." *Atmospheric Environment* 35 (29): 4959–70.

Steiner, Gerald, and Alfred Posch. 2006. "Higher Education for Sustainability by Means of Transdisciplinary Case Studies: An Innovative Approach for Solving Complex, Real-World Problems." *Journal of Cleaner Production* 14 (9): 877–90.

United Nations. 2014. *World Urbanization Prospects: The 2014 Revision, Highlights*. United Nations, Department of Economic and Social Affairs, Population Division.

Engaging the Field Experience

17
Engaging the Field Experience
Integrated, Interdisciplinary, On-Site, Enduring

Benjamin R. Spencer

Public interest design researchers, educators, and practitioners strive to improve the processes, products, and outcomes of the projects they carry out in underserved communities, to disseminate the lessons these projects provide, and to prepare students to do the same. Universities play a critical role in these efforts and, in many ways, provide a nurturing environment for public interest design. At the same time, the structures that govern higher education can inhibit the full potential of public interest design. By enhancing opportunities to pursue public interest design as a form of engaged scholarship, providing incentives for interdisciplinary collaboration, and promoting community-based curricula at home and abroad, educators have the opportunity to strengthen the efficacy of interventions and expand the scope of practice.

Public interest design is a creative, integrative means of investigating and solving complex problems. Iterative and nonlinear, public interest design involves generating knowledge that informs project design and implementation in underserved communities, celebrates the rich complexity of culture and context, and addresses the multivariate challenges that community members face. Within an academic context, where theoretical exploration often takes precedence over hands-on experience, the **Scholarships of Application and Engagement** (SAE) provide a platform for educators to take public interest design out of the classroom and into the field. SAE involve "professional activities such as designs for specific sites and communities where theory and practice interact, vitally renewing each other," "integrating practice of teaching, research, and service," and "bringing the intellectual and technical resources of the university to bear upon a community's pressing needs" (UW CBE 2009, 2).

Universities offer a unique environment to pursue SAE. Their advantages include access to intellectual and financial resources, relatively flexible schedules, and the freedom to pursue activities that fall outside the boundaries of mainstream practice. Still, traditional scholarship is better understood at many universities than project-based research. The significant time and effort it takes to implement SAE projects can go largely unrecognized. Select design programs provide guidelines that specifically call out SAE as a legitimate path for career advancement; however, this practice is not yet widespread (Rottle et al. 2014, 333). University leadership can help by providing incentives, such as tenure and promotion, for the pursuit of these modes of inquiry.

Public interest design research reaches its fullest potential when it brings together multiple disciplines and assimilates participatory, qualitative, and quantitative methods. Participatory activities, such as community mapping, identify community assets, needs, and priorities. Focus-group interviews provide insights into community perceptions and serve as an entry point for relevant quantitative research. Quantitative data, along with participatory drawing and modeling exercises, inform the design and implementation of projects that are evidence based, creative, and community driven. Applied technical research leads to improvements in the performance and accessibility of materials and technologies. Participatory impact assessment allows community members to define and evaluate project successes and failures, while research instruments reinforce the objective validity of outcomes and establish causality between design interventions and their impacts. Coming full circle, lessons learned can be applied to subsequent projects in the same communities, and methods and findings can be disseminated for potential application in diverse contexts.

Teams with varied expertise and skills are necessary. Establishing connections across departmental divisions brings additional disciplines into the fold and grows the donor base to include foundations that invest not only in design but also in health, education, and other areas. Forging close partnerships with nonprofit organizations and leveraging university resources to support the growth of professional public interest design activities blaze a wider path for graduates and seasoned practitioners alike to pursue viable careers in the practice.

Although universities lend themselves to collaboration in many respects, disciplinary and academic insularity remain commonplace. University leadership can provide incentives, such as supporting cross departmental appointments, hiring professors of practice, promoting policies that reward interdisciplinary and interorganizational efforts, structuring budgets to facilitate the flow of financial resources between collaborating schools, and allocating discretionary funds to place-based initiatives (NASEM 2005, 332).

Modeling effective public interest design practices in schools is critical to seeding the expansion of the profession and strengthening its impact in underserved communities. An increasing number of design programs emphasize public interest design in their curricula through studios, design/build projects, and certificate programs. Despite these positive developments, the cultivation of collaboration and community engagement remains an ongoing challenge. With notable exceptions, such as Campbell and Malan's iZindaba Zokudla project (pages 158–164) and Peterson's Huxtable Fellowship (pages 171–177) (described in the Chapters 18 and 20), enrollment in public interest design courses is often limited to one discipline or degree program. Students are typically involved in projects for a limited time and exposed to only a subset of the skills necessary to carry out and critically reflect on projects. A semester is rarely enough time for students to gain a background in relevant theory, familiarize themselves with the nuances of cultural context, and build relationships with community members—let alone design, implement, and assess the impacts of an intervention.

Long-term engagements in the same communities, maintaining a consistent on-site presence, and providing opportunities for interdisciplinary participation in public interest design research at multiple stages of project evolution provide mutual benefits for students and communities. Among other advantages, long-term engagements help communities and design teams establish dialogue and trust. Consistent on-site activities are arguably easier to maintain when universities and communities are situated in close proximity. However, as Gaudio's Healing an Urban Stream project (pages 165–170) illustrates, international efforts where communities face acute challenges and local institutions lack the resources to respond are critically important. Permanent in-country centers for public interest design would provide opportunities for interdisciplinary, cross-cultural groups to pursue long-term, place-based projects. Such in-country centers would represent a potential next step toward the cultivation of integrated public interest design research, education, and practice abroad.

References

NASEM (National Academies of Sciences, Engineering, and Medicine). 2005. *Facilitating Interdisciplinary Research*. Washington, DC: National Academies Press.

Rottle, Nancy, Patsy Eubanks Owens, Benjamin R. Spencer, and Will Green. 2014. "Service-Learning as a Change Agent: Issues and Solutions." Panel presentation (abstract) in EDRA 45, Building with Change, Proceedings of the 45th Annual Conference of the Environmental Design Association, 333, New Orleans, LA, May 28–31.

UW CBE (University of Washington College of Built Environments). 2009. *Tenure and Promotion Processes and Guidelines*. Seattle: University of Washington Department of Landscape Architecture College of Built Environments.

18

iZindaba Zokudla (Conversations About Food)
Innovation in the Soweto Food System

Angus Donald Campbell and Naudé Malan

iZindaba Zokudla (Conversations About Food): Innovation in the Soweto Food System[1] is an interdisciplinary research project initiated by the departments of Development Studies and Industrial Design at the University of Johannesburg (UJ), South Africa. The project aims to create a more sustainable food system in Johannesburg through urban agriculture. In 2013, iZindaba Zokudla conducted a series of public **multi-stakeholder engagement** (Dubbeling, de Zeeuw, and van Veenhuizen 2010) sessions to develop a strategic plan for urban agriculture in Soweto.[2] Appropriate technology was identified as a key requirement for sustainable food-systems change.

In response, an interdisciplinary **service-learning** (Jacoby 2015) course was developed in 2014 to support students and urban farmers in designing appropriate technology for marginalized and resource-poor urban farms. The course, Urban Agriculture and Food Systems Change, was offered to Bachelor of Technology Industrial Design students as a component of their Design Theory 4 and Product Design 4 modules and to Bachelor of Arts Honours Development Studies students in their Participation and Institutional Development module. Urban farmers located at three educational centers in Soweto were identified to take part in the design process. For each site, an interdisciplinary team was assembled that consisted of one industrial design student, between four and seven development studies students, and between three and five local farmers.

The service-learning course was offered to the students with the following learning objectives:

- identify opportunities for technological design through processes of personal immersion and engagement with community partners

- design appropriate technology for resource-poor contexts through collaborative design and social science methods
- critically evaluate the impact of relevant design processes and outcomes

Methodology

The 2014 service-learning course was developed as a direct result of the iZindaba Zokudla multi-stakeholder engagement sessions (see Figure 18.1) (Dubbeling, de Zeeuw, and van Veenhuizen 2010), which began in 2013. The sessions continued in 2014 in conjunction with the service-learning course, resulting in increased articulation and interaction in the complex collective-action project. Broad participation democratized opportunities for developing and refining urban-farm technology, contextualizing and socializing it in the process. Inherent in this methodology was an acknowledgment that technology is part of a local sociotechnical system (Latour 2005), which includes social capital among actors (Malan 2015a), local resources such as land, and city policies (Malan 2015b). This acknowledgment was important to encourage appropriate technological outcomes from the service-learning course (Smillie 2000).

The specific methods used within the service-learning course drew on participatory action research and human-centred design (Campbell 2013; Hussain, Sanders, and Seinert 2010). A step-by-step methodological guide was provided to the students but was sufficiently flexible to encourage improvisation. This methodological guide consisted of three distinct phases: (1) *immersion* in the lifeworld of the farmers (Brand and Campbell 2014; Theron, Wetmore, and Malan 2016); (2) active *engagement* with the farmers; and (3) continual *reflection* on the process (Malan and Campbell 2014).

18.1
iZindaba Zokudla multi-stakeholder engagement session at the UJ Soweto campus. Naudé Malan and Angus D. Campbell, iZindaba Zokudla, Johannesburg, South Africa, 2013.

iZindaba Zokudla (Conversations About Food)

Immersion was encouraged through a range of field visits and theoretical lectures. Engagement was facilitated through different design media, such as drawings, clay, cardboard models, and toys, to enable effective three-way communication between the designers, social scientists, and farmers. Reflection was undertaken using private online student blogs. In each team, the industrial design students were required to focus on the design of the technology, and the development studies students took up roles as team managers, process monitors, and asset and stakeholder mappers.

Learning and Technological Outcomes

Participatory methods enabled students to observe and engage with farmers on each of the sites in order to identify appropriate designs. The process resulted in three prototype technologies over a period of fourteen weeks of teaching time and biweekly field trips to farming sites, farmers' markets, local farming cooperatives, or iZindaba Zokudla multi-stakeholder engagement sessions. The prototypes served as the industrial design students' major project outcome for the semester. The students documented the design process in their blogs, which were integrated with their fieldwork and design development into a final mini-dissertation. The development studies students were required to write four assignments: a contextualization of the current food system in Soweto, their own private reflective blog, a report on their participatory process, and an evaluation of the outcomes of the project.

The three prototype technologies that were realized surpassed all expectations, resulting in the university's Technology Transfer Office provisionally patenting them after the course. They included a self-watering seedling growing system (see Figure 18.2), an off-grid food storage and cooling system (see Figures 18.3 and 18.4), and an off-grid water pump. The seedling growing system was exhibited internationally and included in the publication *Design to Feed the World* (Di Lucchio and Imbesi 2015, 144, 153–4). The off-grid food storage and cooling system has been further validated by an external engineering company, Resolution Circle, to be batch manufactured. This process still continues but is not open to participating farmers to test its appropriateness effectively. Therefore, the water pump was consciously made more accessible. It was documented in an open source manual,[3] which used readily available plumbing components for do-it-yourself manufacture by urban farmers. The manual was printed and disseminated to 150 urban farmers in two of the iZindaba Zokudla engagement sessions and has thus far been viewed seventy times and downloaded thirteen times (Jacobsz, Campbell, and Malan 2014).

The fourteen private student blogs documented the design research process and illustrated how design and societal considerations can be built into technology development. On analysis, it was clear that a methodological structure with defined disciplinary outputs succeeded in meeting the intended learning objectives of the course. Apart from limited interpersonal conflict, students and farmers collaborated amicably.

18.2
Seedling growing system concept discussion at Setlakalana Molepo Adult Education Centre, Jomari Budricks, Angus D. Campbell, and Naudé Malan, Take Root Seedling Growing System for iZindaba Zokudla, Johannesburg, South Africa, 2014.

18.3
Food-storage prototype evaluation with urban farmers from Siyazenzela. Natalia Tofas, Angus D. Campbell, and Naudé Malan, Umlimi Urban Food Storage Unit for iZindaba Zokudla, Johannesburg, South Africa, 2014.

The service-learning aspect of the course led to increased diversity within the student and farmer teams in terms of culture and social class. This was important to encourage appropriate and relevant knowledge outcomes in the postcolonial and postapartheid South African context (Mbembe 2015). Both student groups benefited from learning from each other through collaboration, although depending on team dynamics, some of the development studies students felt that the practical design of the physical technology overshadowed their written theoretical outputs. This conflict required coordination by the lecturers to help bridge the two disciplines.

iZindaba Zokudla (Conversations About Food)

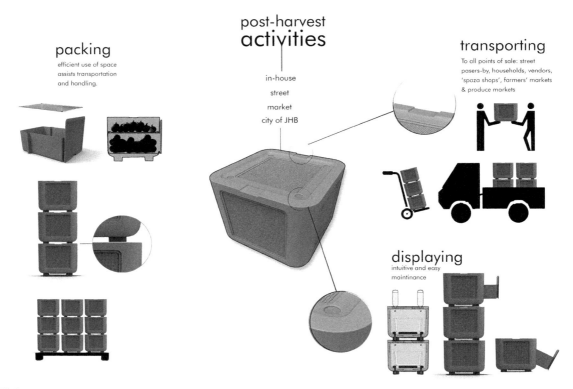

18.4
The evaporative cooled food storage system accommodates the post-harvest activities of food packing, transportation, and display. Natalia Tofas, Angus D. Campbell, and Naudé Malan, Umlimi Urban Food Storage Unit for iZindaba Zokudla, Johannesburg, South Africa, 2014.

Real-world learning, with the associated complexity involved in the interactions between multiple actors, requires sufficient time. The service-learning course somewhat underestimated these time requirements. Even with these shortcomings, the course benefited both the urban farmers, who received more appropriate technology, and the students, who experienced real-world embedding of their own learning—resulting in highly appropriate knowledge outcomes for the next generation of South African citizens.[4]

Notes

1 For more information, see www.designsocietydevelopment.org/project/izindaba-zokudla/ and www.facebook.com/izindabazokudla/.
2 Soweto is a former apartheid nonwhite township on the outskirts of Johannesburg and currently hosts a UJ campus, where the engagement events took place.

3   The open source movement is one where intellectual property is freely shared for broad dissemination; in this case, the manual was licensed under a Creative Commons Attribution-NonCommercial-ShareAlike 4.0 International License.

4   This work is based on research supported by the University of Johannesburg Teaching Innovation Fund and in part by the National Research Foundation (NRF) of South Africa for the Thuthuka, unique grant number 88030 held by Angus D. Campbell and titled, "Designing Development: An Exploration of Technology Innovation by Small-Scale Urban Farmers in Johannesburg," and unique grant number 88059 held by Dr. Naudé Malan and titled, "Innovation in the Soweto Food System: Engaging with Soweto Agriculture." Any opinion, finding, and conclusion or recommendation expressed in this material are that of the authors, and the NRF does not accept any liability in this regard.

References

Brand, Kyle, and Angus Donald Campbell. 2014. "In-Context and Ecology Immersion for Resilience: An Exploration of the Design of a Household Farming Kit." In *Proceedings of the International Union of Architects World Congress: UIA 2014 Durban: Architecture Otherwhere: Resilience, Ecology, Values*, edited by Amira Osman et al., 1332–43. Durban, South Africa: UIA.

Campbell, Angus Donald. 2013. "Designing for Development in Africa: A Critical Exploration of Literature and Case Studies from the Disciplines of Industrial Design and Development Studies." In *Proceedings of the Gaborone International Design Conference (GIDEC) 2013: Design Future: Creativity, Innovation, and Development*. Gaborone: University of Botswana.

Di Lucchio, Loredana, and Lorenzo Imbesi. 2015. *Design to Feed the World: 100 Projects, 50 Schools, 5 Topics*. Milan, Italy: RDesignPress.

Dubbeling, Marielle, Henk de Zeeuw, and René van Veenhuizen. 2010. *Cities, Poverty and Food: Multi-Stakeholder Policy and Planning in Urban Agriculture*. Rugby: Practical Action Publishing.

Hussain, Sofia, Elizabeth B.-N. Sanders, and Martin Seinert. 2010. "Participatory Design with Marginalized People in Developing Countries: Challenges and Opportunities Experienced in a Field Study in Cambodia." *International Journal of Design* 6 (2): 91–109.

Jacobsz, Werner C., Angus Donald Campbell, and Naudé Malan. 2014. *No. 1 in the Izindaba Zokudla Make Your Own Series of DIY Technology Guides: How to Make Your Own Water Pump*. Johannesburg, South Africa: Design Society Development DESIS Lab. www.academia.edu/18855164/No._1_in_the_Izindaba_Zokudla_Make_Your_Own_Series_of_DIY_Technology_Guides_How_to_Make_Your_Own_Water_Pump.

Jacoby, Barbara. 2015. *Service-Learning Essentials: Questions, Answers, and Lessons Learned*. San Francisco: Jossey-Bass.

Latour, Bruno. 2005. *Reassembling the Social: An Introduction to Actor-Network-Theory*. Oxford, UK: Oxford University Press.

Malan, Naudé. 2015a. "Design and Social Innovation for Systemic Change: Creating Social Capital for a Farmers' Market." In *The Virtuous Circle: Design Culture and Experimentation*, edited by Luisa Collina, Laura Galluzzo, and Anna Meroni, 965–78. Milan, Italy: McGraw-Hill Education.

Malan, Naudé. 2015b. "Urban Farmers and Urban Agriculture in Johannesburg: Responding to the Food Resilience Strategy." *Agrekon* 54 (2): 51–75.

Malan, Naudé, and Angus Donald Campbell. 2014. "Design, Social Change, and Development: A Social Methodology." In *Design with the Other 90%: Cumulus Johannesburg Conference Proceedings*, edited by Amanda Breytenbach et al., 94–101. Johannesburg, South Africa: Cumulus Johannesburg.

Mbembe, Achille. 2015. "Decolonizing Knowledge and the Question of the Archive." *Africa Is a Country*. https://africaisacountry.atavist.com/decolonizing-knowledge-and-the-question-of-the-archive.

Smillie, Ian. 2000. *Mastering the Machine Revisited: Poverty, Aid, and Technology*. Rugby, UK: Practical Action Publishing.

Theron, Francois, Stephen Wetmore, and Naudé Malan. 2016. "Exploring Action Research Methodology: Practical Options for Grassroots Development Research." In *Development, Change, and the Change Agent: Facilitation at Grassroots*, edited by Francois Theron and Nthuthuko Mchunu, 317–41. Hatfield, South Africa: Van Schaik Publishers.

19
Building Partnerships and Awareness
Healing an Urban Stream
Brian Gaudio

A large river and its eight subsidiaries run through the city of Santiago, Dominican Republic. These urban streams used to be places for recreation, fishing, and even bathing. Santiago's population has grown in the past fifty years, turning some of these waterways into areas of concentrated poverty with dangerous living conditions. The city also faces serious risk of natural disaster from hurricanes and tropical storms. Low-income communities are often most vulnerable during severe rainfall events, so a US Fulbright Program research project sought to better integrate those communities into the city's disaster-mitigation efforts. This ten-month project, completed at Pontificia Universidad Católica Madre y Maestra (PUCMM), took an interdisciplinary approach to environmental remediation, flood mitigation, and public participation in postdisaster rebuilding.

On November 20, 2012, a torrential downpour hit the city of Santiago, killing three people in a barrio called Yagüita de Pastor (Ponce 2012). Among the deceased was a three-year-old girl who fell in a stream while crossing a makeshift bridge. A young community leader who attempted to save the child also died. The mayor of Santiago held a press conference, stating that he would move the affected families to a safe place and restore the stream to its original state (CDN Channel 37 2012). This never happened. So, in 2016 students from PUCMM's School of Architecture partnered with the US Fulbright program and PUCMM's Center for Urban and Regional Studies (CEUR) to develop a design proposal to bring the community one step closer to recovery. In this case, urban design became a strategy to advocate for a barrio that had been forgotten by local authorities.

Once called "Santiago's campus" because of its public outreach programs, PUCMM had since shifted its focus to building private partnerships. The research project, in a small way, attempted to renew the idea that PUCMM and its students can contribute meaningfully to their city. To graduate from PUCMM, all architecture students must complete two 180-hour internships. The six students who participated on the research team each fulfilled one of the required internships.

Student learning objectives addressed the following:

- synthesize qualitative and quantitative data in field research activities
- understand how to collaborate effectively with community partners
- position design as a tool to advocate for those with limited voices

The project was carried out in two phases, a research phase and a design phase, with the goal of integrating the affected community into the city's environmental resiliency efforts.

Research Phase

The initial research phase began by creating a **basemap** of the neighborhood. Students partnered with the Dominican chapter of Habitat for Humanity to facilitate a **participatory mapping** exercise with thirty residents, who identified businesses, churches, educational facilities, and so on. Students synthesized this information, field-verifying locations during site visits. After establishing the basemap, the interns formed two teams: one investigating qualitative sociocultural issues and the other quantitative environmental issues.

The sociocultural team investigated the barrio's history and partnered with neighborhood teens from the community nonprofit Acción Callejera to conduct interviews with residents. Acción Callejera, which specializes in youth development programs, has worked in the community for over ten years and has a large facility in the barrio. The interviews compared past and present Yagüita, focusing on four important spaces: the park, the stream, the community center, and the school. The teens and architecture students co-created questions, then surveyed twenty-seven residents. This information was translated into two morphological maps: one detailing sectors and land uses in the barrio, the other highlighting a visual history of development (see Figure 19.1).

Through the sociocultural team's research, they learned that Yagüita originated as a repository for people who had been displaced by city infrastructure projects. Yagüita was established in 1950 when Rafael Trujillo, the country's dictator at the time, constructed a monument in downtown Santiago. The thirty families who lived on the site of the future monument were moved to a vacant hillside across the river. By 1960, about 190 families lived in the barrio, and by the 1980s, the population had reached ten thousand (CEUR et al. 1993). According to Juan Parache, Director of Land Use for the City of Santiago, most of the new development occurred in close proximity to the stream despite it being illegal to live within thirty meters of the waterway. Today Yagüita has approximately twenty thousand people. Many of

RESEARCH PHASE

19.1
Morphological maps. Brian Gaudio and research team, Healing an Urban Stream, Santiago, Dominican Republic, 2015.

the newer streets are too small for a garbage truck to pass, and the city has yet to connect a sewage line. Thus, the stream is a repository for waste.

The environmental team tested water quality in the stream and estimated the number of families living in flood and mudslide zones. They referenced the work done by Fundación Dominicana Para la Gestión de Riesgos (FUNDOGER), the city's disaster and risk assessment group. In terms of environmental degradation, FUNDOGER reports that 31 percent of residents living near the stream are served by a garbage truck, while 69 percent use the stream as a dump, and sewage from 49 percent of households flows directly into the water (Peña 2012).

To measure how poor the water quality was, students collected samples from four points along the stream, analyzing them for pH, dissolved oxygen, turbidity, and conductivity. They also brought samples to the local water authority for analysis. Water in the stream was at "code red" levels due to the dangerously high levels of fecal coliform and low levels of dissolved oxygen. At these levels, residents should refrain from coming into contact with the water.

Design Phase

Responsibility for the stream's putrid condition falls equally on the shoulders of city government and residents. Infrastructure alone cannot improve the stream's health; basic environmental education for residents is as important as any physical changes to the stream. At the macro scale, the proposed design outlined 2,200 meters of riparian restoration and erosion control to mitigate flooding and enhance water quality. A microcollection system for trash pickup was designated for areas where roads are too small for garbage trucks. Local *mototaxis* would serve as subcontractors, collecting water cooler–sized waste bins from individual homes and transporting them to trash facilities stationed on the existing garbage route. Pedestrian bridges located at high points along the stream would improve evacuation routes and increase connectivity, while public "soft spaces" along the stream would provide recreation and prevent future residential development in flood-prone areas.

One of those public "soft spaces" was proposed on the site of the collapsed bridge. Today, a bench and a large shade tree sit on the south side of the stream, while three houses remain disconnected on the north side (see Figure 19.2). Dominican Habitat for Humanity met with the three families who live on the north side of the stream and discussed relocating and building new housing for them. The proposal recommends that the land where those houses sit be transformed into a pilot park (see Figure 19.3).

The proposed park's features were derived during a participatory design exercise, in which residents delineated activities and programming they would like to see in the space. The south side of the stream was recommended to become an urban "parklet," with built-in seating for playing dominoes, a patio for barbecues and celebrations, and porous ground cover to reduce runoff. A pedestrian bridge would take visitors across the stream into the approximately twelve-by-fifty-meter

SITE PHOTOS

19.2
Site photos. Brian Gaudio, Healing an Urban Stream, Santiago, Dominican Republic, 2015.

DESIGN PHASE

19.3
Streamside park and urban parklet. Brian Gaudio, Healing an Urban Stream, Santiago, Dominican Republic, 2015.

park. The park would have three distinct spaces: a shaded sitting area, a covered community meeting space, and a small field for unstructured play, all connected by an elevated walkway. Terraced gabion walls would stabilize the soil, and relief channels and berms would offer flood protection. Trees and riparian plants, such as the royal poinciana, would provide shade and help lower the water temperature.

Results

These plans were presented to the affected community, Acción Callejera, FUNDOGER, Dominican Habitat for Humanity, the Rockefeller Foundation's 100 Resilient Cities initiative, and students and faculty of PUCMM's architecture school. The design proposal has not been implemented, and the affected families still live in the line of disaster. The project failed to result in structural changes, but it did build awareness. One architect from Santiago is using the project as a case study for a resiliency plan the city is creating with the US Agency for International Development. Also, one of the six architecture interns designed housing for the families who are still living along the floodplain as her senior thesis. In 2017, Acción Callejera and a team from the University of Florida proposed to work in Yagüita on an environmental education program and a microcollection system. The outcome of this proposed project is unknown.

In the case of postdisaster rebuilding, understanding a place's history, development, and future aspirations can only strengthen the quality of design. When engaging the field experience, it is important to build partnerships with organizations that have already been working on and will continue to work on the issues that the project seeks to address. Listening to residents, analyzing the situation in multidisciplinary fashion, and cultivating the right partnerships can lead to a quality design solution; however, execution of such a design solution may require more long-term commitment and financial resources.

References

Cadena de Noticias Channel 37. 2012. "Sepultan Niña Murió Ahogada en Cañada Hoyo de Elías" (video). Recorded November 21, 2012. www.diariode3.com/sepultan-nina-murio-ahogada-en-canada-hoyo-de-elias/.

CEUR, PUCMM, Programa de las Naciones Unidas para el Desarrollo, and Ayuntamiento de Santiago, eds. 1993. *Proyecto Manejo Ambiental Urbano "Carpeta de Proyectos, Estrategia Barrio Sano."*

Peña, Luis. 2012. *Plan Comunitario de Gestión de Riesgos*. Santiago, Dominican Republic: FUNDOGER.

Ponce, Miguel. 2012. "Inundaciones Dejan Cuatro Muertos y Daños a Viviendas." *El Caribe*, November 20. www.elcaribe.com.do/2012/11/20/inundaciones-dejan-cuatro-muertos-danos-viviendas.

20
Advancing Resiliency
The Huxtable Fellowship in Civic Engagement and Service Learning

Benjamin Peterson

The Ada Louise Huxtable Fellowship at the Boston Architectural College (BAC) promotes design leadership, civic engagement, and service learning across design disciplines. A competitive and selective honors program, the fellowship resides within the BAC's Gateway Initiative and is funded with support from OneWorld Boston and the Cummings Foundation.

As an educational initiative, the Huxtable Fellowship has the following aims:

- mobilize students who have demonstrated an interest in design and community engagement
- facilitate academic and community partnerships, supported by local municipal, nonprofit, and professional organizations
- sharpen the pedagogies of applied learning and refine communication and collaboration skills in the context of public interest design projects
- develop student leaders
- encourage the transfer of skills and experiences through vertical, peer-to-peer mentoring

As an initiative rooted in public interest design and civic engagement, the fellowship reinforces the BAC's commitment to applied learning through collaborative partnerships with Boston's Community Design Resource Center (CDRC) and affiliated nonprofit and community organizations. At its core, the Huxtable Fellowship emphasizes design's utility to foster a community's capacity for meaningful change. The current cohort of diverse, advanced students in both undergraduate and graduate degree programs in architecture developed a program of community-supported outreach and advocacy related to sea level rise and climate change in East Boston.

Advancing Resiliency in East Boston

With a population of over forty thousand densely packed, tightly knit residents, East Boston is uniquely situated to incur the predicted consequences of coastal flooding associated with climate change and sea level rise. The neighborhood is a transport and infrastructure hub, and, as such, agency-based planners have responded to these alarming predictions with the intent to protect city assets (ULI 2015, 9). However, the voices and stories of East Boston residents—long-term dwellers in a classified environmental justice community—have often been excluded from top-down planning agendas of larger, louder stakeholders (Newman et al. 2013, 9).

In partnership with East Boston's Neighborhood of Affordable Housing (NOAH) and the CDRC, the Huxtable Fellows have sought to amplify these often-unheard stories, developing tactics to empower residents to take action and to devise equitable resolutions to their community's specific vulnerabilities.

Learning by Doing: Strategies in Action

To ensure that neighborhood residents have a voice in shaping solutions to their self-identified risks, the Huxtable Fellows have addressed multiple learning objectives:

- identify challenges and verify opportunities through quantitative geospatial research and qualitative ethnographic fieldwork
- provide a foundation for communicating the consequences of sea level rise
- design materials that demystify climate change
- create social cohesion and community consensus through the dissemination of research in public forums

Through these efforts, the fellows uncovered how collaborative planning, focused on replicable and targeted solutions, foregrounds the issue of sea level rise in two ways: as a shared ecological concern and as the impetus for the residents of East Boston to become more resilient collectively.

Design Research: Data as Context

To become trusted allies in community-supported planning efforts, the Huxtable Fellows have oscillated between the roles of the empiricist, data-driven design investigator and the empathetic design listener. East Boston presents a complex and diverse array of conditions that prohibit simplistic design resolutions. As the Huxtable Fellows pursued their efforts, they zoomed in and out of scales, from the macro level of regional ecological, economic, and demographic data to the very micro level of an individual homeowner's dreams and desires. Approaching these complexities as systems has allowed the fellows to recognize patterns, to isolate and synthesize parameters for design prioritization, and to develop tactical and effective approaches to design action curated into accessible, community-vetted, and verified design recommendations.

The fellows began their research in the syntax of percentages, quantities, and geospatial data sets. Confidently, they recited the "facts" to their peers: "In East Boston, the median family income is 58 percent of the statewide median." "Fifty-five percent of East Boston residents do not speak English as their native language." "By 2050, 35 percent of the housing stock in Jeffries Point will be susceptible to flooding." And they visualized this information as articulate—if distant—infographics, maps, and diagrams (see Figure 20.1).

However, while the fellows were canvassing the neighborhoods, a resident in a topographically low street pointed to tattered cardboard covering his grade-level basement windows and stated that at high tides today, he can pick seashells

20.1

After the Huxtable Fellows canvassed East Boston and verified initial findings through in situ meetings with homeowners, they distilled information into diagrams illustrating shared vulnerabilities. Boston Architectural College Huxtable Fellows (Annika Nilsson Ripps, Andres Rincon, David Morgan, Mehran Jahedi, Anna Mezheritskaya, Christine Banister), Huxtable Fellowship in Civic Engagement and Service Learning, East Boston, Massachusetts, 2015.

Advancing Resiliency

out of his dirt-covered basement floor. This encounter immediately humanized the quantitative metrics, and the fellows recognized the need to collect stories. The students used the generated maps, diagrams, and data sets as foundational transcripts for conversations; the quantitative research was enriched by the more qualitative, ethnographic, and narrative data of the social fabric of East Boston. The residents' recollections of storm events, the tangible evidence of prior damage, and the palpable efforts of continued reconstruction supplemented the numbers ascribed to relative scales of vulnerability in East Boston's neighborhoods.

Field Research: Building Consensus Through Engagement

Along with the scientific evidence suggesting East Boston's vulnerability to flooding, other challenges complicate the community's readiness to respond to the complexities of sea level rise and climate change (Kirshen, Ballestrero, and Bosma 2014). The Huxtable Fellows identified issues that included, but were not limited to, the following:

- economically burdened families coupled with high levels of poverty
- linguistic and social isolation
- substantive knowledge deficit related to the climate change science
- overburdened civic organizations and historical lack of organizing support for community-supported planning initiatives
- limited funding for environmental education of residents
- institutional insensitivity to language-related communication challenges

In response, field research became an essential tool both for on-the-ground investigation and as an immediate platform for advocacy and education.

Over multiple weeks, the Huxtable Fellows canvassed East Boston's most vulnerable neighborhoods, developing a system for cataloging existing housing-stock conditions. To clarify initial findings, the students visited with residents in their homes to understand how, where, why, and when water had compromised their living conditions. The information was graphically synthesized (in various languages) as a tool for homeowners and renters to understand concerns and options for future remediation (see Figure 20.2). Research in the field transformed into a service: residents identify the fellows as advocates and knowledge partners and continue to contact the cohort, asking for assessments of their homes and actionable, affordable recommendations for improvement.

Strengthening With Partnerships and Transforming With Capital

The Huxtable Fellows' efforts demonstrate how successful public interest design projects simultaneously galvanize a constellation of stakeholders and catalyze future efforts. The community-supported planning process, developed in partnership with

20.2

The information was graphically synthesized (in various languages) as a tool for homeowners and renters to understand concerns and options for future remediation. Boston Architectural College Huxtable Fellows (Annika Nilsson Ripps, Andres Rincon, David Morgan, Mehran Jahedi, Anna Mezheritskaya, Christine Banister), Huxtable Fellowship in Civic Engagement and Service Learning, East Boston, Massachusetts, 2015.

NOAH, presents a paradigmatic methodology of education, outreach, and action for replicable efforts in other neighborhoods likely to be affected by sea-level rise. The development of an equitable, transparent academic-community partnership has bolstered NOAH's ongoing resiliency-planning efforts. In fact, the Huxtable Fellows have played an important role in demonstrating the effectiveness of NOAH's collaborative efforts, assisting the organization to secure a three-year implementation grant funded by the Kresge Foundation.

The Huxtable Fellowship has been made possible through the generous grant funding of the Cummings Foundation's OneWorld Boston program. Each fellow receives a stipend for participation in the project, with the remaining funding allocated to costs associated with the project's goals, including stipends to support community-member participation in design charettes and community meetings (see Figure 20.3). The fellows have become aware of the catalytic potential of funded work to support or generate other grant funding; multiple funding streams, including the grant recently awarded to NOAH from the Kresge Foundation, not only help guarantee the efficacy of actions but also build capacity among the variety of partners and participants involved in East Boston's resiliency-planning efforts.

Advancing Resiliency

20.3
The Huxtable Fellows orchestrated several community meetings to share findings, generate consensus, and identify priorities for future action. Boston Architectural College Huxtable Fellows, Huxtable Fellowship in Civic Engagement and Service Learning, East Boston, Massachusetts, 2015. Photo: Christian Borger.

Transferring Knowledge and Sharpening Applied Learning Pedagogies

The experience has contributed to the Huxtable Fellows' professional development as they take ownership of their educational and entrepreneurial trajectories. The fellows' tenure has been punctuated by moments of reflective assessment structured as outlets for **metacognitive**, **double-loop learning**[1] to support the continuous refinement of collaboration and communication skills. Each fellow has assumed a mentorship role within less experienced Gateway teams. As "super" teaching assistants, the fellows share knowledge and transfer lessons learned through vertical, peer-to-peer mentoring.

Moreover, the fellowship has cultivated a spirit of self-directed leadership in the realm of public interest design. One fellow is developing a business focused on resiliency retrofitting that aims to educate local contractors in a network of homeowners-consumers who may be affected by rising tides. Another has embarked on a course of research and advocacy exploring resiliency-planning efforts and community engagement in cities affected by similar issues: New York City, New Orleans, and Houston.

At a curricular scale, the fellowship offers an educational experience through applied learning in the civic realm. The fellows have recognized that design thinking and processes situate designers as instigators, facilitators, mediators, and advocates. Moreover, the project identifies complex problems as opportunities for design resolutions that are fortified through engagement with stakeholders in iterative, ongoing processes. Finally, the Huxtable Fellowship reinforces that design leadership requires the ability to communicate and collaborate and the sensitivity to listen, demonstrate empathy, and nurture relationships of trust.

Note

1   *Metacognition* refers to processes of learning that encourage students to think reflectively, and critically, about not only *what* they are learning, but also *how* they are learning. The double-loop learning theory, developed by Christopher Argyris and Donald Schön (1974), uses such critical thinking to evaluate the construction of new knowledges through their application in practice and aims to make decision-making processes more effective through the recognition of productive failures and successes.

References

Argyris, Christopher, and Donald A. Schön. 1974. *Theory in Practice: Increasing Professional Effectiveness*. Oxford, UK: Jossey-Bass.

Kirshen, Paul, Thomas Ballestrero, and Kirk Bosma. 2014. "Adaptation for City Infrastructure: A Case Study of East Boston, Massachusetts." Presentation at EMF Adaptation Workshop: Climate Change and Environmental Justice Communities, Stanford University, CA, July 22.

Newman, Jim (Linnean Solutions), with Sarah Slaughter (The Built Environment Coalition) and Alex Wilson (The Resilient Design Institute). 2013. *Building Resilience in Boston: "Best Practices" for Climate Change Adaptation and Resilience for Existing Buildings*. Boston: Boston Society of Architects. Retrieved from www.massport.com/media/266311/2013-July_Building-Resilience-in-Boston.pdf.

ULI (Urban Land Institute: Boston New England). 2015. *A Technical Assistance Panel Report: Advancing Resiliency in East Boston*. Retrieved from http://boston.uli.org/wp-content/uploads/sites/12/2016/03/Advancing-Resiliency-in-East-Boston-TAP-Report.pdf.

Inclusive Iteration

21
Inclusive Iteration
Participation as Method in Design Theory and Practice
Eduardo Staszowski

A participatory tradition in the history of design is becoming more evident in today's design practice and theory (Bonsiepe 1999). Increasingly, designers are participating in initiatives to address complex environmental, economic, and social issues and are striving to become agents of sustainable change for the public good (Kimbell 2011). From hyperlocal urban issues, such as improving accessibility to municipal services and public goods, to more wicked problems associated with efforts to ensure renewable energy, financial inclusion, or universal health care, a growing number of design-led experiments, practitioners, and pedagogies are convening to challenge the way these problems are framed and solved.[1]

The reality of design as a practice and theoretical paradigm is rapidly shifting. Partnerships involving the public sector, community-based organizations, universities, philanthropies, and commercial associations are adopting methodologies that have been pioneered by designers, such as design thinking and research, human-centered design, and participatory design. The earlier conception of elite designers operating from within the walls of studios inaccessible to many no longer applies. The designer's way of thinking and doing is now distributed, public, collaborative, and practiced in the wild. It is what Ezio Manzini (2015) calls "design, when everybody designs." Designers and nondesigners co-design in search of sustainable solutions and new meanings for everyday life (Penin, Forlano, and Staszowski 2012).

In the midst of this professional and philosophical transformation, designers have found new roles as activists, ethnographers, and social scientists, among others. Designers now advocate for empathy and transparency, as well as build trust among people, environments, and institutions. Designing *with* and not *for* someone is the new axiom that seeks to redefine design by combining expert, tacit knowledge and participation as method, thus transforming the relationship between designers and their clients—a call that is aligned with neighboring disciplines and praxes (Ingold 2013). Designers are blurring professional and disciplinary boundaries, and the process of design, as well as the contexts where it is created, is becoming more open and inclusive (Penin, Staszowski, and Brown 2015).

Despite this optimism and good will, inclusiveness in design is not free of complications. While progress has been made, whether participation will be instituted as a value within design itself is still in question for a number of reasons. Creating truly participatory situations implies shared decision making and the distribution of agency, yet it also implies greater civic engagement, which engenders new challenges and tensions for designers in places often marked by conflict, lack of diversity, protracted social and political processes, and hierarchical structures. As a result, we are seeing projects in which designers and their partners are not only searching for new responses to difficult and novel problems but also designing participatory methods and tools to facilitate the collaborations they are trying to promote.

This section, devoted to the theme "inclusive iteration," sheds light on these developments through the work of design educators who are experimenting with and codifying educational strategies to train future designers to work with a deep sense of and investment in inclusivity within diverse and underrepresented communities. These strategies combine many methods and approaches, such as experience mapping, concept generation, rapid prototyping, evaluation, and negotiation. In an experimental, iterative process, project phases and activities often repeat or overlap, allowing for the disparate needs, motivations, and ideas that exist among the different participants to proliferate and align.

Readers will explore three projects selected to showcase this aspect of pedagogy as it relates to design for the public interest:

- At Lawrence Technological University (pages 189–194), a graduate-level architecture student worked with a nonprofit organization to redesign an interior environment in a way that would contribute to the healing and long-term well-being of individuals recovering from mental illness. The student participated in the development of the community partnership, facilitating the stakeholder engagement process. The comprehensive participatory process that followed included the partner and its clients in the actual construction of the space.
- At Cornell University (pages 182–188), students in interdisciplinary programs on tactical urbanism and creative placemaking worked with a community-based organization in Utica, New York. Focusing on engaging participatory design to propose short-term spatial transformations, the partnership co-created an art and culture festival. The transformations activated ongoing efforts to promote community sustainability and social resilience in the context of fundamental shifts in the experience of work and life.

- At Philadelphia University (pages 195–200), an undergraduate class of architecture, landscape architecture, and interior design students traveled to Johannesburg, South Africa, to develop design proposals for a youth precinct. Collaborating with a broad range of constituents, students built on interviews, investigative site inventories, and asset analyses to conduct a series of community design charettes. Using a pedagogical model grounded in an assets-based approach, the course emphasized the interrogation of otherness and intercultural differences in the context of humanitarian architectural projects.

Note

1 See Public & Collaborative: New York City, http://nyc.pubcollab.org. Public & Collaborative is a program of activities, developed by Parsons DESIS Lab at the New School, to explore how public services in New York City can be improved by incorporating greater citizen participation in service design and implementation.

References

Bonsiepe, Gui. 1999. "Some Virtues of Design." In *Gui Bonsiepe: Interface—An Approach to Design*. Edited by Dawn Barrett, 152–60. Maastricht, Netherlands: Jan Van Eyck Akademie.

Ingold, Tim. 2013. *Making: Anthropology, Archeology, Art, and Architecture*. London: Routledge.

Kimbell, Lucy. 2011. "Rethinking Design Thinking: Part 1." *Design and Culture* 3 (3), 285–306.

Manzini, Ezio. 2015. *Design When Everybody Designs: An Introduction to Design for Social Innovation*. Cambridge, MA: MIT Press.

Penin, Lara, Laura Forlano, and Eduardo Staszowski, 2012. "Designing in the Wild: Amplifying Creative Communities in North Brooklyn." Cumulus Working Papers Helsinki-Espoo 28/12, Publication Series G. 2013, 84–8, Aalto University, School of Arts, Design and Architecture, Helsinki, Finland.

Penin, Lara, Eduardo Staszowski, and Scott Brown. 2015. "A New Generation of Transdisciplinary Thinkers and Practitioners of Design-Led Social Innovation." *Design and Culture* 7 (3): 441–50.

22
"Making" Change *Together*
Rust to Green's Placemaking Praxis

Paula Horrigan

In 2015, Cornell University's Rust to Green (R2G) Capstone Studio (LA 4020/7020) joined forces with the Oneida Square neighborhood in Utica, New York, to co-create the first One World Flower Festival (OWFF), to be held that spring. Since 2010, the studio's professor, Paula Horrigan, has been leading R2G's university–community partnership and teaching its companion capstone service-learning studio. The studio is designed to support the larger R2G New York civic engagement project, also led by Horrigan. R2G aims to catalyze community-driven **placemaking** in upstate New York cities endeavoring to transition from postindustrial "rust" to "green" resiliency (Horrigan 2015). Guided by placemaking (Schneekloth and Shibley 1995) and **democratic civic engagement** (Saltmarsh, Hartley, and Clayton 2009), R2G is deeply rooted in place and, for the past six years, in the city of Utica.

The R2G Capstone Studio emphasizes integration and application of skills and knowledge learned in the landscape architecture major while introducing graduating seniors to R2G's placemaking praxis through undertaking local placemaking projects with Utica partners. The Capstone Studio's 2013 efforts generated the study, "Taking Steps Toward Creative Placemaking: Oneida Square Arts and Culture District" (Horrigan et al. 2013). The study identified ways that **creative placemaking** (Markusen and Gadwa 2010) might drive Oneida Square's integrated environmental transformation—physically, socially, and economically.

The Oneida Square neighborhood anchors downtown Utica's south end and is home to its most diverse population, 38.7 to 51.1 percent of whom are living below the poverty line (US Census Bureau 2016). Oneida Square contains the Mohawk Valley Resource Center for Refugees (MVRCR), the Utica Public Library, and the Munson-Williams-Proctor Arts Institute. In spite of recent physical upgrades, this neighborhood is considered unsafe, socially inactive, and unappealing. Creating an art and culture festival was one of the 2013 study's creative placemaking action ideas. Two years later, R2G's university–community partners moved the idea forward, and in the process, the 2015 R2G Capstone Studio, with eleven students participating, realized the following three learning objectives:

- learn and practice placemaking and democratic community design
- collaborate effectively with others across differences on addressing a local issue, need, problem, or aspiration
- co-create and complete a placemaking project with community partners

Project Goals

The OWFF unfolded as a participatory placemaking process to remake Oneida Square into a safe, inclusive, and welcoming public place. With the festival deadline set for May 9, R2G Capstone Studio students began meeting in early February with the festival planning committee members representing MVRCR, Cornerstone Community Church, Oneida County Health Department, local artists, and Utica schools and businesses. The two staff members of the new Utica-based R2G Urban Studio were on hand to convene the weekly meetings in Utica, which the students in the R2G Capstone Studio attended regularly via Skype.

The following goals were collaboratively developed for the project:

- through the festival, draw attention to Oneida Square's public realm and bring positive energy and affection to a part of Utica currently considered to be unsafe, negative, and neglected
- forge, develop, and expand participation, inclusion, co-creation, and collaboration through all aspects of the festival's making and production to strengthen and build social capital and to catalyze ongoing community-driven revitalization
- expand the visibility and value of art and culture to the neighborhood's sense of place and use art and culture as a primary community development vehicle

Continual dialogue and reflection, which are integral to R2G's approach and process, facilitated progress toward these goals. The R2G Capstone Studio made a total of five trips to Utica, including a weekend-long stay during the festival. Students designed the festival logo and developed its website and social media for disseminating event information, tracking the event as it unfolded, and generating greater participation and buzz. Students also undertook mapping and analyses to assess and develop a festival geography aimed at tactically activating and beautifying the square (see Figure 22.1). Festival elements and programming took shape around the themes of "One World" cultural diversity, flowers, and Mother's Day. A $3,000 grant to the

22.1
R2G Capstone Studio student Zoe Shively, at a community workshop uses a large-scale model to share and generate ideas for the festival's placemaking elements, tactics, and activities. Cornell University R2G Capstone Studio, Utica, New York, 2015.

R2G Capstone Studio from Cornell University's Engaged Learning and Research initiative provided materials for creating low-cost, short-term elements that would spur creativity, experimentation, and new placemaking ideas for Oneida Square. Planning and development over the festival's four-month production period also involved performance programming, obtaining permissions and permits, and overall event promotion and advertising.

The placemaking process fostered widespread inclusion and participation in festival "making" and contributing to the making of change in Oneida Square. Making, an essential and often-underemphasized ingredient of placemaking, fosters community building and the development of a community's social capital (Silberberg 2013).

Festival-planning ideas and prototypes for co-created elements, activities, and programs emerged from three participatory planning and making workshops, which the Capstone Studio organized and cofacilitated. Students made elements such as large sculptural flowers and Aqua-Resin globes, then distributed them to Utica-area youth and artists for further embellishing (see Figure 22.2). Local artists and volunteers designed and assembled other elements, including planters and banners.

Ultimately, the festival's variety of elements and activities arose from the combined efforts of many people and demonstrated the following inclusive iteration strategies:

- undertaking a **dialogic**, community-engaged festival planning and development process through weekly meetings, planning and making workshops, an open

22.2
Sculptural Aqua-Resin globes, seen here being fabricated by Cornell student Sarah Schlichte then painted by a Utica teen, added color and artistry to Oneida Square. Cornell University R2G Capstone Studio, Utica, New York, 2015.

- access website, social media communications, and In Our Backyards (IOBY) fund-raising campaign
- broadening inclusion and participation in "making" through participatory design and making by local artists, youth, adults, seniors, and such groups as MVRCR, Thea Bowman House, Cornerstone Community Church, Fine Arc, Sculpture Space, and Midtown Utica Community Center
- ongoing postfestival placemaking through interviewing and reporting postevaluation; continuing R2G's role in 2016 festival planning; engaging Oneida Square Project in social enterprise business development; continuing neighborhood use of globes, flowers, seats, and planters; and applying for and receiving a 2016 Levitt AMP [Your City] Grant for a free neighborhood summer concert series

"Making" Change Together

Project Results

"It's all about putting some love in Oneida Square," said one attendee as he took in the scene unfolding on May 9, 2015. OWFF created a palpable feeling of optimism for neighborhood residents. By physically and socially transforming the square into an inviting place, the festival took a bold first step in shaping the area's future.

Brightening the square were thirty multicolored planters, designed and constructed by the Cornerstone Community Church's Oneida Square Project. They brimmed with vibrant mixes of newly planted flowers. A team of artists created the sari banners waving from the square's lampposts, and thirty-five giant flower globes, individually painted by area artists and youth, enlivened the sidewalks. A flower-shop mural by Utica high school students brought new life to a derelict building facade. Giant plywood flowers, painted by young and old from the Midtown Utica Community Center and the Fine Arc Day Habilitation program held at the Players of Utica theater, were fashioned into flower totems that appeared to be "growing" throughout the square (see Figure 22.3). Artful custom mosaic trash receptacles found a new home in the square, and their success helped launched a social business enterprise, Oneida Square Public Art and Design,[1] which offers jobs and training in the making of mosaic street furnishings to people with significant barriers to employment.

At the information booth, nearly five hundred crocheted flowers made by seniors during community crochet nights at Utica's Parkway Senior Center were clustered together on a canvas banner so visitors could "pick" one (for free). Local musicians and dancers performed on the sidewalks and in the street. People made use of the 150 flower-topped moveable bucket seats painted by 4-H volunteers and children at the Thea Bowman House after-school program. Giant banners, to be permanently hung on buildings at a later date, portrayed historic seed catalog images and provided a backdrop to a community chalkboard and placemaking station, where Capstone Studio students invited people to share their concerns and hopes for the neighborhood.

While they had originally thought the festival would transform the square for just a single day, the partners quickly changed tack as planning got under way. They decided there needed to be more visible lasting change in the festival's wake. The flower totems, mosaic receptacles, banners, and planters would stay, and a summer watering and maintenance program would keep the flowers thriving. Postfestival feedback particularly emphasized the optimism created by the festival and the positive reception to the many placemaking improvements, which endured. The festival mobilized the community and set in motion creative placemaking and revitalization efforts, including a much-expanded second annual festival and a summerlong free neighborhood concert series the following year.

22.3
Festival placemaking creations, resulting from the three-month-long shared "making" process by university and community partners, ready for assembly and installation in Oneida Square. Cornell University, R2G Capstone Studio, One World Flower Festival, Utica, New York, 2015.

Note

1 For more information on Oneida Square Public Art and Design, see http://oneidasquareproject.com/mosaic-trash-cans/.

References

Horrigan, Paula. 2015. "Rust to Green: Praxis as University-Community Placemaking." *Partnerships: A Journal of Service-Learning and Civic Engagement* 6 (3): 8–28.

Horrigan, Paula, Tarah Brand, Jack Grieshober, Olivia Lerner, Elouise LeVeau, David Torrey de Fresheville, and Yumig Zheng. 2013. "Taking Steps Toward Creative

Placemaking: Oneida Square Arts and Culture District." Report prepared by the Rust to Green Capstone Studio, Cornell University Rust to Green Action Research Project, Department of Landscape Architecture, Cornell University, Ithaca, NY.

Markusen, Ann, and Anne Gadwa. 2010. "Creative Placemaking: A White Paper for the Mayor's Institute on City Design." White paper, National Endowment for the Arts, Washington, DC.

Saltmarsh, John, Matthew Hartley, and Patti Clayton. 2009. "Democratic Engagement." White paper, New England Resource Center for Higher Education, Boston, MA.

Schneekloth, Lynda H., and Robert G. Shibley. 1995. *Placemaking: The Art and Practice of Building Communities*. New York: John Wiley and Sons.

Silberberg, Susan. 2013. *Places in the Making: How Placemaking Builds Places and Communities*. Boston: Massachusetts Institute of Technology. http://dusp.mit.edu/sites/dusp.mit.edu/files/attachments/project/Places-in-the-Making_Executive-Summary-for-web.pdf.

US Census Bureau. 2016. "2009–2013 American Community Survey 5-Year Estimates." Accessed November 14, 2016. http://factfinder.census.gov/faces/tableservices/jsf/pages/productview.xhtml?pid=ACS_14_5YR_S1701&prodType=table.

23
Building User Capacity Through Iterative Processes
Ten Friends Diner

Edward M. Orlowski and Julia Jovanovic

The Activist Architecture and Design Studio (ARC 5824) was conceived in 2007 by Associate Professor Edward Orlowski as a design course for graduate-level architecture, interior design, and urban design students at Lawrence Technological University. Beginning in the fall of 2015, this studio was migrated into the lower-division course work in the Master of Architecture program as a section of Integrated Design Five (ARC 4116): a required course focused on the relationship between architecture and the public sphere.

The class engages students in a dialogue regarding the social, political, and cultural obligations of the design professional. Students apply a model of advocacy design in the face of institutionalized contexts of neglect and economic disadvantage. Participation in the studio, as well as an activist mindset, provides architecture students with an insight into three potential shifts in their views of both their studies and their future careers:

1. The studio presents a pedagogical shift from designer as problem solver to include designer as problem seeker.
2. Engagement with and identification of project constituencies expose students to a definition of *client* that is more expansive than seen in traditional practice; addressing the needs of underserved constituencies is an opportunity for new models of innovative and entrepreneurial practice.
3. Students develop an awareness of the role architects and designers can play in the advancement of the public good and an understanding of how their talents can be brought to bear on environmental issues, community planning, and public policy.

Architecture instructors typically present their students with a design "problem" and give a prescribed building type, program, and physical site to be developed. In the Activist Studio, however, the nature of the problem is unknown at the beginning of the semester, even to the instructor, and is discovered by the student through a sequence of focused assignments and investigations, which encourages intimate engagement with an issue. This close familiarity often results in a personal connection to the cause, which changes the nature of the design approach, transferring the focus from the designer to the client, or constituency. Student Julia Jovanovic's work with the Ten Friends Diner illustrates this shift.

Project Context

In the spring of 2014, Ms. Jovanovic's research largely focused on issues facing children and youth. A staggering statistic indicating high suicide rates among youth in Ontario was uncovered, which directed research toward the topic of mental health. It was discovered that in Canada, one in five individuals has or will suffer from a mental health problem. Mental health care translates to 15 percent of the health-care burden but receives only 6 percent of Canada's health-care budget. Of particular concern was the fact that eleven Canadians per day commit suicide, and 90 percent of these suicide victims have a diagnosable mental health concern.[1]

Her research led Ms. Jovanovic to contact the Mental Health Consumer/Survivor Employment Association of Essex County, which operates publicly as Ten Friends Diner (so named because originally there were ten employees). Ten Friends Diner is a nonprofit organization in Windsor, Ontario, that hires individuals recovering from mental health setbacks, helping them attain the new skills and self-esteem needed to seek permanent employment in the greater community. Many of these **consumer/survivors** (CMHA Ontario et al. 2005) cope with illnesses like schizophrenia, depression, anxiety, and bipolar disorder. Ten Friends Diner is a safe haven for these individuals, allowing them to work while gaining access to peer support and counseling.

Discussions with Ten Friends Diner Executive Director Carolyn Burton revealed a need that could be addressed. Due to budget cuts in 2012, the diner operation was relocated to a different building. The new space, although larger, presented environmental and functional challenges, including poor lighting conditions, deteriorating ceiling insulation, gloomy decor, impeded work flow, high indoor humidity, lack of storage, and disconnected employee areas. These conditions had a direct, significant impact on the well-being and attitude of the consumer/survivors, many of whom suffered from increased anxiety, confusion, and depression. "Our old diner was cozy and warm," one consumer/survivor stated in an on-site interview, "The current diner lacks the home feeling and casts off the sensation of being in an institution. The color is dark and has no welcoming feel." Another noted that "my mood in relation to the old diner was more work effective, brought on happier thoughts and a sense of freedom. I really love the added room in the new diner, but as for motivation, the decor lacks that inspiration."

Project Goals

The main goal for the redesign of Ten Friends Diner was to create a healthy, uplifting, functional environment that would contribute to the healing and long-term well-being of all its occupants. This general goal was refined into specific needs, including redesigning the lighting, fashioning a consolidated work space, reorganizing the work flow, creating additional storage space, mitigating high humidity and deteriorating ceiling conditions, and using the design of the diner to disseminate mental health awareness and inspire future initiatives.

Jovanovic engaged in comprehensive information gathering on a range of mental health topics with various project constituencies through surveys and interviews. Her research included case studies on evidence-based design and how design decisions could affect the physical and mental well-being of users. All research that led to design suggestions was verified with the consumer/survivors, who rejected certain propositions that were anticipated to negatively affect a particular mental health condition.

Project Results

In meetings facilitated by Jovanovic, the consumer/survivors dictated the direction of the design, analyzing their needs and suggesting appropriate solutions (see Figure 23.1). Perhaps the most significant result was that the consumer/survivors felt empowered and inspired to propose design ideas, raise funds, create publicity, and assist in the construction of the project. As required by the course format, Jovanovic maintained a cycle of soliciting ideas from consumer/survivors, presenting design alternatives to all constituencies, recording feedback, and returning with amended proposals for discussion, while documenting and presenting these experiences to her peers. Jovanovic also met the course requirements of using the identification of Social Economic Environmental Design (SEED) Network issues—specifically health, job training, empowerment, and strengthening community—to frame the critical needs of the project and using the **Massive Change story formula** (Bruce Mau Design 2005) to outline the narrative of project engagement.

The community became involved by donating funds, labor, and materials. Volunteers skilled in building trades, marketing, and photography were also critical to advancing the project mission. These donations came about in part because Jovanovic prepared design-vision materials for inclusion in solicitation packages. There were a variety of public and private donors, and the newspaper *Windsor Star* became a primary media partner.

Over the course of several months, the team at Ten Friends Diner raised enough funds to execute the project, addressing all the goals set forth at the conception of the design (see Figure 23.2). While the primary community partners and stakeholders were the consumer/survivors, managers, and customers of Ten Friends Diner, Jovanovic also worked to meet the goals of the Canadian Mental Health Association (CMHA) and the Ontario Ministry of Health and Long-Term Care. Furthermore, the project served as a beacon for other individuals in the Windsor community who suffer from mental health challenges. Finally, Jovanovic

23.1
Preliminary rendering of Ten Friends Diner. Julia Jovanovic, Ten Friends Diner, Windsor, Ontario, Canada, 2015.

23.2
Interior of Ten Friends Diner. Julia Jovanovic, Ten Friends Diner, Windsor, Ontario, Canada, 2015.

self-identified as a stakeholder in the project; she was personally and emotionally engaged in both the process and the impact of Ten Friends Diner.

Jovanovic and Burton collaborated in preparing a written agreement outlining the scope of Jovanovic's design work and the deliverables to be provided by the end of the semester. A portion of each student's final grade depended on meeting such expectations, revealed through assessment by their community partners. Orlowski instituted the requirement of this agreement to provide a sense of closure to the semester; it also allowed for the student and partner to maintain a working relationship after the semester ended, which proved in Jovanovic's case to be ongoing.

Learning Objectives

During the life of the project, Jovanovic met several course learning objectives:

- use statistical and observational tools in research, focusing on identifying a problem, the **ecosystem** that perpetuates the problem, and the affected constituencies
- create and document a participatory design process rooted in professional best practices, demonstrating an awareness of innovative and alternative models of professional practice
- exhibit the ability to engage in inclusive and informed conversations about design in partnership with nonarchitects

23.3
Ten Friends Diner community garden. Ten Friends Diner staff, Ten Friends Diner, Windsor, Ontario, Canada, 2015.

Positive changes were noticed in almost all of the thirty-plus employees of the diner, whose attitude and general well-being significantly improved. Fewer employees missed work or reported heightened anxiety or confusion. As the project was completed, the consumer/survivors were inspired to devise further initiatives, such as a community garden, which was constructed in 2015 (see Figure 23.3).

The successful realization of this project not only created an uplifting, functional environment for healing and business but also directly reinforced the goals of the organization: giving consumer/survivors confidence in their abilities and building their capacity to seek and pursue future opportunities. The design process helped Ten Friends Diner address its programmatic and social objectives.

Note

1 Sources: Statistics Canada, the Ontario Association for Suicide Prevention, and Children's Mental Health Ontario.

References

Bruce Mau Design and the Institute without Boundaries in collaboration with the Canadian Heritage Information Network. 2005. *Massive Change in Action*. Accessed August 23, 2006. www.massivechangeinaction.virtualmuseum.ca (site discontinued).

CMHA Ontario, Centre for Addiction and Mental Health, Ontario Federation of Community Mental Health and Addiction Programs, and Ontario Peer Development Initiative. 2005. *Consumer/Survivor Initiatives: Impact, Outcomes, and Effectiveness*. http://ontario.cmha.ca/public_policy/consumersurvivor-initiatives-impact-outcomes-and-effectiveness/#.WBtm1C0rKpo.

24

Examining Collaborative Efforts to Visualize Community Transformation
Alexandra Youth Precinct Project

Chris Harnish

In 2013, seven undergraduate architecture, landscape architecture, and interior design students from Philadelphia University's College of Architecture and the Built Environment collaborated on a master-plan design proposal for the Alexandra Youth Precinct in Johannesburg, South Africa. To prepare, students completed a two-credit seminar on campus in spring (ARCST 471–1), followed by a one-credit ten-day "short course" (ARCST 471–2) in Alexandra Township.

Sociospatial Contexts

When designers from the Global North engage unfamiliar spatial and cultural contexts in the Global South, essential designer-client relationships and design-problem definitions can be lost in translation. A pedagogical model grounded in **asset-based community design** prepares students to acknowledge and transcend design challenges in these contexts. This model emphasizes research that prioritizes "the diverse factors that affect the quality of human life" (Nussbaum 2011, 14).

This pedagogy also stresses the interrogation of **otherness** (Kapuściński 2009, 13) as an operative factor in the success of cross-cultural design engagements. Too often, well-intentioned public interest architectural projects fall short where people from different cultures engage one another in the shared desire for improved spatial contexts. As designers and educators, we must parse such failures to deliver culturally and formally responsive architecture of significant enduring value in emergent contexts vitally in need of engagement. This pedagogy asks students to confront and transcend cultural boundaries and perceptions in order to be successful in such engagements.

Within the urban boundary of Johannesburg lies the 2.6-square-mile township of Alexandra. The township has long been a spatial manifestation of its nation's complex history, a refuge from and resistance against oppression, and a place of scarcity and insecurity in the face of underdevelopment and undervaluation.[1] Numerous built attempts by outside governmental and nongovernmental organizations (NGOs) to revitalize the Alexandra community have ultimately been underused by local constituents, leading to divisive and debilitating perspectives of design interventions challenging the spatial legacy of apartheid (Swift 1983). To the outside designer wishing to undertake a community-focused development project in Alexandra, the public's wariness forms a complex web—one that must be met with a responsive strategy of authentic community engagement.

Alexandra's 6.4-hectare Youth Precinct is itself a microcosm of these spatial politics and emerging cultural demands. Three community centers, four public schools, and multiple outdoor sports and recreation facilities serve up to 1,500 youth each day. Despite this emphasis on public programming, little consideration was given to precinct planning as a unified whole. The public spaces envelop a series of legally ambiguous private homes, many of which are held by families of original landowners and are still contested today.

Preparatory Seminar

Three primary goals were established for the preparatory seminar. The first goal was to replace students' preconceptions of South Africans with qualitative interpersonal perspectives. Through direct, scaffolded interactions with South Africans over the course of the semester, students came to understand and better interpret cross-cultural relations.

Second, the seminar developed students' understanding of the public interest design methodologies that international groups employ to develop design rationales for humanitarian architectural projects. Students interrogated the design methodologies and outcomes of such projects and presented their findings. The module culminated with presentations of the author's work in South Africa, including one convincing design methodology that nonetheless resulted in a "failed" humanitarian outcome. This humbling dialogue of lessons learned offered students the opportunity to examine and question designed outcomes and to understand the challenges of work in unique contexts.

The third goal was to develop a user-focused research and design methodology for the forthcoming short course in Alexandra. Students tested the model by engaging hypothetical clients in a mock **community design workshop** based on their proposed research methodology. Through this process, students developed research skills and faced the challenges of engaging "others."

On-Site Short Course

The city of Johannesburg and local NGOs prepared the events schedule and recruited participants in advance of the on-site short course. Youth group leaders from the nearby Phutedechaba Community Centre acted as intermediaries between the university students and the precinct's primary user group, Alexandra youth. These youth leaders proved invaluable to establishing a valid dialogue between the students and community stakeholders.

Community participants led a precinct walking tour that successfully initiated authentic human relationships. Students informally engaged participants on positive aspects of their **sociospatial** experience, gleaning specific insights into community perceptions. Students' on-site presence and empathetic attentiveness to constituent testimonies disarmed the prodigiously held community perception of outsiders. Concurrently, students conducted a spatial inventory, quantitatively studying concrete environmental attributes and documenting their findings in notes, drawings, photographs, and video.

Iterative Development and Communication Strategies

Groups gathered in **community engagement workshops** to disseminate the findings, consolidating their insights into concepts that could best summarize shared aspirations for the precinct's future (see Figure 24.1). While these themes may not have revealed specific design solutions, they did "begin close to the ground, looking at life stories and the human meaning" (Nussbaum 2011, 14) of design decisions for real people. The workshops revealed the importance of initiating design from the perspective of human experience, rather than from that of perceived need, and re-formed preconceptions the students may have generated.

Participants designed a text-based mural to communicate the qualitative results of the workshops to the broader Youth Precinct community and to build consensus around the themes that emerged (see Figure 24.2). Over the following two days, participants painted the mural on an exterior wall at the eNtokozweni Community Centre. This experience validated the collegiality of the group, and the mural provided a tangible artifact of Alexandra youth perspective on their community.

Design students then worked in an open-studio setting at the Thusong Community Centre, where participants observed and engaged in the design process. Student-generated design materials including axonometric site drawings and photo montages emphasized clarity and legibility functioning across a diverse group of users. A seven-minute video coproduced with Alexandra youth, particularly resonated with the community constituents. The video and design documents were presented to governmental agencies to heighten awareness of the precinct's condition and to demonstrate the community's capacity to address the issues.

24.1
Community engagement workshop. Alexandra Youth Precinct Project, Alexandra Township, Johannesburg, South Africa, 2013.

24.2
Community mural painting day. Alexandra Youth Precinct Project, Alexandra Township, Johannesburg, South Africa, 2013.

24.3
Community presentation, eNtokozweni Community Centre. Alexandra Youth Precinct Project, Alexandra Township, Johannesburg, South Africa, 2013.

At two points in the process, full-scale community design charettes were held to engage a broad range of constituents in the process; more than fifty people attended each charette (see Figure 24.3). The first charette was presented as a process-based presentation, dedicated to feedback from community members and synthesis of research and design. This process resulted in a diverse range of responses requiring sensitive negotiation and feedback.

Learning Objectives

As a result of this project, students were able to:

- synthesize disparate stakeholder interests
- develop a rigorous and meaningful design proposal focused on the needs and desires of constituencies
- distinguish between complex cultural and spatial contexts

- discover the challenges of community-focused design methodologies while working on-site
- apply methods that incorporate local governing bodies and empower community members

Project Results

The results of this methodology revealed both predictable and insightful design components. Quantitative environmental and security challenges, such as stormwater runoff and poor lighting, were largely predictable and easily solved from the design sense. More nuanced, however, were the qualitative issues of otherness, including contested spatial injustice and poor perception of community-focused architecture based on perceived corruption and hidden agendas by outside governmental forces. As the most critical design issues raised by stakeholders, these perceptions also revealed the necessity for empathy, research and interpretation, and effective feedback loops between constituents and designers in such an in situ practice. This process helped students comprehend the problem of paying attention only to the quantitative in neglect of the qualitative.

The project results were similarly compelling on-site. Heightened awareness of precinct users' needs, assets, and capacities occurred at the neighborhood scale, resulting in community-driven cleanup efforts, improved security measures, and representation in local politics. Governmentally, the proposal resulted in the Johannesburg Development Agency (JDA) implementing the design. Streetlights, sidewalks, and landscaping are now in place, and circulation has been redirected to the proposed route, solving community members' concerns over private property. The JDA is incorporating the Youth Precinct into its designs for a bus rapid transit network and transit-oriented development strategy. The precinct is now a node of cultural development and will be strengthened by these future plans.

Note

1   Field research, May 2013.

References

Kapuściński, Ryszard. 2009. *The Other*. Brooklyn, NY: Verso Books.
Nussbaum, Martha. 2011. *Creating Capabilities: The Human Development Approach*. Cambridge, MA: Harvard University Press.
Swift, Jon. 1983. *Alexandra, I Love You: A Record of Seventy Years*. Braamfontein, South Africa: Future Marketing and Alexandra Liaison Committee.

Evaluating Student Learning

25
Evaluating Student Learning
Engaging Experience to Create Agents of Change

Nadia M. Anderson

The projects presented in this section demonstrate how public interest design courses can be transformative components of professional design education. They expand not only student learning but also professional practice and university–community relationships by creating what Ernest Boyer (1996, 20) describes as "a special climate in which the academic and civic cultures communicate more continuously and more creatively with each other." These courses require evaluation methods that document students' abilities to operate in social contexts with nonexperts and to facilitate social processes, going beyond design pedagogy's typical focus on acquisition of professional knowledge and skills as evidenced by design products.

Because it involves students in work with nonprofessional community partners, publicly engaged design pedagogy is a key area for articulating process-oriented evaluation methods that "think about how people co-create situations of *usefulness* for particular ideas and ways of being/doing" that are part of an "ongoing process of experience" (Cooks and Scharrer 2006, 53). They further demonstrate how these courses influence students' understanding of the role of design in shaping power relationships. They see themselves as agents of change not because they are doing good, but because they break down societal positions about who gives and who receives knowledge and service. Engaged design courses also present opportunities to assess how projects and courses affect community partners and how they contribute to building university-community partnerships. These elements of evaluation articulate the impacts of public interest design pedagogy beyond the classroom, showing its significance within design disciplines in creating opportunities for expanded models of practice.

As all engagement activities are inherently about **partnership**—acting *with* rather than *for* community partners—assessment of engaged design learning must acknowledge the relational nature of this learning. This kind of learning is not an individual activity, but rather "a communicative process ... which cannot be separated from the experience of its occurrence" (Cooks and Scharrer 2006, 44). "By situating learning in the relational and contextual processes through which people make meaning" (45), engaged pedagogy creates opportunities for students to learn to challenge ideas of identity, power, and culture embodied in the built environment. In engaged design courses, the focus of evaluation systems must shift away from technical competency and assistance in favor of "student reflexivity—the recognition of one's location with respect to others and how this affects the production of knowledge and power" (Rios 2011, 125).

In public interest design practice, partnerships between designers and communities replace the expert-client structure of professional relationships with a relational structure in which each partner contributes knowledge and expertise that the other lacks, transforming the relationship from one of patronage or service to one of mutual collaboration. Engaged courses provide opportunities for students to learn in this kind of environment and therefore must be evaluated in terms of how well they create this environment, in addition to how well students learn to think in this way. In other words, evaluating the course itself is part of evaluating student learning. Do students see themselves, as a result of the course, as dialogical people participating in mutual exchange with others, or do they see themselves as individuals separate from others? Achieving the former is requisite for fulfilling the transformative potential of engaged design pedagogy.

Evaluating publicly engaged design courses and their effects on students, community partners, and institution-community relationships is a complex undertaking that requires attention and creativity. Ideally, a combination of evaluation methods is needed to document the range of impacts that these courses can have. Documenting numbers and types of participants in courses, as well as the demographics of the communities involved, demonstrates both the wide-reaching impacts of the courses and their complexity, which extends far beyond the logistics of typical design studios. Quantitative measures are not, on their own, enough to capture the impacts of public interest design courses. Qualitative methods are needed to demonstrate relational and process-based learning, describing participants' feelings and experiences in their own words.

Engaging with communities can provide design students with valuable experiences, but as philosopher John Dewey (1938) notes, experiences alone are not necessarily educational. Structured **reflection**, a key element of service-learning pedagogy, asks students to pause and evaluate their experiences, making connections between the more abstract concepts introduced in course work and the specific experiences acquired through engagement (Hatcher and Bringle 1997, 153–4). Reflections are also valuable as learning evaluations, revealing what students have learned through course experiences and how this learning has affected their understanding of design and its role in society.

The information collected through different evaluation methods can inform larger curricular structures by demonstrating the important roles public interest design courses play in expanding students' understanding of design processes and practices, as well as designers' roles in society. This section presents three examples of how student-learning evaluation supports the transformative capabilities of these courses:

1. The Gateway Initiative program at The Boston Architectural College (BAC) is evaluated statistically, documenting an extraordinary number of students and projects affected by the program. Introduced early in the curriculum, the CityLab and Community Practice courses instill reflexivity in students. Ongoing student reflection and portfolio evaluation throughout the curriculum underscore the BAC's institutional commitment to "understanding design as a social practice" (pages 206–213).
2. The Roche Health Center in Tanzania (pages 214–219) provides an example of the impacts of a complex multiagency and multiyear project on students and local communities. Evaluation of previous decisions is embedded in each stage of project development and associated curricula alongside outside assessment by the Clinton School of Public Service. This combination allows the project to constantly evolve while also documenting the project's positive effects on the community at specific points in time.
3. Students involved in the partnership between Iowa State University and the Iowa Correctional Institution for Women (pages 220–225) reflected on their experiences through surveys designed to reveal how their attitudes changed as a result of the course, illustrating the power of what Abbilyn Miller (2014, 151) calls "the radically engaged classroom." This kind of class, according to Miller, engages issues of profound inequity, creating the potential to break down inequalities on "personal, interpersonal, and structural" levels.

Evaluation of public interest design courses is multi-faceted and complex. It nevertheless needs to be an integral part of these courses and the projects they engage. By demonstrating the impacts of public interest design pedagogy on students and community partners, evaluation also demonstrates the relevance of engaged design in breaking down university/public boundaries and expanding the scope of design practices.

References

Boyer, Ernest L. 1996. "The Scholarship of Engagement." *Journal of Public Service and Outreach* 1 (1): 11–20.

Cooks, Leda, and Erica Scharrer. 2006. "Assessing Learning in Community Service Learning: A Social Approach." *Michigan Journal of Community Service Learning* 13 (1): 44–55.

Dewey, John. 1938. *Experience and Education*. New York: Touchstone.

Hatcher, Julie A., and Robert G. Bringle. 1997. "Reflection: Bridging the Gap between Service and Learning." *College Teaching* 45 (4): 153–8.

Miller, Abbilyn. 2014. "The Politics of Radical Pedagogy: Transforming Power and Seeking Justice." In *Community Matters: Service-Learning in Engaged Design and Planning*, edited by Mallika Bose, Paula Horrigan, Cheryl Doble, and Sigmund C. Shipp, 151–66. Oxford, UK: Routledge.

Rios, Michael. 2011. "Operative Sites for Dialogue and Reflection: The Role of Praxis in Service-Learning." In *Service-Learning in Design and Planning: Education at the Boundaries*, edited by Tom Angotti, Cheryl Doble, and Paula Horrigan, 125–36. Oakland, CA: New Village Press.

26
Assessing Experiential Learning in Design Education
The Practice Department at the Boston Architectural College

Bethany Lundell Garver

Pioneering public interest pedagogy and practice, the Boston Architectural College (BAC) is the oldest **cooperative education (co-op)** program in architecture in the United States. Founded in 1889 by patrons of the Boston Society of Architects and the Massachusetts Institute of Technology, the BAC emerged as a movement "broadening ... the possibilities of architectural training" (Brown 2014, 11), making design education more accessible by allowing students to practice in local offices while simultaneously pursuing course enrichment. From the start, the spirit of public interest design has been integral to the BAC's curriculum, proving to be a sustainable learning tool for aligning design education with ongoing changes in the field.

Scarcely any architectural education models support students in pursuing continuous full-time work while in school (Salama 2015). The BAC, by contrast, has long-standing relationships with design firms, public agencies, and nonprofit organizations who serve as faculty, mentors, and employers for students. Through flexible **work-based learning**, the college offers the only accredited degree-granting programs in the country that complement academic course work with structured qualitative and quantitative assessment of parallel cooperative education. In this way, the community becomes the BAC's extended campus, resulting in 97 percent of graduates being employed in their design fields on graduation day, with many holding leadership positions (The BAC 2016). Thirty-four percent of baccalaureate graduates come from underrepresented populations in architectural education (Cox, Matthews, and Associates 2016).

Learning Model

The Practice Department is a practice-meets-academy environment (Harriss and Widder 2014, 43) that supports the disciplines of architecture, interior architecture, landscape architecture, and design studies as a vital educational component of the BAC. The department itself does not confer degrees; rather, it administers a required curriculum of applied learning cultivated outside the classroom that aligns with process-oriented evaluation. This aspect of the overall curriculum is commonly referred to as the **practice component**.

The Practice Department model encompasses four strategies: *P*artnerships, *R*eflective assessment, *A*pplied learning, and *C*areer support. Using David Kolb's (1984) Experiential Learning Model as a framework, the department promotes public interest design through a lifelong cycle of "concrete experience, observation of and reflection on that experience, formation and synthesis of abstract concepts based on reflection, and active experimentation that tests the concepts in new situations" (Jacoby 2014, 6). The model leverages a multifaceted learning-doing curriculum to build a more productive school-community-profession relationship that prepares future designers for lives of civic responsibility and service (Brown 2014).

Upon completion of Practice Department requirements, students achieve skill levels that reflect integration and synthesis of their academic studies within work-based learning settings. Students will be able to:

- make connections across disciplines among experiences outside the classroom by showing an enhanced ability to broaden perspective and build on prior learning to take on increasingly challenging problems
- exhibit organized preparation and confident delivery of a compelling message with a variety of supporting materials (graphics, written descriptions, and self-reflection) to increase audiences' knowledge and understanding
- collaborate across and among myriad contexts and organizations to accomplish a clear sense of civic identity, independent initiative in engagement activities, and collaborative commitment to community goals

These experiential learning outcomes are measured through students' accumulation of **practice hours**, written and graphic portfolio evidence, and one-on-one **practice assessment** meetings with Practice Department faculty (see Figure 26.1). A sustained high rate of student employment in the competitive field of design is an illustrative metric for evaluating the effectiveness of the model.

Partner Evaluations

The Gateway to Practice Initiative demonstrates how the Practice Department model matches student learning with Kolb's (1984) concept of "concrete experience" that supports real-world issues. Gateway projects are voluntary and progress over two

26.1
This matrix reflects a sequence of requirements for the practice component of each degree program that the Practice Department develops and administers; adapted from a self-assessment matrix in Gelmon, Agre-Kippenhan, and Cress (2013, 169)

Practice Department Requirements and Learning Outcomes Matrix

	New Student	Beginner	Engaged	Advanced
Timeline of Reflective Assessment	Broadly introduced during new student orientation	One-on-one Practice Assessment (PA) scheduled during Community Practice course at the end of the Foundation curriculum	Every student signs up for one-on-one PA appointment prior to thesis preparation	Every student signs up for one-on-one PA appointment prior to graduation
Practice Hours (required minimum)	Some students are eligible to receive credit for prior practice hours	Architecture (0) Interior (0) Landscape (0)	Architecture (2,200) Interior (450) Landscape (600)	Architecture (3,000) Interior (900) Landscape (900)
Skill Level	N/A	Awareness and Understanding	Integration	Synthesis
Experience	None or partial (may have prior practice experience)	Foundational	Some	Deep
Personal Development	Attention on self	Awareness of self in broader context	Linked to others	Big picture
Reflection	None or partial	Broad	Related	Deep and integral
Connection to Community	Individual benefit	Responds to relevant local issues and identifies community assets	Linked to community in a personal way	Facilitates new opportunities for expanded community linkages
Transdisciplinary Approach	Focused on self	Willingness to make personal decisions that reflect awareness of others	Acknowledges appreciation and respect for others	Finds new connections and adapts naturally to others
Professional and/or Civic Engagement	Unknown	Active participant	Organizes next steps and manages tasks	Initiates action on design projects and/or social justice issues
Capacity to Work on Design Teams and with Diverse Communities	Unclear	Partial and directed	Responds to requests that develop context-appropriate action	Imaginative, motivated leader

Source: Bethany Lundell Garver, the BAC Practice Department, Boston, Massachusetts, 2016

semesters. The initiative gives students an opportunity to connect community needs with societal concerns. As multidisciplinary undergraduate and graduate student teams prepare programmatic and schematic design proposals for community-based clients, they simultaneously accrue practice hours. The weekly time commitment for Gateway projects ranges from ten to twenty hours for each student.

Community partners evaluate students' attitudes and designs during presentations, workshops, and written critiques, commenting on how each team's goals and outcomes address community needs and benefit the client's mission. Following students' asset-based designs, feasibility studies, or on-site field observations, clients assess how teams exhibited ethical reasoning, integrity, and professionalism regarding diverse cultural factors. With encouragement from Practice Department faculty, clients offer open dialogue and honest feedback on group efforts, broadening students' interpersonal communication and conflict-resolution skills by exercising their ability to express differing ideas and values respectfully. Evidence of these experiential learning outcomes is enclosed in students' required portfolios.

Since 2008, 1,300 BAC students have engaged in more than one hundred sponsored Gateway projects, resulting in a combined effort surpassing fifty years of full-time work (The BAC 2013). In 2015, the program launched the Ada Louise Huxtable Fellowship for students specifically focused on design in environmental justice neighborhoods. Overall, Gateway builds student capacity to generate future opportunities for inclusive community decision making. These student-community partnerships impart self-confidence and reflection on the impact of design in underrepresented places otherwise unable to attain design services (see Figure 26.2).

Reflective Assessment

One-on-one practice assessments facilitate evaluation of students' work-based experience in specific knowledge areas. To gauge student performance, the Practice Department model relies on partnerships between educators, students, and employers, which are formalized through **Student Learning Contracts** (SLC). The SLC calibrates specific competencies, including critical thinking, presentation delivery, and technical skills. Competencies related to public interest design—such as social interaction, human-centered design, intercultural knowledge, and teamwork—are also measured (see Figure 26.3).

Students report their hours in work-based and applied-learning settings. Then, progress is noted on their academic transcripts, and their compiled portfolio evidence is reviewed in practice assessments. This formal assessment process promotes institutional awareness of students' progress, incremental self-reflection, and identification of skill-development needs relative to students' specific interests.

Applied Learning and Career Support

Abstract concepts of public interest design are distilled into two credit-bearing classes administered through the Practice Department that are required for undergraduate and graduate students in all disciplines: CityLab (FND1006/3006) and Community Practice (FND2007). These foundation courses utilize applied learning projects to expose students to design stewardship and civic engagement *early* in their education (see Figure 26.4). They also introduce students to reflective practice

26.2
Select examples of Gateway to Practice Initiative partnerships at the BAC from 2008–2016.

BAC Gateway to Practice Initiative (Gateway) Community Partners **

- OneWorld Boston
- Boston Society of Architects *
- Asian American Civic Association/Boston Redevelopment Authority (AACU/BRA)
- Allston Village Main Streets,
- American Legion Marsh Post #442
- Arlington Children's Theater
- Belmont Housing Authority
- Benjamin Franklin Institute of Technology
- Boston Chinatown Neighborhood Center *
- Boston Green Academy
- Boston Parks and Recreation
- Boston Public Schools *
- Boys and Girls Club of South Boston
- Boston Redevelopment Authority (BRA); Boston Planning and Development Agency (BPDA) *
- Brockton 21st Century Corporation
- Catherine Aragon
- Charlestown Municipal Garden Association
- Children's Cooperative Montessori School
- Church of the Covenant *
- Citizen Schools *
- City of Boston Mayor's Office *
- Codman Academy *
- The Community Design Resource Center of Boston (CDRC) *

- Division of Capital Asset Management & Maintenance *
- Department of Neighborhood Development *
- Design Museum Boston
- Dorchester Community Food Co-Operative
- Egleston Square Main Streets
- Fair Housing Center of Greater Boston *
- Fenway Community Development Corporation
- First United Parish of Everett
- Four Corners Action Coalition
- Four Corners Main Streets
- Franklin Park Zoo
- Friends of Lake Cochituate *
- Friends of Modern Architecture
- Friends of Modern Architecture Lincoln
- Girl Scouts of Eastern Massachusetts
- Greater Grove Hall Main Streets
- Greater Love Tabernacle Church
- Hale Reservation *
- Hawthorne Youth and Community Center *
- Higginson/Lewis School
- Higher Ground
- Hosmer School *
- Housing Assistance Corporation of Cape Cod *
- ImprovBoston
- Innercity Weightlifters

- Juniper Gardens Condominiums
- Long Way Home
- Maimonides School *
- Massachusetts Department of Transportation (MassDOT)
- Metal Oxygen Separation Technologies
- Metro West Collaborative Developers
- Metropolitan Waterworks Museum *
- Mission Hill K-8 School
- New Brook Farm, Inc.
- New England Conservatory
- Neighborhood of Affordable Housing, Inc. (NOAH) *
- Nuestra Comunidad
- PJ Kennedy School *
- Roca Chelsea
- Roxbury Community Cultural Arts Center
- Salvation Army Harbor Light
- Somerville Community Growing Center
- Stonybrook Neighborhood Association
- Students 4 Students
- Town of Ashland *
- Town of Hamilton Recreation Department
- Transition House
- Triangle, Inc.
- United Neighborhood Design Alliance
- Viet AID
- West Branch Somerville Library
- William E. Carter School *
- William Monroe Trotter Institute at UMASS Boston
- Women's Lunch Place
- YouthBuild Boston
- Zoo New England

Source: Bethany Lundell Garver, the BAC Practice Department, Boston, Massachusetts, 2016

26.3
Student Learning Contract categories and competencies evaluated by the BAC Practice Department.

BAC Student Learning Contract (SLC) Competencies

Core Competencies			Concentration Tracks		
Conceptua-lization	Professional Values and Organization	Representation Tools and Techniques	Public Interest Design, Service, and Research	Practice Management and Design Entrepreneurship	Design Implementation and Project Delivery
• Critical thinking • Investigation, inquiry and analysis • Creative thinking • Problem solving • Programming and feasibility • Site/existing conditions analysis • Use of precedents, reading and research • Social interaction and human-centered design • Intercultural knowledge and competence • Environmental stewardship and global learning • Integrative and applied learning	• Written communication • Oral communication and presentation delivery • Information literacy • Ethical reasoning, integrity and professionalism • Personal time management • Conflict resolution • Interpersonal skills • Teamwork and collaboration • Leadership and service	• Model building and fabrication • Building information modeling • 2D and 3D CAD drafting • 3D illustrative rendering • Web, graphic, or interactive design • Raster and vector image editing • Manual drafting • Freehand sketching • Diagramming	• Mentoring • Teaching and conducting workshops • Civic engagement, service and volunteerism • Writing for grant proposal or design publication • Design competitions • Research project (ideate, document, publish) • Attend community or professional lectures, conferences • Committees and student groups • Professional and community organizations	• Business practices and operations • Team building • Stakeholder roles • Budgeting and accounting • Schedule and work plan development • Project management • Bidding and contract negotiation • Marketing support • Market research	• Planning, zoning or permitting regulations • Schematic design and design development • Engineered systems (service, structural, environmental) • Financial considerations and project cost • Codes and regulations • Technical and construction documents • Material, lighting, FF&E selection • Specifications • Construction administration and observation

Notes:

1. Competencies are evaluated using portfolio evidence gathered by each student and reviewed during scheduled Practice Assessment appointments. Students' practice portfolios exhibit Understanding/Awareness (beginner), Integration (engaged), and Synthesis (advanced) in targeted SLC competencies.

2. Competency-based metrics are adapted from Value Assessment of Learning in Undergraduate Education (VALUE) rubrics from the Association of American Colleges and Universities, National Council of Architectural Registration Boards (NCARB) knowledge areas, Council of Landscape Architectural Registration Boards (CLARB), National Council for Interior Design Qualification (NCIDQ), and Social Economic Environmental Design Network (SEED) principles.

Source: Bethany Lundell Garver, the BAC Practice Department, Boston, Massachusetts, 2016

through pre-course and post-course self-evaluations, portfolio documentation, and preliminary in-class practice assessments.

Career support is offered through Practice Lab, the department's online job database, in addition to advisory meetings with dedicated career services staff, workshops, job fairs,

26.4 Students in the Practice Department's CityLab Intensive course discuss design stewardship in the Rose Fitzgerald Kennedy Greenway with YouthBuild Boston program manager Alex Ho. Bethany Lundell Garver, the BAC Practice Department, Boston, Massachusetts, 2016.

networking events, and annual student employment surveys. Students pursue work-based opportunities that target SLC knowledge areas. Since the Practice Department only approves practice hours accompanied by regular supervisor evaluations, the model also builds closer relationships between students, supervisors, and mentors.

Practice-Meets-Academy Public Interest Futures

Transdisciplinary in nature, the Practice Department reinforces the value of uniting different design disciplines through an intellectual, practical, mission-driven framework that goes beyond a singular perspective. Underscoring the role of designers as collaborators with multiple stakeholders, students learn to become citizens in dynamic, diverse places. By providing a structure for satisfaction of practice-oriented degree requirements via transcript notation, the model shows where, when, and how high-quality public interest design principles are learned. More importantly, it articulates a range of ways for public interest design to fit in the institutional context. This gives students the opportunity to reflect on public interest design engagements the same way they might reflect on more traditional work in design firms, allowing them to examine the relationship between the two with deeper understanding (see Figure 26.3).

By framing public interest design alongside other forms of professional practice, the Practice Department seeks to break down perceptions of *alternative* versus *mainstream* architecture and design-related fields. Accessibility of this type of education inculcates the importance for students, educators, and practitioners to consider more extensive issues that architectural practice can address.

In contrast to "subjective, elitist, ideological, and master-apprentice models [that] still control many architecture studios" (Salama 2015, 9), the Practice Department model shows how creative cooperation in the spirit of design stewardship takes precedence over self-aggrandized individualism. Given its historically significant roots, the model realizes the educational effectiveness of applied learning outcomes combined with rigorous assessment, portfolio evidence, and a foundational curriculum for understanding design as a social practice. Above all, the model proves that excellence in design education can instill a deep, long-lasting culture of collaborative learning that is responsive to environmental and social interests best addressed through an inclusive (rather than autocratic) approach.

References

The BAC. 2016. "BAC in Brief: Fast Facts About the Boston Architectural College." Accessed August 15, 2016. http://the-bac.edu/about-the-bac/bac-in-brief.

The BAC (Boston Architectural College). 2013. "The Gateway Initiative: Annual Report and Recent Projects." http://the-bac.edu/Documents/Departments/Practice/2013/Gateway_Initiatives_final_10.24.2013.pdf.

Brown, Don Robert. 2014. *Designed in Boston: A Personal Journal-History of the Boston Architectural College*. Boston: Boston Architectural College.

Cox, Matthews, and Associates. 2016. *Diverse: Issues in Higher Education*. Accessed August 15, 2016. http://diverseeducation.com/.

Gelmon, Sherril B., Susan Agre-Kippenhan, and Christine M. Cress. 2013. "Beyond a Grade: Are We Making a Difference? The Benefits and Challenges of Evaluating Learning and Serving." In *Learning Through Serving: A Student Guidebook for Service-Learning and Civic Engagement Across Academic Disciplines and Cultural Communities*, edited by Christine M. Cress, Peter J. Collier, and Vicki L. Reitenauer, 163–77. Sterling, VA: Stylus Publishing.

Harriss, Harriet, and Lynnette Widder. 2014. *Architecture Live Projects: Pedagogy into Practice*. New York: Routledge.

Jacoby, Barbara. 2014. *Service-Learning Essentials: Questions, Answers, and Lessons Learned*. San Francisco: Jossey-Bass.

Kolb, David A. 1984. *Experiential Learning: Experience as the Source of Learning and Development*. Englewood Cliffs, NJ: Prentice-Hall.

Salama, Ashraf M. A. 2015. *Spatial Design Education: New Directions for Pedagogy in Architecture and Beyond*. Farnham, UK: Ashgate.

27
Merging Research, Scholarship, and Community Engagement
Roche Health Center

Michael Zaretsky

In 2007 the Roche community (a village of approximately five thousand residents in Tanzania) identified a critical need for a permanent health-care facility. Most people in this region had to walk several hours to access health care. Residents asked the nonprofit Village Life Outreach Project (VLOP) to collaborate on the project. The Roche Health Center (RHC) opened April 1, 2011, and that summer, a two-month external **assessment** of the project studied the impacts of RHC on the Roche community. The assessment concludes:

> [t]he community fully supports the health center, and it is the preferred provider of health care in Roche. The community has taken ownership of it and is proud to be host to the health center. ... Their inclusion in the process of planning, building, and evaluating has helped them take ownership in the project and expect only the best.
>
> (Lucker 2011)

The RHC project emerged as a result of nonprofits, universities, and individuals working together over many years. The project is one of many collaborations between the following partners: VLOP, a Cincinnati-based nonprofit; Shirati Health, Education, and Development (SHED) Foundation, a nongovernmental organization in Tanzania; University of Cincinnati (UC) faculty and students; the Clinton School of Public Service at the University of Arkansas; and residents of three villages in Tanzania—Burere, Nyambogo, and Roche.

VLOP merges research, scholarship, pedagogy, and outreach based on a set of community-engagement principles. Through partnerships, VLOP seeks to improve

27.1
Testing a photo voltaic panel with the RHC committee. Michael Zaretsky/Village Life Outreach Project, RHC, Roche, Tanzania, 2011.

quality of life, health, and education for the residents of rural Tanzania. Tanzanian villagers identify challenges that can be addressed in partnership with VLOP, SHED, UC, and others. UC faculty employ the research and teaching resources of a Research I university to address these issues. These resources include cross disciplinary design, engineering, and social science research to inform design decisions (see Figure 27.1).

VLOP members use several principles when teaching and doing work related to any global project. These principles translate to the following learning objectives in UC courses that engage students with communities in Tanzania:

- assess inherent power imbalances and inequities between Western and non-Western communities, as well as power imbalances within cultures
- evaluate who is benefiting from the design and construction projects
- relate and apply reciprocal learning in context
- analyze cultural, social, economic, constructive, and climatic conditions of work areas
- apply knowledge of existing conditions to all design and construction decisions
- incorporate principles of **appropriate technology** by using materials, tools, and techniques that local residents can replicate
- create meaningful partnerships with local residents and nonprofit partners in all aspects of research, design, and construction
- create design and construction proposals that are informed by the desires of the local community and contextual conditions
- assess all design proposals on their cultural, social, economic, and technical value for the communities with whom we are working

RHC Teaching

Working with other UC faculty, Arup engineers, SHED, and members of the Roche community, students in three RHC graduate architecture studios (ARCH713) explored, developed, tested, and assessed design proposals for the RHC complex between 2008 and 2011. The first studio, in 2008, developed a master plan, infrastructure plan, building system, and clinic designs. In addition to the studio, an external committee consisting of architecture and engineering students, faculty, and practitioners, including engineers at Arup Chicago through the Arup Cause,[1] explored the technical challenges of the inherent design conditions given a lack of electricity, water shortages, minimal availability of materials, few local contractors, and economic limitations.

Students in the following studio, in 2009, further developed the clinic plans and details. The third studio, in 2011, explored the public edge of the complex along the street, conducted a **post-occupancy evaluation** of the clinic, and researched alternative construction methods that could be implemented in the construction of the medical-staff housing.

A subsequent UC Honors course, Humanitarianism: Design Thinking across the Disciplines (SAID3010H), taught in 2011, 2013, and 2015, brought together students from across the university to study and critique humanitarianism and aid to Africa. Students explored how design thinking could provide a relevant approach to humanitarianism for all disciplines and developed projects to be implemented in Tanzania.

Project Assessments

Ongoing assessments and evaluations of previous decisions have informed every step of the RHC project. VLOP has partnered with the Clinton School of Public Service for project assessments since 2010. Spencer Lucker, Masters of Public Service candidate at the Clinton School, spent two months assessing the RHC project through interviews, surveys, data analysis, and observation. The evaluation provided data that covered four areas: demographics, service delivery, community satisfaction, and public opinion. Lucker (2011) stated in the community-satisfaction assessment that "every person who was asked if it [RHC] were an important part of the community either agreed or strongly agreed (seventy-nine out of seventy-nine community members)."

Students from the Humanitarianism course learned about RHC through observations, drawings, and interviews with villagers, patients, and medical staff.[2] This learning led to discoveries of additional needs that had to be addressed to improve the comfort of patients while they were waiting or being examined, such as the need for more seating in the waiting area for family members of patients. Medical-housing construction, which was also influenced by design changes identified in the student assessments from UC and the Clinton School, began in early 2015.

The most important assessment of RHC comes from ongoing dialogue with SHED and the Roche community. The community knows that the project partners are committed and will leave only when the community indicates that they are no longer needed. During a March 2016 visit, villagers pointed out maintenance issues in the clinic that will affect the design of future buildings. For example, the oversized gutter, designed to show villagers how their roofs could be used for water collection, had been repaired several times due to the lack of caulking materials in the region. This knowledge led to a redesign of the gutter, which was implemented in the medical housing.

The clinic does not resemble other buildings in the region, though it is built with local materials and tools (see Figure 27.2). Designing a building that looks different from other buildings in the area was a risk. However, it has been verified many times that the community is proud of this project. They are proud that people come to visit RHC, and they recognize its value beyond its function as a clinic: it is a meeting place for the community (see Figure 27.3).

Pedagogical Outcomes

The student course evaluations for the RHC studios were very positive, with the majority of students stating that this course "made a strong contribution to my education overall."[3] There were several positive comments, such as the following:

27.2
Construction at RHC clinic. Michael Zaretsky/Village Life Outreach Project, RHC, Roche, Tanzania, 2011.

27.3
RHC committee members meeting. Michael Zaretsky, RHC, Roche, Tanzania, 2015.

> This course was extremely successful in the integration of realistic challenges and conditions with the studio curriculum. One of the most successful components of the course was exposing students to these challenges and letting them figure out decisions through trial and error, collaboration with other professionals, and collaboration amongst their studio colleagues.

This type of feedback supports the pedagogical intentions; however, one challenge was that most students in the studios did not actually get to engage the community with whom they were designing.

Two architecture students at UC, Emily Roush Elliott and Jesse Larkins, have completed cooperative (co-op) internships in Tanzania with VLOP. Elliott spent her co-op in Tanzania leading the design and construction of the health clinic in 2010. She returned to UC to complete her Masters of Architecture degree; her thesis was "Avoiding Imposition Through Methods of Making," situated in Roche, Tanzania. Elliott went on to become the first UC student to be awarded an Enterprise Rose Architectural Fellowship. She is already recognized as a future leader in public interest design.

Elliott and her husband started a firm in the Mississippi Delta, and the other VLOP co-op participant, Larkins, began working for their firm immediately following his graduation. Elliott, Larkins, and many other students are testaments to the impact of hands-on public interest design projects within education.

Notes

1. The Arup Cause (www.arup.com/about_us/making_a_difference/communities_and_causes) is a global initiative that exists to reward and encourage Arup's community-centered and educational activities.
2. The students' post-occupancy evaluation was developed using the approach outlined in Preiser et al. (1988).
3. This quote and the following taken from UC course evaluations of RHC design studios, fall 2008, 2009, and 2011.

References

Lucker, Spencer F. 2011. "Evaluation of Roche Health Center, June–August 2011." Evaluation, Clinton School of Public Service, University of Arkansas, Little Rock, AR.

Preiser, Wolfgang F. E., Harvey Z. Rabinowitz, and Edward T. White. 1988. *Post-Occupancy Evaluation*. New York: Van Nostrand Reinhold.

28
Reflecting Through Razor Wire
The Environmental Justice in Prisons Project
Julie Stevens

The Environmental Justice in Prisons Project (EJPP) provides landscape architecture and design students with opportunities to engage the often-misunderstood prison population by working directly with incarcerated individuals and prison staff to design and build therapeutic and productive outdoor spaces. A long-term partnership between the Iowa State University (ISU) College of Design and the Iowa Correctional Institution for Women (ICIW), EJPP uses design/build to expand the social capacity and develop the vocational skills of both students and incarcerated women. No classroom experience or book can provide life lessons and skills like a few months on the front lines, as is evident in the student reflections throughout this chapter.

Between 2011 and 2016, five courses and three design/build projects were completed with ICIW:

Multipurpose Outdoor Classroom (2013)

The ICIW warden selected the first design/build project: a multipurpose outdoor classroom located in a one-acre space at the heart of the new campus. The outdoor classroom was developed in partnership with counselors and women in the intensive treatment programs at ICIW. Three classrooms, a lawn mound, and an aspen grove provide opportunities to bring counseling and classroom activities outdoors, a stark contrast to the bleak building interiors (see Figure 28.1).

28.1
The Multipurpose Outdoor Classroom looking east through one classroom to the lawn mound and aspen grove where students and incarcerated women are working. Environmental Justice in Prisons Project, Iowa State University and the Iowa Correctional Institution for Women, Multipurpose Outdoor Classroom, Mitchellville, Iowa, 2013–2014.

28.2
One crew blurs the lines between students and incarcerated women to create a healing garden for women with special needs. Environmental Justice in Prisons Project, Iowa State University and the Iowa Correctional Institution for Women, Special Needs Healing Garden, Mitchellville, Iowa, 2015.

Staff Decompression Area (2014)

A second project, the Staff Decompression Area, was inspired by watching ICIW staff and officers gather in the parking lot to "decompress" between shifts. This multileveled brick patio was located near the staff entrance, outside the secure perimeter.

Reflecting Through Razor Wire

Special Needs Healing Garden (2015)

Project three, a Healing Garden for women with special needs is designed for individual or small group counseling or respite from mental fatigue. It is located near the health-care building with views and access from the acute and sub-acute mental health units. In addition to the Healing Garden, the crew also established the first production garden, approximately one acre in size (see Figure 28.2).

Reflection as Evaluation and Validation

Reflection is the "intentional consideration of an experience in light of particular learning objectives" (Hatcher and Bringle 1997, 153). Reflection in community engagement is not only a method for assessing student learning but also a means for understanding how the experience has helped to expand students' moral and social capacities.

> When reflection activities engage the learner in examining and analyzing the relationship between relevant, meaningful service and the interpretative template of a discipline, there is enormous potential for learning to broaden and deepen along academic, social, moral, personal, and civic dimensions.
>
> (Hatcher, Bringle, and Muthiah 2004, 39)

Working in a prison is intense, and there is little time to think about the social, emotional, and physical energy flowing between people and the project at hand. Students often are unaware of what they have learned or are unable to articulate their expanded perspectives until they have had some distance from their learning experiences. Therefore, "reflection acts as a bridge between conceptual understandings and concrete experiences" (Felten, Gilchrist, and Darby 2006).

Free writing is used to collect reflections from students in real time, in their most authentic voices. Specific survey questions allow for comparing and contrasting students' experiences. "Through reflection, the community service can be studied and interpreted, much like a text is read and studied for deeper understanding" (Hatcher, Bringle, and Muthiah 2004, 39). These reflections, when shared with the Iowa Department of Corrections (IDOC) and ISU officials, validate continuing and expanding the partnership.

The student reflections quoted throughout this chapter describe the impacts of this partnership. Responses were gathered via a survey of past and current students; the responses were anonymous, as directed by ISU's Institutional Review Board. All students who responded reported a significant shift in their perceptions of incarcerated people.

> Prior to this experience, I felt that all people incarcerated were hardened criminals who were constantly serious and angry. Afterward, I realized many

> of the women in the prison are victims of their own upbringings. ... I definitely viewed these inmates more sympathetically than I did before.

Building Gardens and Social Capital

EJPP is challenging the notion that healthy environments are an amenity rather than a necessity by creating gardens in prisons to improve the health and well-being of incarcerated women and staff. Helphand (2006) summarizes our deep connection to the natural landscape, illustrating why it is essential: "From the long evolutionary perspective, our landscape preference and experience is that of a 'survivor landscape,' one that ultimately sustained life. It's part of what makes us human" (213). EJPP aims to shift tightly held beliefs by listening to the concerns and desires of both prison staff and incarcerated women, educating our community partners about the benefits of access to healthy landscapes, and then building understanding by constructing therapeutic outdoor spaces.

Former ICIW warden Patti Wachtendorf often referred to this partnership as a win-win: the students gain real-world experience, and the prison an improved landscape. More importantly, this winning combination creates understanding and empathy between students and incarcerated people.

This result is not exactly what students were looking to gain when they signed up for a design/build project in a prison. The survey asked students to reflect on what they *hoped* to gain and what they *actually* gained from working with EJPP. Most respondents expressed a desire to gain professional experience with design and construction. Many were candid about wanting a great portfolio project, giving them an advantage over students entering the profession having never planted a tree or built a stone wall. EJPP provides opportunities for hands-on learning, and it does stand out in a portfolio.

> It helped me get a job right out of college at a great firm. The project was extremely unique and gave my interviewers a lot to speak about during my interview.

The following comment represents a common shift in students' priorities from a purely personal agenda to a concern for the greater good:

> Through interaction with IDOC staff and offenders, I gained a deeper understanding and profound respect for the rehabilitative nature of the programs at ICIW. ... It is easy to think of prisons as solely punitive places, meant to separate offenders from the rest of society, but learning about these facilities showed me the emphasis placed on lowering recidivism rates, addressing mental health and/or substance abuse issues, and giving offenders professional and personal skills necessary to successful lives after incarceration.

Learning Outcomes and Project Results

There are the obvious outcomes: physical interventions completed through three complicated design/build projects and the addition of a production garden program. The project has also had often-unseen impacts on students and incarcerated women working side by side to create beautiful spaces in a landscape typically void of life. The women report feelings of accomplishment and pride in providing beautiful gardens and healthy food to fellow residents. Students learn to negotiate power struggles, security protocols, and challenges inherent in any construction project. The real lesson students learn, though, is that few people have access to the benefits of well-designed, healthy environments (see Figure 28.3).

The following three learning objectives represent years of revisions based on the deeply engaged nature of this partnership. Earlier learning objectives were more basic and less meaningful, such as "describe principles of **biophilic design**." The learning objectives now emphasize engagement and social change through design/

28.3
Students adjusted to on-site variables. With time, they learned to consult the entire crew—students and incarcerated individuals alike. Environmental Justice in Prisons Project, Iowa State University and the Iowa Correctional Institution for Women, Multipurpose Outdoor Classroom, Mitchellville, Iowa, 2013–2014.

build, the results of which are apparent in the student reflections that follow each learning objective.

1. Examine personal ethics when working with diverse populations, especially those incarcerated.

   "I think it sets a new precedent for designing environments that heal rather than intimidate or diminish."

2. Develop a restorative and productive prison program *with*, not *for*, the community and client, using intentional design and physical interventions.

   "The greatest impact of this partnership is that it is indeed a partnership, involving ISU, facility staff and wardens, and incarcerated women. If the projects used only design knowledge, security rules, or offender experience, they would not be as strong, but the collaboration builds ownership among all groups. This maximizes impacts and keeps the discussion optimistic and oriented toward restoration and rehabilitation."

3. Translate design concepts into reality through the construction of studio projects, including supervising a construction site, securing materials, handling budgets, and managing client expectations and team dynamics.

"As a designer within a relatively large landscape architectural firm, I am able to navigate the various parts of projects (schematic design, design development, construction documentation, construction observation, etc.) easily because I have seen an entire project come to fruition. My colleagues and managers can trust me to understand a variety of tasks and how they should be completed."

The quotes throughout this chapter represent students' general sentiments over the six years of partnership with ICIW. The very nature of working inside a prison comes with lessons embedded in every wall, path, and planting bed. These reflections affirm that designing and building are vehicles for social understanding and progress.

References

Felten, Peter, Leigh Z. Gilchrist, and Alexa Darby. 2006. "Emotion and Learning: Feeling Our Way Toward a New Theory of Reflection in Service-Learning." *Michigan Journal of Community Service Learning* 12 (Spring): 38–46.

Hatcher, Julie A., and Robert G. Bringle. 1997. "Reflection: Bridging the Gap Between Service and Learning." *College Teaching* 45 (4): 153–8.

Hatcher, Julie A., Robert G. Bringle, and Richard Muthiah. 2004. "Designing Effective Reflection: What Matters to Service-Learning?" *Michigan Journal of Community Service Learning* 11 (Fall): 38–46.

Helphand, Kenneth. 2006. *Defiant Gardens: Making Gardens in Wartime*. San Antonio, TX: Trinity University Press: 213.

Part 3

SEED Academic Case Studies

29
The SEED Process for Academia
Lisa M. Abendroth and Bryan Bell

The nine case studies featured in Chapter 30 offer insights on project-based research and engaged learning. The collection is presented through a consistent framework that allows for comparison and contrast between project profiles and highlights core pedagogical concerns including teaching strategies. Each narrative introduces a project codeveloped between academic and community partners. Some projects are effective short-term efforts bound within one or two semesters. Others reveal the rewards and challenges inherent in the long-term evolution of work with the same partner over time and beyond the confines of an academic schedule. Projects demonstrate the delivery of educational content in community-based contexts. They also exhibit the variety of public interest design pedagogies present across disciplines of design.

Projects were selected by the editors for inclusion in this section from the peer-reviewed international call for project submissions in Part 2. As part of the case study development process, the educators responsible for each project completed the SEED Evaluator as documentation of that project. To generate a useful case study format, the SEED Evaluator creates a common lexicon for the reporting of pedagogy and practice, "process and purpose" (Saltmarsh, Hartley, and Clayton 2009, 6)[1]—a blend which emerges in these projects as students and faculty work collectively with communities beyond the traditional confines of the campus. The following are among one standardized set of documented elements for each project: primary social, economic and environmental issues addressed, the community-based challenge, pedagogical goals, project results, and learning outcomes. An emphasis on teaching strategies illustrates how educators are leading collaborations between partners and students toward specific goals. Project-specific learning objectives[2] provide a tangible connection between teaching strategies and learning outcomes. (Please refer to Appendix A in Part 4, pages 318–327, for an index of learning objectives cross-referenced across chapters from Part 1, Part 2, and Part 3 of this publication.)

The SEED process creates a common means for project documentation and comparison. Originally created as a tool to help converge the community-based interests of stakeholders and design teams, the SEED Evaluator has evolved over time[3] and is being adapted in a variety of contexts including those directed around public interest design education. An online tool available through the SEED Network, it is "an interactive software program that provides a protocol to help guide, document, evaluate, and communicate the social, economic, and environmental outcomes of design projects" (SEED Network 2017). Its embedded methodology constructed around community-identified concerns (driven by participatory practices, design research, and measurement of outcomes) cross-referenced with primary and secondary social, economic, and/or environmental issues can help direct students and educators through benchmarks relevant to any public interest design project. Iterative project phases and the combination of evidence in the form of descriptive writing and supporting documentation offer a much-needed framework for students[4] and those new to community-driven processes.

Notes

1. Saltmarsh, Hartley, and Clayton (2009) argue for "purpose and process" as being fundamental to the specific activity of "democratic engagement," a form of engagement where "democratic values" evinced at all levels of academia, for example, can motivate systemic transformation (6).
2. Bloom's *Taxonomy of Educational Objectives* (1956) has informed the project-specific learning objectives presented in these case study project profiles. The taxonomy represents six levels within the realm of cognition which can synchronize educational methods for identifying goals and assessing learning through curriculum. The levels, which grow in complexity of reasoning, address "(1) knowledge, (2) comprehension, (3) application, (4) analysis, (5) synthesis, and (6) evaluation" (18).
3. The first iteration of the collectively authored SEED Evaluator with software developed by Eric Field was first introduced at the 2010 Structures for Inclusion conference hosted at Howard University.
4. See the case study entitled "A Social Approach to Design" (pages 243–248) where the project faculty adapted aspects of the SEED Evaluator in order to guide student inquiry and project analysis in an interior design seminar.

References

Bloom, Benjamin, ed., Max D. Engelhart, Edward J. Furst, Walker H. Hill, and Davis R. Krathwohl. 1956. *Taxonomy of Educational Objectives: The Classification of Educational Goals*. New York: D. McKay Co., Inc.

Saltmarsh, John, Matthew Hartley, and Patti Clayton. 2009. *Democratic Engagement White Paper*. New England Resource Center for Higher Education. Accessed February 10, 2017. http://repository.upenn.edu/gse_pubs/274.

SEED Network. 2017. "SEED Evaluator 4.0." Accessed February 10, 2017. https://seednetwork.org/seed-evaluator-4-0/.

30
SEED Academic Case Studies
Lisa M. Abendroth and Bryan Bell

A. Design in Partnership With the Lama Foundation
B. Pleasant Street Pedestrian Project
C. A Social Approach to Design
D. Cooperative Education at the Detroit Collaborative Design Center
E. Com(m)a
F. The Farm Rover
G. On Site: Public Art and Design
H. South of California Avenue
I. With Sacramento

Case Study A
Design in Partnership With the Lama Foundation

Design in Partnership With the Lama Foundation is an educational alliance that has resulted in a series of scale-appropriate small structures designed and built by students for seasonal use at a community-based nonprofit organization.

Project-Specific Student Learning Objectives
- develop real-world design skills that are responsive to community-based client needs
- manage differing project needs inclusive of budget, schedule, and environmental efficiency
- experiment with hands-on construction techniques and building practices

Summary
The Program in Environmental Design at the University of Colorado Boulder (CU Boulder) has introduced an alternative to the undergraduate advanced course experience. Third-year architecture, planning, landscape, and design studies majors are provided a series of praxis options—courses that promote interdisciplinary engagement outside the classroom working with community-based partners. Taken as co-requisites in the spring semester, the Lama Foundation Design/Build Studio (six credits) and Seminar (ENVD 3300, three credits) has been offered since 2013 and is one of the pillars of the praxis options (CU Boulder 2017). A separate summer studio (ENVD 3200, six credits) realizes the build component of the extended project. Over the past four summers, students pursuing an emphasis in architecture and community engagement have constructed three small cabins and a bathhouse, all ranging from approximately 93 to 250 square feet at the foundation.

Issues Addressed
Social: Education, Strengthening Community; *Environmental:* Environmental Sustainability

Community-Based Challenge
Located in Questa, New Mexico, the Lama Foundation (LF) is a "spiritual community, educational facility, and retreat center" committed to spiritual education and practice (Lama Foundation 2018). Named after the Spanish community Lama that settled the territory, LF aligns sustainable stewardship of the land with a deep respect for communities and traditions of practice (Lama Foundation 2017). Since the 1996 Hondo fire that ravaged the complex, this intentional community has lovingly reconstructed the center facilities to reflect the ideology and mission of their

30A.1
Interior of the Sky Hut. ENVD junior level praxis students, Sky Hut, Questa, New Mexico, Spring–Summer 2015. Photo: Stephen Cardinale.

work. The accommodations built by CU Boulder students are part of a tradition of environmental stewardship and green construction, core values embedded within the center and its community.

LF has a need for low-impact green infrastructure that embraces the principles of permaculture. New structures need to be fire resistant and rodent proof and reside off the grid. The design and construction of three dwellings and a recently added bathhouse reinforce the sensibilities of the organization and the people it serves: stewardship, service, and deep respect for the earth are fundamental. Students and faculty cultivate an appreciation of the goals and practices of the Lama community in order to translate them into functional, aesthetic designs that reflect this sustainable community and its community of practice.

Pedagogical Goals
Students combine studio course work with a seminar that supports a holistic approach to engaged learning. In the design phase, each project is developed primarily on campus during the sixteen-week spring semester. The course then shifts into a five-week summer session with emphasis on constructing the project on-site. Providing students with the full scope of a design/build practice environment

30A.2
Exterior of Buff Hut. ENVD junior level praxis students, Buff Hut Questa, New Mexico, Spring–Summer 2013. Photo: Stephen Cardinale.

30A.3
Tour of a New Mexico earthship community, 2016, Taos, New Mexico.

30A.4
Architectural model, rendering, and completed showerhouse. ENVD junior level praxis students, Koh Haus showerhouse, Questa, New Mexico, Spring–Summer 2015. Site Photo: Stephen Cardinale.

in a capstone course brings together many desirable skills, including developing construction documents, creating schedules, and estimating budgets, while infusing the project with a functional understanding of sustainable design. Students gain a tangible sense of materials through hand-manipulated outcomes. Each student has a chance to be a leader in at least two team-based tasks (lighting and door construction, for example).

Select Teaching Strategies
- **Site visits**: Students travel on two occasions to the site during the design phase of the project: in January for social and cultural exchange and again in April for the construction of the building foundation. These four-day trips allow the students to get acquainted with the center, stakeholders, and surrounding natural conditions. LF members travel to Boulder mid-semester to review final designs and select a final concept, identifying one design for summer implementation. These mutual activities develop rapport while also building trust between students and the leadership of the Lama community.
- **Working on-site**: Students can enroll in the summer design/build studio to take their design concepts through to implementation. Working at the foundation in the Sangre de Cristo Mountains of New Mexico provides a unique opportunity for students to understand the technical and cultural challenges embedded in the locational context of design/build.
- **Living on-site**: Students camp on-site for an average of twenty-one days each summer during the building phase. During this time, they share in the communal lifestyle of the center and participate in community activities such as daily meetings, meal preparation, and meditation. Living together as a cohort without the distractions of modern life helps students focus on the intentions of the community-based problem.

Project Results and Learning Outcomes
The spring semester ends with students creating a set of construction documents before the summer build phase. Prior to transitioning to the site during the summer, students spend two-and-a-half weeks on campus in prefabrication, construction prototyping, and assembly tasks. Students are exposed to a full range of tools and ways of working through woodworking, computer numerical control (CNC) routing, welding, and laser cutting. Because students are responsible for interior and exterior design/build considerations, the on-campus time allows for experimentation with fabrication and finishing details. The on-site build phase supports formal and informal learning, allowing students to teach and learn from one another while working and living together. Students from previous summers also regularly mentor current students and introduce new or learned concepts. Each year since 2013, an average of sixteen students have participated in the summer construction hosted at the foundation. The Buff Hut (2013), Heiwa Hut (2014),[1] Sky Hut (2015), and KohHaus

30A.5
Construction of the Sky Hut deck. ENVD junior level praxis students, Sky Hut, Questa, New Mexico, 2015. Photo: Stephen Cardinale.

indoor-outdoor bathhouse (2016) were each designed and built over a seven-month scheme.

Partners: Lama Foundation; University of Colorado Boulder Program in Environmental Design

Credits: CU Boulder: senior instructor, Jade Polizzi; adjunct instructor, Stephen Eckert; students, 2013, 2014, 2015, and 2016 Lama Foundation Design/Build Studios and Seminars

Note

1   See Eckalizzi Design's website (www.eckalizzi.com/#!/projects/teaching) for documentation, including images and videos from the 2013 Buff Hut and 2014 Heiwa Hut design/build projects.

References

CU Boulder. 2017. "Praxis." University of Colorado Boulder Program in Environmental Design. Accessed March 30, 2017. www.colorado.edu/envd/program-information/community-engagement/praxis.
Lama Foundation. 2017. "Detailed Information." Accessed January 15, 2017. www.lamafoundation.org/about/12-detailed-about.
Lama Foundation. 2018. "About Lama Foundation." Accessed March 28, 2018. www.lamafoundation.org/about-lama-foundation/.

Case Study B
Pleasant Street Pedestrian Project

The Pleasant Street Pedestrian Project reimagined and transformed underused, sometimes derelict, public spaces into pedestrian-friendly environments that promote community inclusion and empowerment.

Project-Specific Student Learning Objectives
- analyze factors contributing to the inclusion or exclusion of a range of stakeholders in the design process
- create engagement tools that generate site-specific discourse
- use full-scale prototype designs to inspire social and pedestrian activity

Summary
Formerly located within the University of Cincinnati (UC) Research Institute, MetroLAB is a UC School of Architecture and Interior Design (SAID) program established to promote "learning through the process of making, applied research and innovation, and community engagement and impact" (UC DAAP 2018).[1] The graduate architecture course Advanced Integration Studio (ARCH 7005) is a MetroLAB public interest design offering in the College of Design, Architecture, Art, and Planning. In the summer of 2015, course faculty and fourteen students partnered with the Corporation for Findlay Market (CFFM) in the Pleasant Street Pedestrian Project,[2] one of several college-wide initiatives with CFFM to energize community voice along Pleasant Street—a neighborhood vulnerable to development in the heart of Cincinnati. The project launched what was to become a series of faculty- and university-led efforts over the next year to realize the benefits of community inclusion in the built environment.

Issues Addressed
Social: Gathering Spaces, Empowerment, Crime and Safety

Community-Based Challenge
Located just two miles from the UC campus, Pleasant Street encompasses four diverse city blocks connecting the recently redeveloped Washington Park in the south with the historic Findlay Market[3] in the north.[4] It is a corridor in transition, mixing newer condominium development with existing residential and rental properties, as well as many vacant lots. Considered an anchor in the community, CFFM sponsored this initiative to identify and foster social-impact projects that promote community interests. These interests emerged as the social issues previously identified.

Pedagogical Goals
The project's primary goal was to cultivate thoughtful, responsive forms of community engagement that encompassed local residents and organizations

30B.6
The first Pleasant Street event featuring neighborhood mapping. MetroLAB, Pleasant Street Pedestrian Project, Cincinnati, Ohio, 2015.

30B.7
The first Pleasant Street event featuring a photo wall. MetroLAB, Pleasant Street Pedestrian Project, Cincinnati, Ohio, 2015.

(including representatives from several neighborhood organizations), commercial stakeholders, and CFFM (Kern 2016). This goal was accomplished through a variety of instructive pedagogies applied to the creation of three temporary community-outreach events, each corresponding to a phase in the design process. These events were hosted in empty lots on Pleasant Street, which were cleared and improved for this purpose. Produced by the students, each event promoted a distinct objective supporting qualitative data collection. The first event championed getting-to-know-the-community activities such as photo booths, a video-interview station, and neighborhood mapping. Attendees were encouraged to respond to prompts that began to define neighbors' collective place-based interests. The second event included participatory cooking demonstrations, playscapes for children, and lighting installations—activities that brought people together to share ideas and observations. The third event presented design prototypes responding to community input collected at previous events.

30B.8
Construction of Pleasant Street Parklet. MetroLAB, Pleasant Street Pedestrian Project, Cincinnati, Ohio, 2016.

SEED Academic Case Studies

Select Teaching Strategies[6]
- **Learning through making**: The Pleasant Street Pedestrian Project leveraged incremental and to-scale development of concepts that evolved directly from stakeholder feedback. Early in the process, students activated underutilized public spaces, using discarded materials as a viable way to engage community. Discovering that empty lots could not be transformed into permanent gathering spaces, students explored alternative concepts and adapted to the evolving design restraints through iterative making.
- **Applying design research**: Design research was instrumental to experiencing generative project development. Students applied newfound understanding of community-identified challenges obtained through observations, interviews, events, and charettes, and they executed designs with knowledge of materials and construction research. Testing supported design and development, and the results were incorporated into design recommendations and prototypes.
- **Activating community**: The primary goal of the summer session was to activate neighborhood discussion and identify shared public-space interests through sponsored community events (Kern 2016). This strategy was furthered when the Cincinnati-based organization Design Impact hosted a community engagement workshop for students focused on the concept of empathy building, helping to ground understanding of inclusive design. A temporary studio near Pleasant Street offered regular contact between the students and nearby residents.

Project Results and Learning Outcomes
The community's desire for a pedestrian-friendly streetscape directed the MetroLAB students to develop a solution that bridged several considerations, including the need

30B.9
Pleasant Street Parklet at night. MetroLAB, Pleasant Street Pedestrian Project, Cincinnati, Ohio, 2016.

for safe and socially inclusive gathering spaces. Students introduced the design for a *parklet*—a broadening of the sidewalk into one or more parking lanes—at community meetings in 2015, where it garnered enthusiastic support. Students temporarily installed four full-scale prototypes at parking locations on Pleasant Street in early July. The celebration associated with these installations became the conclusive vehicle for collecting valuable stakeholder feedback. In spring of 2016, eleven of the original fourteen students returned to conduct an independent study focused on the construction of the final parklet design. The Pleasant Street parklet was built under a revocable street privilege between the city and CFFM, which required that the structure be modular and allow for disassembly, if needed. The parklet was installed May 29, 2016, with no predefined programming beyond that provided by the community, which will direct its use over time.

Upon conclusion of the summer session, students had acquired new skills in participatory practices and demonstrated agile ways of directing engagement processes that were responsive to the community context. Collaborating with diverse stakeholders, who often had differing views, revealed the complex reality of working in the public interest. Students were exposed to the full scope of project

30B.10
Pleasant Street residents playing chess in the parklet. MetroLAB, Pleasant Street Pedestrian Project, Cincinnati, Ohio, 2016.

SEED Academic Case Studies

30B.11
View of Pleasant Street Parklet from across the street. MetroLAB, Pleasant Street Pedestrian Project, Cincinnati, Ohio, 2016. Photo: Bob Schwartz.

development predicated on community-driven desires and were subsequently challenged to innovate within these parameters.

> **Partners**: University of Cincinnati College of Design, Architecture, Art, and Planning; Pleasant Street Committee; Corporation for Findlay Market; People's Liberty; Pleasant Street residents; Over-the-Rhine Community Housing; Over-the-Rhine Community Council; City of Cincinnati Department of Transportation and Engineering
> **Credits: UC**: MetroLAB studio director and professor, Michael Zaretsky; SAID professor and structural engineer, Tom Bible; students, summer 2015 Advanced Integration Studio and spring 2016 independent study
> **Funding**: UC Pathway B Third Century Materials Grant, People's Liberty, Carol Ann and Ralph V. Haile, Jr./U.S. Bank Foundation

Notes

1   At the time of this project, MetroLAB was operating within the UC Research Institute.
2   See the Pleasant Street Pedestrian Project at www.daap.uc.edu/metrolab/pleasant-street-pedestrian-project.html.
3   Findlay Market was named one of five recipients of the 2016 American Planning Association's Great Places in America award for Great Public Spaces, a designation that considers eight integrated social, cultural, and historical

qualities, among others. See: www.planning.org/greatplaces/spaces/2016/findlaymarket/.
4   Pleasant Street is located in the Cincinnati neighborhood of Over-the-Rhine.
5   See www.dbxchange.eu/node/1416 for elaboration on MetroLAB's strategies.

References

Kern, Jac. 2016. "One Street at a Time: UC's Pleasant Street Parklet Represents a Silver Lining." *UC Magazine*, July 25. http://magazine.uc.edu/editors_picks/recent_features/pleasant_parklet.html.

UC DAAP (University of Cincinnati, College of Design, Architecture, Art and Planning). 2018. "MetroLAB." Accessed May 29, 2018. www.daap.uc.edu/metrolab.html.

Case Study C
A Social Approach to Design

A Social Approach to Design champions a foundational, first-person understanding of the empathic skills necessary for an ethical, human-centered practice in interior design.

Project-Specific Student Learning Objectives
- interpret the context, function, and needs defining projects for underrepresented groups in the field of interior design
- analyze in written and visual form the social, economic, and environmental impact of design projects
- express the ethical and social responsibilities of the interior designer

Summary

The School of Interior Design in the Faculty of Communication and Design at Ryerson University has been ranked one the world's leading programs for interior design study (Pagliacolo 2016). Located in the heart of Toronto, Ontario, the Bachelor of Interior Design program features curricular tracks in six concurrent themes: "communications, art and design history, design dynamics, interior design, professional practice, and technology" (RSID 2016). A final course in the history track is the fourth-year Design Seminar (IRH 401). From 2012 to 2015, one instructor's once-yearly section of this seminar has introduced concepts of public interest design. A Social Approach to Design is a course project that exposes seminar students, often for the first time, to ethical, social, cultural, economic, and environmental dilemmas of design for underserved clients.

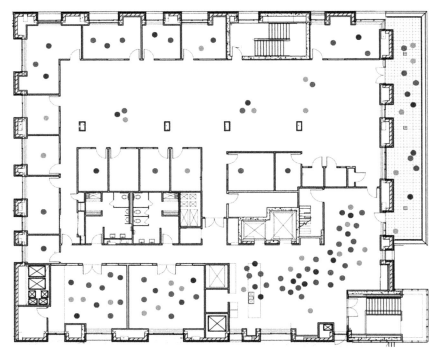

30C.12
This diagrammatic analysis documents the social aspects of the Centre for Social Innovation located on the fourth floor of Daniels Spectrum. More dots are shown in areas that function as open spaces where collaboration and exchange can occur. Design Seminar students, social programming analysis, A Local and Social Approach SEED Evaluation, Toronto, Ontario, Canada, 2015.

Issues Addressed
Social: Education, Civic Engagement, Equity

Community-Based Challenge
As a discipline, interior design is integrated into many expressions of the built and communicative environment. Interior design is central to social well-being as positioned through the nexus of economic and environmental factors; subsequently, students of interior design are in an agile position to leverage social-impact opportunities in their field. Shifting focus from exemplars of international high design to local expressions of design for social justice helped emphasize the criticality of the community-based challenge: students were guided through a local design inquiry that put them in direct contact with built projects conveying a social concern significant to the students' semester study of public interest design.

Pedagogical Goals
The project, A Social Approach to Design, facilitated applied learning through the cityscape of Toronto, enabling interior design students to gain firsthand experience of public interest design in context. A team-based case-study assignment introduced the city as a learning lab. Students were given a list of city organizations where the architectural design or programming might embody social design considerations. Project sites selected for the fall 2015 course included cultural institutions, community centers, temporary housing facilities, and religious organizations (Leu 2015). The class worked

30C.13
Generous hallways function as impromptu gathering spaces for Daniels Spectrum organizations to come together as a single multicultural community. Design Seminar students, social programming analysis, A Local and Social Approach SEED Evaluation, Toronto, Ontario, Canada, 2015.

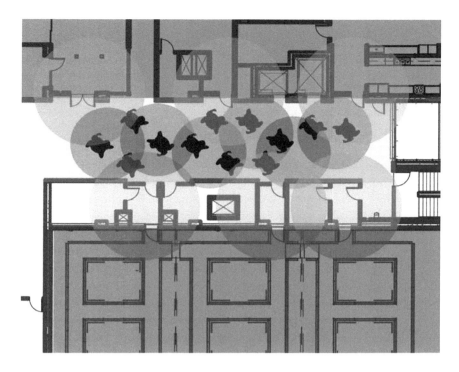

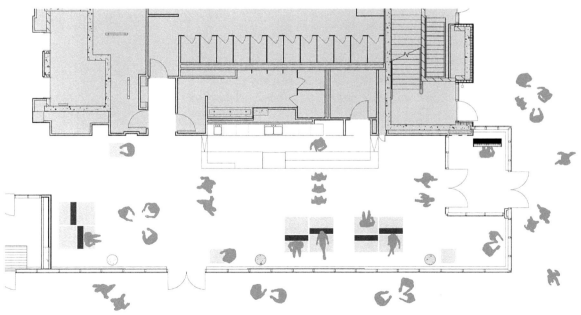

30C.14
This ground floor diagram of the Artscape Lounge and Show Me Love Café in Daniels Spectrum analyzes programming for casual social interaction in an affordable housing neighborhood. Design Seminar students, social programming analysis, A Local and Social Approach SEED Evaluation, Toronto, Ontario, Canada, 2015.

collectively with organizational contacts and corresponding architectural offices to research social priorities manifested through the design of the buildings. The social lens was quickly expanded to include analysis of holistic triple-bottom-line considerations. Student-led teams conducted site visits, meeting with organization staff, building occupants, and architectural-firm representatives. Students thus observed the alignment of design intent, outputs, and impact based on needs driven by the community or client.

Select Teaching Strategies

- **Focused class discussion**: Topical discussions, supported by critical readings and film viewings, introduced themes of social justice in design, focusing on the role of the designer in a contemporary practice. Class discussions of the designer as facilitator versus consultant increased cultural sensitivity and built empathy. Examining processes of engagement and ways in which designers are meeting the needs of clients as communities reinforced the possibilities of working beyond the commercial traditions of interior design.
- **City as learning lab**: Connecting students directly with organizations, stakeholders, and architectural design teams helped realize the value of first-person research. Being able to contextualize the site requirements and to balance those with the organization's needs and the design limitations allowed students to make important connections about the design process, especially pertaining to social, economic, and environmental considerations. Emphasis on local design shifted student learning to a space surrounding the Toronto campus, which helped achieve a secondary but related goal: students developed an understanding of pressing local issues.
- **Design evaluation**: A modified version of the Social Economic Environmental Design (SEED) Evaluator tool guided students in the process of analyzing design outcomes. Reporting on the historic, cultural, and social conditions of the community served by the design solidified students' primary research with field

30C.15

High contrast colors, non-glossy finishes, and indirect lighting helps people who are visually impaired navigate through the facility. Design Seminar students, sensory analysis, Canadian National Institute of the Blind: Case Study Analysis, Toronto, Ontario, Canada, 2013.

contacts. Students researched how the design created positive social, economic, and environmental impact; how it responded to the needs of the community; and how stakeholders were engaged in the design process over the life of the project. Students further identified key issues for their project sites or programs, along with analysis supporting how design outcomes responded to these issues (Leu 2015).

Project Results and Learning Outcomes

Students produced written and visual research based on original discoveries made through site visits. They documented their findings in photographs and drawings to highlight how designs met key issues addressed in the work. Social, economic, and

30C.16
The sense of smell is incorporated at critical junctures within the building: the Fragrance Garden is located near the front entry and the Cafeteria is the heart of the building. Design Seminar students, sensory analysis, Canadian National Institute of the Blind: Case Study Analysis, Toronto, Ontario, Canada, 2013.

30C.17
Adjacent to every room are tactile braille signs to assist staff and visitors navigating through the facility. Design Seminar students, sensory analysis, Canadian National Institute of the Blind: Case Study Analysis, Toronto, Ontario, Canada, 2013.

SEED Academic Case Studies

environmental issues were scrutinized as significant to the combination of factors affecting design results. Diagrams expressed responses to social concerns in gathering and entry spaces, transitional areas, public versus private areas, and programming analyses. Built models further elaborated on manifestations of design meeting social needs. The team-based project output was a comprehensive presentation of findings, accompanied by a booklet detailing the site-specific research results, design and program analyses, and design evaluation using the SEED Evaluator tool.

As a result of this project, students were able to confront issues of ethical and moral responsibility and identify gaps or opportunities for social justice endeavors in their work as interior designers. Students distinguished the diverse contexts that define design in the public interest and translated social, economic, and environmental considerations expressed by stakeholders into design outcomes. Student research documented the importance of building empathy through firsthand observation and working directly with project partners.

> **Partners**: Ryerson University, Faculty of Communication and Design, School of Interior Design; fall 2015 organizations: Salvation Army Harbour Light Ministries; Regent Park Aquatic Centre; Ronald McDonald House; University of Toronto Multi-Faith Centre; Artscape for Daniels Spectrum; Diamond and Schmitt Architects; Maclennan Jaunkalns Miller Architects; Montgomery Sisam Architects; Moriyama and Teshima Architects
> **Credits: Ryerson University**: fourth-year interior design instructor, Christine Leu; students, fall 2012–fall 2015 Design Seminar

References

Leu, Christine. 2015. "RSID Fall 2015 IRH401 Design Seminar." Assignment sheet.
Pagliacolo, Elizabeth. 2016. "8 Top Interior Design Schools: Ryerson University, Toronto." *Azure Magazine*, January 14. www.azuremagazine.com/article/interior-design-schools-ryerson-university-toronto/.
RSID (Ryerson School of Interior Design). 2016. "Bachelor of Interior Design." Ryerson University. Accessed November 23, 2016. http://rsid.ryerson.ca/program.

Case Study D
Cooperative Education at the Detroit Collaborative Design Center

The Detroit Collaborative Design Center (DCDC) provides integrated, engaged learning opportunities for cooperative (co-op) education students pursuing a practice in public interest design; students work side by side with DCDC designers and university faculty on a range of projects serving Detroit communities.

Project-Specific Student Learning Objectives
- use iteration to create effective visual communication presentation materials for public interest design contexts
- practice building trust with stakeholders through a range of community-engagement strategies
- discover the design and administrative practices of a university community design center

Summary
The University of Detroit Mercy (UDM) School of Architecture (SOA) is home to DCDC, a full-service, multidisciplinary, nonprofit community design firm. Among the oldest community design centers in the country, DCDC got its start in 1994 as a neighborhood design studio merging community need with student and professional talent (DCDC 2017). With more than twenty years in practice, DCDC supports a mission of civic engagement and strives for sustainable community outcomes that promote resiliency. DCDC has provided a range of design services to over one hundred nonprofit organizations and low-profit limited liability companies (DCDC 2017). The center is recognized for its commitment to design-facilitation processes and neighborhood-level community-engagement workshops, as well as for its long-term citywide initiatives.

UDM architecture students are required to complete two semesters of co-op internship credit working in a design office.[1] Students typically take Professional Experience I (ARCH 3010) in the third year and Professional Experience II (ARCH 3020) in the fourth year. DCDC provides a special opportunity for co-op students seeking experience in public interest design methodologies. An average of eight to ten architecture students apply for three or four internship positions at DCDC each semester (fall, spring, and summer). Interns contribute to public initiatives and are exposed to the full spectrum of design and community-engagement processes.

Issues Addressed
Social: Civic Engagement, Education, Equity

Community-Based Challenge
The Livernois Community Storefront (LCS), a DCDC project, was a catalyst for community connectivity and renewed neighborhood investment along the Livernois Avenue corridor in northwest Detroit. At the time of this project, the economic decline of the historic Avenue of Fashion, a once-celebrated shopping district, threatened the future vitality and cohesion of the corridor—the connective tissue between stakeholders that include businesses (both long standing and emerging), two universities (including UDM), and community organizations (ULI 2011, 11–12). Reimagining the Livernois Avenue corridor as a vital hub for commerce and

30D.18
Co-op students work on iterations of the wall installation map of the Livernois corridor highlighting local businesses. DCDC, LCS Wall Map, Detroit, Michigan, 2013.

culture prompted the storefront initiative, which operated from May 2013 through September 2014 as a pop-up venue and site for community events (Chadha and Stanard 2013). The sustained momentum of the LCS project in collaboration with local partners has aided in the corridor's on-going revitalization.

Pedagogical Goals
The LCS project provided co-op students with an applied-learning context: the project demonstrated the phases of a community development project during its one-and-a-half-year life. Students supported the launch of the storefront on May 31, 2013, and played an important role in facilitating the space's relationship with the community. Working alongside DCDC designer-educators and UDM SOA faculty, students applied technical skills developed in course work and newly acquired facilitation skills to professional and community-engagement contexts relevant to the LCS project. Students attended client meetings, participated in community-engagement workshops, prepared design documents, and assisted with hands-on design/build projects. The co-op experience through the LCS project and its leaders mentored students in their active engagement with a high-visibility and transparent public project.[2]

Select Teaching Strategies
- **Community engagement**: Co-op students are embedded in the DCDC community design center environment and are expected to participate in project-engagement efforts. Students gained experience incorporating community expertise into design development by documenting and participating in community meetings. They built relationships with local businesses and organizations in street-side conversations that allowed them to practice talking about their work. Students helped organize and staffed storefront events that interfaced with different stakeholder groups. Their activities helped promote LCS neighborhood inclusion, resulting in the creation of organizational items, such as a community bulletin board, calendar of events, and Livernois map.
- **Iterative production**: Co-op students come to the internship with varying levels of proficiency needed to be successful in the DCDC environment. The

30D.19
A co-op student and a project manager assemble the wall map for the LCS. DCDC, LCS Wall Map, Detroit, Michigan, 2013.

30D.20
A DCDC co-op student installs finishing touches on a neighborhood bulletin board. DCDC, Fitzgerald Community Bulletin Board, Detroit, Michigan, 2014.

experience grows competencies and student confidence through an openness to iteration and exploration. Working with other interns and staff, students use skill sharing to accomplish project goals. During the LCS project, students explored iterative production through a variety of team-developed project

SEED Academic Case Studies

30D.21
A co-op student installs exterior lettering on the LCS. DCDC, LCS Facade, Detroit, Michigan, 2013.

components. Tasked with the storefront window design, students created visual concepts, responded to input, developed prototypes, researched implementation options (laser cut vinyl, for example), and ultimately installed the work alongside project managers. Additionally, students workshopped their concepts at a design charette with members of the American Institute of Architecture Students (AIAS) to help determine construction and assembly methods for the Livernois map and community bulletin board installation.

- **Teaching-hospital model**: The teaching-hospital model embedded within DCDC helps co-op students acclimate to the requirements and full scope of professional practice in a project-based public interest design context (Pitera 2014, 10–11). Students actively participate in the range of required interactions that support project decision making and implementation. For the LCS project, students researched, conceptualized, proposed, adjusted, and implemented a series of modest, scale-appropriate projects under DCDC mentorship. Using the methods typically deployed by DCDC and modeling these within their own projects helped realize learning outcomes and student-stated goals. By participating in a studio-based teaching practice, students are afforded hands-on learning in field experiences that promote their education through immersion.

Project Results and Learning Outcomes
During its operation, LCS hosted over one hundred events, including community celebrations and organizational events that promoted and fostered the unique cultural

identity of Livernois. Co-op students were active participants in LCS placemaking efforts that moved well beyond the confines of design/build. The storefront is still functioning as a pop-up space but is no longer run by DCDC.

As a part of the UDM SOA co-op course requirement, students submit monthly evaluations that demonstrate their professional accomplishments and lessons learned. The evaluations are reflective documents that offer insights into students' expectations and the reality of their professional experiences in a community design setting. These evaluations help DCDC project directors and managers regularly adjust to student needs. Student learning objectives provide measures for learning outcomes, which are tracked over the course of the semester. Students exit the co-op internship able to adapt to diverse public interest design requirements, which encompass skills in community outreach, communication, design thinking, and rapid prototyping, among others.

> **Partners**: Detroit Collaborative Design Center, School of Architecture, University of Detroit Mercy; REVOLVE Detroit; Livernois Avenue businesses; University Commons Organization; Challenge Detroit; Detroit Design Festival; Surdna Foundation
>
> **Credits: DCDC LCS Project**: project director, Virginia Stanard; project managers, Ceara O'Leary and Krista Wilson; additional project leaders, Dan Pitera, Christina Heximer, and Monica Chadha; co-op students during 2013 and 2014 semesters

30D.22
The Livernois wall map on the opening day of the LCS. DCDC, LCS Wall Map, Detroit, Michigan, 2013.

SEED Academic Case Studies

Notes

1. Co-op internship credit variables include full time (two credit, three-hundred-hour equivalency over twelve weeks) and part time (one credit, one-hundred-fifty-hour equivalency over six weeks) options.
2. See page 123 of *Syncopating the Urban Landscape*. Author Dan Pitera (2014) shares DCDC's three-pronged model for "knowledge-sharing" engagement, which includes "inform, feedback, [and] exchange"—a model realized in the LCS project with co-op students.

References

Chadha, Monica, and Virginia Stanard. 2013. "Impact Detroit as a Catalytic Converter." American Architectural Foundation. Accessed January 20, 2017. www.archfoundation.org/2013/09/impact-detroit-as-a-catalytic-converter/.

DCDC (Detroit Collaborative Design Center). 2017. "About." University of Detroit Mercy School of Architecture. Accessed January 20, 2017. www.dcdc-udm.org/about/.

Pitera, Dan. 2014. "Amplifying the Diminished Voice." In *Syncopating the Urban Landscape: More People, More Programs, More Geographies*. Detroit Collaborative Design Center, University of Detroit Mercy School of Architecture, 9–12. www.dcdc-udm.org/media/documents/syncopating/Syncopating2014_V1.0_smaller.pdf.

(ULI) Urban Land Institute. 2011. "Detroit, Michigan: Reviving Livernois Avenue as a Thriving Urban Main Street." ULI Daniel Rose Fellowship Program City Study Visit Report, Urban Land Institute, Daniel Rose Center for Public Leadership in Land Use, January 18–21. http://uli.org/wp-content/uploads/2012/06/detroit_2012_rose_F_web.pdf.

Case Study E
Com(m)a

Com(m)a is a multimodal project created in response to the 2010 earthquake in Chile. Students and faculty worked with partner organizations and community members to address reconstruction scenarios appropriate for a postdisaster community, resulting in a series of design/build projects and workshops.

Project-Specific Student Learning Objectives
- recognize how collaborative, community-based design can affirm productive actions
- relate disciplinary practices to global contexts and needs
- formulate solutions that empower student- and community-centered assets

Summary

In 2011 the faculty of the Department of Architecture, Interior Architecture, and Designed Objects (AIADO) at the School of the Art Institute of Chicago (SAIC) selected the Com(m)a project proposal for their annual GFRY Design Studio.[1] A transdisciplinary collaborative initiated in 2005, Motorola and SAIC have partnered through the GFRY Design Studio to support students in public-innovation projects (SAIC 2012). One proposal is selected every year for this high-profile, two-semester-long opportunity where projects are developed from concept through implementation, a process that fosters original thinking and making (SAIC 2012). In spring and summer 2011, twelve graduate students and three undergraduate students, in disciplines such as sculpture, art therapy, interior architecture, architecture, designed objects, and performance, were selected for inclusion in the Com(m)a initiative.

Issues Addressed
Social: Disaster Response, Learning, Local Identity

Community-Based Challenge
On February 27, 2010, an earthquake registering 8.8 on the Richter scale ravaged central Chile. This event destroyed homes in and around the city center of Talca, the historic regional capital of Maule, located approximately 158 miles south of Santiago. The site of the Com(m)a initiative was the Paso Moya neighborhood southwest of

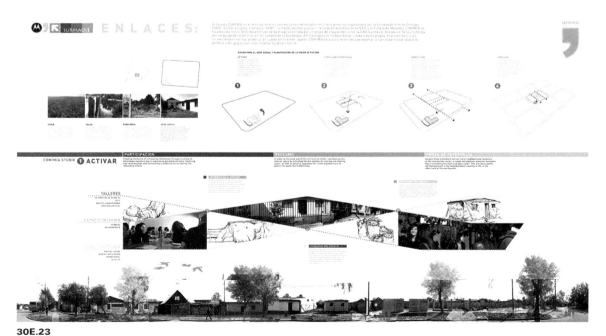

30E.23
An informational board used by Com(m)a Studio students to explain the scope of their project to the local community and to Chilean academic partners. Com(m)a Studio, Enlaces, Talca, Chile, 2011.

SEED Academic Case Studies

30E.24
The public billboard installed on the exterior fence allowed neighbors to leave messages for one another, and the community center to announce events taking place in the neighborhood. Com(m)a Studio, Diario Mural, Talca, Chile, 2011.

Talca's historic center. An alliance between community groups and the Com(m)a team realized substantive connections to this neighborhood where the earthquake revealed social inequity: with the damage to housing came an assault on the social fabric of a community and its local identity.

Nongovernmental organizations, Surmaule, a Talca-based social action and empowerment group, and Reconstruye, an affiliation of professionals and academics committed to the advancement of justly built environments, were project partners (Ciudades 2012). These two groups acted as intermediaries to connect the Com(m)a team with local resources, including the Paso Moya neighborhood association that participated in the process of identifying community need.

30E.25
The *quincho* located in the center of the building courtyard created a shaded public space for neighborhood events and gatherings. Com(m)a Studio, Quincho, Talca, Chile, 2011.

Pedagogical Goals
A goal of the Com(m)a initiative was to teach students how to solve complex embedded social, economic, and environmental problems. In small steps, remotely and on site, students tackled postdisaster response and in the process learned how to empower and mobilize community voice through design. Students were taught that they could be catalysts for positive development and productive conversation. By identifying a complement of community strengths and student abilities, the Com(m)a team developed a program of scale-appropriate, tangible design solutions. Com(m)a subsequently created a GFRY Design Studio precedent for locational learning—learning supported by preparatory activities off-site in advance of working on-site with a host community. Intrapersonal learning nurtured a deep connection to stakeholder needs while application of technical skills realized student potential to facilitate design responses in context.

Select Teaching Strategies
- **Intercultural preparation**: Preparation for cultural immersion came through a series of interventions that grew in scope over time. First, the spring semester course introduced students to the Talca community and the impact the earthquake had in Paso Moya. Next, secondary research provided historical and cultural lenses for generating student understanding and building empathy. With this context, students created initial design proposals that responded to an early appreciation of the issues affecting the community.

SEED Academic Case Studies

30E.26
The front yard of the community center was paved and furnished for families to enjoy the playground equipment also designed and built by Com(m)a Studio students. Com(m)a Studio, Pavimento, Talca, Chile, 2011.

In March the Com(m)a team conducted their first nine-day site visit to Talca where they directed site-mapping and analysis exercises along with programming and design studies in collaboration with community groups. In April the Reconstruye team traveled to Chicago to provide feedback on six project proposals that responded to community-identified need. Reconstruye and Surmaule facilitated weekly Skype meetings with stakeholders and conveyed feedback between the neighborhood association and Com(m)a.

- **Quick-response templates**: Through preliminary and remote research, teams developed working processes, or "templates," that could enable rapid response following a disaster. These strategies were accomplished through an instructor-created "Task, Tool, Jig" methodology. Big problems were broken down into smaller manageable parts appropriate for student initiation. In an effort to scale the enormity of the multisemester project and practice an asset-based strategy, students self-identified individual strengths and related these to team tasks that they could feasibly accomplish within the stated goals and timeline. Connecting the task to tools for execution allowed other students to become technical skill-set collaborators. Jig operated as a systemic framework for guiding design process and implementation. Students were encouraged to work quickly and iteratively while acknowledging the relevance of their own expertise, as well as the expertise of their peers and the community they were working with.

- **Resource mapping**: An emphasis on mapping social and material capital would determine project feasibility. Reconstruye and Surmaule functioned as primary contacts for on-the-ground development and worked with the neighborhood to organize and identify community resources and project goals. Through this asset-based lens, the Paso Moya neighborhood identified two areas for project development: (1) a series of community workshops that encouraged participants to confront grief and loss through the postearthquake rebuilding effort and (2) a series of design/build efforts that addressed improvements at the community center. These projects were developed between April and May; then the team returned to Talca for a three-week (June 20 to July 8) construction and implementation phase. Students worked within the limitations of the local conditions to determine material specification, use, reuse, and recycling or upcycling options available for their on-site construction. Co-creation activities were at the heart of their programming; this required a detailed understanding of the unique capacities of the community with which they were collaborating.

Project Results and Learning Outcomes

Com(m)a resulted in four community-center design/build projects (a *quincho*,[2] a playground, a courtyard, and a participatory message board) and four workshops (art making, art therapy, furniture repair, and video/documentary), conceived to support community members in coping with loss.[3] The final day of construction concluded

30E.27
The day before the group departed, neighbors organized an art sale and barbecue while community partner, Surmaule, provided live music. Com(m)a Studio, Final event, Talca, Chile, 2011.

SEED Academic Case Studies

with a celebration acknowledging the efforts of students and neighbors alike. The Com(m)a team left the neighborhood association with the tools that the team had purchased and guidelines—including blueprints—for continued improvement of the community-center facility. Surmaule monitored facility use and organized community-center events. Projects supported community goals while offering students the chance to gain expertise with technical, hands-on craft and building skills. Student learning came in pluridisciplinary forms emphasizing reciprocity and trust. Intrapersonal skills, such as listening and written and verbal communication, challenged students to adapt new ways of conveying information.

> **Partners**: School of the Art Institute of Chicago, Academic Studio Commissioner and Grant Writer; Motorola Foundation, Grant Provider; Thornton Thomasetti, Structural Design Consultant; Reconstruye; Surmaule; Paso Moya neighborhood association and community members
>
> **Credits: SAIC**: instructors, Odile Compagnon and Paul Tebben; students, spring and summer 2011 GFRY Design Studio

Notes

1. The GFRY Design Studio references a Motorola product-naming structure memorialized by Motorola Chief Marketing Officer Geoffrey Frost (see www.saic.edu/academics/departments/aiado/comma-gfry-10-11).
2. A *quincho* is similar to a pergola and is used as a sheltered gathering space.
3. See the GRFY 2011 website for before (www.odilecompagnon.com/GFRY_2011_COM%28M%29A/AS_WE_FOUND_IT.html) and after (www.odilecompagnon.com/GFRY_2011_COM%28M%29A/AS_WE_LEFT_IT.html) project documentation.

References

Ciudades para un Futuro más Sostenible. 2012. "ONG Reconstruye: Iniciativas en red para reconstruir de forma sustentable (Santiago de Chile, Chile)." Escuela Técnica Superior de Arquitectura de Madrid, Universidad Politécnica de Madrid Grupo de Investigación en Arquitectura, Urbanismo y Sostenibilidad, Departamento de Estructuras y Física de la Edificación — Departamento de Urbanística y Ordenación del Territorio. Accessed October 17, 2016. http://habitat.aq.upm.es/dubai/12/bp4419.html.

(SAIC) School of the Art Institute of Chicago. 2012. "Com(m)a: GFRY 10-11." Accessed December 16, 2016. http://www.saic.edu/academics/departments/aiado/comma-gfry-10-11

Case Study F
The Farm Rover

The Farm Rover is a mobile farming home base that provides shelter, access to basic facilities, secure tool storage, and temporary living space for farmworkers operating in flood-prone farming regions.

Project-Specific Student Learning Objectives
- apply principles of participatory action research (PAR) to a design/build project
- formulate a plan for stakeholder engagement that uncovers needs related to traditional farming practices
- practice community-based strategies for working across political, ecological, and fiscal divides

Summary
The Center for Sustainable Development (CSD) at the University of Texas at Austin School of Architecture (UTASOA) sponsors a summer program in public interest design. The program, which identifies a new challenge every year, consists of two complementary course offerings: a ten-week design studio (Advanced Design/Build Practicum, ARC W696) and a five-week seminar (Community Design Engagement Seminar, ARC F386M). The combination of studio and seminar explore the creative tension between design/build methods and community-based endeavors in support of building trust through a relatively brief period of stakeholder engagement. Reflective and experiential learning between the studio and seminar supports a mix of undergraduate and graduate students in architecture, landscape architecture, and community and regional planning.

In summer 2015, Austin's Office of Sustainability challenged sixteen students to develop a response to urban floodplain farming that connected well-being with access to healthy foods. The challenge evolved into a project, developed in cooperation with two partner organizations: the Multicultural Refugee Coalition (MRC), an organization devoted to the resettlement of the refugee community in Austin; and the New Farm Institute, the nonprofit educational branch of Green Gate Farms (GGF), a certified organic farm committed to sustainable farming in the spirit of community-supported agriculture.

Issues Addressed
Social: Refugee Empowerment; *Economic:* Entrepreneurship; *Environmental:* Environmental Education

Community-Based Challenge
A result of the Balcones Fault, Austin is divided east and west by an escarpment which exposes the city to flooding during storm events. Rapid development of Austin's urban core coupled with the propensity for urban flooding created an

30F.28
Learning from MRC community farmers. UTA summer 2015 Public Interest Design Build Studio and Seminar, Farm Rover, Green Gate Farm, Austin, Texas, 2015.

opportunity for the exploration of a floodplain farming problem scenario (Public Interest Design Summer Program, 2015, 16–19). While this land typically cannot be developed for purposes such as housing, for example, it could provide a sustainable use alternative: urban farming, and thus local food production, in zoned areas that promote the cultivation of land for the purpose of growing fresh, accessible food (Bossin and Frambach 2013).

The mutual interest in promoting urban agriculture reinforces the agency of the partner organizations involved. Austin's Office of Sustainability sought solutions that explored floodplain food production (Public Interest Design Summer Program 2015). Together, MRC and GGF had a need for mobile infrastructure that would provision the productivity, comfort, and well-being of community farmers working in potential floodplain farm zones. These issues were addressed in combination and relative to Austin's floodplain infrastructure.

Pedagogical Goals
While GGF, located east of downtown Austin, is not a floodplain property, it provided an accessible farm location for MRC participants and UTASOA students, who were able to work together on-site in the development of this case study project. This farm has a history of sustainable agriculture, is committed to education and outreach, and was able to facilitate a valuable partnership between project stakeholder groups and students. The on-site farming context was beneficial in connecting students to the traditions, culture, and requirements of refugee farmers relative to the design problem. Over the ten-week summer session, students were exposed to a breadth of skill development that ranged from the interpersonal to the technical.

30F.29
Students building on-site. UTA summer 2015 Advanced Design/Build Practicum, Farm Rover, Green Gate Farm, Austin, Texas, 2015.

30F.30
The Urban Farming rover prototype featuring the kitchenette with integrated cistern, shaded areas for rest, and storage spaces. UTA summer 2015 Advanced Design/Build Practicum, Farm Rover, Green Gate Farm, Austin, Texas, 2015.

Select Teaching Strategies

Faculty constructed learning scenarios that included stakeholders from diverse social, economic, and political contexts. Adopted strategies included those pertaining to research, cultural immersion, and design/build.

- **Research**: Drawing upon principles of PAR, students undertook participant observation, key informant interviews, and spatial mapping to understand

30F.31
A student demonstrates the rolling shade screen. UTA summer 2015 Advanced Design/Build Practicum, Farm Rover, Green Gate Farm, Austin, Texas, 2015.

how refugees' past farming practices might inform this project's design/build outcome (McIntyre 2008).

- **Cultural immersion**: Faculty fostered students' cultural immersion through activities that aimed to expand understanding and bridge differences among diverse stakeholders. Students worked with refugees at gardening plots that included Lanier High School (LHS), Festival Beach Community Gardens (FBCG), as well as the GCF farm site. Understanding the unique needs of this multi-actor farming community was a top requirement.
- **Design/build**: Drawing upon empirical research, students created design concepts that supported intercultural, community-based farming. They were resourceful in creating proposals and solutions that responded to environmental issues and ensured resilient practices. Material reuse and new fabrication thoughtfully responded to community need and context of use.

At the start of the project, students leveraged their research into design concepts that benefited from stakeholder input. From this, students integrated a variety of techniques and theoretical perspectives into predesign development across all three partner organizations. Consistent participation at LHS, FBCG, and GGF allowed for consideration of how existing gardening practices and spaces relate to a range of proposed conditions. By participating in farm work activities alongside MRC project stakeholders, students were encouraged to reflect upon the relationship between design and empathy. Upon selection of design direction, students worked iteratively in teams devoted to one of three areas: (1) "frame" (floor, frame, and roof systems), (2) "fill" (interior components), and (3) "flip" (entry and access points) (Public Interest Design Summer Program 2015, 37–43).

30F.32
The Urban Farming rover prototype features gas-powered hinges which allows an operator to respond quickly to different weather events. UTA summer 2015 Advanced Design/Build Practicum, Farm Rover, Green Gate Farm, Austin, Texas, 2015.

Project Results and Learning Outcomes

The integration of engaged research into the concept, design, and construction of the Farm Rover advanced a model for reflective design practice and provides a multifunctional response to floodplain farming and farmworker necessity (Perkes 2009). Welded to a mobile-home chassis, the portable structure is twenty feet by seven feet; it can support basic human needs and provide tool security and shelter for people working in the field. In this context, the Farm Rover resolves a number of farmworker-related requirements in one single functional system: it provides shade, rain shelter, personal storage for tools, a kitchenette, water supplied by a fifty-five-gallon cistern, a composting toilet, and areas for rest and community gathering. The exterior walls incorporate perforated metal and gas-powered hinges, which allow an operator to respond to various weather events. Technical achievements such as these will be increasingly important for exploring and testing how design disciplines respond to local conditions of global processes.

The students completed the project with recommendations and plans for three variable rover units that respond to the evolving nature of the project and the processes to which it responds. Urban Farming (unit B), which maximizes space for seating while including resting space, was the concept that was built and deployed; two other units, Community Gardening (unit A) and Rural Farming (unit C), each provide spatial enhancement variables for rest, storage, or seating (Public Interest Design Summer Program 2015, 51–55). The students embraced the goal of adaptable use in their programming, anticipating it in the generation of this first prototype. Testing of the Urban Farming unit in floodplain-farming applications is forthcoming.

Partners: University of Texas at Austin School of Architecture; Center for Sustainable Development (UTA School of Architecture); City of Austin Office of Sustainability; Green Gate Farms, New Farm Institute; Multicultural Refugee Coalition

Credits: CSD: studio instructor, Coleman Coker; seminar instructor, Kristine Stiphany; project manager, Sarah Wu; teaching assistant, Kaethe Selkirk; students, summer 2015 Advanced Design/Build Practicum and Community Design Engagement Seminar

References

Bossin, Meredith, and Heather Frambach. 2013. "Grow Food, Grow Local." *Imagine Austin* (blog). Accessed June 13, 2017. www.austintexas.gov/blog/grow-food-grow-local.

McIntyre, Alice. 2008. *Participatory Action Research*. Thousand Oaks, CA: Sage Publications.

Perkes, David. 2009. "A Useful Practice." *Journal of Architectural Education* 62 (4): 64–71.

Public Interest Design Summer Program. 2015. "The Field House: An Investigation into Floodplain Food Production in Austin, Texas." Center for Sustainable Development, School of Architecture, University Texas at Austin. https://www.soa.utexas.edu/publications/2015-pid-report.

Case Study G
On Site: Public Art and Design

Two studio courses—one in public art and the other in public interest design—were joined to afford a unique opportunity for creative placemaking in a suburb of Washington, DC. Ten temporary installations[1] and a neighborhood "Superblock" party became catalysts for community engagement that activated public space and stimulated conversations about the future of the community.

Project-Specific Student Learning Objectives
- develop temporary art and design works that respond to and connect underutilized community spaces
- use art and design to build partnerships and advocate for local engagement
- analyze the physical and psychological meanings of place through interdisciplinary form making

Summary

In spring 2013, the Montgomery Housing Partnership of Montgomery County, Maryland, and the Long Branch Business League approached faculty from the Department of Art and the School of Architecture at the University of Maryland

(UMD) to discuss an idea for a pilot public art and design course focused on the Long Branch neighborhood. Located 3.5 miles northwest of campus, Long Branch is a culturally diverse neighborhood in transition: it is expected to be heavily affected by the forthcoming light rail Purple Line, which will connect Long Branch to the Washington Metro transit system in 2022. This university-community partnership focused faculty and student efforts and neighborhood-created synergies on the potential of placemaking during a time of change.

The course, "On Site: Creating a Sense of Place through Intervention and Transformation," united a three-credit undergraduate advanced sculpture studio

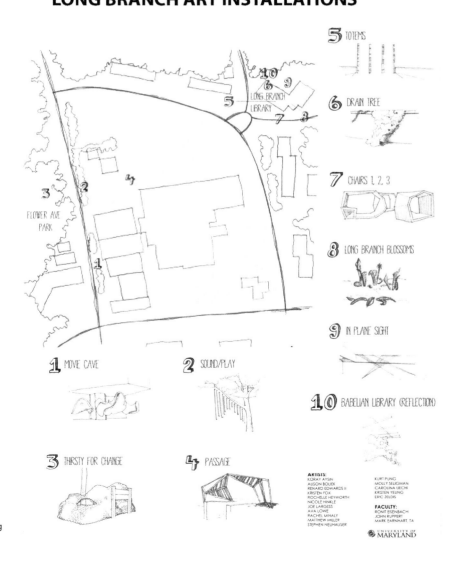

30G.33
A poster created for distribution during the Superblock Party with information and locations of all ten installations. Design: Kristen A. Fox and Alison Boliek Supinski, On Site, Long Branch, Maryland, 2013.

elective (ARTT 4380) with five students and a six-credit graduate architecture studio (ARCH 601) with twelve students. Students, faculty, and community partners together played a critical, timely role in affirming the collective identity of the neighborhood as it prepared to represent itself in local and regional planning and infrastructure-investment discussions.

30G.34
Located in the local playground, discarded plastic bottles were woven together with wire thread to form a translucent pavilion gently formed around existing trees that pierced through the structure's roof. Renard Edwards, Kristen A. Fox, Alison Boliek Supinski, and Kristen Yeung, Thirsty for Change, Long Branch, Maryland, 2013.

Issues Addressed
Social: Local Identity, Strengthening Community; *Environmental:* Capitalizing, Reimagining, and Interconnecting Underutilized Spaces

Community-Based Challenge
The Long Branch neighborhood in Silver Spring, Maryland, is characterized as a first-ring suburb of Washington, DC, and is composed of multiple and diverse communities that support numerous small, locally owned businesses. Challenged by a lack of investment in existing public infrastructure, lack of cultural amenities, and the development of the Purple Line, Long Branch sought to increase the visibility and recognition of its existing assets and anticipated needs in seeking public-private partnerships like the one generated with UMD.

Pedagogical Goals
This first iteration of On Site was a proving ground not only for what might be possible in a community-based public-private partnership of this kind at UMD, but also for the potential of the course to evolve. The faculty recognized the challenges inherent in bringing together undergraduate and graduate students from two related but different disciplines. The benefits of the experience far outweighed any deterrents, however. By emphasizing the shared qualities of their respective disciplines, students were able to fuse sculptural and architectural form making with the spatial conditions of site-specific installation. Beyond the making, students had to understand the complexities of environment, place, and people, and cultures to propose appropriate site interventions responsive to community issues.

30G.35
Composed of neon construction string tied to the upper library courtyard railings and fixed to the ground below, this work converged at different points, creating colorful triangular planes that interacted and intersected with one another and introduced a new spatial geometry to adjacent spaces. Stephen Neuheuser, Matthew Miller, and Kristen Yeung, In Plane Site, Long Branch, Maryland, 2013.

SEED Academic Case Studies

To achieve this goal, students worked in cross disciplinary teams to generate proposals that answered the project challenge: create a sense of place through temporary interventions (Haslam 2013). This prerogative was supported by a series of explorations that bridged two dominant themes in the course: one devoted to formal, material, and spatial explorations and the other to social, cultural, and political issues. Together, these themes helped frame the following activities: research through precedents, site observations, photographic documentation, stakeholder discussion groups, and reciprocal listening; technical skill development exploring formal responses to materiality, building, space, site, and community contexts; conceptual formulations responding to issues, physical environments, community identities, and cultures; and design/build interventions, inviting interactivity, exploration, and discovery.

Select Teaching Strategies

- **On- and off-site project development**: Students were guided through a sequence of assignments, both in the community and on campus, that helped them understand the possibilities for making work driven by community concerns. A combination of research-based inquiries and technical investigations merged *meaning* with *making*. The proximity of Long Branch to campus ensured that students spent time in the community as a structured part of their research practice, which was critical to understanding the scope of embedded issues.
- **Iteration**: Students managed the full scope of project development in each of ten team-developed installations inclusive of early prototyping, full-scale design mock-ups, and installation and de-installation plans. Supported by

30G.36
Through color and form, Chairs 1, 2, 3 encouraged playful interaction—a place to sit, a place to relax, a space to move through—activating the library plaza and unleashing its potential as a community public space. Joseph Largess, Kurt Pung, Rochelle Heyworth Cusimano, and Rachel Mihaly, Chairs 1, 2, 3, Long Branch, Maryland, 2013.

ongoing stakeholder feedback, students tested their work, verified material compatibility, oriented their designs to a specific location, and engaged local partners for required permissions and permits.

- **Communication and documentation**: The Superblock party, held on May 11, 2013, in the Long Branch Library plaza, was a milestone in the semester-long project. Together with faculty and local partners, students organized, promoted and documented the event and served as "project ambassadors," available to discuss their ten interactive works displayed on nearby Flower Avenue. The temporal nature of the project created an opportunity for students to gain experience telling the story of their work using communication and documentation methods so that the ideas and messages lived on.

Project Results and Learning Outcomes

The Superblock party helped reimagine Long Branch public spaces as engaged, vibrant, connected environments—places people want to be. The interactive installations displayed from May 6 to May 20 explored issues relevant to the community's infrastructure challenges and provoked direct engagement with those issues. Since the academic collaboration, Long Branch has continued to affirm its identity through several artistic and cultural enhancement initiatives, including a highly visible mural program and pop-up performances (myMCMedia 2015; Lowry 2016). The pilot offering of this public art and design course has evolved into several subsequent site-based iterations that promote transformative placemaking and collaboration in communities throughout Maryland (Long Branch 2014).

30G.37
The team used hinges to connect the triangular panels to one another with the understanding that the form would stabilize once fixed to the ground. Despite building a series of physical and digital models, the students were amazed to see that the idea worked when tested at full-scale in the studio. Kurt Pung, Matthew Miller, Carolina Uechi, and Rochelle Heyworth Cusimano, Passage, Long Branch, Maryland, 2013.

30G.38
This temporary gateway offered an artful suggestion as to how one might permanently connect disjointed areas of the neighborhood in festive, unique, and beautiful ways. Kurt Pung, Matthew Miller, Carolina Uechi, and Rochelle Heyworth Cusimano, Passage, Long Branch, Maryland, 2013.

Partners: University of Maryland Program in Architecture, School of Architecture, Planning, and Preservation, Department of Art, College of Arts and Humanities, National Center for Smart Growth Research and Education, and Art and Architecture Libraries; Impact Silver Spring; Long Branch Business League; Montgomery County Public Libraries; Montgomery Housing Partnership; Montgomery County Department of Parks; Arts and Humanities Council of Montgomery County

Credits: UMD: architecture faculty, Ronit Eisenbach; studio art faculty, John Ruppert; teaching assistant, Mark Earnhart; students, spring 2013 advanced sculpture and architecture studios

Note

1 See the website Long Branch: Exploring Sites in Transition (http://artinplace.wixsite.com/long-branch/10-installations) for an overview of all ten student projects and subsequent work in Long Branch.

References

Haslam, Maggie. 2013. "UMD Students Debut Public Art Installations." *UMD Right Now*, May 8.

Long Branch. 2014. "Art in Place: 10 Installations, Spring 2013." Accessed December 15, 2017. http://artinplace.wixsite.com/long-branch/10-installations.

Lowry, Sean. 2016. "Paratext and the World of a Work in Public Space: Eisenbach and Mansur's *Placeholders*." *Unlikely: Journal for the Creative Arts*. Issue 2, Field Work, November. http://unlikely.net.au/issue-2/placeholders.

myMCMedia. 2015. "A Project to Beautify the Long Branch Business Community," YouTube video, 2:00. Posted by Montgomery Community Media, July 7. Accessed December 20, 2016. www.youtube.com/watch?v=7FMvvTfHAs0.

Case Study H
South of California Avenue

The South of California Avenue (SOCA) project is a multimodal incubator that has ignited a series of placemaking efforts, generating numerous community-building activities that include the development of a nonprofit organization and a community center in the planning stage.

Project-Specific Student Learning Objectives
- develop community-based leadership skills
- facilitate communication and relationship building with stakeholders by establishing a common design language
- use design to leverage resilient community transformation

Summary
Louisiana Tech University School of Design (LTU SOD) offers two courses that unite its service-learning and social-justice initiatives: the Community Design Activism

30H.39
Runners take to the streets in the inaugural SOCA Sprint 5K. CDAC, SOCA Sprint 5K, Ruston, Louisiana, 2009.

Center (CDAC) is available to graduate architecture students (ARCH 545) and to third- and fourth-year undergraduate architecture students as a repeatable course (ARCH 445). An alternative to a field internship, CDAC promotes engaged learning by providing access to ongoing social-impact projects in Ruston and surrounding communities. One such project is SOCA, a long-term plan initiated in 2008 with a twenty-year vision for the co-creation of a sustainable neighborhood south of campus and California Avenue. SOCA challenges students to take a holistic approach to community design problem solving by exploring embedded contextual themes, such as well-being and education, as an entry point for understanding the social conditions of people and place in the built environment.

Issues Addressed
Social: Education, Gathering Spaces, Strengthening Community

Community-Based Challenge
Ruston has a population of approximately twenty-two thousand people, of which 39.1 percent live in poverty, nearly three times the national poverty rate (US Census Bureau 2016). With this concern at the forefront, SOCA arose out of a reciprocal interest in building community between LTU SOD service-learning capacities and assets in the impoverished neighborhood near campus. Five years of relationship building between university facilitators, students, community partners, and city leaders led to formalizing community interests, including improving education, providing gathering spaces, and strengthening community among others. Addressing

30H.40
CDAC students facilitate painting of fence pickets for the SOCA community garden. CDAC, SOCA, Ruston, Louisiana, 2011.

South of California Ave.

these human issues as design issues became a way of combatting the localized social strain of poverty.

Coalition building by LTU SOD faculty and community partners through the SOCA project resulted in the development of Neighborhoods Unified for Hope (NU-Hope), an independent nonprofit. NU-Hope's mission is to mobilize a constellation of partners and volunteers from across the city who seek to improve their community. CDAC functions as the design arm of the organization; there, student-led projects are instigated and enacted with a variety of partner organizations and stakeholder groups.

Pedagogical Goals

Students are integral to the long-term plan for SOCA. Service-learning activities are woven into course work and articulated based on the stated needs of the community challenge under investigation. Relying on predetermined phases, students explore the following (Singh 2010, 599–600):

- understanding (discovery, research, documentation)
- awareness (promotion of problems, community contacts)
- expertise (best practices, precedents)
- planning (charettes, community discussion, roundtable meetings, fund-raising)
- design (with the community, university, and city)
- implementation (building proposed projects, fund-raising)

30H.41
Completed SOCA garden sign and entry. CDAC, SOCA community garden, Ruston, Louisiana, 2011.

SEED Academic Case Studies

These phases reinforce SOCA student learning objectives and emphasize the cultivation of leadership skills, design facilitation through relationship building and communication, and collaborative transformation of resilient communities.

Select Teaching Strategies
- **Teaching leadership**: Student teams tackle new or ongoing SOCA initiatives determined by community feedback and input. These challenges are framed through the six phases (listed earlier) and offer opportunities for students to engage in conversations and work with the community. Leadership skills are nurtured through students' ability to observe, listen, and discover—intrapersonal proficiencies that can build confidence by bridging understanding

30H.42
A student helps with arts and crafts projects at the 2016 block party. NU-Hope, SOCA block party, Ruston, Louisiana, 2016.

and fostering mutual respect through shared goals. Students can then apply leadership skills through the mentored organization, design, and promotion of events that build awareness of and generate funds for SOCA projects.

- **Building trust**: Teaching leadership skills works hand in hand with building trust between students and stakeholders. A series of CDAC-sponsored annual events has helped build that bond, including fall block parties, a five-kilometer run, and year-round community-service outreach. Students become embedded in the neighborhood by participating in activities that promote inclusion and build fellowship.
- **Developing citizen designers**: CDAC students are given opportunities to identify with and share the interests of the community. Shifting emphasis from building structures to building relationships creates a space for connecting with people and their needs where design problems and solutions emerge from the community context. The multiyear engagement process of SOCA is ongoing, with long-term benchmarks that support students in expanding skills beyond the technical. To understand their in-progress design challenges, students typically use methods like qualitative observations and analysis, interviews, mapping and diagraming, asset-based design, local media and government support, and stakeholder advisory groups.

Project Results and Learning Outcomes
Since 2008, SOCA has produced results ranging from community-interest events to planning and implementing a community garden, which has since served as an impromptu meeting space. Through these scaled developments and in the creation

30H.43
CDAC students review feedback from a community meeting and discuss next steps to pursue. CDAC, SOCA project, Ruston, Louisiana, 2017.

SEED Academic Case Studies

30H.44
Rendering of the proposed Hope House. CDAC, NU-Hope, Hope House, Ruston, Louisiana, 2017.

of NU-Hope, the need for a community center has emerged. In collaboration with the city, which donated land for the center (Bergeron 2017), the Hope House will serve as a gathering space, provide educational outreach, and strengthen community ties by hosting programs of interest to the neighborhood. This project has spurred others activated by a desire for enhanced connectivity, including redeveloping an abandoned rail line as a shared-use path and planning sidewalks that promote safe walking and biking. Students demonstrate learning in these initiatives through participation and leadership, in weekly reflective journal entries, and in the results of their diverse community design activities. Students are actively engaged in designing the Hope House and procuring the necessary support for the project to be considered a success to the neighborhood and the city.

> **Partners**: Louisiana Tech University School of Design Community Design Activism Center; Neighborhoods Unified for Hope; City of Ruston; North Central Louisiana Master Gardeners; North Central Alliance Partners in Prevention; Paul E. Slaton Head Start Center; Kiwanis of Ruston; Rotary Club of Ruston; North Central Louisiana Arts Council; Origin Bank; First National Bank; Ruston High School; local churches; local drug court; and numerous other organizations across the city
>
> **Credits: LTU SOD**: lead instructor and director of CDAC, Kevin J. Singh; students, CDAC (since 2008)

References

Bergeron, Nancy. 2017. "Aldermen Approve Revitalization Projects: Community Gardens, Center Aim to Unite Neighborhoods." *Ruston Daily Leader*, March 7.
Singh, Kevin. 2010. "Rebuilding a Community: Social Justice, Diversity, and Design." In *98th ACSA Annual Meeting Proceedings, Rebuilding*, 597–603. Association of Collegiate Schools of Architecture. Accessed November 7, 2016. http://apps.

acsa-arch.org/resources/proceedings/uploads/streamfile.aspx?path=ACSA.AM.98&name=ACSA.AM.98.72.pdf.

US Census Bureau. 2016. "Quick Facts: Ruston City, Louisiana." Accessed November 9. www.census.gov/quickfacts/table/IPE120215/2266655.

Case Study I
With Sacramento

As both an urban intervention project and a participatory action tool, With Sacramento leverages design process as an entry point for capacity building through shared decision making and inclusive coproduction of design.

Project-Specific Learning Objectives
- demonstrate the value of perseverance over time in constructing meaningful project results
- distinguish between research speculations and long-term prevailing outcomes
- formulate design process as a means to effectuate collaborative design thinking and coproduction

Summary
In spring of 2014, the Center for Public Interest Design (CPID) at Portland State University's School of Architecture formed a multiyear partnership with community

30I.45
What if a bus stop was reimagined as a community center? CPID, With Sacramento, Sacramento, California, first bus stop anticipated in fall 2017.

SEED Academic Case Studies

organizations and the city and county of Sacramento, California. Initiated by the Sacramento Area Council of Governments (SACOG), this collaborative brought together CPID students, local governments, and the Sacramento-based organizations La Familia Counseling Center and Mutual Assistance Network (MAN) to strategically address issues of disinvestment in Sacramento.[1] Driven by social, economic, and environmental challenges and their public health impacts, the With Sacramento project asserts an inclusive process for assessing immediate and long-term community needs. The project leverages anticipated cap-and-trade carbon tax credits for California public-transit improvements in the South Sacramento and Del Paso Heights neighborhoods. CPID graduate architecture students, undergraduate seniors, summer interns, and student fellows contributed to the ongoing research and development of this project.

Issues Addressed
Social: Strengthening Community; *Economic:* Access to Services; *Environmental:* Sustainability

Community-Based Challenge
SACOG worked with CPID to identify South Sacramento and Del Paso Heights as ideal partner neighborhoods, each with strong organizational alliances through La Familia and MAN. The state of California had identified the regions these communities are located near or within as "disadvantaged" and eligible for access to the Greenhouse Gas Reduction Fund (CALEPA 2014, 20). Characterized by urban infrastructure disinvestment, these communities vocalized needs and opportunities around community well-being and quality of life. Through student-generated community engagement and outreach, vacant properties, safety, and access to goods and services emerged as critical issues (CPID 2016). Public-transportation accessibility

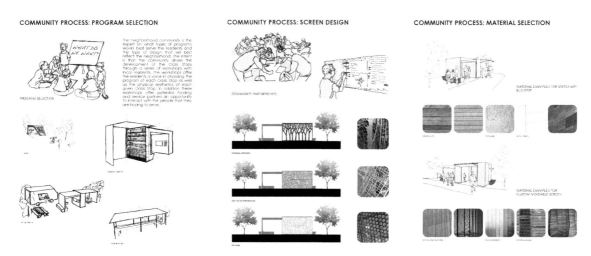

30I.46
Designing a participatory process for transit stop design that can offer community amenities, identity, and gathering spaces. CPID, J. Nicole De Jong, With Sacramento, Sacramento, California, first bus stop anticipated in fall 2017.

was identified as a significant factor of community interest and became a focal point for CPID research—one potentially supported by California's cap-and-trade legislation.

Pedagogical Goals

With Sacramento proposes multiple opportunities for focused pedagogy. As a multifaceted, embedded community-based project, it offers students a unique applied context for honing outreach and research skills, working on-site with stakeholders through a variety of engagement techniques. The project also realizes the value of design process as a gateway to building relationships, community networks, and communication platforms. These nontechnical skills are not only necessary but vital when designing with public constituents.

Because CPID establishes longer-term project partnerships, students experience projects at various stages of research and development, replicating the qualities of real-life work and enhancing students' understanding of workflows, project roles, and life cycles. CPID also underscores team building between individuals and student cohorts; by emphasizing responsibility to project goals, CPID constructs a legacy of knowledge among participating students beyond the conclusion of the academic term. Project faculty have facilitated additional goals: practicing methods of coproduction and design; using human values to motivate design thinking; and researching, building, and deploying a range of low- and high-tech tools to deepen community engagement.

Select Teaching Strategies

- **Amplify community voice**: Students explored varied engagement techniques supporting the open inclusion of diverse stakeholder groups. Students relied on community-organization networking and the inherent social capital

30I.47
Community input as design research. CPID, With Sacramento, Sacramento, California, ongoing.

SEED Academic Case Studies

generated with residents at engagements in Sacramento. Students canvassed neighborhoods and used mapping and diagramming to document their findings. They conducted observations and interviews, participated in public forums, created interactive games, and used descriptive writing, drawing, and asset-based design to verify the voice of the community. Students also helped refine the With Sacramento online engagement tool, which provides enhanced access beyond direct contact with project partners.

- **Systemic integration**: CPID emphasizes the concept of integration within the curriculum and in its projects. This concept is manifested in project problems and possible solutions where students evaluate social, economic, and environmental factors and the impact of these on the stakeholders. Students are encouraged to look holistically at the design intervention and consider systems, processes, and programs that expand solutions through design and development.

- **Scale appropriateness**: Students are guided through a planning process that frames small-scale design interventions as a way to build capacity and effectiveness with communities facing large-scale concerns. The incremental development of a project teaches students about the possibilities of modularity and the progressive organic growth of ideas toward long-term goals. Controlling project scale (or tackling smaller aspects of a project) helps students work through problem solving and application scenarios iteratively, which serves both long-term planning goals and specific small-scale interventions.

30I.48
An architecture student speaks with Del Paso Heights residents about how they travel to, from, and within their community. CPID, With Sacramento, Sacramento, California, ongoing.

30I.49
Diagram of project concept from vacant lot to pop-up shop to building. CPID, Woodrow Merkel, With Sacramento, Sacramento, California, ongoing.

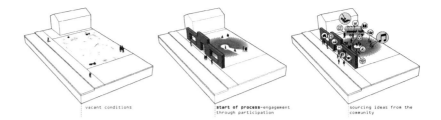

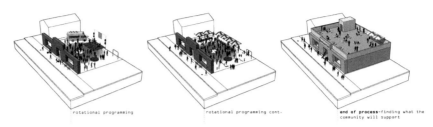

Project Results and Learning Outcomes
Since 2014, With Sacramento has generated the following outputs:

- research materials representing both neighborhoods
- a series of low-tech participatory events
- visioning documents
- a master plan for a sports facility in Del Paso Heights
- reappropriation of an unused school for community activities
- a design guide that empowers the local community and designers to participate in community-centric public-transit infrastructure

The design guide promotes multifunction bus shelters: bus stops that are also community centers. Four bus-shelter concepts have been presented, each functioning as an in situ community center and gateway to the neighborhood.

With Sacramento also collaborated with Ecosistema Urbano, using its Local(in) platform (Ecosistema Urbano 2010; CPID 2016, 80–90) to customize an online engagement tool specific to this project. This version of the community engagement tool is currently in testing prior to full release. Once launched, the tool will further support including the widest breadth of community voice.

Students have participated in all phases of the project to date. Learning outcomes in the form of design proposals indicate a wide and deep understanding of community civic engagement techniques coupled with the requirement for coalition building through local, organizational, and political outlets relevant to this project (CPID 2016, 46–79). Design solutions respond to a varied set of circumstances and requirements, from large scale to small. Finally, the importance of a well-articulated design process that responds to the community context is evident; students engaged with and promoted the inclusion of their partners in this work where commonly held values were tangible.

>**Partners**: Center for Public Interest Design, Portland State University School of Architecture; La Familia Counseling Center; Mutual Assistance Network; South Sacramento and Del Paso Heights residents; Sacramento Area Council of Governments
>
>**Credits: CPID**: instructors, Sergio Palleroni, B.D. Wortham-Galvin, and R. Todd Ferry; students since spring 2014, graduate-level Urban Design Studio (ARCH 580), undergraduate Urban Design Studio (ARCH 480), summer internships, and student fellowships; Ecosistema Urbano; Place Studio

Note

1   See the With Sacramento project at www.centerforpublicinterestdesign.org/cpid-sacramento-transit-guide/.

References

CALEPA (California Environmental Protection Agency). 2014. "Designation of Disadvantaged Communities Pursuant to Senate Bill 535 (De León)." www.calepa.ca.gov/files/2016/10/EnvJustice-GHGInvest-Documents-SB535DesCom.pdf.

CPID (Center for Public Interest Design). 2016. *Community-Centered Transit Stop Planning Guide*. Portland State University School of Architecture, July 21.

Ecosistema Urbano. 2010. "Local(in), Online Mapping Tool." Accessed January 16, 2017. http://ecosistemaurbano.com/portfolio/localin/

31
Afterword
A Public Interest Design Educational Platform

Thomas Fisher

To see one possible future for public interest design, we need to understand the disruptions that are coming to both higher education and to the design professions. In their book *Platform Revolution*, authors Geoffrey Parker, Marshall Van Alstyne, and Sangeet Paul Choudary (2016) describe how digital platforms like Spotify have disrupted the music business, Facebook the news media, and Airbnb the hospitality industry. These authors further argue that any information-intensive, highly fragmented field that has a few gatekeepers and a lot of information asymmetry will likely find itself transformed by digital platforms that allow people to share information without the need of intermediaries. These authors do acknowledge that highly regulated, resource-intensive industries that have high failure costs will resist disruption longer, but they insist that even those will eventually get disrupted.

Consider both higher education and the design professions in this light. Both remain information intensive in the control and delivery of knowledge, both have great information asymmetries with students or clients seeking the knowledge of professors or practitioners, both are highly fragmented with many entities competing for tuition dollars or fees, and both have gatekeepers determining who gets admitted or licensed. Both, in other words, stand poised for a tremendous digital disruption, which has already begun. Free courses on online services like Udacity, Coursera, and edX have raised doubts in the minds of some debt-burdened students as to the value of traditional higher education.[1] And although less evolved, on-demand design services on sites like allaDIYally, Zoom Interiors, and SpoonCity have shown how platforms can help people connect directly with professionals at a much lower cost.[2]

Such sites have yet to have a major impact on either higher education or the design professions. But the hospitality industry would have said the same about

Airbnb in 2009, before it became the largest hotelier in the world without owning any real estate, or the taxi industry the same about Uber before it became larger than any taxi company in just a few years. The surest way to get disrupted by a platform business is to deny the threat and to assume that the old gatekeeping of information can last in the face of the digital revolution well under way.

Is it in the public interest for higher education to continue to charge high tuition rates and to deliver knowledge mainly to tuition-paying students when we now have the ability to distribute information much more widely for free? While public interest design may need to adapt itself, for pragmatic reasons, to the current gate-keeping model of higher education, does the platform revolution coursing through the global economy represent an opportunity for us to use design thinking to imagine more equitable and accessible forms of education, with the public interest in mind? Likewise, is it in the public interest for the design professions to continue to charge high fees for one-off designs for the relatively few clients that can pay the freight when hundreds of millions of people living in substandard housing, unsafe neighborhoods, and impoverished conditions need these services far more than the rich? Does public interest design represent an opportunity to rethink our practice models, embracing the entire human population as potential clients?

Which brings us back to public interest design. While many public interest design projects in school reflect the good intentions and great passion of the people involved—the faculty, students, and community members—this work still largely occurs within the traditional higher education system, with its studio-based curriculum and its semester or quarter schedule. As a result, the outcomes of public interest design education remain limited in scope and by no means meet the enormous need for this work that exists in communities around the world. Schools still largely focus on the design of individual shelters or site-specific developments, for example, while rarely attempting to redesign the systems or policies that would enable the best ideas to get implemented and widely adopted. If public interest design is to have the impact we all hope that it will, we need to do both.

The same is true of the professional context within which public interest design occurs. While a growing number of architecture and design firms encourage their staff to take part in pro bono efforts and occasionally take on projects that benefit communities most in need, this too remains just a drop in the bucket in terms of the demand for these services. Nor do we—professors and practitioners alike—talk nearly enough about how to change that situation. We give well-deserved recognition and awards to the best public interest design projects, but we rarely talk about how we could deliver public interest design services at scale. Might a request for ideas on how to scale up a project or proposal become a standard part of public interest design awards programs? From that perspective, we might do better *not* recognizing the beautiful one-off projects or awarding the dedicated people doing this work if it lulls us into complacency, thinking that we have done the best that we can do and all that we can do.

Producing public interest design at a scale commensurate with the need will require a transformation of our educational system and our design practices—something that seems likely to happen, given our vulnerability to the "platform revolution." So we need to ask: How can we can appropriate the coming digital disruption and use it to greatly expand the reach and impact of public interest design? The answer lies in turning public interest design into its own platform.

An admirable attempt at this happened in 2007, when Cameron Sinclair and Kate Stohr started the Open Architecture Network. That platform provided a digital commons where designers and communities could share innovative solutions to diverse public interest design challenges and collaborate on projects of mutual interest. While Sinclair and Stohr's organization, Architecture for Humanity, and the Open Architecture Network no longer exist, they had the right idea, and the notion of a public interest design platform remains of interest to many.[3]

Other platform-like sites have arisen more recently. The Social Economic Environmental Design (SEED) Network[4] has videos of case studies of award-winning projects, a tools section outlining methods and engagement strategies via the SEED Evaluator software, and an overview of the SEED evaluation process. And the Impact Design Hub,[5] in a transition as of this writing, has evolved from being more like a publication, with well-written articles and a jobs section where people can look for or post work opportunities, to being more like a digital platform, with curated open source content, interactive conversations among participants, and assessments of public interest work in particular places (Crepeau 2014). Both sites serve as invaluable sources of ideas and information for students, professors, and practitioners.

The disruptive implications of the platform revolution have only very recently become apparent, and there remains little incentive to embrace it among those who have prevailed in the old economy, via the tenure system of higher education or the licensing system of architectural practice. Nor do students trying to succeed in these systems have much power to change them, however out of sync the old rules are with the on-demand, networked world that increasingly surrounds us. As a result, we get the current condition of well-meaning and often well-done public interest design projects that may inspire many but that serve a very few, creating another kind of inequality.

By not doing much to alter the conditions under which higher education and professional practice now get done, the design community has created a situation in which we will suffer from the disruption of the new economy more intensely, the longer we wait. And we should not wait, since doing so does a disservice to the millions of people who can benefit from this work. It is not our discomfort with institutional change, but their discomfort living in terrible and even terrifying conditions that matters most, and giving them a platform that empowers them to improve their own lives seems like the only practical and ethical way forward. To this end, the emergence of the Open Architecture Collaborative[6] out of the Architecture for Humanity affiliates offers an excellent model: a network of committed people

Afterword

doing important work outside of the institutional restrictions of higher education and licensure.

So what might a public interest design *education* platform look like, one that could sustain itself financially as well as pedagogically? It would provide access to anyone who wants to learn something about this field or who has something to teach others. That accessibility has become increasingly possible in all but the most remote or impoverished locations, with roughly 40 percent of the world's population now connected to the Internet (Internet Live Stats 2016). A public interest design educational platform would also allow people to share ideas, information, and strategies, whether for educational or professional purposes, as well as to offer public interest design services that, like on the legal services platform Avvo,[7] might present as a menu of options with minimum prices often much lower than traditional fees. It might work more like eBay or Etsy and provide an open marketplace for education or design services that lets individuals, wherever they are around the world, deal directly with one another.

Such a platform could serve as a model for education more generally. Rather than follow the standard model of expecting students to come to campuses to learn, a public interest design platform would accommodate the wide range of informational needs of people by allowing them to stay where they are, accessing knowledge when required and sharing with others what they know. Research shows that students have greater motivation and achieve better outcomes when involved in project-based, design-oriented active learning, and a platform that allows public interest design students to learn in place and learn by doing would be better than much of what happens now in traditional classrooms and studios (Darling-Hammond 2008).

A widely accessible digital platform for public interest design education would also alter the equation of teacher and learner. It would let everyone show their work, post questions to colleagues, and respond to the inquiries of others, making everyone both a student and a teacher, depending on the situation. This would help build the knowledge base of public interest design and make the best ideas available to whoever wanted to adapt them to their particular needs.

A platform like this would also affect the way in which ordinary people access design services. While the authors of *Platform Revolution* acknowledge that a small percentage of professionals will continue to serve the world's wealthiest individuals and organizations, they also argue that a platform-based economy will lead a sizable percentage of professionals in a field like architecture to serve a much wider segment of the global population while working for much lower fees. In the context of current business models, that may sound disheartening. But if design professionals shift the model from providing one-off solutions for the few to generating prototypical solutions for the masses, we will also discover a lucrative line of work.

The key to financial sustainability in a platform economy lies in providing as much value as possible to as many people as possible. For public interest design, that means not only sharing ideas and information, but also developing ways to measure the value created by the work, something that this nascent field has yet to do in any systematic way. Most practitioners who do this work know the transformative effect it can have on the lives of people and the fates of communities. But we need to document that not just with anecdotes and stories, but also with data that show how much public interest design can reduce negative indices like poverty and criminality and enhance positive ones like security and opportunity. The gathering and sharing of these data as part of a person's participation in the platform could be one of its greatest values.

Another part of its value will depend on how many people participate in it. Unlike early platform efforts—like ArchVoices.org, whose labor intensiveness offset its true usefulness—success may now lie in appropriating existing platforms and populating them with useful and inspiring content. Teaching and practicing through sites like Facebook, Coursera, or Skillshare[8] would allow us to focus on physical design and let others handle the digital architecture.

It may sound odd to posit public interest design, now a relatively minor part of the profession, as a model for where design education and practice must go, but I do not think educators and practitioners have much choice. The validity of professions—be it the teaching professions or the design professions—increases according to the scope of their mission and the scale of their impact. Other professions have taken on global challenges like public health or human rights, while the design professions retain an educational and practice model still focused mainly on serving the rich. Unless the design professions and design education take on the global challenge of providing safe shelter and secure settlements for every person on the planet, regardless of ability to pay, ours will be a field much smaller and less relevant than it has been in the past.

Notes

1 See www.udacity.com, www.coursera.org, and www.edx.org.
2 See http://alladiyally.com, www.arc-max.com, and www.spoon.city.
3 See "Converge: Exchange—A Platform for Public Interest Design in Chicago," produced by Arbuckle Industries, filmed March 18–19, 2009, http://vimeo.com/7077745.
4 See http://seednetwork.org.
5 See http://impactdesignhub.org.
6 See www.openarchcollab.org.
7 See www.avvo.com.
8 See www.skillshare.com.

References

Crepeau, Katie. 2014. "Expanding the Impact Design Movement." *Impact Design Hub*. August 6. https://impactdesignhub.org/2014/08/06/feature-expanding-the-impact-design-movement/?feature_id=19063.

Darling-Hammond, Linda. 2008. *Powerful Learning: What We Know About Teaching for Understanding.* San Francisco: Jossey-Bass.

Internet Live Stats. 2016. "Internet Users." Accessed August. www.internetlivestats.com/internet-users/.

Parker, Geoffrey, Marshall Van Alstyne, and Sangeet Paul Choudary. 2016. *Platform Revolution: How Networked Markets Are Transforming the Economy and How to Make Them Work for You.* New York: W. W. Norton.

Part 4
Appendix

Glossary

This glossary is predominantly composed of entries authored by contributors representing themes central to Part 2 of this publication. These contributors were invited to submit terms and correlating definitions based on the innovative issues addressed within their work. These are especially relevant given the interrelated nature of Part 2 chapters and serve to effectively bridge concepts from throughout the publication.

The glossary entries that follow are credited to the respective chapter author(s) in Part 2, signified by in-text chapter and page numbers that are cross-referenced in this publication. In these chapters, glossary terms are indicated in bold type. Other entries have been provided by the publication editors with the intention of supporting overarching theories or models relevant to the entire scope of publication content. Citations evident throughout submitted glossary entries acknowledge the plurality of ideas from beyond this publication and as represented in the associated reference list.

active listening: "Suspending our own thought processes and making a conscious effort to understand another person's position. Using our body language, eye contact, and where appropriate, verbal cues—short questions or comments—we can help the speaker formulate their thoughts and reassure them they are being listened to" (Seeds for Change 2009). *See* Clark and Agrawal, Chapter 11, page 118.

allyship: "An active, consistent, and arduous practice of unlearning and re-evaluating, in which a person [with] privilege[s] seeks to operate in solidarity with a [group of people who have been] marginalized" (adapted from Anti-Oppression Network 2015). *See* Clark and Agrawal Chapter 11, page 120.

apprentices in training: Individuals enrolled in a job-skills training program that will prepare graduates to emerge into traditional apprenticeships with practitioners of a professionally recognized trade. *See* Folan, Chapter 10, page 113.

appropriate technology: A technology is considered appropriate when it is designed and built to align with the local, cultural, and economic conditions of a given group in a sustainable, replicable manner. (For more on appropriate technology, see Hazeltine and Bull 2003.) *See* Zaretsky, Chapter 27, page 215.

assessment: A systematic evaluation of specific activities or conditions of a given project or program. Assessment is often completed by a third party who is not one of the entities involved in the design or creation of the project or program. *See* Zaretsky, Chapter 27, page 214.

asset-based community design: An approach informed by asset-based community development whereby communities are empowered to direct their own innovation and change by leveraging existing or underutilized assets toward long-term sustainable outcomes (Collaborative for Neighborhood Transformation, n.d.). *See* Harnish, Chapter 24, page 195.

basemap: An initial scale drawing that includes pertinent project baseline information such as topography, building footprints, streets, sidewalks, and bodies of water. A basemap is a working drawing in that it is not meant for presentation but acts as a preliminary site plan. These drawings are commonly requested at the beginning of a project in architecture school. *See* Gaudio, Chapter 19, page 166.

biophilic design: Using forms, functions, and patterns in nature to design and build structures, landscapes, and other nonhuman objects. Biophilic design connects our developmental needs with our instinctual needs to associate with and love other living beings. *See* Stevens, Chapter 28, page 224.

case clinics: A small-group guided process designed to support new ways of seeing beyond challenges (Presencing Institute 2016). *See* Grocott and McEntee, Chapter 15, page 142.

community design workshop: A method or event whereby designers work with community constituents in response to a design proposal. Initially, this may include exercises where constituents participate in the design process. It may also be used as a feedback loop, gaining constituent response to an initial design proposal. *See* Harnish, Chapter 24, page 196.

community engagement workshop: A method or event whereby designers work with community constituents to research and develop critical design criteria that may inform a design proposal. Such workshops typically do not include design processes, but rather cultural and spatial research, trust building between the designer and constituents, and quantitative baseline research that may be used in evidence-based design research. *See* Harnish, Chapter 24, page 197.

consumer/survivor: An individual who is currently receiving mental health services or is a survivor of psychiatric intervention (or is both); the term is associated with consumer/survivor initiatives, programs run for and by people with mental health problems. *See* Orlowski and Jovanovic, Chapter 23, page 190.

cooperative education (co-op): An organized method of linking formal classroom instruction with practical experience in a work setting. There are two common educational approaches: the alternating method, where a student attends school for a term and then works for a term, and the parallel, or concurrent method, where a student's class schedule is structured to accommodate both school and work in the same day or week. The term was coined by Herman Schneider, dean of engineering at the University of Cincinnati, in 1906. *See* Garver, Chapter 26, page 206.

creative placemaking: An approach that positions arts and culture as primary drivers of placemaking projects and multisector collaboration as key to the projects' success. Creative placemaking amplifies and develops the physical and social character of a place, from the neighborhood to the regional scale, around its arts and culture diversity and distinctiveness. *See* Horrigan, Chapter 22, page 182.

cultural probes: Physical objects or materials used to invoke interactive responses and discussion among respondents during user observation, research, and interviewing (Gaver, Dunne, and Pacenti 1999). *See* Chan, Chapter 16, page 151.

democratic civic engagement (DCE): (1) A movement in higher education institutions concerned with their public purpose and how they educate college students to become responsible citizens. DCE describes the passionate engagement of students in civic life within and outside their academic atmosphere as intense and in close connection with people and their problems. DCE is inclusive in the identification of problems and the co-creation of solutions, and it is respectful of the knowledge brought by others. Finally, DCE is transformative because it focuses on the processes and purposes of the engagement, not just on the activities in which students and community members are involved (Fitzgerald et al. 2012; Boyte and Fretz 2010; Saltmarsh, Hartley, and Clayton 2009). *See* Pacheco, Chapter 12, page 122. (2) A framework that puts democracy front and center in civic engagement in higher education, fostering reciprocity and a *with*, not *for*, relational dynamic between those on campus and those in the community. In DCE, universities and communities employ democratic processes (means) to work with one another on alleviating public problems and advancing democratic purposes and culture (ends). *See* Horrigan, Chapter 22, page 182.

Design for Deconstruction (DFD): Denotes responsible practices in managing end-of-life building materials to minimize consumption of raw material. Designers support these practices by considering and employing strategies that incorporate harvested materials or facilitate future adaptation and reuse of new material (Morgan and Stevenson 2005). Also referred to as *Design for Disassembly*. Also see the US Environmental Protection Agency and US Green Building Council guidelines. *See* Folan, Chapter 10, page 115.

design/build: An approach where the range of skills from designing to building and fabrication are addressed in construction projects that serve to educate students through contextual hands-on learning, often conducted with community partners.

design thinking: "Design thinking," as defined by the design firm IDEO and taught at Stanford University's Hasso Plattner Institute of Design (d.school), is a human-centered approach to problem solving. The approach includes mindsets and methods that empower interdisciplinary teams to understand problems by making use of empathy-cultivating interviews and observations of users in the field, synthesizing insights, facilitating brainstorms and ideation, and testing ideas through prototypes (Miller 2015; Brown 2017). *See* Chan, Chapter 16, page 148.

dialogic: A process or space that is consciously enabled by placemaking praxis and that creates the conditions for people to dialogue and ultimately act together in setting and realizing transformative agendas for their environments. It involves, among other things, participation and inclusion, back-and-forth exchanges, reflection, and ongoing cycles of confirmation and interrogation *See* Horrigan, Chapter 22, page 184.

double-loop learning theory: Developed by Christopher Argyris and Donald Schön (1974), the theory uses critical thinking to evaluate the construction of new knowledge through its application in practice and aims to make decision-making processes more effective through the recognition of productive failures and successes. *See* Peterson, Chapter 20, page 176.

ecosystem: In the context of problem identification, refers to the social, environmental, economic, historical, and political elements, entities, and relationships that create and perpetuate the problem. This social context can be linear (cause and effect), web-like, or cyclical. Identification of the components of the ecosystem allows designers and community partners to recognize opportunities for effective interventions. *See* Orlowski and Jovanovic, Chapter 23, page 193.

edge effect: Changes in population or community structures occurring at the boundary of two habitats (Levin 2009, 780). *See* Folan, Chapter 10, page 111.

experiential learning: Any activity that puts college students in contact with people, their places, and their problems as part of a learning scenario. In the case of projects undertaken within the design studio, students also connect with and explore the tectonic qualities of materials and tools (Butko and Cricchio 2014; Allen 2012; Kolb 1984). *See* Pacheco, Chapter 12, page 122.

human-centered design: Human-centered design, which can be distinguished from user-centered design, maintains a focus on advancing human dignity in a way that enables human beings to thrive and exist under diverse circumstances (Buchanan 2001). *See* Chan, Chapter 16, page 147.

identity literacy: The capacity to identify, acknowledge, and discuss the intersectional power dynamics of one's own identities and the identities of others, including but not limited to racialization, gender, documentation status, and class. (Center for Art + Public Life 2017). *See* Clark and Agrawal, Chapter 11, page 118.

impact-driven design: An iterative, human-centered design process in which a project establishes a core mission that achieves considerable strides toward greater societal goals. *See* Benimana, Chapter 14, page 135.

intercultural competencies: Skills that allow people to relate to and interact with others whose social or cultural contexts are distinct with the purpose of fostering a "democratic culture" of communication and understanding through "intercultural dialogue" (Bergan and van't Land 2010). *See* Hartig and Pawlicki, Chapter 13, page 133.

intrapersonal skills: Skills that focus on interior perspectives and self-insight. Distinct from the interpersonal skills that form the basis of social intelligence, these personal skills include empathy, curiosity, willingness to be challenged, knowing to ask for help, being proactive, and cultural awareness. *See* Grocott and McEntee, Chapter 15, page 141.

learning objectives: Goals that define measureable (educational) benchmarks within a project, course, or program of study.

learning outcomes: Specific changes in an individual's awareness, knowledge, skills, motivations, or levels of functioning (adapted from Corporation for National and Community Service, n.d.).

Massive Change story formula: A narrative structure developed by Bruce Mau (2005) and the Institute Without Boundaries that outlines various components of a design problem and its response; this framework allows designers to identify and describe the situation they are addressing, the codeveloped solution, the design team members, the project users, the realization process, and the impact of the design proposal. *See* Orlowski and Jovanovic, Chapter 23, page 191.

metacognition: The processes of learning that encourage students to think reflectively and critically about not only *what* they are learning but also *how* they are learning. *See* Peterson, Chapter 20, page 176.

mindset: A self-perception that people hold about their talents and aptitudes. A growth mindset is when people believe that basic abilities can be developed through practice and perseverance. A fixed mindset is when people believe that qualities, like intelligence or talent, are fixed (Dweck 2006, ix, 6–7). *See* Grocott and McEntee, Chapter 15, page 141.

multi-stakeholder engagement (MSE): A methodology to encourage sustainable interventions into systemic problems. To achieve this, MSE requires the facilitated involvement, sharing, co-creation, innovation, and learning together of four sectors of society: knowledge-based institutions, governmental units, businesses, and societal or community groups (Dubbeling, de Zeeuw, and van Veenhuizen 2010; Peterson 2013; Global Innoversity 2014). *See* Campbell and Malan, Chapter 18, page 158.

otherness: The innate human recognition of unfamiliar persons or places based on similarity versus difference from oneself. The success of cross-cultural design projects often relies on transcending otherness toward identified commonality (Kapuściński 2009). *See* Harnish, Chapter 24, page 195.

outcomes: "Changes resulting from a program's activities or services; [quantifiable] changes in knowledge, attitude, behavior, or condition" (Corporation for National and Community Service, n.d., 12).

outputs: "The direct products or program activities and may include types, levels, or targets of services to be delivered by the program" (Corporation for National and Community Service, n.d., 10). Examples include activities, products, and participation.

participatory mapping: The act of involving local community members in spatially analyzing their town, city, or area. This method for data collection uses residents' tacit knowledge to gain a better understanding of the area. This technique is often used when outside researchers are planning to implement a community-based project in a particular neighborhood or town. *See* Gaudio, Chapter 19, page 166.

partnership: Acting *with* rather than *for* community partners. Also referred to as *engaged design partnership*. *See* Anderson, Chapter 25, page 203.

placemaking: A process and practice (professional or lay) that, above all, values co-creation and collective participation by citizenry and groups in shaping their environments. Placemaking acts to build social capital and realize placemaking projects (permanent, temporary, or tactical) wherein materials, activities, and meanings combine to foster greater place attachment, identity, and belonging for users and inhabitants. *See* Horrigan, Chapter 22, page 182.

post-occupancy evaluation (POE): A systematic process of evaluating a building or built project at some period after it has been occupied or is otherwise in use. Aspects such as operations, performance, and relevant factors of design may be evaluated in a POE. (For more on POE, see Preiser, Rabinowitz, and White 1990.) *See* Zaretsky, Chapter 27, page 216.

practice assessment: An incremental one-on-one meeting between a student and a practice adviser where the student's work-based experience is documented and learning outcomes in specific knowledge areas are measured. *See* Garver, Chapter 26, page 207.

practice-based learning: A pedagogical approach employing immersive, collaborative, and participatory learning experiences to expose students to real-world problems in context-specific, place-specific, real-world settings. Also referred to as *hands-on education*, **service-learning**, or *learning by doing*. *See* Davis and Weikert, Chapter 9, page 107.

practice component: A required portion of a curriculum program that is dedicated to tracking and evaluating students' work-based learning experience and associated practice hours (see also **practice hours**). It should appear on student transcripts alongside academic component requirements and grades. The term was coined by Don Brown at the Boston Architectural College in 2003 after several iterations, including "work/study," "work/school," "work curriculum," and "practice curriculum" (Brown 2014, 138). *See* Garver, Chapter 26, page 207.

practice hours: Reportable hours describing the amount of time students spend engaged in specific knowledge areas during work-based learning experiences. Hours are approved by a supervisor and tracked on student transcripts. *See* Garver, Chapter 26, page 207.

public interest design: "A design practice composed of three tenets—democratic decision making through meaningful community engagement, an issue-based approach, and the requirement for design evaluation" (Abendroth and Bell 2016, 308).

radical empathy: Requires active and integrated interaction with someone whose values and experiences are potentially different from oneself in order to gain insights into individual behaviors, complex historical events, and the interconnectedness of the various surrounding communities (adapted from Fuglei 2015). *See* Clark and Agrawal, Chapter 11, page 119.

reflection: (1) When students pause and evaluate their engaged design experiences so as to connect these specific experiences to broader concepts and constructs. *See* Anderson, Chapter 25, page 203. (2) An activity providing students and project participants with an opportunity to review and evaluate an experience or activity through free writing or by responding to specific questions. This introspective technique can be used immediately after the experience or activity is complete or after some time has passed. *See* Stevens, Chapter 28, page 222.

Scholarships of Application and Engagement (SAE): Emphasize a reciprocal understanding of the relationship between theory and practice. They place value on the application of knowledge, while at the same time recognizing that the "act of application" itself generates knowledge. The SAE stress the importance of purpose in academic pursuits; promote the interdependence of teaching, research, and service; and prioritize knowledge generation that engages stakeholders beyond the academy to address critical societal challenges. When sanctioned by universities, the SAE provide a foundation for the design, implementation, evaluation, and contemplation of public interest design interventions as legitimate academic pursuits (Boyer 1990, 23; Boyer 1996, 19). *See* Spencer, Chapter 17, page 155.

SEED Certification: "Third-party evaluation and resulting recognition of compliance with SEED standards (mission and principles) at an exemplary level" (Abendroth and Bell 2016, 308).

SEED Evaluator: "An online communication tool that translates the SEED process allowing communities, audiences, and designers to define goals for design projects and then measure project achievement through a third-party review" (Abendroth and Bell 2016, 308).

serious play: Facilitated play-based activities designed to develop and enhance skills, such as collaboration, creativity, and self-awareness. *See* Grocott and McEntee, Chapter 15, page 142.

service-learning: "A form of experiential education in which students engage in activities that address human and community needs together with structured opportunities for reflection designed to achieve desired learning outcomes" (Jacoby 2015, 26). *See* Campbell and Malan, Chapter 18, page 158.

Social Economic Environmental Design (SEED) Network: "A principle-based group of individuals and organizations dedicated to building a culture of civic responsibility and engagement in the built environment and the public realm" (SEED Network 2017).

social literacy: A designer's understanding of the context, levels of complexity, and interconnectedness of social problems, their potential root causes, and the various possible methods for addressing them. Students develop social literacy through both classroom and practice-based learning by being exposed to a diversity of people, social issues and themes, movements, organizations, contexts, and theories of change, in order to challenge their own and others' worldviews and to develop the understanding, humility, and cultural sensitivity needed to design appropriate and impactful community-based interventions. *See* Davis and Weikert, Chapter 9, page 107.

sociospatial: The engagement of societies with the public and private spaces they occupy. A symbiotic relationship is formed between a community and its space as the community engages, occupies, forms, and transforms its physical environment. At the same time, the physical environment informs and shapes society through its public space and public–private edges. *See* Harnish, Chapter 24, page 197.

Student Learning Contract (SLC): A set of specific competencies intended to serve as a guide for students as they navigate a range of work-based learning experiences. The SLC is used to help direct students' future objectives and career growth and is the basis for evaluating their performance. *See* Garver, Chapter 26, page 209.

work-based learning: An educational strategy that involves interactions with industry or community partners linked to classroom-based instruction. It does not mean that the experience has to occur in a workplace or as part of a workday. *See* Garver, Chapter 26, page 206.

References

Abendroth, Lisa M., and Bryan Bell, eds. 2016. "Glossary." In *Public Interest Design Practice Guidebook: SEED Methodology, Case Studies, and Critical Issues*, 306–9. New York: Routledge.

Allen, Stan. 2012. "The Future That Is Now: Architecture Education in North America Over Two Decades of Rapid Social and Technological Change." *Places Journal*, March. Accessed July 21, 2016. https://placesjournal.org/article/the-future-that-is-now/.

Anti-Oppression Network. 2015. "Allyship." Accessed August 1, 2016. https://theantioppressionnetwork.wordpress.com/allyship/.

Argyris, Christopher, and Donald A. Schön. 1974. *Theory in Practice: Increasing Professional Effectiveness*. Oxford, UK: Jossey-Bass.

Bergan, Sjur, and Hilligje van't Land, eds. 2010. *Speaking Across Borders: The Role of Higher Education in Furthering Intercultural Dialogue*. Council of European Education Series, no. 16, back cover summary. Strasbourg, France: Council of Europe Publishing.

Boyer, Ernest L. 1990. *Scholarship Reconsidered: Priorities of the Professoriate*. New York: John Wiley and Sons.

Boyer, Ernest L. 1996. "The Scholarship of Engagement." *Journal of Public Service and Outreach* 1 (1): 11–20.

Boyte, Harry C., and Erick Fretz. 2010. "Civic Professionalism." *Journal of Higher Education Outreach and Engagement*, 14 (2): 67–90.

Brown, Don Robert. 2014. *Designed in Boston: A Personal Journal-History of the Boston Architectural College*. Boston, MA: Boston Architectural College.

Brown, Tim. 2017. "Design Thinking." IDEO University (website). Accessed April 20. www.ideou.com/pages/design-thinking.

Buchanan, Richard. 2001. "Human Dignity and Human Rights: Thoughts on the Principles of Human-centered Design." *Design Issues* 17 (3): 35–39.

Butko, Daniel, and Anthony Cricchio. 2014. "Designing the Build Experience Through Inhabitable Deliverables: Three Case Studies Housing Project-based Instruction." Paper presented at the 102nd annual meeting of the Association of Collegiate School of Architecture, Miami Beach, FL, April 10–12.

Center for Art + Public Life. 2017. "What We Do." California College of the Arts. Accessed March 29. http://center.cca.edu/about.

Collaborative for Neighborhood Transformation. n.d. "What Is Asset-Based Community Development (ABCD)." Asset-Based Community Development Institute. Accessed March 17, 2017. https://resources.depaul.edu/abcd-institute/publications/publications-by-topic/Documents/What%20isAssetBasedCommunityDevelopment(1).pdf.

Corporation for National and Community Service. n.d. "How to Develop a Program Logic Model." 10–12. (Adapted from the W.K. Kellogg Foundation Evaluation Handbook, 2004.) Accessed May 9, 2017. www.nationalservice.gov/sites/default/files/upload/OpAC%20Logic%20Model%20draft%20in%20progress.pdf.

Dubbeling, Marielle, Henk de Zeeuw, and René van Veenhuizen. 2010. *Cities, Poverty, and Food: Multi-Stakeholder Policy and Planning in Urban Agriculture*. Rugby: Practical Action Publishing.

Dweck, Carol. 2006. *Mindset: The New Psychology of Success*. New York: Ballantine Books.

Fitzgerald, Hiram, Karen Bruns, Steven Sonka, Andrew Furco, and Louis Swanson. 2012. "The Centrality of Engagement in Higher Education." *Journal of Higher Education Outreach and Engagement*, 16 (3): 7–27.

Fuglei, Monica. 2015. "Radical Empathy: Teaching Students to Walk in Others' Shoes." *Concordia University—Portland*. Accessed August 1, 2016. http://education.cu-portland.edu/blog/news/teaching-radical-empathy/.

Gaver, Bill, Tony Dunne, and Elena Pacenti. 1999. "Design: Cultural Probes." *Interactions* 6 (1): 21–29.

Global Innoversity. 2014. "Concept Statement and Working Agreements." Accessed June 16, 2016. http://globalinnoversity.org/wp-content/uploads/2014/02/Concept-statement-and-working-agreements-v3.pdf (site discontinued).

Hazeltine, Barrett, and Christopher Bull, eds. 2003. *Field Guide to Appropriate Technology*. Atlanta, GA: Elsevier Science.

Jacoby, Barbara. 2015. *Service-Learning Essentials: Questions, Answers, and Lessons Learned*. San Francisco: Jossey-Bass.

Kapuściński, Ryszard. 2009. *The Other*. London: Verso.

Kolb, David. 1984. *Experiential Learning: Experience as the Source of Learning and Development*. Englewood Cliffs, NJ: Prentice-Hall.

Levin, Simon A. 2009. *The Princeton Guide to Ecology*. Princeton, NJ: Princeton University Press.

Mau, Bruce. 2005. "Massive Change in Action." Institute without Boundaries in collaboration with the Canadian Heritage Information Network. Accessed August 23, 2006. www.massivechangeinaction.virtualmuseum.ca (site discontinued).

Miller, Peter. 2015. "Is 'Design Thinking' the New Liberal Arts?" *The Chronicle of Higher Education* (website), March 26. Accessed April 10, 2017. http://chronicle.com/article/Is-Design-Thinking-the-New/228779.

Morgan, Chris, and Fionn Stevenson. 2005. *Design for Deconstruction*. SEDA Design Guidelines for Scotland, no. 1. Glasgow: Scottish Ecological Design Association. www.seda.uk.net/assets/files/guides/dfd.pdf.

Peterson, H. Christopher. 2013. "Fundamental Principles of Managing Multi-Stakeholder Engagement." *International Food and Agribusiness Management Review* 16 (Special Issue A): 11–22.

Preiser, Wolfgang F. E., Harvey Z. Rabinowitz, and Edward T. White. 1990. *Post-Occupancy Evaluation*. New York: Van Nostrand Reinhold.

Presencing Institute. 2016. "Case Clinic." Accessed August 14. https://uschool.presencing.com/tool/case-clinic.

Saltmarsh, John, Matthew Hartley, and Patti Clayton. 2009. *Democratic Engagement White Paper*. Boston, MA: New England Resource Center for Higher Education.

SEED Network. 2017. "About SEED Network." Accessed March 15. https://seednetwork.org/about/.

Seeds for Change. 2009. "Active Listening." Accessed August 1, 2016. www.seedsforchange.org.uk/activelistening.

Biographies

Editor Biographies

Lisa M. Abendroth is a professor and coordinator of the Communication Design program at the Metropolitan State University of Denver in Colorado, USA. She is a SEED Network founding member, a SEED Evaluator coauthor, and a recipient of the SEED Award for Leadership in Public Interest Design. Abendroth lectures and presents the SEED methodology and case studies in diverse educational contexts, including the Public Interest Design Institute. Her research across design disciplines includes writing, curating, and critically assessing solutions that address underserved people, places, and problems. Along with Bryan Bell, Abendroth is coeditor of the *Public Interest Design Practice Guidebook: SEED Methodology, Case Studies, and Critical Issues* (2016). She holds degrees from Virginia Commonwealth University, USA, and the Rhode Island School of Design, USA.

Bryan Bell founded the nonprofit organization Design Corps in 1991 with the mission to provide the benefits of design for the 98 percent without architects. His current work includes research on the field of public interest design and the SEED Network, which Bell cofounded. His work has been supported by the American Institute of Architects (AIA) College of Fellows Latrobe Prize and through a Harvard Loeb Fellowship. Bell has published three books in the field, and he organizes the Public Interest Design Institute and the Structures for Inclusion conference series. He was awarded a National AIA Award and was a National Design Award finalist. His work has been exhibited at the Venice Biennale and the Cooper Hewitt, Smithsonian Design Museum. Bell holds degrees from Princeton University, USA, and Yale University, USA, and is an associate professor in the School of Architecture at North Carolina State University, USA.

Contributor Biographies

Robin Abrams is a professor of architecture at the School of Architecture of the North Carolina State University College of Design. She is a registered architect specializing in inner-city revitalization, housing, and urban design. She is an AIA Fellow and member and a licensed member of the American Society of Landscape Architects (ASLA). Abrams earned a degree in urban studies from Northwestern University, a master's degree in community and regional planning and a master of architecture degree from the University of Texas at Austin, and a PhD in landscape from the University of Sheffield, England. She has worked in the field of urban design in Austin, Texas, since 1979. During that time, she has produced over thirty master plans. In addition to work in the United States, Abrams has consulted on projects in Mexico, Japan, and England.

Shalini Agrawal is an associate professor at California College of the Arts and assistant director of the Center for Art + Public Life. Agrawal, trained as an architect, has twenty years of experience facilitating a diversity of communities and is the cofounder of Architreasures in Chicago. Her practice, MAC Studio Landscape Architecture, engages communities in the design of public spaces.

Mariana Amatullo is an associate professor of strategic design and management at Parsons School of Design at The New School. She also serves as the cochair of the management initiative at The New School, a university-wide effort focused on a new vision of management education for the twenty-first century driven by principles of design, creativity, and social justice. Amatullo joined The New School in August 2017 after sixteen years at ArtCenter College of Design in Pasadena, California, where she cofounded and led its award-winning social innovation department, Designmatters. She is the recipient of the inaugural 2012 DELL Social Innovation Education award and was named one of *Fast Company*'s Co.Design 50 Designers Shaping the Future and the Public Interest Design 100. Amatullo holds a PhD in management from the Weatherhead School of Management at Case Western Reserve University, where she is a scholar in residence. Her research focuses on the impact of design on social innovation and organizational practice. She also holds an MA in art history and museum studies from the University of Southern California and a *licence en lettres* degree from the Sorbonne University, Paris.

Nadia M. Anderson is associate professor of architecture and urban design and director of the City Building Lab at the University of North Carolina at Charlotte. Her work focuses on publicly engaged design as a vehicle for social empowerment and environmental resilience, ranging across scales, from the detailing of modular affordable housing to studies of regional local-foods systems. Anderson is a licensed architect who practiced in Chicago, Warsaw, and Vienna from 1994 to 2005 before moving to full-time academic work. She received her master of architecture degree from the University of Pennsylvania in 1994 and her BA from Yale University in 1988.

Jeremy Beaudry is an experience design strategist at the University of Vermont Medical Center in Burlington, where he leads a human-centered design for healthcare practice. Previously, he was a professor of design and director of the Design for Social Impact master's degree program at the University of the Arts in Philadelphia. His research and design practice focuses on creating collaborative tools and methods with organizations, communities, and leaders in the service of systems-wide change and innovation efforts. He has lectured and publicly presented projects at the intersection of social impact design, health, and design education in national and international venues.

Christian Benimana is the Rwanda programs manager at MASS Design Group and the director of the African Design Centre in Kigali. He has led the design on many design/build projects, including the Neo-Natal Intensive Care Unit at Rwinkwavu Hospital in Rwanda and the Maternity Waiting Village in Malawi. He taught at the architecture school of the former Kigali Institute of Science and Technology and is currently the chairman of both the Education Board of the Rwanda Institute of Architects and the Education Board of the East African Institute of Architects.

Peter Miles Bergman graduated in 1996 with a BA from the University of California, San Diego. He has worked as a screen printer, hand stripped film for packaging, trafficked newspaper ads, jockeyed PDFs for web offset printing, and written features as a contributing editor. After a decade covered in ink, he returned to school in 2007 to pursue an MFA in visual communication from the School of the Art Institute of Chicago. As an associate professor of art in the Communication Design program at Metropolitan State University of Denver, Bergman combines an academic interest in design with professional experience in print publishing to teach typography, publication design, and packaging while maintaining an active exhibition practice and small press publishing imprint under the name *is* PRESS.

Gene Bressler was appointed head of the Department of Landscape Architecture at North Carolina State University College of Design in 2006. Bressler teaches the First-Year Fall MLA Design Studio along with Professor Art Rice. His areas of research and teaching focus on urban growth, sustainable development, and the planning and design strategies for challenging suburbia. Bressler serves on the college's Annual Urban Design Forum. Since 2010, Bressler has corepresented NC State on the Blue Ridge Road District Planning and Design task force. In 2006, Bressler was recognized with the national award Outstanding Administrator of the Year by the Council of Educators in Landscape Architecture (CELA) for his leadership and contributions to teaching. In 2007, he was awarded Fellow by the ASLA.

Angus Donald Campbell is head of the Department of Industrial Design at the University of Johannesburg. His design research focuses on innovation at the nexus of social, ecological, and technological systems within the South African context, which led him to cofound the Design Society Development DESIS Lab and interdisciplinary research project iZindaba Zokudla (Conversations about Food).

Deland Chan is a transdisciplinary educator, urban planner, and designer with a passion for urban sustainability and human-centered design. As the assistant director of Urban Studies for Community-Based Learning and a cofounder of the Human Cities Initiative at Stanford University, she teaches project-based courses open to undergraduate and graduate students from all disciplines, with a focus on experiential learning. Chan completed her undergraduate studies in urban studies and sociology at Stanford University and her graduate studies in city and regional planning at the University of California, Berkeley.

Megan Clark is a former senior manager of student programming and strategic partnerships at the California College of the Arts Center for Art + Public Life. Clark received her master's degree in sustainable design at the University of Texas at Austin. She has helped launch community-engagement programs in Texas and California, and she develops community-engagement workshops for students, faculty, and design professionals.

Lee Davis is an author, designer, and social entrepreneur. He is currently codirector of the Center for Social Design and faculty in the Master of Arts in Social Design program at the Maryland Institute College of Art. Davis is cofounder and served for sixteen years as co-chief executive officer of NESsT, an incubator for social enterprises across Central Europe and Latin America. Davis is a trustee of the Winterhouse Institute, dedicated to advancing design education for social impact, and a social enterprise fellow at the Yale School of Management. He is a 2004 recipient of the Skoll Award for Social Entrepreneurship and a 1988–1989 recipient of the Thomas J. Watson Fellowship.

R. Todd Ferry is associate director and senior research associate at the Center for Public Interest Design within the Portland State University School of Architecture. His research and work investigate how social needs can be addressed by architecture in underserved communities. Recent work includes a sustainable community center for seniors in Inner Mongolia, China; a mobile stage for the Portland Opera bringing the arts to more communities; and the POD Initiative offering new visions for addressing homelessness regionally. This work is incorporated into Ferry's teaching through architecture studios and courses on design thinking, public interest design, and an introduction to architecture.

Thomas Fisher is a professor in the School of Architecture at the University of Minnesota, as well as the Dayton Hudson Chair in Urban Design and the director of the Metropolitan Design Center at the university's College of Design. He was recognized in 2005 as the fifth most published writer about architecture in the United States and has been recognized four times as a top design educator by the journal *Design Intelligence*. He has published nine books, more than fifty book chapters and introductions, and more than four hundred articles in professional journals and major publications. His newest book, *Designing Our Way to a Better World*, was published in May 2016 by the University of Minnesota Press.

John Folan is an architect, professor, and executive director of PROJECT RE_, an amalgam of designers, builders, and material specialists committed to realizing latent potential through design. Since 2008, he has held the T. David Fitz-Gibbon Chair at Carnegie Mellon University, where he founded and is director of the Urban Design Build Studio. Through his work with the UDBS, Folan has collaborated with challenged urban communities in western Pennsylvania on the development and implementation of catalytic projects through participatory design processes. His private professional practice focuses on place-based, social, economic, and environmental issues in architecture and urban design.

Bethany Lundell Garver is the director of Applied Learning at the Boston Architectural College, teaching courses in urban design and community engagement. Garver directs the CityLab program and helped develop the reflective assessment process for the BAC's Practice Department. Garver was educated at Harvard University in urban design and at Auburn University in architecture and interior architecture, and her work spans design, research, practice, and policy. Drawing from expertise leading projects in Boston, San Francisco, New York, and the American South, Garver employs a learning-by-doing approach to expanding design stewardship for more healthy, equitable, and sustainable communities. She is a licensed architect, National Council of Architectural Registration Boards certificate holder, and an elected board member of the Association of Collegiate Schools of Architecture and the Boston Society of Architects AIA chapter.

Brian Gaudio is a cofounder of Module, a housing start-up in Pittsburgh. In 2015, he was a Fulbright Scholar in Santiago, Dominican Republic. Gaudio directed *Within Formal Cities*, a documentary about the housing crisis in South America, which debuted in 2016. He has worked as a designer at the Gulf Coast Community Design Studio and in the Blue Sky Department at Walt Disney Imagineering. Gaudio graduated summa cum laude from North Carolina State University with a bachelor of architecture degree, where he was a Park Scholar, started a nonprofit organization, and was a finalist for the Harry S. Truman Scholarship.

Dan Gottlieb is an associate professor in the Environmental Design department at ArtCenter College of Design. He has successfully led multiple grant-funded courses and programs, including the award-winning Safe Agua initiative to design innovative water solutions for Latin American communities with no running water. Gottlieb was awarded ArtCenter's 2012 Great Teacher Award and the 2007 Nuckolls Fund for Lighting Education Grant, and he has led international educational collaborations, including the Pacific Rim Projects in Tokyo, Japan, with Tama Art University. He is a leader of the design studio Padlab and is an internationally respected expert in materials research and innovation, illumination technology and design, and spatial installation design. Gottlieb received his master of architecture degree from the Yale School of Architecture.

Lisa Grocott is head of design at Monash University and director of WonderLab, a design and learning research lab. She spent the past twelve years at Parsons School of Design in New York, where she was the dean of academic initiatives and, for the past six years, core faculty in the Transdisciplinary Design MFA program.

Anthony Guido is a hybrid industrial designer and design educator focused on transformative products, services, and systems. As program director of the MDes Design for Social Impact program at the University of the Arts in Philadelphia, Guido works on the development of creative, human-centered design tools and methods for learning in a rapidly changing world. Following industrial design studies at the Ohio State University, he began his design career working in Europe, the United States, and Japan for several large companies, start-up ventures, and universities. He received a master's degree in strategic sustainable development from the Blekinge Institute of Technology in Sweden.

Maggie Hansen is director of the Small Center for Collaborative Design, where she leads a team of creative makers, doers, and educators working for a better city. Hansen's work in professional practice in New York at Nelson Byrd Woltz Landscape Architects and her background in architecture, landscape architecture, and contemporary art contribute to an interdisciplinary ethos. Her design research investigates how the work of engaging urban hydrology, restoring cultural spaces, and supporting native ecosystems can contribute to civic life and community identity. Hansen holds a BA from the University of Chicago and master's degrees in architecture and landscape architecture from the University of Virginia.

Chris Harnish is an associate professor of architecture at Thomas Jefferson University in Pennsylvania. He teaches and practices resilient humanitarian architecture and community development in southern Africa, including participatory design methodologies and high-performance, low-tech design strategies. His work with communities results in architectural projects that include the following: the Piet Patsa Community Arts Centre, Viljounskroon, South Africa; the Youth with a Vision Children's Centre, Dennilton, South Africa; the eNtokozweni Community

Centre, Alexandra, South Africa; and the Malamulo Hospital in Thyolo and Blantyre, Malawi. In 2016, Harnish was awarded a Fulbright Scholar Fellowship to teach design methods for cross-cultural humanitarian development at the University of Malawi Polytechnic in Blantyre.

Ursula Hartig holds a master's degree in architecture (*diplom-ingenieur*) from the Technische Universität in Berlin. Since 1997, she has been a research fellow and teacher for design and construction in the Department of Architecture and a project manager and director of TU Berlin's DesignBuild Studios, which include the planning, realization, and documentation of buildings in Mexico and Afghanistan. In 2004, Hartig founded CoCoon, a sector for intercultural and interdisciplinary teaching, research, and practice in the field of the built environment. In 2012, she directed the symposium DesignBuild-Studio: New Ways in Architectural Education in Berlin, was coordinator of the dbXchange.eu web platform, and is currently a professor at the Hochschule München.

Penny Herscovitch is an associate professor in the Environmental Design department at ArtCenter College of Design. Herscovitch is a Los Angeles-based designer and design educator. She is a leader in the design studio Padlab, whose work encompasses materials research and innovation, illumination, and spatial installation design. She has lectured and taught internationally, and her work has been published extensively. Herscovitch conducts research and writes for renowned institutions and firms, including Morphosis Architects. She was awarded the 2007 Nuckolls Fund for Lighting Education Grant and the 2012 Great Teacher Award. She has led international educational collaborations, including the Pacific Rim Projects in Tokyo, Japan, with Tama Art University and the award-winning Safe Agua project with Designmatters and the Innovation Center of TECHO. She received her BA in architecture from Yale University.

Paula Horrigan, emerita professor of landscape architecture at Cornell University, works to advance democratic placemaking and the public purposes of design and higher education through her community-engaged education and scholarship. Placemaking praxis, action research, and service-learning guide her Rust to Green project, which aims to advance placemaking across scales in postindustrial upstate New York. Horrigan is a fellow of both the ASLA and the CELA, and she is coeditor of *Service-Learning in Design and Planning: Educating at the Boundaries* (2011) and *Community Matters: Service-Learning in Engaged Design and Planning* (2014).

Jeffrey Hou is professor of landscape architecture at the University of Washington, Seattle, where his work focuses on design activism, public space, and cross-cultural placemaking. Hou is an author and editor of *Greening Cities, Growing Community:*

Learning from Seattle's Urban Community Gardens (2009), *Insurgent Public Space: Guerrilla Urbanism and the Remaking of Contemporary Cities* (2010), and *Transcultural Cities: Border-Crossing and Placemaking* (2013). In a career that spans the Pacific, Hou has worked with indigenous tribes, farmers, and fishers in Taiwan; neighborhood residents in Japan; villagers in China; and inner-city immigrant youths and elders in North American cities.

Jamer Hunt collaboratively designs open and flexible programs for participation that respond to emergent cultural conditions. He is the vice provost for Transdisciplinary Initiatives at the New School, where he was founding director (2009–2015) of the graduate program in Transdisciplinary Design at Parsons. With Paola Antonelli at the Museum of Modern Art, he was co-creator of the award-winning curatorial experiment and book *Design and Violence (2013–15)*, as well as a collaborator on the symposia HeadSpace: On Scent as Design and Design and the Elastic Mind. He is currently completing a book manuscript on scale, complex systems, and the unruliness of everyday experiences.

Julia Jovanovic was born in a small village in Bulgaria and immigrated to Canada at the age of eleven. Her passion for art and architecture led her to pursue a master of architecture degree from Lawrence Technological University. Her graduate work focused on themes of environmental and social sustainability. Inspired by the process and execution of the Ten Friends Diner project, Jovanovic has launched and operates R3 Design, a small design practice focusing on interior, exterior, and landscape design and renovation in Windsor, Ontario, Canada. She also teaches design and technical course work at LTU.

Sharon Lefevre is an assistant professor and director of University Common Curriculum at the University of the Arts in Philadelphia. She is the author of *The Heirloom House* (2015) and for three years has written for the *Nantucket Chronicle*. Her articles include "Finders-Keepers," "Aloft," and a series on the island's workforce-housing challenge. Lefevre was an assistant film editor and producer of documentary films for Kufic Films, Smith-Kline in-house productions, and HBO documentary shorts. She won first prize in the Philadelphia Film Festival for *King of the Junkmen*. She holds degrees from Princeton University and Columbia University.

Naudé Malan is senior lecturer in development studies in the Department of Anthropology and Development Studies at the University of Johannesburg. He is the lead researcher and convener of iZindaba Zokudla (Conversations about Food) and a cofounder of the Design Society Development DESIS Lab. He has published on urban agriculture, food systems change, participatory development, user-centered design, human rights, social security, and science policy. Malan holds a PhD in development studies from the University of Johannesburg in Johannesburg, South Africa.

Tracy Manuel is a multimedia designer. At the intersection of storytelling and media, her work includes an iterative, design-based approach to community radio and an undergraduate honors thesis exploring the social, artistic, and political capabilities of Instagram. At the Center for Design in the Public Interest at the University of California, Davis, Manuel helps patients, providers, and entire communities improve communication about chronic pain.

Michael McAllister is an associate professor at the University of the Arts in Philadelphia, where he teaches, consults, and runs independent projects focusing on design with and for people living with disabilities. He has over twenty years of experience in product development focused on office furniture for Knoll. At Syracuse University, he cofounded COLAB, a center for interdisciplinary explorations, and served as director of design and innovation. His design work has received multiple awards and has been supported through a National Endowment for the Arts grant. His work with gesture-based interfaces is exhibited at the Newseum in Washington, DC, and at the Walker Art Center in Minneapolis, Minnesota.

Kate McEntee is a social design researcher with a practice focused on asking the right questions. She graduated with an MFA in transdisciplinary design from Parsons School of Design and is currently a lecturer and design research fellow in the faculty of Art Design and Architecture at Monash University in Melbourne, Australia.

Rahul Mehrotra is professor of urban design and planning at the Harvard Graduate School of Design. In 1990, he founded RMA Architects in Mumbai, India. Driven by a commitment to advocacy in Mumbai, his firm has initiated several unsolicited projects. Mehrotra coauthored *Bombay: The Cities Within*, *Banganga: Sacred Tank*, *Public Places Bombay*, *Bombay to Mumbai: Changing Perspectives*, and *Architecture in India Since 1990*. Based on the recommendations in Mehrotra's study *Conserving an Image Center: The Fort Precinct in Bombay*, the historic Fort area in Mumbai was declared a conservation precinct in 1995—the first such designation in India.

Jonas Milder is founder and principal of Milder Office, a design and production company based in Philadelphia. Milder Office distributes its own furniture system and also consults on the programming and design of work and learning environments. Milder has been a full-time faculty member in the Industrial Design Department at the University of the Arts in Philadelphia since 1997. He served as chair of the undergraduate industrial design program between 2002 and 2006 and directed the Master of Industrial Design program between 2007 and 2012. Milder earned a bachelor's degree in industrial design from the College for Design in Schwäbisch Gmünd, Germany, and a design diploma from the University of the Arts in Berlin, Germany.

Kelly Monico received her MFA from the University of Denver in 2005. She is currently an associate professor of art at Metropolitan State University of Denver, where she teaches in the Communication Design program. Her design practice embodies human-centered design and data visualization, with the majority of her creative projects drawing on the use of repetitive actions and patterning as a means to study human behavior. Her work has been featured in numerous exhibitions, including *Craft Tech/Coded Media* at the Boulder Museum of Contemporary Art, *Design After Dark* presented by the Design Council of the Denver Art Museum, and *URB11* at the Kiasma Museum of Contemporary Art in Helsinki, Finland.

Edward M. Orlowski is an associate professor of architecture at Lawrence Technological University and past president of the Association for Community Design. He holds a master of architecture degree from the University of Michigan. He directs courses focusing on design ethics and practice within a model of activism, and he has presented papers both in the United States and abroad on activist design paradigms. Orlowski is a member of the SEED Network and Architects, Planners, and Designers for Social Responsibility. He is the founding director of the public interest design and research lab Atelier Mule.

Pedro Pacheco is a full time professor at Tecnológico de Monterrey and has worked for over twenty years developing pedagogical scenarios to help undergraduate and graduate students connect theory and practice in the planning, design, and construction of housing and community infrastructure for underserved groups. These pedagogical explorations have evolved into Impulso Urbano, a service-learning program co-created by Pacheco where architecture students apply their knowledge to the service of low-income groups in Mexico. Impulso Urbano also works with students and professors from other departments and institutions in recognition of the fact that the built environment is a complex phenomenon that requires insight from other disciplines.

Sergio Palleroni is a professor of architecture and founding director of the Center for Public Interest Design at Portland State University. His research and fieldwork serve communities in need worldwide through his educational initiatives for design students. To that end, he cofounded the BASIC Initiative, a service-learning education program that since 1988 has focused on collaborative work with communities in need in much of the world. Palleroni has received recognition from several countries for this work, including the US National Design Award in 2005, the Latrobe Prize in 2011, and finalist for China's Tang Prize in 2015.

Nina Pawlicki is a teaching and research fellow at the School of Architecture at Technische Universität in Berlin and is part of CoCoon, a studio for intercultural and interdisciplinary teaching, research, and practice. With a particular interest in actor-driven processes in the design of social spaces, she ran design/build projects in Mexico, Mongolia, Jordan, and Berlin. In 2013, Pawlicki coinitiated the European DesignBuild Knowledge Network, funded by the European Union, and in 2012, she cohosted the symposium DesignBuild-Studio: New Ways in Architectural Education. Pawlicki studied architecture at TU Berlin and the Pontificia Universidad Católica de Chile and has a wide range of architectural experience.

Sarah Perrault is an associate professor in the University Writing Program at the University of California, Davis, and codirector of the UC Davis Center for Design in the Public Interest. Her research interests include public science communication, writing pedagogy, rhetorical theory, and how rhetoricians and designers can work together to do public interest design work. She has a PhD in rhetoric and composition, an MFA in creative nonfiction writing, a BA in anthropology, and an enduring interest in interdisciplinarity.

Benjamin Peterson is the director of Practice Instruction at The Boston Architectural College and is responsible for the development and delivery of a curriculum in practice focused on civic engagement. Peterson directs the college's Gateway Initiative, a program that provides design opportunities for students to work with community partners as clients and collaborators. He received a BA in anthropology and environmental studies from Bowdoin College and a master of architecture degree from the Rhode Island School of Design, with studies focused on the intersections of architecture, landscape, and infrastructure. Peterson serves on the board of directors of the Community Design Resource Center of Boston and sits on the advisory board for the citywide master-planning process for Cambridge, Massachusetts.

Susannah Ramshaw is the associate director of Designmatters at ArtCenter College of Design, where she develops and leads new strategic programming to support the curricular expansion of the Designmatters minor. Ramshaw has held artistic and educational positions at the Colburn School of Music, the Los Angeles Philharmonic, and the Chicago Architecture Foundation. She has developed experiential learning programs for college students, piloted online learning platforms for elementary teachers and students, and developed a music therapy program for communities on Skid Row in Los Angeles. A classically trained trumpet player, Ramshaw received a bachelor of music degree from DePauw University and studied at the University of Music and Performing Arts in Vienna, Austria.

Benjamin R. Spencer is an associate professor in the University of Washington, Department of Landscape Architecture, an adjunct associate professor in the University of Washington, Department of Global Health and director of the Informal Urban Communities Initiative. Spencer's work is collaborative and interdisciplinary. It integrates research, practice, service, and teaching and explores the relationship between the built environment, ecology, and health in developing urban communities. It champions design and technology as vehicles for human well-being, environmental regeneration, and social justice. His recent and ongoing projects include the community-driven participatory design and implementation of public space, garden, and point of use water interventions in informal urban communities in Peru and Cambodia.

Eduardo Staszowski is an associate professor of design strategies at Parsons School of Design at The New School. Staszowski is cofounder and director of the Parsons Design for Social Innovation and Sustainability Lab, and his current research interests center on the intersection of design, social innovation, and public policy, which has as its core the development of experimental yet practical approaches to enhancing participation in policy development and public service design. He holds a PhD in design from the Politecnico di Milano in Italy.

Julie Stevens is an assistant professor in landscape architecture at Iowa State University. Her research and teaching priorities are centered on improving the health of people and landscapes by creating mutual stewardship through engaged design. Beginning in 2011, she has partnered with the Iowa Department of Corrections to create restorative and productive landscapes in Iowa's prisons. With teams of dedicated students and offenders, the Environmental Justice in Prisons Project has expanded the production gardens and completed three therapeutic gardens at the Iowa Correctional Institution for Women. The project is now extending these efforts to other prisons in the state with the help of evidence-based design and programming.

Susan Verba directs the Center for Design in the Public Interest at the University of California, Davis, and is an associate professor in the Department of Design. Her work focuses on information design that directly benefits the public, exploring issues of health, safety, civic and community participation, and accessibility. She is also principal and founder of Studio/lab, where she leads research-based projects and advocates for the value of design in corporate, nonprofit, and government communications.

Mike Weikert is founding director of the Center for Social Design and Master of Arts in Social Design at the Maryland Institute College of Art. In 2008, he established MICA's Center for Design Practice, a multidisciplinary, project-based studio bringing together students and outside partners to collaborate on innovative solutions to social problems. Previously, Weikert served as cochair of the graphic design department at MICA, partner and creative director at Atlanta-based Iconologic, and design consultant to the International Olympic Committee. In 2011, he was nominated for the Cooper-Hewitt National Design Award, and in 2014, he received the Ashoka U–Cordes Innovation Award.

Emilie Taylor Welty is a Tulane University professor of practice who manages design/build projects at the Small Center for Collaborative Design and is a practicing architect in New Orleans, Louisiana. Taylor Welty's recent studios include the Grow Dat Youth Farm and LOOP's Gathering Pavilion. Her education includes a technical background from the University of Southern Mississippi and a master of architecture degree from Tulane. Taylor Welty's creative practice includes making as a generative design method at the intersection of formal and informal design. She leads a firm called Colectivo in New Orleans with Seth Welty and Dan Etheridge.

Daniel Winterbottom is a landscape architect and professor of landscape architecture at the University of Washington. He holds a bachelor's degree in landscape architecture from Tufts University and a master's degree in landscape architecture from the Harvard Graduate School of Design. His research interests include the landscape as a cultural expression, ecological urban design, community participatory design, service-learning, and restorative-healing landscapes. In 1995, he developed a program to design and build projects that address the social or ecological concerns of marginalized communities. Winterbottom has written and contributed to many books on sustainable design and building. Notably, *Therapeutic Gardens: Design for Healing Spaces* (2015), coauthored with Amy Wagenfeld, received the 2016 EDRA Great Places book award. He was honored as an ASLA Fellow in 2011.

Michael Zaretsky is associate dean in the College of Design, Architecture, Art, and Planning and associate professor in the School of Architecture and Interior Design at the University of Cincinnati. He is a licensed architect, the director of the MetroLAB public interest design/build program, and the design director of the Roche Health Center in rural Tanzania with the nonprofit Village Life Outreach Project. His research is focused around culturally, economically, technologically, and environmentally responsive public interest design projects for underserved communities. Zaretsky's published work includes dozens of articles and conference presentations, as well as the books *Precedents in Zero-Energy Design* (2009) and *New Directions in Sustainable Design* (with Adrian Parr, 2010). He is currently writing *Design Beyond Borders*, a book that explores how international design/build projects engage those in communities where they are working.

Reading List

Abendroth, Lisa M. and Bryan Bell, eds. 2016. *Public Interest Design Practice Guidebook: SEED Methodology, Case Studies and Critical Issues*. New York: Routledge.

Amatullo, Mariana, Bryan Boyer, Liz Danzico, and Andrew Shea, eds. 2016. *LEAP Dialogues: Career Pathways in Design for Social Innovation*. Pasadena, CA: Designmatters at ArtCenter College of Design.

Angotti, Tom, Cheryl Doble, and Paula Horrigan, eds. 2011. *Service-Learning in Design and Planning: Educating at the Boundaries*. Oakland, CA: New Village Press.

Argyris, Christopher, and Donald A. Schön. 1974. *Theory in Practice: Increasing Professional Effectiveness*. Oxford, UK: Jossey-Bass.

Awan, Nishat, Tatjana Schneider, and Jeremy Till. 2011. *Spatial Agency: Other Ways of Doing Architecture*. London: Routledge.

Bell, Bryan, ed. 2003. *Good Deeds, Good Design: Community Service Through Architecture*. New York: Princeton Architectural Press.

Bell, Bryan, and Katie Wakeford, eds. 2008. *Expanding Architecture, Design as Activism*. New York: Metropolis Books.

Bose, Mallika, Paula Horrigan, Cheryl Doble, and Sigmund C. Shipp, eds. 2014. *Community Matters: Service Learning in Engaged Design and Planning*. New York: Routledge.

Boyer, Ernest L., and Lee D. Mitgang. 1996. *Building Community: A New Future for Architecture Education and Practice. A Special Report*. Princeton, NJ: The Carnegie Foundation for the Advancement of Teaching.

Boyer, Ernest L. 1997. *Scholarship Reconsidered: Priorities of the Professoriate*. The Carnegie Foundation for the Advancement of Teaching. San Francisco, CA: Jossey-Bass.

Brause, Caryn. 2017. *The Designer's Field Guide to Collaboration*. New York: Routledge.

Dewey, John. 1938. *Experience and Education*. New York: Touchstone.

Dolgon, Corey, Tania D. Mitchell, and Timothy K. Eatman. 2017. *The Cambridge Handbook of Service Learning and Community Engagement*. Cambridge, UK: Cambridge University Press.

Feldman, Roberta, Sergio Palleroni, David Perkes, and Bryan Bell. 2011. *Wisdom from the Field: Public Interest Architecture in Practice*. FAIA Latrobe Prize Research Report. Washington, DC: College of Fellows of the American Institute of Architects.

Findley, Lisa. 2005. *Building Change: Architecture, Politics and Cultural Agency*. London: Routledge.

Fisher, Thomas. 2016. *Designing Our Way to a Better World*. Minneapolis: University of Minnesota Press.

Fisher, Thomas. 2010. *Ethics for Architects: 50 Dilemmas of Professional Practice*. New York: Princeton Architectural Press.

Freire, Paulo. 1970. *Pedagogy of the Oppressed*. New York: Seabury Press.

Gardner, Howard, Mihaly Csikszentmihalyi, and William Damon. 2002. *Good Work*. New York: Basic Books.

Hammett, Jerilou, and Maggie Wrigley, eds. 2013. *The Architecture of Change: Building a Better World*. Albuquerque: University of New Mexico Press.

Harriss, Harriet, and Lynnette Widder. 2014. *Architecture Live Projects: Pedagogy into Practice*. New York: Routledge.

Hatcher, Julie A., and Robert G. Bringle. 1997. "Reflection: Bridging the Gap between Service and Learning." *College Teaching* 45 (4): 153–58.

Hatcher, Julie A., and Robert G. Bringle, eds. 2012. *Understanding Service-Learning and Community Engagement: Crossing Boundaries Through Research*. Charlotte, NC: Information Age Publishing.

Horton, Myles, and Paulo Freire. 1990. *We Make the Road by Walking: Conversations on Education and Social Change*, edited by Brenda Bell, John Gaventa, and John Peters. Philadelphia, PA: Temple University Press.

Hou, Jeffrey, Benjamin R. Spencer, Thaisa Way, and Ken Yocom, eds. 2015. *Now Urbanism: The Future City Is Here*. New York: Routledge.

Hou, Jeffrey, ed. 2013. *Trans-cultural Cities: Border Cross and Placemaking*. New York: Routledge.

Jacoby, Barbara. 2015. *Service-Learning Essentials: Questions, Answers, and Lessons Learned*. San Francisco: Jossey-Bass.

Keshen, Jeff, Barbara E. Moely, and Barbara A. Holland. 2010. Research for What?: Making Engaged Scholarship Matter. Charlotte, NC: Information Age Publishing.

Kolb, David A. 1984. *Experiential Learning: Experience as the Source of Learning and Development*. Englewood Cliffs, NJ: Prentice-Hall.

Latour, Bruno. *Reassembling the Social: An Introduction to Actor-Network-Theory*. Oxford, UK: Oxford University, 2007.

Latour, Bruno, and Peter Weibel, eds. 2005. *Making Things Public: Atmospheres of Democracy*. Cambridge, MA: MIT Press.

Manzini, Ezio. 2015. *Design When Everybody Designs: An Introduction to Design for Social Innovation*. Cambridge, MA: MIT Press.

Margolin, Victor, Nynke Tromp, Bert van Meggelen, and Max Bruinsma. 2015. *Design for the Good Society: Utrecht Manifest 2005–2015*. Rotterdam, Netherlands: nai010 publishers.

Oppenheimer Dean, Andrea. 1998. *Proceed and Be Bold: Rural Studio After Samuel Mockbee*. New York: Princeton Architectural Press.

Oppenheimer Dean, Andrea. 2002. *Rural Studio: Samuel Mockbee and an Architecture of Decency*. New York: Princeton Architectural Press.

Palleroni, Sergio. 2004. *Studio at Large: Architecture in Service of Global Communities*. Seattle: University of Washington Press.

Papanek, Victor. 1983. *Design for Human Scale*. New York: Van Nostrand Reinhold.

Papanek, Victor. 1971. *Design for the Real World: Human Ecology and Social Change*. New York: Pantheon.

Poggenpohl, Sharon, and Keiichi Sato. 2009. *Design Integrations: Research and Collaboration*. Bristol, UK: Intellect Ltd.

Resnick, Elizabeth. 2016. *Developing Citizen Designers*. New York: Bloomsbury Academic.

Saltmarsh, John, Matthew Hartley, and Patti Clayton. 2009. *Democratic Engagement White Paper*. Boston: New England Resource Center for Higher Education.

Schneekloth, Lynda H., and Robert G. Shibley. 1995. *Placemaking: The Art and Practice of Building Communities*. New York: John Wiley and Sons.

Schön, Donald A. 1985. *The Design Studio: An Exploration of Its Traditions and Potentials*. London: RIBA Publications for RIBA Building Industry Trust.

Simonsen, Jesper, and Toni Robertson, eds. 2013. *Routledge International Handbook of Participatory Design*. New York: Routledge.

The National Task Force on Civic Learning and Democratic Engagement. 2012. *A Crucible Moment: College Learning and Democracy's Future*. Washington, DC: Association of American Colleges and Universities.

Appendix A
Learning Objective Index

Learning Objective Index

This index cites over 160 learning objectives assembled from the documented pedagogies in this publication.[1] Cross-referenced throughout, learning objectives vary according to design discipline and reflect learning and assessment indicators at the level of a program, course, or project respectively.[2]

When taken as a whole, the index provides important documentation about the nature of pedagogy, goals and methods, as well as desirable learning attributes. Collating these objectives is a move toward a comprehensive view of public interest design education.

Part 1

Educating the Next Generation of Social Innovators: Designmatters at ArtCenter
Mariana Amatullo, Dan Gottlieb, Penny Herscovitch, and Susannah Ramshaw

See pages 22–33

Safe Agua Course Series Learning Objectives (p. 25):

- Use field research to develop a sense of empathy and to give further insight to the problem by understanding core values, aspirations, physical environments, and so on
- Engage community members, stakeholders, and audiences in the co-creation and prototyping phases of the design process
- Develop sustainable, scalable solutions with a potential for real-world outcomes
- Develop radically affordable products and services for base of pyramid families who are living on under two dollars per day
- Develop a sustainable business plan, including sourcing, pricing, and marketing
- Research and identify potential partners and manufacturers to bring the products to market

Changing Practice, Practicing Change: The Graduate Certificate in Public Interest Design at Portland State University
R. Todd Ferry and Sergio Palleroni

See pages 34–45

Introduction to Public Interest Design Seminar Learning Objectives (p. 37):

- Analyze foundational definitions, history, and present trends in the field of public interest design
- Develop engagement strategies in underserved communities to identify issues, map assets, and work toward a collective solution
- Demonstrate knowledge of funding models for public interest design projects
- Interpret the fundamentals of sustainability
- Demonstrate real-world experience on a public interest design project
- Compare metrics for creating and evaluating the efficacy of a public interest design project

A Comprehensive Public Interest Design Curriculum: College of Design, North Carolina State University

Public Interest Design Certificate Learning Objectives (p. 51):

- Analyze precedents of how public interest design can be a meaningful part of professional practice
- Describe one model of professional practice in public interest design
- Identify public need for design that can address community challenges
- Identify a design project's social, economic, and environmental impact on a community

Appendix A: Learning Objective Index

319

Bryan Bell, Robin Abrams, and Gene Bressler See pages 46–58	• Identify stakeholders and assets that can address project challenges • Test a step-by-step method of working with a community as a design partner • Apply a collaborative process with multiple stakeholders
Connecting Classrooms and Publics: The University of California, Davis, Center for Design in the Public Interest Susan Verba, Sarah Perrault, and Tracy Manuel See pages 59–69	*Professional Practice and Ethics Course Learning Objectives (p. 63):* • Explore notions of design agency as a way to gain insight into the role of the designer, present and future • Probe ideas of meaningful work and the value of making "with" rather than "for" • Connect theory and practice • Consider ethical issues in planning and carrying out user-centered research and activities that engage the public in the design process • Discuss different ways to define and evaluate success in a project and explain how they are appropriate for different situations
Design (Education) to Create Meaningful Change: The Design for Social Impact Master's Program at the University of the Arts Anthony Guido with Jeremy Beaudry, Jamer Hunt, Sharon Lefevre, Michael McAllister, and Jonas Milder See pages 70–81	*Program Pedagogical Goals (p. 76–77):* • Practice dsi through real-world design projects in partnership with businesses, government agencies, nonprofit organizations, and community groups • Examine the contextual, theoretical, and historical evolution of dsi practices and techniques and relate these to current philosophies and best practices in the field • Foster a collaborative, participatory co-design process that places people at the center of the design process • Use design tools for community engagement, conversation, and collective learning to facilitate a participatory co-design process • Develop emotional intelligence, facilitation, and leadership skills that support the design student's ability to maneuver effectively in complex organizational and social situations • Relate expertise in the use of a range of design methods and tools drawn from a variety of design disciplines • Use design-research methodologies to understand the specific stakeholders, context, and issues of a given design opportunity • Apply inductive reasoning through quantitative and qualitative research data to identify patterns, insights, and design opportunities • Construct iteratively developed design prototypes in a range of fidelities and formats that can be tested with stakeholders • Develop clear metrics and assessment criteria to evaluate the impact of design interventions and prototypes • Analyze fundamental business and entrepreneurial practices as they apply to the field of design • Create visually compelling, narratively rich documentation and presentations that effectively communicate the design process and project outcomes

Collaborating for Change in New Orleans: Small Center for Collaborative Design *Maggie Hansen and Emilie Taylor Welty* *See pages 82–92*	*Design/build Courses Learning Objectives (p. 87):* - Plan a project from an initial client–partner interview through design to completion of construction - Develop basic construction skills (including welding, woodworking, details, and joinery), with emphasis on understanding the logic of material assembly and design details - Manage a limited materials budget and construction timeline - Delegate responsibilities across a team
From the Ground Up: Envisioning an MFA in Public Interest Design at Metropolitan State University of Denver *Lisa M. Abendroth, Kelly Monico, and Peter Miles Bergman* *See pages 93–104*	*Select Studio and/or Seminar Learning Objectives (p. 99–101):* - Defend premises and principles evinced in ethical public interest design practices - Analyze how place, community, and culture fuse in the creation of social, economic, and environmental design issues - Synthesize discoveries into a program protocol - Develop leadership skills that support the designer's ability to succeed in facilitation - Plan and establish a protocol for field-research activities - Analyze case studies to support thesis research, test hypotheses, and expand critical awareness of issues embedded within design problems - Evaluate bias within assessment scenarios and determine ways to represent inclusivity of participant voices in outcomes - Design artifacts and visual responses that empower communities and build collective knowledge - Relate contexts for project evaluation and analysis whereby historical, critical, and theoretical implications are evident

Part 2

The Edge Effect: PROJECT RE_ *John Folan* *See pages 111–116*	*Cited Learning Objectives (p. 114):* - Develop understanding of complex socioeconomic community contexts - Demonstrate leadership through technical and hands-on skills - Create capacity through design-intent documentation and prototyping skills
Preparing to Design With: IMPACT Orientation *Megan Clark and Shalini Agrawal* *See pages 117–121*	*Cited Learning Objectives (p. 120):* - Apply inclusive language and regular reflection on power dynamics and privilege - Employ active listening rather than a team's fixed vision to evolve relationships and projects - Practice new communication tools among teammates and with community partners - Experiment with responsiveness and flexibility

Democratic Civic Engagement: The USAER XXXIV Training Center for Special Education *Pedro Pacheco* *See page 122–129*	*Cited Learning Objectives (p. 123):* • Build trusting relationships with diverse stakeholder groups by engaging in formal and informal encounters for learning with utc users • Facilitate communication and design outcomes through participatory strategies, in which users were viewed as experts • Generate understanding in academic and community-centered endeavors that helps identify meaningful opportunities for action • Interpret the public purpose and realize the impact design can have on underserved groups
Creating Design Leaders: The African Design Centre *Christian Benimana* *See pages 135–140*	*Cited Learning Objectives (p. 137–139):* Understanding Context: • Apply observation and information-collection skills to determine, list, and prioritize the real issues faced by the community • Scrutinize which of these issues can be addressed through design • Illustrate the limitations and the internal and external factors that may affect the success of the project • Identify contextual opportunities for impact-driven design solutions • Develop tools to use for including the community in the design process Critical Thinking: • Define the parameters of the design solution intervention • Apply an iterative, human-centered design process to solve systemic problems • Translate the process and ideas into practical design solutions • Formulate strategies for scaling the impact of the conceived design solutions Leadership: • Participate in forums in which discussions on solutions to the world's problems take place • Defend the ability of impact-driven design methodology to solve societal problems • Demonstrate leadership through team-building activities to resolve challenges • Demonstrate the ability to understand problems, seek advice, and make design decisions that maximize their positive impact • Develop effective ways to advocate for appropriate impact-driven design solutions to global issues

Teaching *Intra*personal Development, Improving Interpersonal and Intercultural Skill Sets: The Transforming Mindsets Studio *Lisa Grocott and Kate McEntee* *See pages 141–146*	*Cited Learning Objectives (p. 141–142):* • Recognize the influential role mindsets play in the context of learning • Facilitate case clinics to underscore how learning how to learn is key to thriving personally and professionally • Use serious play to enhance social and emotional co-creation skills
Addressing Air Pollution Impacts on Senior Citizens in Beijing, China: The International Urbanization Seminar *Deland Chan* *See pages 147–153*	*Cited Learning Objectives (p. 149–150):* • Comprehend scientific knowledge • Analyze a real-life problem • Synthesize field research into effective ways of addressing air pollution impacts on seniors
iZindaba Zokudla (Conversations About Food): Innovation in the Soweto Food System *Angus Donald Campbell and Naudé Malan* *See pages 158–164*	*Cited Learning Objectives (p. 158–159):* • Identify opportunities for technological design through processes of personal immersion and engagement with community partners • Design appropriate technology for resource-poor contexts through collaborative design and social science methods • Critically evaluate the impact of relevant design processes and outcomes
Building Partnerships and Awareness: Healing an Urban Stream *Brian Gaudio* *See pages 165–170*	*Cited Learning Objectives (p. 166):* • Synthesize qualitative and quantitative data in field research activities • Understand how to collaborate effectively with community partners • Position design as a tool to advocate for those with limited voices

Advancing Resiliency: The Huxtable Fellowship in Civic Engagement and Service Learning *Benjamin Peterson* *See pages 171–177*	*Cited Learning Objectives (p. 172):* • Identify challenges and verify opportunities through quantitative geospatial research and qualitative ethnographic fieldwork • Provide a foundation for communicating the consequences of sea-level rise • Design materials that demystify climate change • Create social cohesion and community consensus through the dissemination of research in public forums
"Making" Change *Together*: Rust to Green's Placemaking Praxis *Paula Horrigan* *See pages 182–188*	*Cited Learning Objectives (p. 183):* • Learn and practice placemaking and democratic community design • Collaborate effectively with others across differences on addressing a local issue, need, problem, or aspiration • Co-create and complete a placemaking project with community partners
Building User Capacity Through Iterative Processes: Ten Friends Diner *Edward M. Orlowski and Julia Jovanovic* *See pages 189–194*	*Cited Learning Objectives (p. 193):* • Use statistical and observational tools in research, focusing on identifying a problem, the ecosystem that perpetuates the problem, and the affected constituencies • Create and document a participatory design process rooted in professional best practices, demonstrating an awareness of innovative and alternative models of professional practice • Exhibit the ability to engage in inclusive and informed conversations about design in partnership with nonarchitects
Examining Collaborative Efforts to Visualize Community Transformation: Alexandra Youth Precinct Project *Chris Harnish* *See pages 195–200*	*Cited Learning Objectives (p. 199–200):* • Synthesize disparate stakeholder interests • Develop a rigorous and meaningful design proposal focused on the needs and desires of constituencies • Distinguish between complex cultural and spatial contexts • Discover the challenges of community-focused design methodologies while working on site • Apply methods that incorporate local governing bodies and empower community members
Assessing Experiential Learning in Design Education: The Practice Department at the Boston Architectural College	*Cited Learning Objectives (p. 207):* • Make connections across disciplines among experiences outside the classroom by showing an enhanced ability to broaden perspective and build on prior learning to take on increasingly challenging problems • Exhibit organized preparation and confident delivery of a compelling message with a variety of supporting materials (graphics, written descriptions, and self-reflection) to increase audiences' knowledge and understanding

Bethany Lundell Garver

See pages 206–213

- Collaborate across and among myriad contexts and organizations to accomplish a clear sense of civic identity, independent initiative in engagement activities, and collaborative commitment to community goals

Merging Research, Scholarship, and Community Engagement: Roche Health Center

Michael Zaretsky

See pages 214–219

Cited Learning Objectives (p. 215):

- Assess inherent power imbalances and inequities between western and non-western communities, as well as power imbalances within cultures
- Evaluate who is benefiting from the design and construction projects
- Relate and apply reciprocal learning in context
- Analyze cultural, social, economic, constructive, and climatic conditions of work areas
- Apply knowledge of existing conditions to all design and construction decisions
- Incorporate principles of appropriate technology by using materials, tools, and techniques that local residents can replicate
- Create meaningful partnerships with local residents and nonprofit partners in all aspects of research, design, and construction
- Create design and construction proposals that are informed by the desires of the local community and contextual conditions
- Assess all design proposals on their cultural, social, economic, and technical value for the communities with whom we are working

Reflecting Through Razor Wire: The Environmental Justice in Prisons Project

Julie Stevens

See pages 220–225

Cited Learning Objectives (p. 225):

- Examine personal ethics when working with diverse populations, especially those incarcerated
- Develop a restorative and productive prison program *with*, not *for*, the community and client, using intentional design and physical interventions
- Translate design concepts into reality through the construction of studio projects, including supervising a construction site, securing materials, handling budgets, and managing client expectations and team dynamics

Part 3

University of Colorado Boulder

Design in Partnership With the Lama Foundation

See pages 232–236

Project-Specific Learning Objectives (p. 232):

- Develop real-world design skills that are responsive to community-based client needs
- Manage differing project needs inclusive of budget, schedule, and environmental efficiency
- Experiment with hands-on construction techniques and building practices

University of Cincinnati

Pleasant Street Pedestrian Project

See pages 237–243

Project-Specific Learning Objectives (p. 237):

- Analyze factors contributing to the inclusion or exclusion of a range of stakeholders in the design process
- Create engagement tools that generate site-specific discourse
- Use full-scale prototype designs to inspire social and pedestrian activity

Ryerson University **A Social Approach to Design** *See pages 243–248*	*Project-Specific Learning Objectives (p. 243):* • Interpret the context, function, and needs defining projects for underrepresented groups in the field of interior design • Analyze in written and visual form the social, economic, and environmental impact of design projects • Express the ethical and social responsibilities of the interior designer
University of Detroit Mercy **Cooperative Education at the Detroit Collaborative Design Center** *See pages 248–254*	*Project-Specific Learning Objectives (p. 249):* • Use iteration to create effective visual communication presentation materials for public interest design contexts • Practice building trust with stakeholders through a range of community-engagement strategies • Discover the design and administrative practices of a university community design center
School of the Art Institute of Chicago **Com(m)a** *See pages 254–260*	*Project-Specific Learning Objectives (p. 254):* • Recognize how collaborative, community-based design can affirm productive actions • Relate disciplinary practices to global contexts and needs • Formulate solutions that empower student- and community-centered assets
University of Texas at Austin **The Farm Rover** *See pages 261–266*	*Project-Specific Learning Objectives (p. 261):* • Apply principles of participatory action research to a design/build project • Formulate a plan for stakeholder engagement that uncovers needs related to traditional farming practices • Practice community-based strategies for working across political, ecological, and fiscal divides
University of Maryland **On Site: Public Art and Design** *See pages 266–273*	*Project-Specific Learning Objectives (p. 266):* • Develop temporary art and design works that respond to and connect underutilized community spaces • Use art and design to build partnerships and advocate for local engagement • Analyze the physical and psychological meanings of place through interdisciplinary form making
Louisiana Tech University **South of California Avenue** *See pages 273–279*	*Project-Specific Learning Objectives (p. 273):* • Develop community-based leadership skills • Facilitate communication and relationship building with stakeholders by establishing a common design language • Use design to leverage resilient community transformation

Portland State University **With Sacramento** *See pages 279–284*	*Project-Specific Learning Objectives (p. 279):* • Demonstrate the value of perseverance over time in constructing meaningful project results • Distinguish between research speculations and long-term prevailing outcomes • Formulate design process as a means to effectuate collaborative design thinking and coproduction

Notes

1. Chapter 1, "Whole-Systems Public Interest Design Education: Department of Landscape Architecture, University of Washington" by Jeffrey Hou, Benjamin R. Spencer, and Daniel Winterbottom is not represented in the index due to chapter formatting considerations. Please see pages 8–21 for specific in-text references to pedagogical goals and learning outcomes provided by these authors.
2. The editors referred contributors to Bloom's *Taxonomy of Educational Objectives* (1956) as a framework for informing a scaffold of incremental cognitive considerations in learning.

Appendix B
Program Considerations Index

Program Considerations Index

The following considerations offer insights relevant to starting a new educational program or evaluating an existing program in public interest design. Points are organized according to university, college, department, course, project, and community concerns. These illustrate how the potential for tapping into existing assets or underutilized resources can activate multisector opportunities beneficial to sustained community–academic exchange.[1]

University	• Examine links between the university strategic plan and intended public interest design programming
	• Establish and work with university-wide partnerships (internal and external)
	• Seek out university service-learning designations for course work, should they be available
	• Consult with university civic engagement, applied learning, and/or strategic partnership offices for guidance and tools for course and programmatic planning
	• Promote knowledge-sharing between university units and community partners
	• Identify the potential for long-term partnerships through university-level affiliations
	• Evaluate university funding sources that promote program viability
	• Advocate for accreditation standards that address community partnerships and engaged learning outcomes
College	• Strategically assess college-level needs, opportunities, and requirements relative to public interest design programming and/or curriculum development
	• Evaluate college funding sources that promote program viability
	• Work across the college to activate transdisciplinary academic relationships vital to community-based efforts
	• Work with the college-level curriculum committee to identify gaps across the college and specific to engaged learning
Department	• Develop regularly offered required course offerings in public interest design
	• Teach across the department curriculum to activate transdisciplinary relationships vital to pedagogy and the field
	• Set internal department level goals for long-term engagement projects
	• Consider the feasibility of embedded course programming through a community design center or other on-site community-level program presence
	• Evaluate department funding sources that promote program viability
	• Consider (business) models for department programming, such as a nonprofit and/or center, that facilitate community-based outreach

Course	• Design interactions to establish partnerships beyond single semester confines
	• Embed cultural immersion pedagogies into course work well in advance of actual community and/or on-site engagement
	• Critically assess the value of time spent on site and the frequency of contact between students and partners
	• Recognize the time required for partnership facilitation and planning—adjust as necessary
	• Adjust and be agile to the responsive needs of the evolving project requirements
	• Empower students to see themselves as university–community ambassadors and ultimately leaders
	• Practice culturally appropriate interactions, communications, and behaviors regularly with students
	• Incorporate activities that stress active listening and reflective journaling
	• Use design thinking and strategy to inform process
	• Emphasize collaboration between student teams, cohorts, levels and disciplines
	• Function as a faculty mediator and facilitator
	• Proactively create and collect permissions for work produced in courses by students with partners that easily facilitates open sharing thereafter
	• Verify the mutuality of project goals and learning objectives between partners and students is understood
	• Use the assessment of learning outcomes to grow the program and adjust pedagogies
	• Introduce the seed evaluator as a tool for guiding public interest design methods in educational contexts
Project	• Consider the project in context
	• Assess the viability of the project through diverse models (such as a start-up)
	• Establish a memorandum of agreement between educational leaders and project partners
	• Create an agreement of expectation specifically for students which details the unique nature of the experience and its subsequent requirement for professionalism
	• Document project processes with detail and care—activate students in this process so they understand the value of translation and storytelling thereafter
	• Ensure a sound and well-planned engagement methodology
	• Determine best practices for knowledge dissemination of project outcomes
	• Embrace a moderate pace in project evolution understanding the work may evolve slower than typical
	• Create evaluation standards specific to the project goals and learning objectives

Community	- Work with partners to codevelop appropriate interactions ensuring inclusive participation across stakeholder groups
- Identify who needs to be at the table, including community liaisons important to the project, community leaders, nonprofit organizations, educational outlets, and other local service outlets
- Demonstrate respect and the value of others
- Communicate expectations to primary stakeholders directly involved in the project
- Create a request for proposal process for vetting and reviewing community projects
- Ensure a protocol is established that documents the value of the partnership
- Work with communities to create a clear methodology and process for project development
- Introduce the SEED Evaluator as a tool for inclusive decision making
- Use an issue-based approach that helps clarify goals based on social, economic, and environmental factors
- Educate others by creating replicable processes for future community adoption
- Generate reciprocal learning opportunities between students and partners
- Participate in the sharing economy
- Work across sociocultural, economic, and environmental divides
- Identify strategies for immersion with the community
- Remember to acknowledge successes and challenges
- Celebrate
Accreditation Resources	- **American Society of Landscape Architects**, Accreditation Standards for First-Professional Programs in Landscape Architecture www.asla.org/uploadedFiles/CMS/Education/Accreditation/.LAAB_ACCREDITATION_STANDARDS_March2016.pdf
- **Council for Interior Design Accreditation**, Professional Standards 2017 https://accredit-id.org/wp-content/uploads/2017/01/II.-Professional-Standards-2017.pdf.
- **National Association of Schools of Art and Design**, NASAD Handbook 2017–2018. https://nasad.arts-accredit.org/accreditation/standards-guidelines/handbook/.
- **Planning Accreditation Board**. PAB Accreditation Standards and Criteria Approved March 3, 2017. www.planningaccreditationboard.org/index.php?s=file_download&id=500

- **National Council of Architectural Registration Boards**
  www.ncarb.org.
- **The National Architectural Accrediting Board**, 2014 Conditions for Accreditation.
  www.naab.org/accreditation/2014_Conditions.

Note

1   For a model of highly accessible and clearly documented academic engagement resources, please see Liz Kramer's work for the Office for Socially Engaged Practice at Washington University in St. Louis, Sam Fox School of Design and Visual Arts. Learn more at http://samfoxschool.wustl.edu/engage and https://sites.wustl.edu/insidesfs/engagement/.

Image Credits

Front Cover Images (left to right):

Row one:

Alexandra Youth Precinct Project, Alexandra Township, Johannesburg, South Africa, 2013. Photo: Chris Harnish.

Urban Design Build Studio, PROJECT RE_, Pittsburgh, Pennsylvania, 2015. Photo: John William Gott, Urban Design Build Studio.

Row two:

Environmental Justice in Prisons Project, Iowa State University and the Iowa Correctional Institution for Women, Multipurpose Outdoor Classroom, Mitchellville, Iowa, 2013-2014. Photo: Julie Stevens.

MetroLAB, Pleasant Street Pedestrian Project, Cincinnati, Ohio, 2016. Photo: Michael Zaretsky.

University of Washington Design/Build Program, Puget Sound Veterans Administration Healing Garden, Seattle, Washington, 2016. Photo: Daniel Winterbottom.

Row three:

MASS Design Group, Mubuga Primary School, Musanze, Rwanda, 2015. Photo: MASS Design Group.

CPID, With Sacramento, Sacramento, California, ongoing. Credit: Center for Public Interest Design.

Row four:

Jomari Budricks, Angus D. Campbell, and Naudé Malan, Take Root Seedling Growing System for iZindaba Zokudla, Johannesburg, South Africa, 2014. Photo: Angus D. Campbell.

University of Colorado Boulder ENVD junior level praxis students, Buff Hut, Questa, New Mexico, Spring–Summer 2013. Photo: Stephen Cardinale.

Kurt Pung, Matthew Miller, Carolina Uechi, and Rochelle Heyworth Cusimano, Passage, Long Branch, Maryland, 2013. Photo: Ronit Eisenbach.

Chapters

1 Whole-Systems Public Interest Design Education: Department of Landscape Architecture, University of Washington
- 1.1 Daniel Winterbottom
- 1.2 Daniel Winterbottom
- 1.3 Daniel Winterbottom
- 1.4 Informal Urban Communities Initiative Team
- 1.5 David Witte
- 1.6 Informal Urban Communities Initiative Team

2 Educating the Next Generation of Social Innovators: Designmatters at ArtCenter
- 2.2 Designmatters at ArtCenter
- 2.3 Stephen Swintek
- 2.4 Designmatters at ArtCenter

3 Changing Practice, Practicing Change: The Graduate Certificate in Public Interest Design at Portland State University
- 3.1 Diagram: Center for Public Interest Design
- 3.2 R. Todd Ferry, Center for Public Interest Design
- 3.3 Center for Public Interest Design
- 3.4 Center for Public Interest Design

4 A Comprehensive Public Interest Design Curriculum: College of Design, North Carolina State University
- 4.2 Courtesy of North Carolina Museum of Art; sculpture: *Gyre* by Thomas Sayre

4.7   Project: Priyanka Bista and Marco Cestar

4.11 Photo: Randall Lanou; project: Randall Lanou, Ellen Cassilly, Erik Mehlman, Scott Metheny, Anya Noelle Shirley Aikman, Morgan Claire Cooney, Kevin Douglas Diamond, Zhendong Ding, Zachary Scott Hoffman, Kim Janiszewski, Kimberly Lynn Johnson, Laura Katherine Liang, Yi-Chang Liao, Aaron Bonner Longo, Joshua Clifford Molter, Myriam Nasr, Marty Warren Needham, Brandon Scott Porterfield, Nicholas Todd Roberts, Bryan Taylor Seef, Meredith Ann Smith, Brittany Leigh Spangler, and Nicholas Thor Strickland

5 Connecting Classrooms and Publics: The University of California, Davis, Center for Design in the Public Interest

5.1   Tracy Manuel, UC Davis Center for Design in the Public Interest

6 Design (Education) to Create Meaningful Change: The Design for Social Impact Master's Program at the University of the Arts

6.2   Jonas Milder

6.3   Dominic Prestifilippo

6.4   Georgia Guthrie, Alaina Pineda, Donovan Preddy, and Dominic Prestifilippo

7 Collaborating for Change in New Orleans: Small Center for Collaborative Design

7.1   Small Center

7.2   Small Center

7.3   Small Center

9 Fundamental Skills: Developing Social Literacy Through Practice-Based Learning

9.1   ©2018 Winterhouse Institute

10 The Edge Effect: PROJECT RE_

10.1 John Folan, Urban Design Build Studio

10.2 Urban Design Build Studio

10.3 John William Gott, Urban Design Build Studio

11 Preparing to Design With: IMPACT Orientation

11.1 Shreya D. Shah, Saltwater Training

12 Democratic Civic Engagement: The USAER XXXIV Training Center for Special Education

12.1 Pedro Pacheco

12.3 Carsten Krohn

Image Credits

13 Intercultural Competencies: Teaching the Intangible
- 13.1 Credit: European DesignBuild Knowledge Network; photo: Peter Fattinger

14 Creating Design Leaders: The African Design Centre
- 14.1 MASS Design Group
- 14.2 MASS Design Group
- 14.3 MASS Design Group

15 Teaching Intrapersonal Development, Improving Interpersonal and Intercultural Skill Sets: The Transforming Mindsets Studio
- 15.1 Mathan Ratinam
- 15.2 Credit: Sophie Riendeau
- 15.3 Mathan Ratinam

16 Addressing Air Pollution Impacts on Senior Citizens in Beijing, China: The International Urbanization Seminar
- 16.1 Deland Chan
- 16.2 Adriana Baird
- 16.3 Leqi Sun

18 iZindaba Zokudla (Conversations About Food): Innovation in the Soweto Food System
- 18.1 Angus D. Campbell
- 18.2 Angus D. Campbell
- 18.3 Angus D. Campbell
- 18.4 Illustration: Natalia Tofas

19 Building Partnerships and Awareness: Healing an Urban Stream
- 19.1 Brian Gaudio
- 19.2 Brian Gaudio
- 19.3 Brian Gaudio

20 Advancing Resiliency: The Huxtable Fellowship in Civic Engagement and Service Learning
- 20.1 Credit: Boston Architectural College Huxtable Fellows; photo: Benjamin Peterson
- 20.2 Credit: Boston Architectural College Huxtable Fellows
- 20.3 Christian Borger

22 "Making" Change Together: Rust to Green's Placemaking Praxis
- 22.1 Sarah Schlichte
- 22.2 Paula Horrigan
- 22.3 Paula Horrigan

23 Building User Capacity Through Iterative Processes: Ten Friends Diner
- 23.1   Rendering: Julia Jovanovic
- 23.2   Steven Rost
- 23.3   Steven Rost

24 Examining Collaborative Efforts to Visualize Community Transformation: Alexandra Youth Precinct Project
- 24.1   Chris Harnish
- 24.2   Chris Harnish
- 24.3   Chris Harnish

26 Assessing Experiential Learning in Design Education: The Practice Department at the Boston Architectural College
- 26.1   Bethany Lundell Garver, Boston Architectural College
- 26.2   Bethany Lundell Garver, Boston Architectural College
- 26.3   Bethany Lundell Garver, Boston Architectural College
- 26.4   Bethany Lundell Garver

27 Merging Research, Scholarship, and Community Engagement: Roche Health Center
- 27.1   Chas Wiederhold
- 27.2   Richard Elliott
- 27.3   Michael Zaretsky

28 Reflecting Through Razor Wire: The Environmental Justice in Prisons Project
- 28.1   Julie Stevens
- 28.2   Julie Stevens
- 28.3   Julie Stevens

30 SEED Academic Case Studies
- 30A.1   Stephen Cardinale
- 30A.2   Stephen Cardinale
- 30A.3   Madigan Wells
- 30A.4   Model and photo: Kyra Traxler; rendering: Shannon Carlin; site photo: Stephen Cardinale
- 30A.5   Stephen Cardinale
- 30B.6   Design and construction: MetroLAB students; photo: Michael Zaretsky
- 30B.7   Design and construction: MetroLAB students; photo: Michael Zaretsky
- 30B.8   Design and construction: MetroLAB students; photo: Michael Zaretsky
- 30B.9   Design and construction: MetroLAB students; photo: Michael Zaretsky
- 30B.10 Design and construction: MetroLAB students; photo: Matthew Andrews
- 30B.11 Design and construction: MetroLAB students; photo: Bob Schwartz

30C.12 Architect of record (floor plans shown): Diamond Schmitt Architects; case study analysis: Katrina Clancy, Nicole Davison, Maria Krynicki, Sean McKay, and Emily Weir
30C.13 Architect of record (floor plans shown): Diamond Schmitt Architects; case study analysis: Katrina Clancy, Nicole Davison, Maria Krynicki, Sean McKay, and Emily Weir
30C.14 Architect of record (floor plans shown): Diamond Schmitt Architects; case study analysis: Katrina Clancy, Nicole Davison, Maria Krynicki, Sean McKay, and Emily Weir
30C.15 Architect of record: Sterling Finlayson Architects with Shore Tilbe Irwin and partners; case study analysis: Jennah Jeong Ha, Jawon Kang, and Lisa Kee
30C.16 Architect of record: Sterling Finlayson Architects with Shore Tilbe Irwin and partners; case study analysis: Jennah Jeong Ha, Jawon Kang, and Lisa Kee
30C.17 Architect of record: Sterling Finlayson Architects with Shore Tilbe Irwin and partners; case study analysis: Jennah Jeong Ha, Jawon Kang, and Lisa Kee
30D.18 Detroit Collaborative Design Center
30D.19 Detroit Collaborative Design Center
30D.20 Detroit Collaborative Design Center
30D.21 Detroit Collaborative Design Center
30D.22 Detroit Collaborative Design Center
30E.23 Com(m)a Studio Team
30E.24 Com(m)a Studio Team
30E.25 Com(m)a Studio Team
30E.26 Com(m)a Studio Team
30E.27 Com(m)a Studio Team
30F.28 Kristine Stiphany
30F.29 Coleman Coker
30F.30 Coleman Coker
30F.31 Alison Steele
30F.32 Alison Steele
30G.33 Design: Kristen A. Fox and Alison Boliek Supinski
30G.34 Renard Edwards, Kristen A. Fox, Alison Boliek Supinski, and Kristen Yeung; photo: John Ruppert
30G.35 Stephen Neuheuser, Matthew Miller, and Kristen Yeung; photo: Ronit Eisenbach
30G.36 Joseph Largess, Kurt Pung, Rochelle Heyworth Cusimano, and Rachel Mihaly; photo: John Ruppert
30G.37 Kurt Pung, Matthew Miller, Carolina Uechi, and Rochelle Heyworth Cusimano; photo: Ronit Eisenbach

30G.38	Kurt Pung, Matthew Miller, Carolina Uechi, and Rochelle Heyworth Cusimano; photo: John Ruppert
30H.39	Bill Willoughby
30H.40	Kevin Singh
30H.41	Kevin Singh
30H.42	Kevin Singh
30H.43	Kevin Singh
30H.44	Ethan Robison (rendering), Rosa Schellinger, and Lane Walters
30I.45	Center for Public Interest Design
30I.46	Center for Public Interest Design, J. Nicole De Jong
30I.47	Center for Public Interest Design
30I.48	Center for Public Interest Design
30I.49	Center for Public Interest Design, Woodrow Merkel

Index

Page numbers in *italic* indicate a figure and page numbers in **bold** indicate a table.

Abendroth, Lisa M.: "Public Interest Design Education Open Forum" 5n4; *Public Interest Design Practice Guidebook* 5n2, 63
Acción Callejera 166, 169
active listening 118, 120, 144
Activist Architecture and Design Studio *see* Lawrence Technological University, Activist Architecture and Design Studio
Adams, Karina 41–42
African Design Centre 133, 135–40, *136*; construction using the MASS Lo-FAB building process 138; critical thinking 138; leadership 138–9; learning objectives 137–9; Mubuga Primary School Project *137*, 139–40; program curriculum 135–7 ; understanding context 137–8; women creating mats *137*; see also MASS Design Group
Airbnb 285, 286
air pollution in Beijing, China 133, 147, 148, 150, *150*, 151, 152; *see also* International Urbanization Seminar
Albert and Tina Small Center for Collaborative Design *see* Small Center for Collaborative Design
allaDIYally 285
Allen, Tania *55*
allyship 120
Amatullo, Mariana 31n1
American Indian Resilience project *42*, 43, *44*; Crow Indian Reservation 43, *44*; Northern Cheyenne Reservation 42, *42*, 43, *44*
American Institute of Architects 48
American Institute of Architecture Students 252
American Institute of Graphic Arts (AIGA) 97
American Society of Landscape Architects 18
Anderson, Erik: Hands in the Mist 33
Anderson, Nadia M. 4
apprentices in training 113–14
appropriate technology 158, 159, 162, 215
Architects Without Borders (AWB)–Seattle 15, 17, 18
Architecture for Humanity 287
ArtCenter College of Design, Designmatters 22–31, 31n1, 32nn2–4, 32nn5–7; department curriculum overview 23–4; Department of Humanities and Sciences 24; department philosophy 22–3; Media Design Practices 23; Safe Agua course series 24–30 (*see also* Safe Agua course series; Safe Agua Peru)
artifact sustainability 109
Artscape for Daniels Spectrum 248
Arup Cause 216, 219n1
assessment 2, 16, 57, 72, 77, 96, 97, 100, 101, 174, 176, 192, 203, 204, 287; course and program assessment 55–8; external 214; participatory impact 17, 156; practice 207, **208**, 209, 212; project 216–17;

quantitative 206; reflective 209; rigorous 212; risk 167; self- 56, 63, *208*; student 217; student self- *56*
asset-based community design 195
asset-based designs 209, 277, 282
asset-based lens 259
Austin, Texas 261, 262; Balcones Fault 261; Office of Sustainability 262, 265; *see also* The Farm Rover; University of Texas at Austin School of Architecture (UTASOA), Center for Sustainable Development

Balcones Fault 261
basemap 166
BaSiC *see* Building Sustainable Communities Initiative
Beaudry, Jeremy 71, 73
Beaufort, North Carolina 54
Beijing, China: air pollution impacts on senior citizens 133, 147, 148, 150, *150*, 151, 152; *see also* International Urbanization Seminar
Bell, Bryan 48, 68; *Expanding Architecture* 1; Public Interest Architecture seminar SEED case study *53*; Public Interest Design Incubator Studio *52*; *Public Interest Design Practice Guidebook* 5n2, 63; Public Interest Design Seminar 56
Bell, Daniel: *The Coming of Post-Industrial Society* 72
Bell, Travis, 45n1
Benimana, Christian 133, 135
Bible, Tom 242
Biomedicas y Medioambientales 20n1
biophilic design 224
Bloom, Benjamin: *Taxonomy of Educational Objectives* 61, 63, 68n2, 229n2, 327n2
Bogotá, Colombia 24
Boston Architectural College (BAC): Gateway Initiative program 150, 176, 204
Boston Architectural College (BAC), Ada Louise Huxtable Fellowship 150–76, *173*, *175*, *176*, 209; advancing resiliency in East Boston 172; design research 172–4; field research 174; learning by doing 152; strengthening with partnerships and transforming with capital 174–5; transferring knowledge and sharpening applied learning pedagogies 176
Boston Architectural College (BAC), Practice Department 206–13, *208*, *210*, *211*, *212*; applied learning and career support 209–12; Gateway 207, 209, *210*; learning model 207; partner evaluations 207–9; practice-meets-academy public interest futures 212–13; reflective assessment 209
Boston Society of Architects 206
Boyer, Ernest L. 48, 202

Buffalo, Peggy Wellknown 43
Building Sustainable Communities Initiative (BaSiC) 34–35
Burnette, Charles 71, 72

California College of the Arts, Center for Art + Public Life 117, 118; IMPACT Orientation 110, 118–20
Campbell, Angus D. *161*, *162*, 163n4
Campbell, Donald 157
Campus Compact 94; Indicators of an Engaged Campus 95
Canadian Mental Health Association 192
Capstone Studio 180, 182–7, *185*, *187*; "Taking Steps Toward Creative Placemaking" 182
Carnegie Community Engagement Classification 94
Carnegie Foundation 6
Carnegie Mellon University 107; Urban Design Build Studio 110, 111–12, *116*, *112*, 113, 115
Carpenter, William 11–12
case clinics 142, 143, 144, *144*, 145
Cassilly, Ellen C. *57*
Center for Art + Public Life 117, 118; IMPACT Orientation 110
Center Pole Foundation 43, *44*
Centre for Social Innovation *244*
Centro de Investigaciones Tecnologicas 20n1
Cerro Verde, Peru *27*, 28, *29*, 30
Chadha, Monica 253
Challenge Detroit 253
Chan, Deland 133
changing practice, practicing change *see* Portland State University, Center for Public Interest Design (CPID), Graduate Certificate in Public Interest Design
Chile: earthquake 244–6, 257, 259; *see also* Com(m)a; Paso Moya; Santiago
Choudary, Sangeet Paul: *Platform Revolution* 285, 288
Circle Food Store 91, 92
City of Cincinnati Department of Transportation and Engineering 242; *see also* Pleasant Street Pedestrian Project
CJ *see* Construction Junction
Clark, Erica 31n1
Clayton, Patti 229n1
Coker, Coleman 266
collaborating for change *see* Small Center for Collaborative Design
Colorado *see also* Metropolitan State University of Denver (MSU Denver), Master of Fine Arts; University of Colorado (CU) Boulder
Colorado Commission on Higher Education 93

Index 341

Com(m)a 254–60; art sale and barbecue 262; community-based challenge 255–6; credits 260; definition 254; front yard of community center *258*; informational board *255*; intercultural preparation 257–8; issues addressed 255; partners 260; pedagogical goals 257; project results and learning outcomes 259–60; project-specific student learning objectives 254; public billboard *256*; quick-response templates 258–9; *quincho 257*, 259, 284n8; resource mapping 259; select teaching strategies 257–9; summary 255; *see also* Paso Moya; School of the Art Institute of Chicago
Community Design Resource Center (CDRC) 150, 151
community design workshop 196
community engagement workshops 197, *198*, 240, 249, 250
community sustainability 109, 181
Compagnon, Odile 260
connecting classrooms and publics *see* University of California, Davis, Center for Design in the Public Interest
Construction Junction (CJ) 112, 114, 115; *see also* edge effect; PROJECT RE_
consumer/survivors 190, 191, 192, 194
cooperative education (co-op) 206; *see also* Detroit Collaborative Design Center
Cooperative Education at the Detroit Collaborative Design Center 248–54
Cornell University, Rust to Green Capstone Studio 180, 182–7, *185*, *187*; Oneida Square 182, 183, 184, 185, *185*, 186, *187*; project goals 183–5; project results 186
Corporation for Findlay Market 237, 242, 284n3; *see also* Pleasant Street Pedestrian Project
Council of Educators in Landscape Architecture 18
Coursera 285, 341
creative placemaking 180, 182, 183, 186, 266
Crow Indian Reservation 43, *44*
cultural probes 75, 151
Cummings Foundation 150; OneWorld Boston program 175

Davis, Lee 3
Davis, Liz 31n1
Del Paso Heights neighborhood 280, 284
democratic civic engagement 110, 122–8, 182; building relationships of trust 123; facilitating design and communication 124–6; generating understanding in academic and community-centered endeavors 126–7; model of interagency collaboration *124*; *see also* Impulso Urbano program; USAER XXXIV Training Center for Special Education
Denver, Colorado *see* Metropolitan State University of Denver (MSU Denver), Master of Fine Arts
Department of City and Metropolitan Planning, University of Utah 121
Design/Build Capstone Studio 9, 10
Design Corps 6n7, 45n2
design (education) to create meaningful change see
Design for Deconstruction 115
Design in Partnership With the Lama Foundation 232–6; architectural model, rendering, and completed showerhouse *234*; Buff Hut exterior *234*; community-based challenge 232–3; credits 236; definition 232; issues addressed 232; New Mexico earthship community *234*; partners 236; pedagogical goals 233; project results and learning outcomes 235–6; project-specific student learning objectives 232; select teaching strategies 235–6; Sky Hut deck *236*; Sky Hut interior *233*; summary 232
Designmatters *see* ArtCenter College of Design
design thinking 72, 74, 99, 148, 176, 179, 216, 253, 279, 281, 286
Design Thinking for Social Innovation course 36, 38
design with *see* IMPACT orientation
Detroit Collaborative Design Center (DCDC), cooperative education 248–54, *251*; community-based challenge 249–50; community engagement 250; co-op student installs exterior lettering on LCS *252*; co-op student installs finishing touches on neighborhood bulletin board *251*; credits 253; definition 249; iterative production 250–2; Livernois wall map *255*; partners 253; pedagogical goals 250; project results and learning outcomes 252–3; project-specific student learning objectives 249; select teaching strategies 250–2; student co-ops work on iterations of wall installation map of Livernois corridor *250*; summary 249; wall map for LCS *250*; teaching-hospital model 252; *see also* Livernois Community Storefront
Detroit Design Festival 253
Dewey, John 203
dialogic 184
Diamond and Schmitt Architects 248

Dominican Republic: Community-Based Design course 94; Habitat for Humanity 166, 168, 169; *see also* Santiago
double-loop learning theory 176
Dunne, Anthony 73

Earnhart, Mark 272
East Boston, Massachusetts 172–3, *173*, 174, 175, *175*; Neighborhood of Affordable Housing (NOAH) 172, 175, 176
eBay 288
Eckalizzi Design 284n1
Eckert, Stephen 236
ecosystem 25, 50, 193
edge effect 111–16, *112*; *see also* PROJECT RE_
educational platform 285–9
edX 285
Eisenbach, Ronit 272
Eliseo Collazos Community Center 17, *18*, *19*
Environmental Design Research Association 18
Environmental Justice in Prisons Project 220–5; buildings gardens and social capital 223; Iowa State University 204, 220, *221*, 222, 223, *224*, 225n2; learning outcomes and project results 224–5; reflection as evaluation and validation 222–3
evaluating student learning 202–4
experiential learning 22, 32, 122, 124, 133, 152, 206–13, 261; *see also* Boston Architectural College (BAC), Practice Department
Etsy 288

The Farm Rover 261–6; community-based challenge 261–2; credits 266; cultural immersion 264; definition 261; design/build 264; issues addressed 261; Multicultural Refugee Coalition farmers *263*; partners 265–6; pedagogical goals 262; project results and learning outcomes 265; project-specific student learning objectives 261; research 263–4; select teaching strategies 263–4; student demonstrates rolling shade screen *264*; students building on site *263*; summary 261; Urban Farming rover prototype *264*, *265*; *see also* Multicultural Refugee Coalition; University of Texas at Austin School of Architecture (UTASOA), Center for Sustainable Development
Federal Highway Administration 72
Ferry, R. Todd 45n1, 284
Field, Eric 229n3
field experience engagement 155–7; *see also* Huxtable Fellowship; iZindaba Zokudla; Pontificia Universidad Católica Madre y Maestra
financial sustainability 109, 288
First National Bank 278
Fisher, Thomas 1, 64
Flournoy, Bill, Jr. *47*, *48*
Fog Water Farms 18, *18*, *19*; funding 20n3
Folan, John *116*
Fox, Andrew *54*
Fox, Sam 121
Freire, Paulo: *Pedagogy of the Oppressed* 4
Fundación Dominicana Para la Gestión de Riesgos (FUNDOGER) 167, 169
fundamental skills 3; *see also* edge effect; IMPACT orientation; social literacy development through practice-based learning; USAER XXXIV Training Center for Special Education

Garver, Bethany Lundell *210*, *211*, *212*
Gaudio, Brian: Healing an Urban Stream 157, 165–94, *167*, *168*
GiraDora 28, *29*, *30*
Go Health Fellowships 20n1
GoldSmith, Stephen 119, 121
Greater New Orleans Fair Housing Action Center 90, 92
Green Gate Farms (GGF) 261, 262, *263*, 264, *264*, *265*, 266; *see also* The Farm Rover
Greenhouse Gas Reduction Fund 280
Grocott, Lisa 133, *143*, *144*
Grow Dat Youth Farm 91, 92
Guido, Anthony 71
Guthrie, Georgia 78

Habitat for Humanity: Dominican 166, 168, 169
Haile, Ann 242
Haile, Ralph V., Jr. 242
Hart, Stuart L. 32n8
Hartig, Ursula 3
Hartley, Matthew 229n1
Harvard Graduate School of Design (GSD) 48–9, *49*
Healing an Urban Stream 165–94, *167*, *168*; design phase 167–9; research phase 166–7; results 169; US Fulbright Program 165; *see also* Pontificia Universidad Católica Madre y Maestra
Heximer, Christina 253
Horrigan, Paula 182
human-centered design 23, 25, 28, 71, 73, 74, 75–6, 77, 94, 96, 133, 138, *147*, 148, 152, 179, 209
Human Cities 148, *149*, 152n2

Humanitarianism: Design Thinking course 216
Hunt, Jamer 71, 72
Huxtable Fellowship, Ada Louise 150–76, *173*, *175*, *176*, 209; advancing resiliency in East Boston 172; design research 172–4; field research 174; learning by doing 172; strengthening with partnerships and transforming with capital 174–5; transferring knowledge and sharpening applied learning pedagogies 176

identity literacy 118, 120–1
impact-driven design 135–6, 137–8, 139
IMPACT Orientation 110, 118–20, 134; context 118; learning objectives and outcomes 120; Spectrum of Spectrums 119, *119*
Impact Silver Spring 272
Impulso Urbano program 125, *125*, *127*, 128n3; *see also* democratic civic engagement; USAER XXXIV Training Center for Special Education
inclusive iteration 3, 179–81, 184; *see also* Cornell University, Rust to Green; Lawrence Technological University, Ten Friends Diner; Philadelphia University, Alexandra Youth Precinct Project
Informal Urban Communities Initiative (IUCI) 9, 10, 15–19; design communication 16; design matters 16–17; Fog Water Farms 18, *18*, *19*, 21n3; funding 21nn1–2; hands-on implementation 16; informal urban development 15; interdisciplinary collaboration 16; long-term relationships 16; multiscalar thinking 16; outcomes 17–18; participatory design 16; pedagogical goals 15–17; personal resilience 16
intercultural competencies 3, 131–3; map presenting project, actors, and organizations *132*; *see also* African Design Centre; International Urbanization Seminar; Transforming Mindsets Studio
International Urbanization Seminar 133, 147–52, *149*, *150*, 152n1; Clean Air Asia 147, *149*, 149, 151, 152; Clean Air Campaign 133, 148, 149–51, *150*, 152; inclusive urban future 147–8; learning objectives and outcomes 149–51; lessons learned 152; seminar structure 148–9; teaching strategies 151
intrapersonal skills 141, 142, 260
Iowa Correctional Institution for Women 204, 220, *221*, 224
Iowa State University 204, 220, *221*, 222, 223, *224*, 225n2

Iquitos, Peru 17, 18, 21n1
iZindaba Zokudla (Conversations About Food: Innovation in the Soweto Food System 157, 158–62; food–storage prototype evaluation *161*; learning and technological outcomes 160–62; methodology 159–60; multi-stakeholder engagement session 158, *159*, 160; post-harvest activities *162*; seedling growing system *161*

Jane Place Neighborhood Sustainability Initiative 91, 92
Johannesburg *see* iZindaba Zokudla (Conversations About Food: Innovation in the Soweto Food System; Philadelphia University, College of Architecture, Alexandra Youth Precinct Project; University of Johannesburg
Johannesburg Development Agency 200
Jovanovic, Julia 190, 191, 192, 193

Kessler, Mark 68n1
Kiwanis of Ruston 278
Kolb, David 207
Koo, Helen 68n1
Koshalek, Richard 31n1
Kramer, Liz 121
Kresge Foundation 175, 176

La Familia Counseling Center 280, 284
Lama Foundation 232, 236; Design/Build Studios and Seminars 232, 236; *see also* Design in Partnership With the Lama Foundation
Landscape Architecture Foundation Olmsted Scholars Program 21n1
Lanou, Randall S. 57
Lawrence Technological University, Activist Architecture and Design Studio 180, 189–1995; learning objectives 193–4; project context 190–1; project goals 191; project results 191–3; Ten Friends Diner 190, 191, *192*, *192*, 194, *195*
Learning Mindset Case Clinic 143
learning objectives 4, 15, 49, 52, 56, **56**, 57, 63, 96, 99, 100, 101, 103n11, 120, 123, 137–9, 142, 149–51, 158–9, 161, 166, 172, 183, 193–4, 199, 215, 222, 224, 229, 229n2, 232, 237, 243, 249, 253, 254, 261, 266, 273, 276, 279; Public Interest Design seminar 37; Safe Agua 25
learning outcomes 2, 4, 23, 28, 30, 96, 109, 120, 144, 145, 207, **208**, 209, 212, 224–5, 228, 229, 235, 240; 247, 252–3, 254, 259, 265, 271, 277, 283
Leite, Margarette 42, 45n1
Leu, Christine 248

Lima, Peru 9, 18, 20, 20n3, 24, 28; see also Fog Water Farms
Livernois Community Storefront (LCS) 249, 250–2, *250*, *251*, 253, *253*, 254, *255*, 284n6
Lomas de Zapallal 9, 17
Long Branch Business League 266
Long Branch neighborhood in Silver Spring, Maryland 266–72; Purple Line 267; Superblock Party 266, *268*, 271; see also On Site; University of Maryland
Louisiana Tech University School of Design (LTU SOD), Community Design Activism Center (CDAC) 274–5, 277, 278, *278*; see also South of California Avenue
Lucker, Spencer F. 216

Maclennan Jaunkalns Miller Architects 248
Malan, Naudé *159*, *161*, *162*; "Innovation in the Soweto Food System" 163n4
Manuel, Tracy 66
Marshall School of Business Brittingham Social Enterprise Lab, University of Southern California 25
MASS Design Group 135, 136, *136*, *137*, 139–40; see also African Design Centre
Massive Change story formula 191
McAllister, Michael 78
McEntee, Kate 133
Mental Health Consumer/Survivor Employment Association 190
Merkelbach, Eichbaum 45n4
metacognition 177n1
MetroLAB 237, 240, 242, 284n2; see also Pleasant Street Pedestrian Project
Metropolitan State University of Denver (MSU Denver), Master of Fine Arts 93–102; Communication Design undergraduate program 94; core courses in year one 99–100; core courses in year two 100–1; Dominican Republic Community-Based Design course 94; interdisciplinarity of Public Interest Design MFA 97–101; Phase One 102, 103; program curriculum overview 98; program opportunities and next steps 101–102; program pedagogical goals 96–101; proposed two-year MFA program **98**; structure of Public Interest Design MFA 97; visioning the future 94–7
Milder, Jonas 71, 73
mindsets 120, 141, 142–4, 145, 189
Mitgang, Lee D. 48
Mobley, Sue 119, 121
Mockbee, Sam 91
Monterrey Tec (Tecnológico de Monterrey) 122, 123, 124–5, 126, 128nn2–3; see also democratic civic engagement; Impulso Urbano; USAER XXXIV Training Center for Special Education
Montgomery County, Maryland: Arts and Humanities Council 272; Department of Parks 272; Public Libraries 272; see also On Site
Montgomery Housing Partnership 266, 272; see also On Site
Montgomery Sisam Architects 248
Moriyama and Teshima Architects 248
Motorola Foundation 255, 260, 284n7; see also Com(m)a; School of the Art Institute of Chicago
Multicultural Refugee Coalition 261, 262, *263*, 266; see also The Farm Rover
multi-stakeholder engagement 158, 159, 160
Mutual Assistance Network 280, 284

National Association of Schools of Art and Design (NASAD) 94, 97
National Center for Smart Growth Research and Education, and Art and Architecture Libraries 272
National Institutes of Health Fogarty Global Health Fellowship Program 21n1
National Research Foundation 163n4
Neighborhoods Unified for Hope (NU-Hope) 275, 278, *278*
New Farm Institute 261, 266; see also The Farm Rover
North Carolina State University Coastal Dynamics Design Lab Studio 54, *54*
North Carolina State University College of Design, Public Interest Design Certificate 46–58; addressing a new educational need 48–50; course and program assessment 55–8; Design/Build Lab *57*; DIY Cartography 54, *55*; flexible course work 52–5; program curriculum overview 50–1; program pedagogical goals and outcomes 51; program philosophy 46–8; Public Interest Architecture seminar *53*; Public Interest Design Incubator *52*; Public Interest Design Seminar 52, 56, **56**; Studio School of Architecture (SOA) 50; Triangle Greenway 47, 48
North Central Alliance Partners in Prevention 278
North Central Louisiana Arts Council 279
North Central Louisiana Master Gardeners 278
Northern Cheyenne Reservation 42, *42*, 43, *44*

O'Grady, Visocky: *The Information Design Handbook* 60
O'Leary, Ceara 253

Oneida Square 182, 183, 184, 185, *185*, 186, *187*
On Site 266–72; Chairs 1, 2, 3 *270*; colorful triangular planes *270*; communication and documentation 271; community-based challenge 269; credits 272; definition 266; issues addressed 269; iteration 270–1; on- and off-site project development 270; partners 272; pedagogical goals 269–70; plastic bottle pavilion *268*; project results and learning outcomes 271;project-specific student learning objectives 266; select teaching strategies 270–1; summary 266–7; Superblock Party 266, *268*, 271; temporary gateway *271*; triangular panels hinged together *271*
Ontario, Canada: youth suicide 190
Ontario Ministry of Health and Long-Term Care 192
Open Architecture Collaborative 287
Open Architecture Network 287
Origin Bank 278
Orlowski, Edward 189, 192
otherness 99, 181, 195, 200
Outpatient Radio 66, *67*
outputs 2, **26**, 96, 97, 98, 103n7, 161, 162, 246, 283
Over-the-Rhine Community Housing 242; *see also* Pleasant Street Pedestrian Project
Over-the-Rhine Community Housing 242, 284n4; *see also* Pleasant Street Pedestrian Project

Pallasmaa, Juhani: *The Eyes of the Skin* 10
Palleroni, Sergio 34, 35, 43, 45n1; *Studio at Large*, 45n3
Papanek, Victor: *Design for the Real World* 2
Parache, Juan 166
Parker, Geoffrey: *Platform Revolution* 285, 288
Parsite DIY Skatepark 91, 92
Parson's School of Design 141; *see also* Transforming Mindsets Studio
participatory mapping 166
partnerships 9, 24, 25, 32n4, 71, 73, 74, 76, 86, 109, 112, 114, 116, 117, 120, 139, 156, 169, 172, 179, 193, 203, 204, **210**, 215, 222, 223, 224, 225, 262, 266; academic-community 175; campus-community 95; collaborative 122, 151; community 37, 78, 99, 100, 145, 151, 180; community-designer 121; cross-community 110, 112; external 31n1; long-standing 43; long-term 220, 280; multi-year 279; private 165; public-private 269; student-community 209; student-university-community 4; trusting 123; university-community 182, 202, 267
Paso Moya, Chile 255–6, *257*, *259*, *260*; *see also* Com(m)a
Paul E. Slaton Head Start Center 278
Pawlicki, Nina 3
Penda, Alaina 78
People's Liberty 242; *see also* Pleasant Street Pedestrian Project
Perrault, Sarah 59, 63
Peterson, Benjamin: Huxtable Fellowship 150–76
Philadelphia University, College of Architecture, Alexandra Youth Precinct Project 181, 195–200, *198*, *199*; eNtokozweni Community Centre 197, *199*; iterative development and communication strategies 197–9; learning objectives 199; preparatory seminar 196; project results 200; sociospatial contexts 195–6
Phnom Penh, Cambodia 17, 21n2; Pongro Senchey 17
Pitera, Dan 253
placemaking 180, 182, 183, 184, *184*, 185, 186, *187*, 253, 266, 271, 273
Pleasant Street Committee 242; *see also* Pleasant Street Pedestrian Project
Pleasant Street Pedestrian Project 237–43; community-based challenge 237; credits 242; definition 237; first event *238*, *239*; funding 242; issues addressed 237; neighborhood mapping *238*; Parklet at night *241*; Parklet construction *240*; Parklet view from across the street *241*; partners 242; pedagogical goals 237–9; photo wall *239*; project results and learning outcomes 240–2; project-specific student learning objectives 237; residents playing chess in Parklet *241*; select teaching strategies 240; summary 237
Polizzi, Jade 236
Pongro Senchey 17
Pontificia Universidad Católica Madre y Maestra (PUCMM), School of Architecture 165–6, 169; Center for Urban and Regional Studies 165; design phase 167–9; research phase 166–7; results 169
Portland State University, Center for Public Interest Design 279–83; *see also* With Sacramento
Portland State University, Center for Public Interest Design (CPID), Graduate Certificate in Public Interest Design 34–45, 45n1, 45n3; American Indian Resilience project *42*, 43, *44*; electives 38; fieldwork 39; program curriculum

overview 35–9; program outcomes 41–5; program pedagogical goals 39–40, *40*; program philosophy 34–35; Public Interest Design seminar 36–8; Student Fellows 39–40, 42, 43; Talks 39; *see also* Adams, Karina; Weber, Reid
post-occupancy evaluation 216, 219n2
practice assessment 207, **208**, 209, 212
practice-based learning 3, 107, 109; *see also* social literacy development through practice-based learning
practice component 207, *208*
practice hours 207, **208**, 212
Pralahad, C. K. 32n8
Preddy, Donovan 78
Prestifilippo, Dominic 78
Proactive Recovery Community Structures 52
PROJECT RE_ 110, 111–16, *116*; capacity, entrepreneurship, and ripple effect 115–16; embedded understanding 114–15; entry marquee illustrating edge effect *112*; exterior view of community room, studio, and entrance hall *114*; leadership by example 115; partnering to impact at scale 112–14; *see also* edge effect
public interest design curriculum 2, 28, 107; *see also* North Carolina State University College of Design
public interest design definition 1, 103n7
public interest design pedagogy 1–4
Puget Sound Veterans Administration Healing Garden 12–14, *13*, *14*
Pyramid theory 33n8

Queen, Sara *55*

Raby, Fiona 73
radical empathy 119
Reconstruye 256, 258, 259, 260; *see also* Com(m)a
reflection 38, 74, 101, 120, 144, 145, 151, 160, 183, 207, **208**, 220, 224, 225; critical 132; evaluation and validation 222–3; self- 207, 209; structured 203–4
reflection-in-action 24
Regent Park Aquatic Centre 248
Remás Project 78–9, *79*
REVOLVE Detroit 253
Riley, David 43
Riverdale school 142
Robert Rauschenberg Foundation 21n3
Roche Health Center 204, 214–19; pedagogical outcomes 217–19; project assessments 216–17; teaching 216; *see also* Shirati Health, Education, and Development (SHED) Foundation; Village Life Outreach Project

Rockefeller Foundation: 89 Resilient Cities 169
Ronald McDonald House 248
Rotary Club of Ruston 278
Ruppert, John 272
Ruston, Louisiana 274, 278; High School 278; Kiwanis 278; Rotary Club 278; *see also* South of California Avenue
Ryerson University: Faculty of Communication and Design 243, 248; School of Interior Design 243; *see also* A Social Approach to Design

Sacramento, California 38, 381; Del Paso Heights neighborhood 280, 284; South Sacramento neighborhood 280, 284; *see also* With Sacramento
Sacramento Area Council of Governments(SACOG) 280, 284
Safe Agua course series 24–30; evolution of programming 27; learning objectives 25; pedagogical goals 25; timeline, activities, and milestone **26**
Safe Agua Peru *27*, 28, *29*, *30*, 32n7; GiraDora 28, *29*, *30*
Saltmarsh, John 229n1
Salvation Army Harbour Light Ministries 248
Sam Fox School of Design and Visual Arts, Washington University 121
Sanders, Elizabeth 73
Sankofa Community Development Corporation 88, 92
Sankofa Mobile Market 88, *89*, 90, *90*
Santiago, Chile 24, 255
Santiago, Dominican Republic 165–6, 169; Healing an Urban Stream *168*
Scholarships of Application and Engagement 3, 155
Schön, Donald 1–2
School of the Art Institute of Chicago (SAIC) 255, 260; GFRY Design Studio 255, 257, 260, 284n7; *see also* Com(m)a; Motorola
Seattle, Washington 8, 11; Architects Without Borders 15, 17, 18; Chinatown-International District 9–10; South Park 42; *see also* University of Washington
SEED (Social Economic Environmental Design) academic case studies 231–83; Com(m)a (*see also* Com[m]a) 254–60; Cooperative Education at the Detroit Collaborative Design Center 248–54 (*see also* Detroit Collaborative Design Center: cooperative education); Design in Partnership With the Lama Foundation 232–6 (*see also* Design in Partnership With the Lama Foundation);

The Farm Rover 261–6 (*see also* The Farm Rover); On Site 266–72 (*see also* On Site); Pleasant Street Pedestrian Project 237–43 (*see also* Pleasant Street Pedestrian Project); A Social Approach to Design 243–9 (*see also* A Social Approach to Design); South of California Avenue 273–8 (*see also* South of California Avenue); With Sacramento 279–84 (*see also* With Sacramento)

SEED (Social Economic Environmental Design) Evaluator 4, 228, 229, 246, 248, 287; 4.0 102n4, 229

SEED (Social Economic Environmental Design) Network 4, 37, 45n2, 94, 95, 102n4, 229, 287; issues 191; principles 95, 102n3

SEED (Social Economic Environmental Design) process for academia 228–9

Selkirk, Kaethe 266

senior cities in Beijing, China: air pollution impacts 133, 147, 148, 149, 150, *150*, 151, 152; *see also* International Urbanization Seminar

Sennett, Richard 10–11

serious play 142, 144

service-learning 8, 9, 10, 17, 34, 43, 83, 97, 109, 122, 124, 158, 159, 161, 162, 182, 273, 274

Shaull, Richard 4

Shirati Health, Education, and Development (SHED) Foundation 214, 215, 216, 217

Sinclair, Cameron 287

Singh, Kevin J. 278

Skillshare 341

Small Center for Collaborative Design 82–91; building capacity and community 85–6; program curriculum overview 83–7; program philosophy 82–3; Sankofa Community Development Corporation 88, 92; Sankofa Mobile Market 88, *89*, 90, *90*; student skill development and learning objectives 86–7

SOCA *see* South of California Avenue

A Social Approach to Design 243–9; aids to help visually impaired navigate facility *246*; Artscape Lounge and Show Me Love Café *245*; braille signs *247*; community-based challenge 244; credits 248; definition 243; generous hallways functions as gathering spaces for Daniels Spectrum organizations *245*; issues addressed 244; partners 248; pedagogical goals 244–6; project results and learning outcomes 247–8; project-specific student learning objectives 243; select teaching strategies 246–7; sense of smell incorporation *247*; social aspects of Centre for Social Innovation *244*; summary 243

Social Design Pathways 107, 108, *108*, 109n3

Social Economic Environmental Design *see* SEED

social innovation 74; Design Thinking for Social Innovation 38; *see also* ArtCenter College of Design, Designmatters; Centre for Social Innovation

social literacy 3, 107, 108, 109, 110

social literacy development through practice-based learning 107–110; artifact sustainability 109; community sustainability 109; financial sustainability 109; Social Design Pathways 107, 108, *108*, 109n3; student sustainability 109; *see also* Winterhouse Institute

sociospatial: contexts 195–6; experience 197

South of California Avenue (SOCA) 273–8; block party *277*; building trust 277; CDAC students reviews feedback *278*; community-based challenge 274–5; community garden *275*, *277*; credits 278; definition 273; developing citizen designers 277; Hope House 278, *278*; issues addressed 274; Neighborhoods Unified for Hope (NU-Hope) 275, 278, *278*; partners 278; pedagogical goals 275–6; project results and learning outcomes 277–8; project-specific student learning objectives 273; select teaching strategies 276–7; Sprint 5K *273*; summary 273–4; teaching leadership 276–7; *see also* Louisiana Tech University School of Design

South Sacramento neighborhood 280, 284

Soweto 162n2; *see also* iZindaba Zokudla (Conversations About Food: Innovation in the Soweto Food System

Spectrum of Spectrums 119, *119*

Spencer, Benjamin R.: *Engaging the Field Experience* 3

SpoonCity 285

SQWater 18

Stanard, Virginia 253

Stanford University, International Urbanization Seminar 133, 147–52, *149*, *150*, 152n1; Clean Air Asia 147, 149, *149*, 151, 152; Clean Air Campaign 133, 148, 149–51, *150*, 152; Human Cities Expo 148; inclusive urban future 147–8; learning objectives and outcomes 149–51; lessons learned 152; seminar structure 148–9; teaching strategies 151

Stanford University, Program on Urban Studies: Human Cities 148, *149*, 152n2

348 *Index*

Staszowski, Eduardo 3
Stiphany, Kristine 266
Stohr, Kate 287
structures for inclusion 64, 66, 102n3
Structures for Inclusion conference: 2010 229n3; 2015 6n7; 2016 5n4
Student Learning Contract 209, **211**
student sustainability 109
Surdna Foundation 253
Surmaule 256, 258, 259, 260; see also Com(m)a

Tanzania 214, 215, 216, 218; see also Roche Health Center
Team Visible Youth 120
Tebben, Paul 260
TECHO 24, 28; Innovation Center 24, 28
Ten Friends Diner 190, 191, 192, *192*, 194, *195*
Thomasetti, Thornton, 260
TIP see Trade Institute of Pittsburgh
Toronto, Ontario 243
Trade Institute of Pittsburgh (TIP) *112*, 113, 114–15; see also edge effect; PROJECT RE_
Transforming Mindsets Studio 133, 141–5; blog post *143*; inside the activities 142; Performance Gym 142–4, *143*, *144*; proposing preferred futures 142–3; Prospective Writing 142, 145; student response 144–5; surfacing limiting beliefs 143–4; Theory U framework *144*; tuning behavior patterns 144
Trujillo, Rafael 166
Tsinghua University, Department of Construction Management and Information Art and Design 148, 150, 151
Tufte, Edward R.: *Envisioning Information* 60
Tulane City Center see Small Center for Collaborative Design
Tulane School of Architecture 82, 83; see also Small Center for Collaborative Design
Tulane University 83, 121

Udacity 285
UDBS see Urban Design Build Studio
UDM see University of Detroit Mercy
UNICEF Innovation 23
United Nations 32; Solutions Summit 135
University Commons Organization 253
University of California, Davis, Center for Design in the Public Interest 59–68; challenges and successes 65–8; course pedagogical goals 64–5; design for understanding 60–3; Outpatient Radio 66, *67*; professional practice and ethics 63–4; program curriculum overview 60–4; program philosophy 59–60
University of Cincinnati 214; College of Design, Architecture, Art, and Planning 242 (see also Pleasant Street Pedestrian Project); Pathway B Third Century Materials Grant 242; Research Institute 237, 284n2 (see also MetroLAB); School of Architecture and Interior Design (see also MetroLAB; Pleasant Street Pedestrian Project); see also Roche Health Center
University of Colorado (CU) Boulder 232, 236; Program in Environmental Design 232, 236; see also Design in Partnership With the Lama Foundation
University of Detroit Mercy (UDM) School of Architecture 249, 250, 253; Professional Experience I 249; Professional Experience II; see also Detroit Collaborative Design Center; Livernois Community Storefront
University of Johannesburg (UJ) 158, *159*, 162n2; Teaching Innovation Fund 163n4; see also iZindaba Zokudla (Conversations About Food: Innovation in the Soweto Food System
University of Maryland (UMD), Program in Architecture, School of Architecture, Planning, and Preservation, Department of Art, College of Arts and Humanities 266, 267; see also On Site
University of Texas at Austin School of Architecture (UTASOA), Center for Sustainable Development 261, 262, 265, 274; see also The Farm Rover
University of the Arts, Design for Social Impact Master of Design Studies 70–80, *76*; additional cross-linked DSI course examples 76; design for social impact 73–4; DSI design methods sequence 75, *75*; origination 72; program pedagogical goals 76–7; program background and strategic evolution 71–4; program curriculum overview 74–5; program outcomes 77–8; program philosophy 70–1; rebooting the graduate program 72–3; Remás Project 78–9, *79*; roadmap *80*; toward strategic design and community engagement 73
University of Toronto Multi-Faith Centre 248
University of Washington Center for One Health Research 21n1
University of Washington, Department of Global Health Thomas Francis Jr. 21n1
University of Washington, Department of Landscape Architecture 8–19; design/build studio outcomes 11–14; design/build

studio pedagogical goals 11; design/build studios 10–4; Ecological Urbanism Studio 9; fabricating community amenities 13; fog collecting 18, 19; fog-water-irrigated community park in Eliseo Collazos 19; Global Innovation Funds 21nn1–2; Informal Urban Communities Initiative 9, 15–19; LARC 402 9; LARC 403 9; LARC 474/475 9; LARC 501 9; LARC 502 9; LARC 503 9; LARC 561 10; LARC 570 10; LARC 571 10 photo-preference exercise 13; program curriculum overview 9–10; program philosophy 8–9; Puget Sound Veterans Administration Healing Garden 12–14, 13, 14; Urban Agriculture Studio 9

University of Washington Global Innovation Funds 21n1

Urban Design Build Studio (UDBS) 110, 111–12, 112, 113–14, 115–16, 116

USAER XXXIV Training Center for Special Education (UTC) 109, 122–27, 127; building relationships of trust 123; facilitating design and communication 124–6; generating understanding in academic and community-centered endeavors 126–7; model of interagency collaboration 124; see also Impulso Urbano program

U.S. Bank Foundation 242

US Fulbright Program 165

UTC see USAER XXXIV Training Center for Special Education

Van Alstyne, Marshall: *Platform Revolution* 285, 288

Verba, Susan 59, 63

Vidal, Alejandro 132–3

Village Life Outreach Project (VLOP) 214, 215, 215, 216, 217, 219

Wakeford, Katie: *Expanding Architecture* 1; Public Interest Architecture seminar SEED case study 53

Washington DC 266, 269; see also On Site

Weber, Reid 42

Weikert, Mike 3

whole-systems approach 8–19, 152n2; see also University of Washington

Wilson, Krista 253

Windsor, Ontario 190; see also Ten Friends Diner

Winterbottom, Daniel 9

Winterhouse Institute 109n1; Social Design Pathways 107, 108, 108, 109n3

Winterhouse Symposium on Design Education for Social Impact 108

With Sacramento 279–84; definition 279; bus stop as community center 280, 281; community-based challenge 280–1; community input 281, 283; community voice amplification 281–2; credits 284; issues addressed 280; partners 284; pedagogical goals 281; project results and learning outcomes 283–4; project-specific learning objectives 279; scale appropriateness 282; select teaching strategies 281–2; storefront for community 281; summary 279–80; systemic integration 282; see also Portland State University

Women With a Vision 90, 92

work-based learning 206

Wortham-Galvin, B. D. 45n1, 284

Wu, Sarah 266

Zaretsky, Michael 217, 218, 242

Zoom Interiors 285